Inventing the
Immigration Problem

Inventing the Immigration Problem

THE DILLINGHAM COMMISSION AND ITS LEGACY

Katherine Benton-Cohen

HARVARD UNIVERSITY PRESS

Cambridge, Massachusetts

London, England

2018

Any views, findings, conclusions, or recommendations expressed in this publication
do not necessarily reflect those of the National Endowment for Humanities
or any other organization.

Library of Congress Cataloging-in-Publication Data

Names: Benton-Cohen, Katherine, author.

Title: Inventing the immigration problem : the Dillingham Commission and its
legacy / Katherine Benton-Cohen.

Description: Cambridge, Massachusetts : Harvard University Press, 2018. |
Includes bibliographical references and index.

Identifiers: LCCN 2017052663 | ISBN 9780674976443 (hardcover : alk. paper)

Subjects: LCSH: United States. Immigration Commission (1907–1910)—Influence.
| United States—Emigration and immigration—Government policy. | United
States—Emigration and immigration—Social aspects. | Demographic
surveys—United States. | United States—History—1901–1953.

Classification: LCC JV6483 .B48 2018 | DDC 325.7309/041—dc23

LC record available at https://lccn.loc.gov/2017052663

For Julius and Asher

Contents

Inventing the
Immigration Problem

Introduction

In April 1910, Henry Cabot Lodge wrote to a friend, "I am now a member of the Immigration Commission, which has been carrying on the most exhaustive inquiry into the subject which has ever been made." The aristocratic senator shared his friend Theodore Roosevelt's passion for imperialism abroad. But where Roosevelt had mixed feelings about immigrants, Lodge did not; he had been the legislative leader of the immigration restriction movement since his election to the House in 1887 and then to the Senate six years later.[1]

Like his more famous colleague Lodge, Senator William P. Dillingham, the U.S. Immigration Commission's chair, championed both imperialism and immigration restriction. The small-town aristocrat was a former Vermont governor who also shared Lodge's rock-ribbed Republicanism and Puritan New England stock. Along with seven other men, Lodge and Dillingham would oversee the largest study of immigrants ever conducted in the United States—the so-called Dillingham Commission.

The Dillingham Commission's work has shaped immigration policy ever since. It produced forty-one volumes of reports, summarized in a brief but potent set of recommendations that was far more restrictive than its own evidence supported.[2] Within a decade, almost all of these policy initiatives were implemented into law. They included a literacy test, a quota system that varied by nationality, the continued exclusion of Asians, and a panoply of new immigration rules. The commission's reforms effectively ended mass immigration from 1924 until the passage of the Hart-Celler Act of 1965. Between 1881 and 1924, approximately twenty-four million immigrants came to the United States; during the twenty-five years that followed, fewer newcomers arrived than in 1907 alone.[3] Even though its overt racial biases have been eliminated, the architecture built by the commission still undergirds federal immigration policy.

The Dillingham Commission was a fact-finding body of unprecedented size and scale, one of the largest investigative projects ever undertaken by the federal government, even to this day. It had notoriety and a large budget. Both attracted social scientists and political activists of all stripes, even those who opposed its aims. Its range was broad and deep. It demonstrated the federal government's capacity as a massive and growing knowledge-acquisition apparatus. The federal Bureau of Immigration and Naturalization, which it vastly expanded, became a quintessential example of the administrative state. (In 2017, after many name changes, relocations, and splits, it inhabits the Department of Homeland Security.) The laws fashioned from the commission's recommendations required elaborate record-keeping apparatuses, byzantine bureaucracy, internal courts, and broad administrative authority.[4]

The commission's work reflected the circumstances and priorities of a particular moment in American history and American Progressivism, a moment characterized by mass immigration, the birth of modern social science, and an aggressive foreign policy that fostered a newly robust notion of federal power both within and beyond the nation's borders. The commission's recommendations also marked a final turn from an immigration policy driven by the foreign-policy priorities of the executive branch to one dictated by legislators' concerns about domestic labor politics.

In 1911, commission member Jeremiah Jenks repackaged its voluminous findings into a mainstream book, *The Immigration Problem: A Study of American Immigration Conditions and Needs.* The book's title asserted the commission's fundamental assumption: immigration was a "problem," and it was the job of the federal government to fix it. The digest was reprinted in six editions through 1926 and received broad readership, and this idea of an "immigration problem" became the way Americans understood the commission's work.[5]

The commission's Progressive Era formulation of an "immigration problem" for federal power to solve has become so indelibly imprinted that its logic—immigration problem; federal government solution—now seems entirely natural. Consider, for example, the irony of President Donald Trump's then-adviser Stephen Bannon's 2017 call for a dramatic expansion of federal immigration enforcement and exclusion even as he demanded a "deconstruction of the administrative state."[6] But conceiving of immigration as a "problem" in America was an invention, and one deeply embedded in the way that both bureaucrats and elites saw the relationship between social science and public policy in the Progressive Era. Indeed, the word "expert" did not gain traction until the 1870s. It was, like the "problem" those experts determined to solve, a product of its era.[7]

As the United States continues to struggle with an immigration system that dissatisfies almost everyone, the Dillingham Commission deserves new attention. Its story shows that the federal government's current role as an administrative leviathan in its enforcement of immigration was neither accidental nor inevitable. Americans have become so used to the narrative of mass migration as a public policy problem to be managed using federal bureaucratic power that hardly anyone—right, left, or center—questions it. Nor do we question why lawmakers ever saw fit to establish an immense governmental architecture to enforce immigration policy in the first place.[8] The federal "immigration problem" is a product of a bygone era that casts a long shadow not just on the current immigration system but also on our collective imaginations.

The Dillingham Commission's Progressive Era confidence in nonpartisan expertise, and its success in implementing its recommendations, appears quaint in the political polarization and gridlock of the twenty-first century. Many of the commission's ideas—and certainly its language—are antiquated. Yet perhaps its most striking element is the unwavering faith its members and staff maintained in their own objectivity. The methods, conclusions—and above all, certitude—of the newly ascendant social sciences appear hubristic in our more critical and cynical age.

Yet even the commission's assertions of objectivity produced inconsistent interpretations and contradictory data. The men and women of the Dillingham Commission were not of one voice. But its final recommendations were so brief, decisive, and restrictive—and so quickly successful—that the behind-the-scenes debates about the nature and impact of immigration in the United States were swiftly obscured. The commission's recommendations called for restrictions based on "quality and quantity" to maintain "economic opportunity" and the "well-being of our people."[9] But much of the commission's research sprawled in an erratic, lively, and internally contradictory mess, far beyond its specific goal and agenda, and it was largely ignored in the commission's own stark recommendations for restriction.

The commission's nine appointees and three hundred odd staff varied in their perspectives and priorities. Some favored restriction; others did not. A majority were conservative Republicans, some were Democrats, and a few were Socialists. One staffer helped found the Communist Party of America. But even as they varied in their policy and political perspectives, they came to a near-consensus about the need to establish new apparatus to exert federal power over millions of immigrants. The vast federal bureaucracy they envisioned has endured and swelled in the century since. Progressive Era experts called immigration a "problem" and created a framework for federal bureaucracy to solve it with a confident swagger that belied the contradictions of their own research footings.

This is the Dillingham Commission's legacy to us.

The Commission and Its Critics

From February 1907 until its final reports were issued in early 1911, the Dillingham Commission investigated what it called "the general effect, in a broad sense, of the new immigration movement upon the people, the industries, and the institutions of the United States." As authorized by Section 39 of the Immigration Act of 1907, the commission had nine appointed members. Three "experts" were chosen by President Theodore Roosevelt: California businessman William R. Wheeler and economists Jeremiah Jenks and Charles Neill. Speaker of the House Joseph Cannon chose three congressmen: John Burnett (D-AL), William Bennet (R-NY), and Benjamin Howell (R-NJ). Three senators (Dillingham, Lodge, and Asbury Latimer [D-SC]), were chosen by Vice President Charles Fairbanks in his capacity as the Senate president. A few people among the appointees and staff members were well known—Lodge, for example, and anthropologist Franz Boas—but most were unknown outside policy and academic circles. Many were academic economists. Women made up more than half of the commission's workforce and authored several of the reports.[10]

The Dillingham Commission. The nine original members of the commission and their chief aides. None was an immigrant. *Front row:* Asbury Latimer, Henry Cabot Lodge, William P. Dillingham, Benjamin F. Howell, Charles P. Neill. *Back row:* William W. Husband, Jeremiah Jenks, Morton E. Crane, William S. Bennet, James Burnett, and William R. Wheeler.

The Dillingham Commission decided early on to focus on fieldwork and statistics in the social-science vein rather than use the traditional legislative strategy of holding hearings. It organized its tables and data around a comparison of recently arrived "races" (its term)—such as the Slovaks and Italians—with long-established ones such as the English and Germans. The final reports' twenty-nine thousand pages explored topics that sprawled the full reaches of the Progressive Era mind. In addition to twenty reports on immigrants in American industries, thick with mind-numbing and undigested tabulations, the reports considered everything from the head size of new immigrants to conditions on transatlantic steamships to prostitution, debt peonage, crime, schools, agriculture, philanthropic societies, other countries' immigration laws, and immigrant women's "fecundity." Even without reading the volumes, the American public could learn in widespread newspaper coverage—from Los Angeles to New York to Berea, Kentucky—about glove making in the Hudson Valley, sex peddling in Chicago and San Francisco,

Japanese fruit farming in rural California and Washington, households and family wages across the Midwest and coal country, the smuggling of Chinese immigrants through California, Mexico, and Canada, and peonage investigations in southern lumber camps—to name just a few of the myriad topics. The commission's first major project began in May 1907—a summer-long investigation of emigration ports and sending cities across Europe. Over the next three years, the commission and its staff visited or gathered data on all forty-six states and several territories, including Hawaii. By its conclusion, the commission—which had "no limit on the time . . . or on the expense it may incur"—had spent nearly a million dollars, a shockingly large figure in 1911.[11]

The commission did not lack for media attention in its own time, or subsequently. In addition to the regional and national press coverage, in 1910 and 1911, the commission was the subject of special issues of the influential policy journal *Survey,* as well as many editorials by both participants and observers. Throughout the research, Boston's Immigration Restriction League (IRL), a clubby group of Harvard alumni close to Lodge (who had four degrees from there), served as watchdog.

From the other side, in defense of immigrants, came the first extended analysis of the commission's findings, even before the public laid eyes on it. With access to an advance copy, the American Jewish Committee (recently formed to combat restriction) hired Russian Jewish émigré and Harvard-trained economist Isaac Hourwich to analyze the reports. In 1912, Hourwich produced a thorough rebuttal of the statistical methods that the reports used to demonstrate that "new" immigrants were less successful than the "old."[12]

The Dillingham Commission's paradigm of "old immigrants" versus "new immigrants" has shaped the study of immigration ever since. Both categories referred to Europeans: "old immigrants" had come mostly from Ireland, Germany, and Scandinavia in the mid-nineteenth century. In contrast, the commission assumed the mostly Jewish, Italian, and Slavic "new immigrants" to be less assimilable and more "alien." In its own words, the commission "paid but little attention" to "the old immigrant class" as a topic of policy. For decades, this so-called hoary distinction between old and new was axiomatic in histories of immigration. But the dichotomous model implicitly defined Asian and Mexican immigrants as "other" in ways that have continued to structure immigration policy and to produce a racial subtext about "illegal aliens" to the present day.[13]

The subsequent replication in historical literature of the old versus new immigrant paradigm—"one of the great shibboleths of American immigration history," as one scholar put it—obscured the fact that the commission did in fact talk about other immigrants, especially Asians.[14] Perhaps because Asian immigration was banned entirely, and because it was a regional issue, few scholars note that the Dillingham Commission was sufficiently interested in Chinese, Japanese, and what it called "Hindoo" (South Asian) immigrants to devote three volumes to the American West and Pacific Coast states.[15] The commission owed its very existence to a compromise wrought by a diplomatic disagreement with Japan. In fact, two of Roosevelt's three appointees—Cornell economist Jeremiah Jenks and San Francisco businessman William R. Wheeler—he considered to be Asia experts.

In contrast to its intense interest in Asia, the commission had almost no interest in Mexico or Mexican immigrants. Mexico's president, Porfirio Díaz, was a close American ally, and before the Mexican Revolution broke out in 1910, the Mexican population in the United States was concentrated almost entirely in the American Southwest. From 1898 to 1910, Mexicans ranked just 28th of 39 immigrant groups. Arizona and New Mexico were still territories and were treated like overseas colonies. Five years before the Dillingham Commission, Lodge had opposed statehood for New Mexico because its people were of "a different race," whose success, in his view, would only encourage Puerto Ricans, Hawaiians, and Alaskans to press for statehood.[16]

In any case, immigrants crossing the overland borders from Mexico and Canada were considered so unimportant—and minimal—that the federal government did not even count them until 1908. The U.S. census did not include them in preprinted lists of national origins. The "old immigrant versus new immigrant" template, based on far more numerous Europeans, distorted the commission's understanding of Mexicans. A typical statistical table's preface explained that the "best method" for understanding its data was "to separate the foreign-born races . . . into two groups; the first to be known as the older immigrants, including the English, Irish, Scotch, French, and Germans, and the second group to be known as the more recent immigrants . . . except the Mexicans, who for obvious reasons should not be classified with either the recent or less recent immigrants of European origin." The reasons were so obvious they did not merit comment, at least for the commission's members and analysts.[17]

Even the commission's analysis of Europeans has continued to receive criticism. Following Isaac Hourwich's 1912 response, more than a century of scholarship by historians and political scientists has mentioned—and usually condemned—the Dillingham Commission's work. In 2011, the *New York Times* proclaimed, "Forty-one volumes, all of it garbage." In a 2013 interview on National Public Radio, prominent sociologist Richard Alba called the reports "overtly racist."[18]

The best analysis remains that of the great Harvard historian Oscar Handlin (himself the son of immigrants). In 1952, Handlin won the Pulitzer Prize for his influential book *The Uprooted: The Epic Story of the Great Migrations That Made the American People.* It famously began, "Once I thought to write a history of the immigrants in America. Then I discovered that the immigrants were American history." On the heels of the book's success, Handlin produced a memorandum for Harry S Truman's Presidential Commission on Immigration and Naturalization. Handlin argued that Congress should rescind the discriminatory national-origins quotas. He blamed their passage in part on the Dillingham Commission's reports, which he described as "neither impartial nor scientific." The Dillingham Commission, on whose basis Congress had passed the quota laws, had taken "for granted the conclusions it aimed to prove—that the new immigration was essentially different from the old and less capable of being Americanized."[19]

Since Handlin's time, the Dillingham Commission has made cameo appearances in many articles and chapters, usually as an example of nativism and racism. The commission is the subject of only one other book, an essential overview by Robert Zeidel. Zeidel calls for a "rationalist" and "policy-oriented interpretation" that moves beyond cultural arguments over racism and bias. Like Handlin before him, Zeidel focuses on the "old" and "new" immigrants. For many decades this approach seemed logical, but ignoring Mexicans and Asians is no longer tenable.[20]

My approach draws on Hourwich, Handlin, and Zeidel, but also benefits from more recent thinking about immigration, state power, and politics. In the last few decades, many scholars have rethought the histories of race and citizenship in the United States. Instead of thinking about "waves" of European immigration, historians have focused on the Chinese Exclusion Act of 1882 as a turning point in immigration history. Nativism has drawn renewed attention, and recent debates about immigration have fueled investigation of past "crisis moments." New interpretations have produced valuable insights about the fluid meaning of race, state power, and legal categories of citizenship and alienage. The Dillingham Commission, too, offers this new literature something fresh—an opportunity to explore how a discrete group of policy makers analyzed diverse groups' comparative worth to their new homeland in a global context.

At least three new avenues of inquiry distinguish my treatment of the Dillingham Commission from earlier treatments. First, a vast scholarship on state power has accompanied the "transnational turn" in American historiography. Most historians "too easily dismiss immigration policy as a domestic matter," as historian Donna Gabaccia puts it. The Dillingham Commission convened during an era of global migration. Its experts brought bureaucratic knowledge from studying or administering the economies, education systems, and immigration policies of the Philippines, Puerto Rico, Hawaii, and Panama: these experiences colored how they saw immigrants. In addition to chairing the Senate Immigration Committee, Senator Dillingham served on the Committee on Territories. Henry Cabot Lodge chaired the Senate Philippines Committee and lent its conference room to the Dillingham Commission for its meetings. The commission made its own extended investigation abroad. Senator Dillingham's chief of staff compiled a volume comparing U.S. immigration laws with other "receiver" nations, such as Canada and Argentina. In considering all these research avenues, this book transforms a topic and set of sources (the commission's reports) familiar to historians of domestic immigration history into part of the story about how Americans thought about immigrants and the world.[21]

New scholarship on the nature of federal governance has also shaped my work. It would be impossible to explain the Dillingham Commission without reference to the twin emergence in the Progressive Era of modern social science and federal bureaucracy. In recent years, practitioners of "American political development" (or APD, to its subscribers) have focused on state-making and the escalation of federal power that governance—including that of immigration

A rare photograph of some members of the Dillingham Commission, their wives, and staff arriving by dinghy from the S.S. *Canopic* on their tour of Europe in the summer of 1907.

policy—required. Government commissions, a Progressive Era creation, are of special interest to historians of public policy and the state. President Theodore Roosevelt loved commissions. He created, among others, commissions to combat corruption on Ellis Island, to quell labor conflict in the anthracite coal industry, to repopulate rural America, to investigate the stockyard conditions described in Upton Sinclair's *The Jungle,* and to begin the conservation movement. Economic commissions in particular became a kind of cottage industry of the Progressive Era.[22] I count the Dillingham Commission among these, since its conclusions focused on the economic impact of new immigrants, and almost all of its major players were economists. Among them was Roosevelt's first appointee, Cornell University professor Jeremiah Jenks, who served on and wrote several volumes for the very first federal economic commission, the U.S. Industrial Commission of 1898–1902.[23]

Other writers have scrutinized the worship of objectivity by reform politicians and social scientists of the era, and many have identified the nation's first generation of women to earn university degrees as crucial to public policy in the early twentieth century. Scholars in Europe, especially, have theorized a "history of the modern fact" (especially in quantitative form) as something crafted and shaped by people, not simply observed or noted. "Knowledge is a historical phenomenon," as one put it. "The history of knowledge explores what people in the past understood by the idea of knowledge and what they defined or accepted as knowledge." More than forty years of women's history scholarship now makes it possible to see the women who constituted the majority of the commission's staff and helped produce this knowledge. Along with the men who hired and promoted them, they helped pioneer women's federal employment.[24]

Third, this book takes regional difference and politics seriously. Not since John Higham's classic 1955 study of nativism, *Strangers in the Land*, have historians paid sustained attention to regional differences in attitudes about immigration policy. Before 1907, southern legislators—who desperately wanted new labor forces—mostly opposed immigration restriction. The American West, too, was generally more open to European immigration, even as it remained in the vanguard of anti-Asian agitation. The South's outsized influence in Congress not only ensured it two permanent spots on the Dillingham Commission; it also meant that an enthusiasm for what was known as "distribution" policy—distributing immigrants away from the crowded eastern seaboard and industrial areas rather than restricting them from entry—permeated the commission's work. Jewish organizations in Europe and the United States mobilized to send Jewish immigrants to underpopulated regions of the South and West. In 1887, Lodge claimed, "True Americanism opposes the further use of Western lands to invite immigrants," but his views were not, even as one close friend put it, those of "the average man."[25]

On Race

This book relies on work on the history of race. Hundreds of studies approach race as "the history of an idea in America," in the words of pioneering scholar Thomas F. Gossett. In 1963, Gossett posited that ideas about racial difference were not timeless; "race theory," he argued, "had up until fairly modern times no firm hold on European thought." Gossett pinpointed imperial Spain's encounter with the New World as a turning point in racial division and theories. Thanks to Eric Hobsbawm, we understand the ensuing era of racial theory's development as simultaneously—and not coincidentally—the age of nationalism. Gossett's study of the early twentieth century did a great service by labeling Progressive Era social scientists for what they were: racists and eugenicists—even by the standards of the time.[26]

Gossett, writing during the civil rights movement, seemed to falter, however, when it came to explaining the distinction between prejudice against "new immigrants" and that against African Americans, Latinos, and Asians. In 1900, the term "race" meant both more and less than it does today: more, because the idea that race was a hierarchy was stronger, but also less, because "race" was often used where today most people would say "ethnicity" ("Italian race," "Greek race," "Irish race"). In that usage, race meant something stronger than what ethnicity would come to mean, but much less than when it was affixed to "black," "white," or even "Mexican" (which belonged in an overlapping category between legal whiteness and social inferiority).

By the 1990s, the burgeoning field of whiteness studies offered new insights into the subtleties of racial thinking.[27] But being of the "Irish race" never equated to the legal and social inequalities of being African American, either before or after the Civil War. Still, thinking about immigrants both as legally white and as frequent victims of discrimination was an important innovation. Some historians have distinguished between race and color: a new immigrant from southern or eastern Europe—for example, an Italian— could be discriminated against on the basis of race but still benefit from being white.[28]

The word "race" was both ubiquitous and contested in the Dillingham Commission's era because ideas about science, heredity, and acquired characteristics were fluid and undergoing great passionate debate. Some people used it simply to refer to a group united by custom, geography, and appearance; others, to claim that one group was biologically inferior or superior to another. Some—influenced by scientific racism and, especially by the 1910s, eugenics—made claims about hereditary characteristics of body, intelligence, and morality that fueled the exclusion of southern and eastern Europeans with the quota laws in the 1920s. In 1907, eugenics was just starting to infiltrate the United States; its influence peaked by the 1920s.²⁹ A shorthand definition of eugenics might be the "science of race improvement." In the words of Harvard climatologist and early enthusiast Robert DeCourcy Ward in 1910, "Eugenics has to do with breeding human beings for the betterment of the human race." A more restrictive immigration policy, in Ward's view, was essential to the "prevention of the unfit" in the United States.³⁰

To add to the confusion, although many scientists were busy disproving Lamarckian ideas about heritable characteristics (which argued that an acquired trait such as developed biceps or the effects of an infectious disease could be inherited by offspring), these ideas still had adherents, even as newer ideas about evolution and about a distinction between genetic and acquired characteristics were growing.

Unfortunately, adherents of all different kinds of theories used the same word—race—to delineate people. One observer might blame environment for, say, Bohemian iron miners' poverty and ill health; another might blame their inherently inferior qualities as the cause of poor outcomes. Both could describe their subjects as belonging to the "Bohemian race" but mean very different things by it—biological deficits, or mere cultural tendencies that marked a lack of assimilation to American norms.

The lines between racial hierarchy, eugenics, social Darwinism, and racism blurred. Some eugenicists and social Darwinists embraced the idea of the "survival of the fittest" without seeing it in purely "racial" terms—some fine specimens might be Italians, others Anglo-Saxons, perhaps even a Jew or an Indian. When Theodore Roosevelt spoke of an "American race," he often qualified it as an amalgam of the best ingredients. Among the thousand young men Roosevelt chose for his Rough Riders regiment from fifty thousand applicants, fifty were perfect specimens of white Anglo-Saxon Protestantism in the form of Ivy League athletes. On the other hand, Roosevelt also chose an equal number of American Indians, a Jew, and an Italian. He chose no African

Americans or Asians. This was racism, yes, but not the kind that saw some European races as eugenically inferior to others.

No accounting of the use of the term "race" would be complete without reference to the Dillingham Commission's *Dictionary of Races or Peoples*. Originally intended as a field guide for the commission's agents, the project was directed by a husband and wife team, Daniel and Elnora Folkmar, who had experience in both colonial administration and eugenics. On its very first page, the dictionary used "ethnical" (a term only two decades old that only rarely appeared in the commission's volumes), "race," and "nation" interchangeably. (A similar approach can be seen in the dictionary's title.) But the dictionary was not completed until after most of the commission's field reports, so its definitions had little meaningful impact on the commission's employees. It did, however, attract a lot of attention—for example, a two-page illustrated feature in the *New York Times* promised the dictionary would offer a "good deal of a revelation to the ordinary American citizen."[31]

The Dillingham Commission's working definition of "race" was not overly fixed, made little recourse to science, and was less rigid than eugenicists might have defined it. The opening volume of the final reports specified that the "Commission, like the Immigration bureau, uses the term 'race' in a broad sense, the distinction being largely a matter of language and geography, rather than one of color or physical characteristics," that defined "more restricted racial classifications." For the purposes of the commission, "such classification is obviously without value, and is rarely employed."[32]

The way the commission used the word "race"—and tried to distance itself from any fixed definition of it—argues against the widespread and ahistorical assumption that eugenics was a prime mover for the commission. Many overviews of the period lump the commission's work with the era immediately following, when eugenics was unquestionably ascendant. The result is an exaggeration of eugenics' role in the commission's assumptions and conclusions. While members of the commission (especially Lodge) and staff (Joseph A. Hill, Elnora Folkmar, Alexander Cance, and even Franz Boas) were interested in eugenics, a close search of the reports and the private papers of both the staff and their critics (such as the IRL) reveals a marked general absence of eugenic thinking. It was simply too early for eugenics to have emerged as the historical bête noire behind the commission's conclusions. Some of the most prominent early eugenicists of the day even lamented the absence of racial explanations in the commission's studies.[33]

Immigration's Laissez-Faire History

In the early twentieth century, as Gary Gerstle has argued, the American people struggled to reconcile a tradition of "civic nationalism" and "racial nationalism"—one built on equality and democracy, the other on inequalities.[34] Nowhere, I would argue, was the contestation of those two ideas more evident than in the Dillingham Commission's work. Its most important architects, among them economists Jeremiah Jenks and W. Jett Lauck (who oversaw the industrial reports), believed passionately in civic ideals of republican democracy and saw the treatment, conditions, and behavior of new immigrants as challenging those ideals. The commission's forty-one volumes represent its researchers' "objective" attempts to reconcile these two implicit intellectual traditions. Those who were most concerned about immigrants at home as well as the American administration of colonial people overseas—like Jenks—thought the most about civics and democratic government.

Yet immigration restriction was a new and largely untested idea. Only in the years immediately preceding the Dillingham Commission's work did large-scale federal restrictions on entry seem a feasible solution to the "immigration problem," because they required an expansion of federal power and a reversal of a laissez-faire policy toward immigrants.

This point requires a brief detour into the history of immigration law. With only the rarest of exceptions, the United States—whose early colonial settlements had names such as "New Amsterdam," "New England," and "New Sweden"—had unquestioningly recruited, welcomed, and incorporated immigrants into the body politic. There were no numerical limits on immigrants, no federal inspections, no head taxes, no rules of entry. Even during the "Know-Nothing" nativism of the 1850s, when many Americans vilified the immigrant Irish, no federal laws forbade their entry. Legal residency—even voting—usually did not require citizenship. Naturalization, including that of the Irish, was done in local state courts, usually pro forma, and sometimes en masse. (Naturalization was federalized in 1906; a key sponsor of the law, Congressman Benjamin Howell, was appointed to the Dillingham Commission the following year.) The anti-Irish nativism of the 1850s did not yield federal restrictions (though some state and local barriers to the Irish existed), and it was targeted almost entirely at one group, even as Scandinavians and Germans (including Catholics) continued to arrive with little opposition. In 1864, when the North desperately needed more laborers, President Abraham Lincoln inserted a new plank into the Republican Party's platform, stating that "foreign immigration, which in the past has added so much to the wealth, development of resources, and increase of nations, should be fostered and encouraged by a liberal and just policy." That year, Congress passed a bill to encourage immigration, the only one of its kind in American history.[35]

Among those who arrived as contract laborers—a category presumed to be something less than free—were the Chinese, spurred on by treaties that encouraged them to come do western railroad work. A campaign for Chinese exclusion flared up in California and across the West in the 1870s (much of it instigated by Irish immigrants). It characterized the Chinese as distinct from other immigrants. The Chinese Exclusion Act of 1882, which barred only workers, became the first federal law to forbid immigrants on the basis of race and class. (An 1875 law banning prostitutes had targeted Chinese women in all but name.) It also marked the beginning of regional politics' effect on national immigration policy. The Chinese continued to be considered, in immigration policy and in the increasingly racial thinking that undergirded it, a race apart. Yet even Chinese exclusion was passed initially as a temporary measure.

In the scholarship dominated by the "old versus new" framework of European immigration, this story has not gotten a full telling.[36] Mexican and Asian immigration occupied a peripheral place in these histories in part because, in a reverse echo of the policy makers of the early twentieth century, much of the formative literature was as interested in proving the successful assimilation of the "new immigrants" as it was in the topic of immigration itself. But Asians and Mexicans seemed less "meltable": indeed, by the 1980s, calls for multiculturalism in the academy elicited a viscerally negative response from John Higham, once the foremost historian on nativism.[37]

In addition to the Chinese Exclusion Act, Congress passed another formative immigration law the same year. The Immigration Act of 1882 marked the moment when "the Federal government first took control of immigration" from the piecemeal oversight of the states, in the words of IRL leader Prescott F. Hall. To keep out what Hall called "the dependent, defective and delinquent classes," the law laid down the first federal restrictions on immigrants on the basis of health, poverty, and criminal background. It also instituted a small head tax to fund a newly created federal Bureau of Immigration. In practice, the law excluded few people, but it did effectively make immigration per se a federal matter for the first time. Even then, the Supreme Court first explicitly upheld the federal government's right to regulate immigration only in 1889. The Bureau of Immigration, first housed under the Department of the Treasury, was not founded until 1891. The first federal port of entry, Ellis Island, opened in 1892—it is, quite literally, a monument to federal immigration policy. Before that, immigrants arrived at ports that belonged to the states.[38] Most important, until 1921, no numerical quota for immigrants existed anywhere in federal statute. Before Chinese exclusion, there was no such thing as an illegal alien.

After 1882, Congress passed a few laws regulating immigration (notably in 1885, 1891, and 1903). These laws were narrow and incremental, focusing on certain categories of "bad" immigrants (such as the Chinese, contract laborers, criminals, prostitutes, anarchists, polygamists, and people with certain diseases). For all the trepidation by immigrants about the medical inspections at Ellis Island, over 98 percent of them passed.[39] New laws regulated the quality of immigrants, not the quantity, and as Chinese exclusion shows, could be highly racialized. As Jewish lobbyists at the time explained, these statutes were "regulatory," not "restrictive."[40] They hardly constituted a comprehensive, numbers-based immigration policy, and the regulatory approach allowed opponents of immigration restriction to argue that everything was under control already.

In this era, opponents of restriction found strong support in the executive branch—regardless of the party of its inhabitant. Presidents did not like restrictive laws; they needed the votes of naturalized citizens and their children, and as a diplomatic matter, they did not want to anger foreign allies. In 1897, led by Henry Cabot Lodge, Congress passed a law requiring male immigrants to be able to read and write in their own language (the literacy test). President Grover Cleveland vetoed it. In his message to Congress, Cleveland called the restrictive measure "a radical departure from our national policy relating to immigration," which "encouraged those coming from foreign countries to cast their lot with us" and obtain "the blessings of American citizenship." The nation's success and "stupendous growth, [is] largely due to the assimilation and thrift of millions of sturdy and patriotic adopted citizens."[41] In other words, the literacy test was a solution in search of a problem.

Even the arrival of unprecedented millions of new immigrants at the turn of the twentieth century did not lead inexorably to the idea that the federal government must—or even could—restrict them. Organized opposition to the new immigrants began to emerge, but it was not universal. Nativist organizations such as the Sons of the Golden West reinvigorated the anti-Asian sentiments of the Chinese exclusion era and organized against Japanese and Koreans. Craft labor unions called for the restriction of unskilled immigrants, and three Harvard alumni founded the IRL in 1894. Anti-Catholicism and anti-Semitism were ubiquitous. Yet even in the face of growing opposition, many Americans argued against restrictions. Some claimed, as had Grover Cleveland, that immigration was no problem at all, or even that it was the source of the United States' strength and uniqueness. Others believed it was a problem, but only in the crowded northeast. Moreover, many believed that regulating such a massive phenomenon was beyond the ken of the federal government, which in the nineteenth century had been thought of more in terms of its limits than its possibilities. The phrases "immigration question" and "immigration problem," much less "immigration policy," for example, barely appeared in print in the United States before 1900.[42]

Racial thinking surely motivated the commission's most important recommendation: a quota system that would restrict "the number of each race arriving each year" based on a percentage of arrivals in the past years, and "the limitation of the number of immigrants arriving annually at any port." But historical accounts that blame racial prejudice alone for the commission's call for restrictions are insufficient. Instead, it was the collision of unprecedented numbers of immigrants with the emergence of new ideas about the federal government's capacity and social scientists' ability to find solutions to problems.[43]

I do not pretend that this book tells everything about the Dillingham Commission; twenty-nine thousand pages confound summary or tidy conclusions.

And like much of the federal government, the commission was internally inconsistent. The chapters that follow combine collective biography and policy history to focus on people particularly important to how the commission turned out—Jeremiah Jenks and W. Jett Lauck, for example. I necessarily focus more on the thinkers than the people they thought about. A new telling of the creation of the commission finds its roots not in a crisis over European immigration, but as part of a response to anti-Asian discrimination in California. I reveal how the Dillingham Commission helped spur the creation of the modern Jewish lobby to challenge restrictions and the labeling of Jews as a separate race. I delve into the empathetic approach the young economist W. Jett Lauck brought to the twenty reports on immigrants in industry, even as he recommended restriction. I also show the simultaneous influence of women on the commission, and of the commission on women, by telling the stories of the majority of the staff members who were female—including several report authors, supervisors, and undercover investigators. I consider the strange ironies of the famed anti-racist Franz Boas's work for a commission often accused of racism. The book concludes with a case study of the commission's enthusiasm for a scheme to replace African American sharecroppers in the Mississippi Delta with imported Italians—a scheme led by LeRoy Percy, a future member of the commission. An epilogue traces the legislative legacies of the commission's work.

One reason that few scholars have explored the Dillingham Commission in greater depth is that the research material is at once overwhelming and incomplete. The sheer mass of forty-one volumes is a turnoff. Worse, as far as anyone knows, the commission has no papers in the National Archives. According to an internal memo, Congress granted the Department of Labor permission to destroy the commission's records during World War I, and it is assumed they are gone. Among the records were likely hundreds of photographs.[44] It may be that the commission's papers contained something worth hiding, or it may simply be that in an era before the creation of the National Archives in 1934, when there were no requirements to save federal records, Wilson was just cleaning house. Some commission paperwork is cross-referenced in the Bureau of Immigration papers. I have also supplemented the reports themselves with the private papers of commission members and staff contained in over two dozen archives from Burlington, Vermont, to

Baton Rouge, Louisiana, and from Stanford to Harvard.[45] Several female employees' papers, never before examined, proved to be a rich source. These collections, both large and ephemeral, helped me piece together the commission's internal workings. I also created a biographical database of the commission's members and the three hundred staff. Although it is incomplete, it reveals common patterns of social-science training, public reform work, and federal employment at home, abroad, and in U.S. colonies. The result is perhaps the deepest analysis of a federal commission of the era yet conducted.

I learned that the researchers who produced all this knowledge did not abandon it. They used it in subsequent decades, not just in the Immigration Service but also far beyond it—on the Federal Reserve Board, on women's rights campaigns, in the field of cultural anthropology, for union campaigns for a living wage and the rise of the welfare state, in the Secret Service and FBI, and for race relations in the American South, to name just a few.

Although I have cast a wide net, I do not claim to have brought in the whole haul. This book is not a comprehensive history or overview of the commission's reports. Such an attempt would be both redundant—because the reports are widely available in printed and digitized form—and stultifying. Rather, I am interested in revealing the structural and ideological roots of federal immigration policy in the Progressive Era, with its simultaneous suspicion and celebration of immigrants, fear of government power and confidence in public policy, need for manual labor and valorization of expertise. The result, I hope, is a series of illustrative episodes, individuals, and investigations that clarify not only how the Dillingham Commission was a product of its time but also how its influence on immigration policy still lingers.

1

---◯◯◯◯---

The Professor and the Commission

Cornell University economist Jeremiah Jenks was the most important, though not the most famous, of the nine appointed members of the Dillingham Commission. Theodore Roosevelt valued Jenks for his ambition and practicality, but these were not characteristics everyone admired. In 1898, Beatrice and Sidney Webb had visited Ithaca, New York, to see Cornell University, where Jenks chaired the Department of Political Economy. Jenks and his wife hosted the English couple. The Webbs were influential Fabian Socialists who would later cofound the London School of Economics; Professor Jenks, in contrast, was a small-town midwesterner who had been educated in Germany. He was ambitious, accomplished, and good-looking, but the Englishwoman was not impressed. Jenks and his family, Beatrice Webb wrote in her travel diary, were "what we should call in England ultra lower-middle class." They had "detestable" accents, "ugly" clothing, and she found their presence in the intellectual world "grotesque and almost revolting." Jenks seemed to be a "self-controlled and sensible fellow," she conceded, and "anxious to get at the actual living fact." She liked that Jenks did "not rest content . . . with mere book knowledge." On the other hand, he had "a purely business brain" that made him seem "singularly out of place as a Professor." He did not act like an intellectual—too "pushing and enterprising," more like a "corn dealer or timber merchant," like his family back in Michigan. Worst of all, his "dominant purpose" seemed to be not academia but appointments to government service. "It is perhaps difficult with English prejudices," Webb conceded, "to be fair to such a man in such a position."[1]

In the Progressive Era United States, Jenks was a prototype fast becoming a stereotype. Four years after Beatrice Webb's put-downs, the *Atlantic Monthly* judged more favorably what it called this "newer type" on campus now "everywhere in existence." In the 1902 article "College Professors and the Public," the anonymous author described "the expert who knows all about railroads and bridges and subways; about gas commissions and electrical supplies; about currency and banking, Philippine tariffs, Venezuelan boundary lines, the industries of Porto Rico, the classification of the civil service, the control of trusts." No scholar should "entangle himself overmuch" with public affairs, the author warned, but neither should he shy from being "practical" or from "helping to carry forward the detailed work of governmental departments." "Academicians," the author concluded, should contribute to the "pervasive, aggressive, all-modifying spirit of Christian democracy."[2]

The *Atlantic Monthly* author claimed to have chosen these topics—Philippine tariffs, the industries of Puerto Rico, trusts, practicality, Christian democracy—"almost at random," but they were an actual accounting of Jenks's works and interests. Jenks began his career in public service in New York State, when the then governor, Theodore Roosevelt, appointed him to a commission studying tax reform. From 1898 to 1902, Jenks served as "primary academic adviser" for the United States Industrial Commission, which economist John Commons called the nation's first "brain trust." There, Jenks oversaw the investigation of corporate trusts (his academic specialty), where he conducted hearings, collected statistics, and wrote and edited reports. In 1899, he was appointed to be an expert in Asia for the U.S. Treasury. From then on, Jenks split his time between the ivory tower and public appointments that took him all over the world. Within a few years, Jenks had represented the federal government in visits to more than a dozen colonies and countries. Along the way, he became an authority on international fiscal policy, colonial administration, and international arbitration. He also learned about colonial race relations.[3]

Jenks was the first among many social scientists—"entrepreneurial bureaucrats," as one scholar has dubbed them—in the employ of the federal government by the early twentieth century. He was more a bold implementer than an original thinker. As he cultivated favor with the president, dipped in and out of academia and public service, and encouraged his Cornell University

Jeremiah W. Jenks (1856–1929). The Cornell University professor, appointed by Theodore Roosevelt to the Dillingham Commission, oversaw most of its work and shaped its priorities and methods.

colleagues to do the same, Jenks pioneered the role of the social scientist as government consultant. His academic work gets little attention today, but he left enduring legacies both in the economics profession and in federal fiscal and economic policy.[4]

The Dillingham Commission's unique power to create consensus around the idea of an "immigration problem" had a singular and lasting impact on immigration bureaucracy and law. From the beginning, Jeremiah Jenks was at the center of that process. He played the largest role among the commission's members. He made many of the motions at meetings.[5] As a seasoned government expert, Jenks supervised most of the commission's early investigations, including those on congestion in cities, on charitable associations, and on "excluded classes" of immigrants. These latter groups included the Chinese, criminals, and prostitutes and their procurers—who came under the purview of a massive undercover study of so-called white slavery. In response to that report, Jenks coauthored model legislation for what would become the

Mann Act of 1910 to combat sex trafficking. He also supervised a volume on the history of immigration laws.[6] With fellow commission member Congressman William Bennet of New York, Jenks revised the immigrant homes report, as well as a report about the Immigration Service's boards of special inquiry, which handled challenges to deportation orders. These projects built on Jenks's legal training. His faith in corporate organization, his exposure to undercover investigations by municipal reformers, and his interest in Asian affairs all left their stamp on the work.

Jenks did much of the hiring for the commission, including that of W. Jett Lauck, who oversaw the immigrants in industries report that comprised half the commission's total work (Lauck wrote fifteen of the reports). Jenks championed the appointment of anthropologist Franz Boas to undertake the study of immigrant head and body measurements. And he served on the committee that oversaw the editing of the reports, which meant that the final versions carried his stamp of approval.

Jenks brought to the commission a confidence in academic expertise, a broad view of state power, a mind influenced by colonial administration, and a reflexive emphasis on practicality. He held a career-long interest in the dangers of corruption and the responsibilities of citizenship, both common themes among Republican reformers. The commission was nonpartisan, but its work was situated right where Jenks was, at the crossroads between Progressive Republicanism and social-science specialization. He belonged to a Republican Party that was less laissez-faire than corporatist, one that favored protective tariffs and robust imperial policy: it was a party that stood both for big business and for big government. In the era of what historian Alan Trachtenberg has called "the incorporation of America," Jenks often compared the federal government to a corporation.[7] He was a promoter of muscular Christianity, a cheerleader for American imperialism, a specialist on trusts and monetary policy, and a major figure in the National Civic Federation—a Republican prototype for the modern think tank.

Jenks and his family personified an era of dizzying change, including their own ascent from "ultra lower class" to the Ivy League and the halls of government. Historians have argued over what the Progressive movement is or was, but few have doubted that the period it encompassed, roughly the two decades preceding World War I, witnessed the birth of modern America. The Republican Party had abandoned Reconstruction but still ran the federal government. The majority—if a decreasing one—of Americans still lived in small towns or on farms. But thousands of miles of new railroads had collapsed time and space and had made restless Americans an even more transient people. Even Jenks, with his venerable stock (he was named for an ancestor who was a veteran of the American Revolution), got itchy feet—moving from Michigan to Illinois to Indiana to New York, to say nothing of his world travels. Cities swelled, factories and mines thrummed with new workers and new machinery, and colleges and universities pulsed with new students both male and female (Mrs. Jenks had a college degree). At every level of government, policy makers and public workers tried new programs and reforms, while the population expanded 21 percent—the fastest growth of any decade in the twentieth century—from seventy-six million in 1900 to ninety-two million in 1910.[8]

The birthrate among native-born white Americans such as the Jenks family fell throughout the twentieth century. Instead, new immigrants made up most of the population growth.[9] In 1901, sociologist Edward A. Ross labeled this combination of events "race suicide," a term President Roosevelt quickly adopted. Poverty and ethnic violence in Europe only accelerated the pace of new immigration already fueled by industrial demand. Immigration began to rise sharply after 1880. By 1910, almost 15 percent of the total U.S. population was foreign-born, a proportion never exceeded since, even at the height of immigration in the early twenty-first century. Although as many as one-third of the migrants later returned to their home country, they lived, worked, prayed, and played during their time in the United States in ways that often concerned and sometimes enraged other residents.[10]

These new immigrants, who were heavily recruited by major manufacturers and labor agents to fuel the Second Industrial Revolution, were as much a symptom of change as its cause. They crowded into city slums, worked factory floors, blasted ore in mines, and commanded the curiosity and concern of philanthropist reformers and government researchers. In all, around twenty-four million immigrants arrived in the United States between 1880 and 1920. The peak year was 1907, with 1.2 million migrants counted at the nation's ports. That year boasted another significant shift. In 1882, fewer than one in eight arrivals had come from southern and eastern Europe. But in 1907, that percentage was officially reversed, with four out of five newcomers—Italians, Jews, Slavs, Greeks, Hungarians—hailing from the region.[11]

In February 1907, President Theodore Roosevelt appointed Jenks to serve on the new U.S. Immigration Commission. Jenks ranked as the first among many university-trained technocrats hired by what would become known as the Dillingham Commission. Many of the new hires had already studied the peoples, implemented the new economies, and governed the school systems of the United States' new colonies. These squadrons of experts helped create the modern American state. In the early twentieth century, imperialism and immigration laws—which governed steamships under foreign flag, regulated foreign consulates, and encouraged other countries to match their laws to that of the United States—worked together to magnify federal power at home and abroad, and to advance the nation's position in the world.[12]

Several key commission staffers had previously worked in or studied Puerto Rico, the Philippines, and East Asia or went to these places immediately after their stints at the commission.[13] In 1907, Jenks wrote a chapter on American rule in the Philippines for *Colonies of the World,* part of a book series on the history of nations edited by Henry Cabot Lodge.[14] One of the first things the commission's members did was to embark on a summer-long tour of European ports and sender cities to evaluate how the U.S. government might shape the migration process overseas.[15] The commission's secretary, Dillingham's former chief of staff William Walter Husband, authored a report comparing U.S. laws to those of other receiving countries and urged parity between U.S. laws and those of Canada and Mexico.[16] Jenks and his cohort were eager to turn the federal government into a laboratory for reform and social perfection. They had been trained to do so.

"The Doctrine of the Open Mind"

Jenks belonged to the first cohort of Americans to earn PhDs. His education was typical of a generation of academics. Born in St. Clair, Michigan, in 1856, Jenks graduated from the University of Michigan in 1878. He taught high school and college literature classes in classical languages and German and read law to pass the bar before moving to Germany to study political economy at the University of Halle. With its seminar style of instruction and an emphasis on rationalism over religion, Halle was a forerunner for modern graduate research and a model soon copied by universities in the United States.[17]

In 1885, with doctorate in hand, Jenks embarked on brief teaching stints across the Midwest, before being appointed to a chair in political economy at Cornell University, where he taught from 1891 to 1912. From there, he moved to New York University. He headed its Division of Oriental Commerce and Politics while continuing in government service until his death in the 1920s.[18]

Jenks's experience in Asian affairs bridged two eras. Previously, the executive branch had managed immigration policy as a function of diplomacy. In the new reality, one that had been emerging since the Chinese Exclusion Act of 1882, Congress increasingly dictated an immigration policy that reflected domestic lobbying and domestic economic concerns. Regulating immigration responded to nativist constituents, but it was also a way to regulate the labor market without regulating businesses, which was ideologically undesirable, as well as more likely to face opposition from a conservative Supreme Court.

Long before his work at the Dillingham Commission, Jenks participated in the creation of the modern field of economics in the United States. In 1885, just after he finished his doctoral degree, he became a charter member of the American Economic Association (AEA). In the nineteenth century, fields that are clearly demarcated today—political science, history, economics, and sociology—had shared one professional organization. The AEA was one of several professional guilds founded during the Progressive Era by doctors, historians, lawyers, and intellectuals eager to differentiate and solidify their expert "brands." Jenks's own department at Cornell University split around this time.[19]

The AEA's founders included not only academics such as Jenks but also liberal Protestant ministers who wanted to "repudiate laissez-faire as a scientific doctrine," as prominent economist Francis A. Walker put it. The AEA's members—both laymen and academicians—hoped to meld the Christian Social Gospel movement with professional social science by retaining the Enlightenment tradition of economics as an outgrowth of the field of moral philosophy. In Great Britain, political economy had been associated with the liberalism of John Stuart Mill and the observation of economic laws rather than with practical applications and reform. But, like Jenks, most of the so-called New School economists had been trained in Germany. Their approach to statecraft reflected a pragmatic American twist on their graduate training. A German education, wrote AEA founder Richard Ely, taught Americans about "linking book knowledge and practical experience." German university education, one American student explained, "begins with the idea of service to humanity."[20]

Jenks's dissertation adviser at Halle, Johannes Conrad, was considered the father of German historicism—the school of thinking that rejected British classical economics. Conrad advised many Americans, including Ely. At Halle, Jenks wrote his dissertation on formative American economist Henry C. Carey. An admirer of Alexander Hamilton, Carey was an early critic of laissez-faire economics and its deductive reasoning, a proponent of protective tariffs. In a way, Carey offered an American version of the German historicist school of economics. His most famous work, *Principles of Social Science* (1858–1859), was an appropriate topic for Jenks, who would become an advocate of a strong central government and historicist approaches.[21]

New research universities in the United States expanded on the models established in Germany by combining undergraduate and graduate training and by adding practical training in fields such as business, engineering, agriculture, and social work. In the first few decades of the AEA's existence, seven current or former Cornell University professors, including Jenks, served as the organization's president. At Cornell, Jenks's original title was "assistant professor of political, municipal, and social institutions." He taught classes not in basic economics but on municipal government and "the principles of politics." His overseas work proved useful for courses in "comparative politics," "Political and Social Conditions in the Far East," and one on "the later territorial acquisitions—the Philippine Islands, Guam, Porto Rico, Samoa and the Hawaiian Islands," with a "brief discussion of the situation regarding Cuba and Panama." He later added courses on economic legislation, international law, and "Modern Questions in International Politics."[22]

The AEA's 1885 statement of principles had listed the "development of legislative policy" as one of its goals. At the time, this statement in favor of reform activism was potentially radical: for many old-guard economists, laissez-faire was more than just orthodoxy—it was a litmus test for "whether a man were an economist at all," as Francis Walker put it. The new economists were called "heterodox" for precisely that reason. It is no accident that the modern social sciences developed in an era that confronted the social effects of industrialization. Unprecedented problems seemed to necessitate unprecedented solutions.[23] Jenks and his commission staff were, as political scientist Elisabeth Clemens has described, "skilled administrators, academic reformers, and men [and women] of talent who stumbled into public service at a time when careers were not clearly defined."[24]

Yet even true believers in the AEA's mission worried about economists who were "too ready to assert themselves as advocates." (In their preface to *The Immigration Problem,* Jenks and Lauck described themselves "not [as] advocates, but [as] interpreters of facts.") These men wanted to make economics and public policy a science that was compatible with Christian morality and ethics. American universities were less closely tied to the state—even to the idea of the state—than was the case in Germany, but new graduate programs at places such as Johns Hopkins University, Cornell University, the University of Chicago, and the University of Wisconsin maintained a sense of practical mission.[25]

By the turn of the century, the relationship between economic theory and Christian reform in the AEA had faded but not disappeared. Bruising battles over tenure and freedom of speech had made many academics shy away from controversy, instead fashioning themselves as objective experts. Jenks, who would serve as president of the AEA from 1906 to 1907, continued to articulate his religious beliefs even as the field of economics grew more secular. In addition to policy-oriented publications, in 1906, he published the *Political and Social Significance of the Life and Teachings of Jesus.* "The Christian religion has proved itself practical in politics," he wrote in the preface. "God cannot be left out as a factor in public affairs." Two years later, during his tenure with the commission, Jenks wrote a pamphlet, "Life Questions of High School Boys," that was used as a text for hundreds of YMCA study courses. Chapter titles included "The Sex Problem," "The Self-Centered Man," and "Social Service in the Community." The section on politics asked, "Can a person be a good citizen without taking an active part in politics? Did Jesus take part in the political movements of his day? Why did he follow that plan?" In 1911, Jenks chaired a committee that updated the Boy Scouts' oath. To underscore masculine Christianity, they added the line "to keep myself physically strong, mentally aware, and morally straight." Jenks wrote and spoke about the relationship between Christianity and public policy for his entire career.[26]

The moral spirit of the early AEA had morphed into a new, Progressive sensibility that idealized objectivity and expertise. One president of the AEA in the 1890s called the economist a man who could stand objective "above the clouds of prejudice." Such an outlook did not deny moral interests and causes, and Jenks subscribed to this view. "Experts have their personal opinions," he wrote in 1909, "but they surely are entitled to a more careful hearing than those people who have not been trained." Jenks became "the trusted adviser not alone of governments but also of business," according to his obituary in an Ithaca newspaper. "Through it all, he maintained the doctrine of the open mind."[27]

Although Jenks's academic work ranged widely, it was connected by a tone of expert conviction and an emphasis on practicality. Starting in the 1890s, Jenks published on civic election reform, the Chinese monetary system, the international gold standard, trusts and monopolies, and the similarities of the Philippines and American Indian reservations as "dependencies."[28] Over time, three overlapping themes developed in Jenks's work: monetary policy and finance, East Asia, and government administration in both colonial and domestic contexts. His views about political economy suggested an acceptance of the rights of corporations to pursue profits, an interest in the macroeconomic effects of trusts and monopolies, an investment in the principles of Christian social gospel, and concerns about the international impact of industrial capitalism in the United States.

As his government service sent him abroad, Jenks gradually moved from his early work on the trust issue to a concentration in Asian affairs and colonial governance. On sabbatical from Cornell University between 1901 and 1902, he toured the world for the War Department, "investigating on the way the government of dependencies in general, and the money and labor questions in the Orient in particular" operated. He then went to Mexico to consult on the gold standard there. As a member of the Commission on International Exchange, "he spent four months visiting leading statesmen and financiers in London, Paris, the Hague, Berlin, and St. Petersburg." In 1903–1904, he traveled to Japan, "the Philippines, China, Great Britain, France, Germany, Holland, and Russia" to lobby for China's gold standard. By 1907, he had visited "Egypt, Burma, the Straits Settlements, the Federated Malay States, Java, [and] Sumatra" to research colonial policy. After the Dillingham Commission, he worked on the enabling legislation for the Federal Trade Commission. He later traveled throughout Asia and South America and served as an economic adviser at the Paris Peace Conference in 1919. He had become one of the nation's leading colonial technocrats.[29]

Although the Republican reform crowd contained some anti-imperialists, most saw the colonies as a tabula rasa for testing new forms of Progressive government and stamping out corruption. Many like-minded academics found colonial administration an ideal opportunity for implementing their expertise. The head of the first Philippines Commission (1898) was Jenks's boss, Charles Kendall Adams, the president of Cornell University and a champion of academics in the public service. Jenks, too, got in early. As chair of an AEA committee on colonial governance in 1899, he recommended the use of experts to create new fiscal systems and the importation of labor to offset native "inefficiencies." His academic work led to his appointment in 1901 as a special commissioner for the War Department to compare English and Dutch colonial administration and to study possible models for governance of the Philippines.[30]

Colonialism—or "expansion," in its supporters' words—was, to Jenks's mind, intrinsic to the American experiment. Even "our forefathers felt, as practically all other strong peoples have felt, the necessity of expansion," Jenks wrote. "This is a perfectly natural ambition," beginning with the "fact that the whites of America were going to take away the land of the Indians. The only question of dispute has been the way in which they take it." Jenks lauded the United States' approach to colonialism: "We are trying to make the Filipinos fit for self-government by dealing justly with them, educating them," and letting them experiment with democracy, he told an audience at Columbia University. "No other nation has ever attempted an experiment of that kind to anything like the same extent." The English and Dutch had at first "been disposed to laugh at our policies" there, but now they "were eager to learn more." Jenks believed in electoral democracy as a way of advancing civilization. Colonialism made sense to him—"the nation with the greatest power is likely to be the one with the best means, and perhaps the strongest ambition to advance civilization from the modern point of view." Like others appointed to colonial posts, Jenks also brought ideas from the provinces back to the mainland. In an article on antitrust legislation in the United States, for example, Jenks suggested a measure based on Puerto Rico's regulation of corporations.[31]

Jenks developed expertise in fiscal and monetary policy in East Asia. In 1903, the War Department dispatched him to negotiate the Boxer Rebellion indemnities in China, and he served a year on the Commission on International Exchange. In that capacity, he worked to put China on the gold standard and created a plan for using the indemnities to fund scholarships for Chinese students to come to the United States. His own Cornell University hosted more students than any other school.[32] Here again, Jenks hoped to connect the international with the domestic, and the diplomatic with the intellectual.

Jenks's overseas work also shaped his views on immigration, particularly his unfettered embrace of centralized federal power. At the turn of the twentieth century, most Americans were comfortable with "external power" exercised in diplomacy and imperialism but less so with federal programs at home. As a result, the United States was, as historian Andrew Cohen points out, "a state far stronger at and beyond the border" than inside it. For a thinker such as Jenks, who prided himself on being "practical," the United States' outward power should be turned inward if that produced the best results. Indeed, immigration policy projected U.S. power as much outward as inward; political scientist Aristide Zolberg called the federal government's attempts to regulate immigration passenger ships as early as 1819 a form of "remote control" of immigrants beyond U.S. borders. The power the United States exercised abroad became an important model for how the state might regulate foreign peoples coming to and within its own borders. With all of Jenks's colonial travels and administration, he thought about immigrants and economics in a global context. His colonial experience of modernity also shaped his belief in the federal government's right to exercise power around the globe.[33]

Jenks's practicality fueled his lifelong advocacy for a public role for economists, even as the AEA's roots in social reform withered. The opening page of his *Principles of Politics* (1909) cited Theodore Roosevelt's maxim that the only thing worse than "the sincere but unpractical radical reformer" was the "corrupt politician." In contrast, "practical reformers," who were willing to learn from experts, were ideal citizens.[34]

Jenks participated in many of the leading reforms of the Progressive Era. Some of his earliest academic publications concerned urban political corruption and local government. He belonged to the National Municipal League, a haven for Republican political reformers and activist social scientists. The league's New York City branch, which investigated urban vice, shaped Jenks's views on white slavery and crime. He also served as vice president of the National Consumers League, led by industrial reformer Florence Kelley and devoted to improving women's working conditions. His experience with reform organizations, as well as coeducational Cornell University, prepared him for the Dillingham Commission's becoming one of the pioneers of women's federal employment.[35]

Jenks believed in bringing the ivory tower to the public. In the 1890s, at the University of Indiana, he had been an early participant in the extension movement, traveling weekly from Bloomington to Indianapolis to teach a night course. At New York University, he started a government-consulting firm, the Near Eastern Bureau, as well as the Hamilton Institute, a distance-learning venture that offered courses and published handsome (and expensive) volumes such as *Credit and the Credit Man, Domestic and Foreign Exchange, Accounting Principles,* and *Advertising Campaigns.*[36]

As president of the AEA in 1906 and 1907, Jenks wed academic economics to the field of business. His first presidential address to the group, "The Modern Standard of Business Honor," perfectly blended practicality and morality and would probably have made Beatrice Webb blanch. Unlike more radical fellow founders of the AEA, Jenks was basically a conservative. Open to some limits on academic freedom, he belonged to the Rooseveltian school of embracing corporate regulation to save capitalism, not destroy it. In 1907, he advised his fellow economists to avoid "some inclusive scheme of social reorganization" but not to be cowardly, either. "We ought not to be swayed at all by fear that we shall be called either socialists or scientific anarchists." For Jenks, expertise and advocacy were as compatible as capitalism and reform. That is, they were compatible, and having practical problems to solve sharpened one's intellectual tools. It also offered professional opportunity for economists insecure about their status as scientists and "torn between the conflicting claims of scholarship and public service."[37]

The tension between these "conflicting claims" shaped the careers of Jenks and the other economists who worked for the commission. Advocacy muddied the waters of "pure" science. Jenks in particular had his detractors. Some of his colleagues dismissed him—sometimes viciously—as a competent expert-for-hire, but with "no use for the refinements of current economic theory" and "still less use for the developing refinements of statistics." His courses at Cornell University were entirely practical, not abstract or theoretical. Another colleague suggested Jenks was trying to find evidence to support his desired conclusions. At least once, Jenks admitted as much, when he remarked, late in the commission's work, "I have been trying during the last two years not to make up my mind, because, officially at any rate, whatever it may be otherwise, I am not allowed to have any mind to make up."[38]

Some of the critiques of Jenks came from colleagues with a more theoretical bent and a contempt for government employees. He seems to have rubbed many people the wrong way. One of Jenks's harshest critics was his former Cornell University colleague Walter Willcox, who served in various government capacities, including as statistician for the U.S. Census Bureau. Willcox described Jenks's AEA presidential address of 1906 as "the veriest twaddle," "not even grammatical," and "pitched to the level of high school students." If the AEA's presidency "goes through an intellectual cycle," Willcox remarked, it had a "crest" at its founding and "a trough with Jenks' twenty years later." Another economist accused him of "slip-slopping through life." These views reflected disdain for Jenks's willingness to advise on such a wide range of issues and to write popular tracts. But Jenks had fans, too, and not just Roosevelt. One professional admirer praised his "good sense and sound judgement." Politicians and businessmen liked his "candor and fairness." Even Willcox described Jenks's early work on trusts as important and influential. He appears to have been a good manager, an underappreciated and underrepresented skill in academia.[39]

The guiding themes in Jenks's academic work shaped his direction of the commission. In his AEA presidential addresses, Jenks rejected laissez-faire philosophy and explored the moral dimensions of capitalism—especially among large firms and trusts. He articulated a broad view of the state, whose "aim" was "to secure for its citizens not merely life, but abundant life of the highest type: economic prosperity and moral excellence." The government's "duty" was to "forbid the use by business men of any means which are injurious to the public interest." It must avoid "special favors to the strong" and "prevent dishonest practices of those whose wealth comes not from service but from plunder and fraud." But he also defended private profit and capitalism, pointing out that being wealthy was not a crime.[40] His talk was a brief for Republican "good government," moderate corporate regulation, and the maintenance of a free-market system.

It did not preclude a strong federal government. Jenks's rejection of rigid laissez-faire dogmatism informed his belief that the federal government had a right—even an obligation—to regulate immigration as a constitutional and politically acceptable way to regulate the labor force. If the federal government had the power to regulate trusts, then surely it had the plenary power to regulate immigration (as a function of its powers to manage foreign policy).

Learning about the Immigration Problem

No single member of the Dillingham Commission was more important than Jenks. Yet besides *The Immigration Problem* and a couple of related articles and talks, most of Jenks's lifework focused on other topics. Alongside his enthusiasm for state power came a way of racial thinking reflected in his writings, recommendations, and exposure to American colonialism. Jenks had what historian Paul Kramer has called an "imperial way of seeing."[41]

Jenks's views about comparative civilization and racial fitness for democracy determined his conclusions about whether new immigrants could be integrated into the American body politic. His stance on suffrage made it clear, for example, that some people—mostly African Americans, some women, and many immigrants—were not ideally suited for democracy and at the very least needed a period of tutelage. He also suggested that it might make sense to bar immigrants from suffrage in places where prejudice might demoralize other citizens or lead them to violence. The commission's final recommendation included placing limits on those who "by reason of their personal qualities or habits, would least readily be assimilated or would make the least desirable citizens."[42]

In 1909, Jenks was invited to give a talk on "the racial problem in immigration" at the National Conference of Charities and Corrections. Appearing alongside immigrant advocates such as Jane Addams and Grace Abbott, Jenks asked, "What is this problem of the immigrant?" "Most of us have something like a race feeling," he admitted; "to put it another way, we have a racial prejudice." "How proud most of us are of being Anglo-Saxons!" Some scholars have cited these lines to characterize Jenks as a believer in eugenics. But his speech continued in a different direction, toward a critique of that viewpoint: it is "very hard to find," he explained, the rational basis of those beliefs. People tend to prefer "persons who are like us," and "persons who are unlike us we disapprove of." The cosmopolitan diplomat and social scientist knew that was dangerous ground on which to make public policy, since "this racial feeling is simply an unconscious feeling which we have never reasoned out."[43]

The Dillingham Commission, Jenks promised, would study not only which races were "better fitted for American citizenship than others" but also the value of diverse immigrants to the nation. "There are advantages that will come from people who are different from us, and the greater the difference, the greater the advantage." Immigrants deserved "sympathy" and "common understanding," not prejudice, and the commission would seek facts to avoid "misunderstandings." An immigration policy crafted on general principles, he continued, would be much better than the current system, in which "the principle of selection is personal" and dependent on the individual decisions of individual immigration agents (another way of saying that the criteria were subjective and qualitative, not quantitative).

Above all, Jenks told his sympathetic audience, "I think we can see how extremely complicated these racial matters are." It was, he urged, "extremely important . . . that we set aside racial prejudice," and adopt an "impartial spirit" to determine "the best solution for our country of our immigration problem *and how it can be best regulated by law* [emphasis added]." Above all, the commission sought to study the "extremely difficult" task of crafting and enforcing "legislation that shall do justice for all and inflict no needless suffering."[44] Jenks's use of the word "race" was almost entirely synonymous with "nationality." In 1911, in an article publicizing the commission's restriction recommendations, he went further: "I have no sympathy for the race-prejudice which leads so many of our wage-earners and others to look with contempt upon the 'dago,' or the Chinaman, or the Jew."[45] It was possible to favor immigration restriction without invoking eugenics, a pattern that in fact characterized many—though not all—of the commission's volumes.[46]

Contrast Jenks with some of the nation's most prominent social scientists. Towering among them were University of Wisconsin sociologist Edward A. Ross and economist John R. Commons, whose ideas about labor law, the welfare state, and social science left a formidable legacy. They were also—even by the standards of their day—engaged in rather viciously racialized thinking. Ross was fired from Stanford University after reportedly claiming at an anti-Japan rally that it would be better to shoot the Japanese at ships in harbor than it would be to let them in. Commons favored immigration exclusion because, he argued, the very survival of democracy was at stake; in his words, "race differences are established in the very blood and physical constitution." Although men such as Ross and Commons held theories of government and economics considerably to the left of Jenks, their racial theories were far more extreme. On a personal level, Ross and Jenks were something close to enemies. No one on the commission—maybe not even Henry Cabot Lodge, who had to deal with public opinion—had public views as vehement as the most famous economists of the day. It cannot be an accident that these men were not picked for the commission—Commons, for instance, had run the U.S. Industrial Commission a few years earlier, where Jenks worked for him. Jenks and his colleagues on the Dillingham Commission believed too heartily in their own objectivity, but they certainly held more temperate views than did more prominent men such as Ross and Commons.[47]

The Progressive Era birthed the modern state, as well as modern politics, lobbying, and think tanks. Thanks to Jenks, the National Civic Federation (NCF) had a far greater influence on the commission than did the still-nascent field of eugenics. Jenks combined his roles as advocate and expert as a charter member in the NCF, founded in 1899 by corporate leaders worried about the growing antitrust movement. NCF's charter statement promised to "organize the best brains of the nation" to solve "some of the great problems related to industrial and social progress"; to cultivate "the most enlightened public opinion; and when desirable, to promote legislation therewith."[48]

The NCF was a lobbying organization—the most powerful one in the United States. It promoted legislation, but not too much. It was also a think tank that operated as a centrist corporate arm of the Republican Party. Membership was a who's who of the era: Vincent Astor, Andrew Carnegie, attorney general Charles Bonaparte, Elihu Root, and President William H. Taft, among others. Under the leadership of its director, Ralph Easley, the NCF sought to blunt radical organizing and government regulation by promoting cooperation between big business and the conservative craft unions of the American Federation of Labor, whose president, Samuel Gompers, was a member. At its peak, one-third of the nation's biggest corporations belonged to the NCF.[49]

The NCF embraced the use of experts and praised their objectivity even as it leveraged their loyalty to business principles and Republican politics. The AEA nurtured a close relationship with the NCF as a living laboratory for their new economic ideas. The think tank, like those of today, also offered a revolving door to government service. In addition to Jenks, active members of the NCF included Secretary of Commerce and Labor Oscar Straus, AEA leader and Dillingham staff member Roland Falkner, and fellow Dillingham Commission member Charles Neill.[50]

Jenks was a major figure at NCF, where he could exercise his belief in "a climate of acceptance for large corporations under government regulation." The NCF "particularly appealed to Jeremiah Jenks," according to one historian, because his German training and legal education meant that he "was always more interested in practical questions than in theory." Jenks emphasized that the NCF committees he chaired did not forbid "expressions of opinion in the form of conclusions." But their "great desideratum" was "verified, comparable facts," necessary to finding out "what is needed in the way of legislation and administrative methods." In 1899, Jenks keynoted the new organization's conference on trusts. In 1908, he represented the NCF on a presidential committee to draft antitrust legislation. He served on and headed several other committees, including its executive council. His influence on the Federal Trade Commission Act of 1914 grew from his work on an NCF committee that had lobbied for corporate-friendly solutions to regulating interstate trade.[51]

The NCF also offered Jenks his first exposure to immigration policy. In December 1905, it held its inaugural conference on the topic, with meetings focused on medical inspection, return migration, industrial impact, and distribution policy. The conference also explored whether "the exclusion of Chinese Coolie labor [should] be made more rigid" and "extended to Japanese and Corean [*sic*] labor," and, if so, how "the admission of exempted classes of

Asiatics, such as scholars, merchants and tourists" should be regulated.[52] These last two questions were ones in which Jenks was particularly interested. Notably, none of these questions assumed the need for broader immigration restriction, although they did presuppose administrative oversight.

In August 1906, Jenks oversaw a new standing immigration department for the NCF, which he staffed with fellow academics. He also chaired its subcommittee on legislation and enforcement. In addition to reviewing Asian exclusion policy, Jenks's division focused on three aspects of what it called "white immigration": "the character" of new immigrants, "the administration of the present laws," and "a plan for distributing the immigrants to the South and West." This agenda reflected a "moderate" stance on immigration policy, one based on improving the "quality" of individual immigrants and stressing enforcement of current laws.[53]

Within the year, however, NCF's agenda had moved toward restrictionism. The committee's fall 1906 meeting was devoted to two debates. One asked, "Is Further Restriction of Immigration Desirable?" An afternoon session proposed, "Granted for Argument's Sake That Further Restriction of Immigration Is Desirable, Are Any of the Measures before Congress Adequate?"[54] The NCF conference coincided with Congress's debates over the 1906 immigration bill that would create the Dillingham Commission.

The NCF's own "thorough study of the *problem of immigration*" was dissolved into the Dillingham Commission. As an NCF publicity pamphlet explained, in 1907, "all the work," as well as two members, Jenks and Neill, "were therefore turned over to that Commission." NCF leaders were relieved to divest themselves of the issue, which pitted its corporate members, who generally favored open immigration, against many labor unions and influential advocacy groups, such as the Immigration Restriction League (IRL). In 1906, Jenks had tried to recruit IRL leader Joseph Lee to join the NCF, but Lee had rebuffed him with charges that the group was too pro-immigration.[55]

Jenks built the Dillingham Commission around his work for the NCF. The commission's early field study on congestion in cities drew on the concern over urban conditions that spurred calls for distributing immigrants to rural areas, a hobbyhorse of the NCF and other Republican civic reform organizations. A report comparing U.S. immigration legislation with other countries was based on a similar compilation Jenks completed for the NCF. Jenks also brought from NCF a list of philanthropic organizations that worked at Ellis Island, which became the backbone of a commission report on charitable associations. These groups were also heavily represented among those solicited to contribute policy recommendations to the commission for its final volume. Finally, Jenks chaired the commission's subcommittee on "Evasions of the Law," later titled the "Committee on Excluded Classes," which focused largely, as NCF put it, on the "character" of new immigrants. These rather oblique titles referred to a wide variety of people already barred from entry into the United States: criminals, anarchists, polygamists, and prostitutes and their procurers. As chair of this committee, Jenks managed the extensive investigation into white slavery, which he staffed mostly with women.[56]

The largest of the "excluded classes" were the so-called coolies barred by the Chinese Exclusion Act of 1882. Jenks had little exposure to domestic policy before 1905, but his fiscal policy work in China spurred a particular interest in what he and his NCF colleagues called "the Asiatic phase" of the immigration problem.[57] First at the NCF, then for the federal government, Jenks became a student of Asian immigration whose enthusiasm bordered, in his work for the commission, on overzealousness.

The Chinese Exclusion Act barred laborers but allowed businesspeople, scholars, diplomats, and ministers to travel to the United States. The frequent harassment over entry papers that the latter groups received amounted to an early form of racial profiling. In 1905, Chinese merchants in Shanghai called a boycott of American trade goods to protest the indignities of the law's entrance and documentation requirements. With the NCF, Jenks helped President Roosevelt forge an agreement with China to end the boycott. In working out the deal, Jenks reiterated the Republican Party line that the United States should "exclude only the classes that we consider dangerous to our interests," such as "the coolie class"—but not merchants, academicians, and ministers.[58]

At the same time, Jenks was working on an NCF investigation into the smuggling of excluded Chinese across the Mexican and Canadian borders, sometimes with assistance from corrupt U.S. immigration officials. These "contraband Chinese" became the nation's first illegal immigrants. The handful of "Chinese inspectors" hired to search for them were the precursors to Border Patrol, which was not established until 1924.[59]

Where there is smuggling, there is corruption—the bugbear of good government or so-called goo goo Republicans, such as Roosevelt and Jenks. Jenks wanted to ferret it out: he was, literally, a Boy Scout. In 1906, President Roosevelt appointed Jenks and fellow NCF member Charles Neill to a committee to investigate, among other things, Chinese smuggling in California. (The committee also examined corruption at Ellis Island and peonage immigrant labor in the South.) When Congress balked at funding the committee, Roosevelt convinced a millionaire NCF official to open his own wallet for the federal investigation. Jenks brought his research to the commission the following year.[60]

The 1907 immigration law had given the commission broad license to "make full inquiry, examination, and investigation." It could call witnesses, subpoena "persons and papers," and travel at home and abroad to pursue "all matters pertaining to the subject."[61] It would be the biggest inquiry of its kind.[62] In short, Jenks could do almost anything he wanted.

In the summer of 1907, with carte blanche powers and generous funding from the commission, Jenks launched an amateur detective campaign to root out smuggling and corruption in San Diego, California, and Ensenada, Baja California.[63] He traveled to San Diego, where he managed to hire an old friend, a physics professor at Stanford University with no relevant experience; stay the deportation of several suspects and witnesses; and supersede the authority of the Bureau of Immigration. After two years, he had produced no proof of a conspiracy and had ruffled official feathers from Washington to California. But "when you come to think of it," one government lawyer pointed out to a colleague, "what else could you expect?" With a cast of characters that included immigration agents from San Diego to New York, government lawyers, the Los Angeles district attorney, the local press, and the commission's "somewhat nebulous agents," there were "enough elements to the problem to bring about all the misunderstanding and confusion that one could well desire." In March 1909, charges against the federal agent suspected of corruption were dropped and his resignation was accepted. Jenks's report was "placed on file" with the commission, but none of his work appeared in the final reports. Jenks and his allies at the NCF always believed that other federal agencies had tampered with their work, "even going so far that Professor Jenks's own telegrams and letters were opened by Secret Service men from other federal departments."[64] The affair reflected the internal contradictions of a state apparatus that relied in equal parts on bureaucracy and force of personality, as well as the reality that the "federal government" was rife with competing interests and internal conflict.

Although Jenks's sleuthing yielded no actual results, his zeal did reveal the priorities that shaped the commission: he saw few limits on his power, and he placed special emphasis on Asian immigration and government "efficiency"—the Progressive Era's code for clean government. From a legal perspective, Jenks held a broad view of an executive power framed mainly in international affairs and foreign policy. In practical terms, he used power in the form of his own person as an expert appointed by the president.

Beatrice Webb had gotten many things about Jeremiah Jenks right, but she had also missed the point. Jenks personified the interaction between the "Professor and the Public" in Progressive Era America. He parlayed his relationship with Theodore Roosevelt in New York into three decades of federal appointments. As a result, he shaped the modern—and lasting—articulation of a federal "immigration problem" in the United States. Yet his appointment to the Dillingham Commission was largely by happenstance, no doubt due to his newly minted expertise in Asian immigration. This expertise had special importance, because the commission's creation—although it is remembered for its study of southern and eastern Europeans—was a direct consequence of a diplomatic crisis with Japan that led to the exclusion of Japanese laborers in the Gentlemen's Agreement.

2

⊗⊗⊗

The Gentlemen's Agreement

The lives of two men—Jeremiah Jenks and Yamato Ichihashi—connect the Dillingham Commission to its little-known origins in U.S.-Japanese relations and the American West. While the midwesterner Jenks climbed the ranks of academia and government, the young Japanese immigrant Ichihashi graduated from high school in San Francisco, attended Stanford University, and worked as an interpreter and translator for the Dillingham Commission. After graduate school at Harvard University, Ichihashi would return to Stanford University as a professor and become a preeminent scholar of Japanese Americans.

Jenks and Ichihashi had much in common, but their differences were more telling. Both men believed in American higher education and social science. Both saw immigration policy and foreign policy as closely connected, believed that domestic legislation shaped immigrants' lives in important ways, and held a special interest in Asian immigration. Both also found personal and professional promise in federal power. Yet here their lives diverged. For Jenks, those possibilities were realized. Ichihashi found only frustration, marginalization, and exclusion.

Most studies of the Dillingham Commission ignore its interest in Asian migration. In the years just after the Russo-Japanese War, the diplomatic importance of the Japanese—and the populist uprising against them in the American West—yielded attention that far exceeded their tiny percentage of the immigrant population. The commission devoted three volumes (vols. 23–25) of its reports to "Japanese and other races" in the Pacific Coast states. In 1911, the director of the western reports, H. A. Millis, summarized the "three immigration

Yamato Ichihashi (1878–1963). A Japanese immigrant who earned a PhD
from Harvard University and who became a professor at his undergraduate
alma mater, Stanford University, Ichihashi served as research assistant and
interpreter for the three volumes on the Pacific Coast and American West.

problems" that the commission believed needed legislative remedies. The
first was European immigration; the other two pertained to excluding
Asians. The opening lines of the volumes on the West read, "Special emphasis
was placed upon Japanese immigration by the agents of the Commission attached to the western office maintained in San Francisco." These priorities
have not survived in most retellings of the commission's origins or goals.[1]

Ichihashi was one of four Japanese immigrants hired as translators and interpreters by Henry Millis, a Stanford economist who became the superintendent of the commission's reports on the Pacific Coast states. Ichihashi and his colleagues were anonymous to readers: although the volumes thanked the American agents by name, as well as the Japanese consulate and media for "the fullest cooperation," no names were listed for the "four Japanese students who at different times have served it as interpreters and translators."[2] Still, Millis's reports clearly evinced sympathy with the Japanese, in keeping with many other cosmopolitan elites in the United States.

The commission served as a bridge from a nineteenth-century tradition of a minimalist federal immigration policy driven by international diplomacy, to an emerging twentieth-century reality of restrictive legislation dictated by domestic politics.[3] In spite of the trend toward restriction, the commission's own investigations of Japanese immigrants—aided by Japanese students such as Ichihashi—challenged the stereotypes held by local and national officials alike. This contradiction was only one of many gaps that would emerge between the commission's findings and its eventual recommendations. In the end, however, as Ichihashi's life showed, restriction policies would prevail. Although Ichihashi and his Japanese coworkers at the commission were indispensable to its production of knowledge, they did not benefit from it.

On April 18, 1906, just after five o'clock in the morning, San Franciscans woke to the earth roiling underneath them hard enough to be felt from Oregon to Los Angeles. The earthquake struck with no advance warning, no modern communication technology, and no system of federal relief. Fires erupting from exploding gas mains destroyed what the earthquake had not. Three thousand lives were lost, and three-fourths of San Francisco's residents were left homeless. Many of these were immigrants with shallow roots in the country. The U.S. Army took control of the response, but private relief—including $246,000 from Japan, the largest donation from a foreign nation—provided the bulk of assistance.[4]

Japan received little thanks for the relief that it gave, and its immigrants got little but grief. The disaster unmasked the racism and social divisions of urban life in chaos. It destabilized institutions and gave free rein to those willing to use fear and prejudice to seize social and political control. In the

years before 1906, the influx of Japanese immigrants in San Francisco—
their population had grown sevenfold from 1900 to 1907 to over eleven
thousand—increased their visibility at a time when nerves were already
frayed. After the disaster, violence against Japanese residents increased dramatically. Most victims were laborers. A mob assaulted and stoned two professors visiting from Tokyo's Imperial University who had come to study
the disaster recovery.[5]

Japanese emigrants, almost all of them men, began coming first to
Hawaii—usually as contract labor—after the Chinese Exclusion Act of 1882.
Although Japan had informally discouraged emigration to the United States
since 1900, the American annexation of Hawaii in 1898 meant that Japanese workers already there could use the islands as "a stepping stone" to the
U.S. mainland. There was no way to restrict those already in Hawaii from
coming to the mainland, because they were not technically immigrants. Hawaiian advertisements and broadsides lured Japanese to California. In 1906
alone, two-thirds of the seventeen thousand Japanese who entered the mainland United States came from Hawaii. They had "American fever," according
to the *Hawaiian Star.* By 1909, more than half the Japanese in the United
States lived in California, where they made up as much as 7 percent of the
male working class. For the first time, there were nearly as many Japanese in
the mainland United States as there were in Hawaii, around seventy thousand.
Yet they were barely present outside the Pacific Coast.[6]

In the aftermath of the San Francisco earthquake and fire, a decidedly local
act set in motion the events that helped create the Dillingham Commission.
In October 1906, San Francisco's school board issued a resolution for administrators to "send all Chinese, Japanese, and Korean children to the Oriental
Public School." Since the turn of the century, San Francisco's labor leaders
and nativists had been demanding that Japanese immigrants be excluded, like
the Chinese had been since 1882. Public rumblings about segregating Japanese schoolchildren began in 1905. The Japanese and Korean Exclusion
League and Native Sons of the Golden West held fiery meetings and sent
dozens of petitions to Congress. The Exclusion League, funded by the
Socialist-leaning Building Trades Council, found free publicity in the yellow
journalism of the conservative *San Francisco Chronicle.*[7] It also pressured the
school board for months to craft a segregation order. Then, on April 18, 1906,

San Francisco's cataclysmic earthquake and fire upended race relations in the West's largest and most important city.

"Taking this as a God-given opportunity," as one scholar in Japan put it, the school board announced its segregation policy six months after the quake. The decree applied to a population of just ninety-three Japanese children scattered across twenty-three public schools. The Japanese government maintained that the Treaty of 1894, which granted Japan a status equal to "most favored nation," made the school board's segregation measure illegal. Japanese diplomats protested, and some people warned of war. More likely was a trade war, which Roosevelt could not afford in a recession year. With this opinion as justification, Japanese residents of San Francisco boycotted the new "Oriental School." Privately, however, the U.S. State Department's highest-ranking lawyer, Solicitor James B. Scott, doubted Japan's argument could succeed. A local act affecting fewer than one hundred children exploded into an international diplomatic crisis. The incident led, in the winding manner of political compromise, to the passage of the Immigration Act of 1907, which news stories called the "Japanese immigration bill" because of its so-called coolie measure to restrict Japanese laborers.[8] The law also created the Dillingham Commission.

San Francisco nativists forced the segregation issue on Roosevelt at a sensitive time. America's acquisition of Hawaii had made it a conduit for Japanese immigration to the U.S. mainland. Meanwhile, in 1905 Japan had decisively defeated Russia in the Battle of Tsushima, demonstrating itself as a military empire worthy of attention. The next year, Roosevelt won the Nobel Peace Prize for his role in brokering an end to the Russo-Japanese War. After 1906, the United States and Japan had firmly established themselves as Pacific world powers. Japan's modernism and scientific advancements rivaled those of its Western counterparts. Ichihashi later called the "civilizational developments" of the United States and Japan "strikingly parallel." Japan possessed, like the United States and Europe, "highly developed industrial and political institutions." His remarks echoed the Japanese state's efforts to highlight its society's commonalities with the United States in class structure. The last thing Roosevelt wanted was to be at odds with a potential competitor for control of the Philippines, Guam, and Hawaii because of a local school board policy.[9]

The San Francisco schools imbroglio became the first serious crisis in U.S.-Japanese relations—worse, in Theodore Roosevelt's words, than "any of the other rather stormy incidents" during his presidency. It also highlighted the disconnect between elite diplomats and working-class white nativists. Roosevelt, Secretary of State Elihu Root, and Secretary of Commerce and Labor Oscar Straus (whose purview included the Bureau of Immigration), needed Japan—if not as an ally, then as something short of an overt enemy. All three men had been strong supporters of Japan in its conflicts with both Russia and China, albeit in the race language of the era: "The Japs were yellow-skinned," Straus and Roosevelt joked with each other, "but the Russians were yellow all the way through." Upper-class Americans such as Roosevelt, Root, and Straus read popular magazine articles that questioned whether the Japanese were "Mongolians" like the almost universally denigrated Chinese. The commission's *Dictionary of Races or Peoples* would claim that the Japanese's "Mongolian traits are much less pronounced" than those of the Chinese. Two years earlier Roosevelt had written to diplomat John Hay, "What nonsense it is to speak of the Chinese and Japanese as of the same race! They are of the same race only in the sense that a Levantine Greek is of the same race with Lord Milner," the consummately British colonial administrator.[10]

These were views that belonged to both American and Japanese elites. Historian Paul Kramer has labeled the distance between the low racism of San Franciscans and the high cosmopolitanism of diplomats in both countries a "countervailing 'civilizing' politics" that left room for the class "elevation" of certain small numbers of otherwise inferior groups. "To keep out the Japanese does not in any way imply that Americans look down upon the Japanese," Jenks explained in the popular magazine *Outlook* (which Theodore Roosevelt helped edit) in 1911. "It simply implies, in the first place, that the two peoples are different. . . . In other words, it is a willingness to face facts." He continued, "The educated Japanese and educated Americans mingle each with the other on terms of absolute equality and with absolute friendship at the present day . . . Scholars from Japan come here and are welcomed exactly as American scholars are welcomed in Germany." But both countries agree "that there shall be no immigration *en masse*." Still, he reiterated, "there is no feeling but respect, and indeed admiration, for the wonderful Japanese people."[11]

Ichihashi's own words showed how these views dovetailed with Japanese class consciousness, as well as with the racial politics of the Meiji period in Japan. In 1913, Ichihashi wrote a pamphlet for Japanese-American immigrant societies in which he explained that the relationship between "whites and Japanese is not analogous to that of whites and Negroes. Caucasians and Japanese are, to begin with, much closer. The Japanese race already contains considerable white blood," and "many a Japanese of high social rank could easily pass for an Italian or Spaniard." But most working-class white San Franciscans would not have agreed with these assessments. One called the Japanese "more servile than the Chinese, but less obedient and far less desirable. They have most of the vices of the Chinese but none of the virtues."[12]

In 1906, the local action of the San Francisco school board had reverberated across the Pacific before Washington even noticed. Within ten days of the proclamation, the American ambassador to Japan wired the State Department that "all newspapers here publish dispatches about agitation in San Francisco for exclusion of Japanese." Europe published news on it as well. The telegram caught both Root and Roosevelt off guard, because, in the president's words, the issue was "so purely local that we never heard of it here in Washington."[13]

Roosevelt called the people of San Francisco "idiots" and "infernal fools" for "insult[ing] the Japanese recklessly." Throughout 1906 and 1907, Roosevelt's private writings revealed his increasing belief that for San Franciscans, racism was the root of the problem. Roosevelt addressed the matter in his December 1906 message to Congress, in which he claimed that segregating Japanese students "from the public schools of San Francisco is a wicked absurdity." By the height of the crisis, Roosevelt decided that the school blowup was "partly [about] labor, and partly a deep-rooted racial antipathy, the extent of which fairly astounds me."[14]

Roosevelt did not share the "racial antipathy" of the protesters. Even if he had, he needed to placate Japan. For years, Roosevelt and Lodge had discussed how to restrict Chinese and Japanese immigration while preserving diplomatic relations. Roosevelt assailed the "criminal stupidity" of the San Francisco anti-Asian activists yet supported in principle a ban on Chinese and Japanese laborers.[15] At the same time, the president, like many other diplomatic and intellectual elites, also favored granting Japanese immigrants the right to naturalize—he had said as much in his December 1906 address to Congress. Popular sentiment on the Pacific Coast remained adamantly opposed. Roosevelt, Root, and Straus determined that federal legislation would be needed to quell the Japan crisis.

Passing the Law

While San Francisco recovered from natural disaster and seethed over Japanese immigration, back in Washington, Congress was mired in debate over immigration legislation. In February 1906, two months before the San Francisco earthquake, Vermont's William Dillingham, chair of the Senate Immigration Committee, had introduced a new comprehensive immigration bill. The final version included several policies promoted by moderate restrictionists of both parties. It raised an immigrant-entry head tax from $2 to $5 (later reduced to $4) and barred new categories of people from immigrating (such as "idiots," "feeble-minded persons," and prostitutes). It created a federally funded Division of Information to encourage distribution policy by offering new immigrants information about underpopulated regions—which moderates on immigration hoped could prevent numerical restriction laws. Most controversially, the bill contained a literacy test for immigrants in their own language. The Senate passed the bill in late May, and it was sent to the House.

Henry Cabot Lodge, the father of the literacy test, had first introduced a literacy bill to Congress in 1891, when he served in the House, and he and Roosevelt had discussed it for years. The Immigration Restriction League (IRL), whose most public member was Lodge, lobbied assiduously for the test.[16] Dillingham had not included the literacy test in his original bill, but it was added during the debates.

The House of Representatives, where August Gardner, Lodge's son-in-law, sponsored the 1906 immigration bill and served on the immigration committee, proved a more challenging environment than the Senate for passing the bill. The "attitude" of the two chambers "toward the immigration question differed radically," as the commission explained in its own history of the 1907 law. Dozens of House members relied on immigrants for their seats. Equally important, Joseph Cannon of Illinois, the powerful Republican Speaker of the House, was a longtime foe of restriction. The Republican Party was split between elite reformers and restrictionists, such as Lodge and Dillingham, and an old guard wary of new federal power, such as Cannon. In the House, proposals for a federal immigration commission had already emerged as a way to delay restrictive legislation, including one by Missouri Republican and German immigrant Richard Bartholdt. Later, the commission itself described its creation as "an admission that the evidence at hand was insufficient to warrant a congressional verdict" on changing immigration policy.[17]

If the Dillingham Commission was a delaying tactic, it also genuinely reflected Progressive Era enthusiasm for "expertise." Speaker Cannon hated experts, but he disliked the literacy test even more. Cannon introduced an amendment to the House bill to replace the literacy test with an immigration commission, funded by the new head tax. He bullied several members to support the bill or to sit out the vote, and the new version eked its way through the House.[18] The House and Senate remained at an impasse over the literacy test, and the bill sat in conference committee for six months.

Then the San Francisco crisis broke. Roosevelt wanted to end the city's school segregation order in exchange for the Japanese government's ceasing to issue passports to the United States (what became known as the Gentlemen's Agreement). Japan was open to negotiation on the point. Roosevelt saw in the stalled immigration bill a potential vehicle to deliver his plan. While the bill was in conference, Roosevelt inserted language that also allowed him to keep out Japanese immigrants who tried to come to the United States while they held passports to Canada or Mexico. One journalist called it the "California compromise."[19]

Roosevelt had never been wedded to the literacy test. Even Lodge, whose two great causes were diplomacy and immigration restriction (he was a member of and later chaired the Senate Foreign Relations Committee), found that the immigration bill divided his loyalties. At first he defended the literacy test in the conference committee. But the Japan crisis changed everything. As conference committee member William Bennet recalled, Elihu Root came to Capitol Hill and told the committee, "Gentlemen, you've got to stop your squabble over the literacy test—adopt your Immigration Commission. We didn't want any war with Japan, and so we said all right." Lodge dropped the literacy test and helped Root compose the amendment that would become the Gentlemen's Agreement. Back at the Capitol, Lodge and his allies "lectured and censured" their fellow conference committee members for three days to bring them to heel.[20]

The fight in Congress took two months of horse trading and arm-twisting. Ideology, partisanship, regional difference, and racism motivated the skeptics. Supporters and critics alike noted the bill's expansion of presidential authority. The Bureau of Immigration already held "tremendous administrative power," in the private words of its overseer, Oscar Straus. Letting Roosevelt use the executive branch to stanch Japanese immigration extended federal power even further.[21]

Moreover, the bill mixed foreign policy with what many members saw as a domestic matter. Those in the executive branch were fine with this. After all, as Straus wrote to his brother during negotiations, "Foreign relations are quite closely connected with Japanese and Chinese immigration matters." But to many members of Congress, Asian segregation and exclusion were domestic, even local, efforts to protect the "American standard of living," in which other countries—or the president, for that matter—had no business interfering. Roosevelt, in the view of Texas senator Charles Culberson, was holding "this authority as a club to compel the San Franciscans to admit Japanese children to their schools, refusing to exclude the Japanese coolies." "In plain words," Culberson claimed, "a foreign power has browbeaten the Government of the United States and browbeaten a sovereign State of this Union into a surrender of its rights to control its own affairs."[22]

Even some politicians sympathetic to Japan hesitated to interfere in California's local school governance. Presidents less imperious than Theodore Roosevelt, both before and afterward, have been frustrated by their powerlessness to prevent states from actions that affected immigration policy. "The Japanese government looks to the [U.S.] federal government to prevent discriminatory treatment of its subjects," Henry Millis observed. But "our political organization is a poor one for dealing with international questions. States may do things of serious international importance, and the federal government does not have power to stay their hands." Presidents avoided binding legislation in favor of using immigration policy as a diplomatic bargaining chip. Rutherford Hayes vetoed an early Chinese exclusion measure; Cleveland had vetoed a literacy test in 1897. Taft and Wilson would do so as well (Wilson twice, though the second time, in 1917, Congress overrode his veto).[23]

Congress, in other words, felt differently than presidents did. The ad hoc nature of Roosevelt's proposal, which gave the executive branch power over which Congress had no control, elicited sharp opposition. Some nativists resented the impermanence of the proposed agreement, which could at least theoretically be changed at the chief executive's whim. House Minority Leader John Sharp Williams of Mississippi asked how Congress could be assured that the president could not or would not choose to let more Japanese in: "I do not want another section of this country cursed as the South has been cursed, with an almost insoluble race problem, and I warn you now it will be a worse one than ours." Another senator complained, "The proposed legislation as a permanent proposition would not be worth the paper upon which it is written." "There can be no doubt," he continued, "as to what the people of the West will demand. It will be the exclusion of Japanese laborers and coolies from the United States and its colonies. That and nothing less." Executive agreements were something less.[24] Much of the opposition was rooted in region and race. Lodge's central role did not help: no Southern Democrat could have forgotten Lodge's sponsorship of the infamous "force bill" of 1890, which had proposed federal supervision over southern elections to ensure black voting rights.

Some opponents of the bill insisted that the issue was racial purity— not just competition with white laborers (which the Gentlemen's Agreement was intended to curtail). As Senator Williams explained, "I am with the Californians . . . I want the Pacific slope kept a white man's country [applause] . . . The influx of another and a radically different race," even one that might "be not only equal, but superior, means another race problem for another portion of this Republic."[25]

Alabama Democrat John Burnett, who served on and would later chair the House Immigration Committee and was soon appointed to the Dillingham Commission, articulated the connection between partisan ideology and racism. The bill, in his view, was "obnoxious" to anyone who opposed giving the president "autocratic powers." Burnett was "duty bound, as I see it, to vote against the report. The big stick which it permits the President to hold over the States may sometime be wielded to the overthrow of the most sacred institutions of the South"—that is, racial segregation. "This constant trenching on the reserved rights of the States," Burnett concluded, "is becoming more dangerous with every Republican Administration." The measure gave "the

President a discretionary power to be used as a bludgeon to force a sovereign State to forego its sovereign right to maintain separate schools." The "precedent," he warned, might be applied "some day in Mississippi."[26] Executive power wielded anywhere, even in foreign affairs, could be used at home.

This "common cause" narrative reflected political point-making, not reality. The Mississippian Williams, claiming to be "with the Californians on the separate school issue," deigned to speak for Californians as if they had one voice. But many Californians supported the compromise. Even as San Francisco launched its segregation measure, Los Angeles coolly proceeded with integration. After the earthquake, many Japanese in San Francisco moved to Los Angeles, whose Japanese population soon outgrew San Francisco's. In 1906, the *Los Angeles Times* reported, "Chinese and Japanese laborers are a blessing rather than a menace." The Los Angeles school superintendent called Japanese students "quiet, well behaved pupils, who set a good example to the others." There was "no Japanese question here." As one newspaper noted, "No protest has been raised by politicians or newspapers." The Dillingham Commission's own analysis of the Bay Area school controversy concluded that "in most localities Japanese pupils and the pupils of other races associate with little or no friction." Attitudes toward the Japanese, the commission reported, varied considerably across the West—from San Francisco's furious anti-Japanese efforts, to Colorado, where "opinion . . . varies all the way from extreme race antagonism to extreme favor," to the "extremely cosmopolitan" Wyoming coalfields, where "few race antipathies are present."[27]

By the end of January, Roosevelt still did not have a deal with the school board or the Japanese government. On February 9, the San Francisco school board members and the mayor—out on bail for corruption charges—were summoned to Washington to meet with the president and Root. Even as the three men met in the White House, Japanese laborers from Hawaii continued to arrive at San Francisco ports. Many were fleeing an outbreak of bubonic plague. Root leaned on the conference committee's Republicans. Secretaries Straus and Root dined with the Japanese ambassador and his German wife. The San Francisco schools agreed to withdraw the segregation order if Japanese immigration ceased. Roosevelt wrote to his son, "Slowly and with infinite difficulty and frequent setbacks, I am getting both the Californians and Japan into an attitude that will permit of a solution."[28]

Finally, on February 18, the revised Immigration Act of 1907 passed both houses, and the president signed it. Two days later, Roosevelt issued an executive order refusing admission to Japanese and Korean laborers with passports to Mexico, Canada, or Hawaii. So began the Gentlemen's Agreement—a name that aptly reflected the "civilizing" politics that underlay it. Wives and children of those Japanese already in the United States were allowed passage, a concession to the importance of establishing families. Within weeks, plans for the commission were under way.[29]

The San Francisco crisis pitted the international relations of competing empires against the rough-and-tumble politics of domestic immigration legislation. The transition was difficult for statesmen used to high diplomacy and suspicious of nativist congressmen. Elihu Root had lobbied for the bill, but as the nation's chief diplomat he viewed the move toward legislative control over immigration policy as at best a necessary evil. In April 1907, Root addressed a group of international lawyers regarding "the real questions" about the Japan crisis. "The practice of diplomacy," he observed, "has ceased to be a mystery confined to a few learned men who strive to give effect to the wishes of personal rulers, and has become a representative function answering to the opinions and the will of the multitude of citizens." Diplomats had the "experience of centuries" to use "rules and customs . . . essential to the maintenance of peace and good understanding between nations." But these rituals, he complained, "have little weight with the new popular masters of diplomacy."[30]

Root counseled his elite audience that "information, understanding, leadership of opinion in these matters, so vital to wise judgment and right action in international affairs, are much needed." Even so, he said, "it is a pleasure to be able to say" that relations between the United States and Japan remained in "perfect good temper, mutual confidence, and kindly consideration"—a view at considerable odds with Roosevelt's secret preparations for possible war. Root was concerned about local and state actions against immigrants' rights, as well as about Congress's move toward legislating what had once been the purview of diplomats. Many of the government's powers were divided, but, as he pointed out, "in international affairs there are no states; there is but one nation." The United States and Japan had a treaty that guaranteed their citizens equal rights. Treaties are "made by the national government," and so "there can be no question of state's rights." But what, Root asked, "was to be the effect upon that proud, sensitive, highly civilized people across the Pacific, of the discourtesy, insult, imputations of inferiority and abuse aimed at them in the columns of American newspapers and from the platforms of American public meetings?" After all, "We introduced Japan to the world of western civilization." He applauded "the genius of the race that in a single generation adapted an ancient feudal system of the far East to the most advanced standards of modern Europe and America." He worried that "angry and resentful feelings" were "inevitable if the process which seemed to have begun was to continue." Root finished with a warning about popular sentiment and immigration policy: "It is hard for democracy to learn the responsibilities of its power; but the people now, not governments, make friendship or dislike, sympathy or discord, peace or war, between nations." "A world of sullen and revengeful hatred," he warned, "can never be a world of peace."[31]

Crafting the Commission

In reality, the Dillingham Commission—like all government commissions—was a middle ground between mass rule and autocracy. Elected officials appointed its members, who were granted wide latitude to operate outside of democratic accountability. Commissions were the quintessential Progressive idea, designed to balance democracy with efficiency and nonpartisan expertise. Commission member William Bennet promised, "We adopted as our watchword, 'We are not afraid of a fact.'" California businessman William R. Wheeler, appointed by Roosevelt, concurred that they just wanted to "learn the facts."[32]

The Dillingham Commission was by nature political—and partisan. Seven of its members were Republicans, and two were Democrats. According to Jenks, at the beginning of their work, "several members of the Commission were strongly inclined not to restrict immigration further," while others—especially Lodge and Burnett—were vocal supporters of new limits.[33] Many of the commission's priorities reflected those of the Republican Party: reforming the civil service (by investigating corruption in the Immigration Service), for example, and investigating white slavery (borrowing from civic-reform club efforts to eradicate vice in New York, Chicago, and elsewhere). In large part, the commission's work, as Jenks's involvement showed, matched the mission of a Rooseveltian Republican Party that championed government expertise, executive power, protection for U.S. corporations, and a muscular foreign policy that extended American influence around the globe. All these views were integral to how the commission did its work and to the conclusions it reached.

Both parties harbored a variety of policy stances about immigration. Most of Congress's southern delegation opposed further federal restrictions. Burnett— who represented working-class steelworkers in Birmingham—was an exception. In the nineteenth century, Republicans were more closely associated with restriction than the Democrats, but they backed away from party-wide stances as immigrant coalitions developed within the party. Richard Bartholdt, the Republican who had originally proposed the commission in Congress, was a German immigrant. Even Lodge, Washington's most prominent proponent of restriction, proved willing to compromise—to the great irritation of the IRL. Dillingham, who chaired the Senate Immigration Committee, was considered only a "moderate restrictionist"; his counterpart in the House, Benjamin Howell—also named to the commission—was a strong restrictionist. Howell had sponsored the Naturalization Act of 1906, which federalized and tightened the procedures for becoming a citizen. In contrast, fellow House appointee Republican William Bennet of New York was prominently pro-immigrant.[34]

Not one commissioner was an immigrant, or of southern or eastern European stock. Bennet had a large Jewish constituency in upper Harlem, but his own roots were deep in Puritan Connecticut. The Irish Catholic Charles Neill, who served as U.S. commissioner of labor and was a former professor at Catholic University, was the only non-Protestant, and the only first-generation American. Roosevelt thought that members of recent immigrant groups could not be "objective." He told the leader of a prominent nativist organization that the appointments "must be high class men," by which he excluded racist populists as well as new immigrants.[35]

At least two members of the Dillingham Commission owed their appointment directly to the Japanese crisis. One was Jenks, with his extensive experience in Asian affairs. The other was William R. Wheeler, the Californian businessman, because he wanted "to see California represented on this commission." Wheeler was in the hardware and railroad business and had served as California's immigration commissioner, a statewide position created in the

1870s, before the federal Chinese Exclusion Act, to keep "unfit" Chinese out of California. His appointment was a sop to the anti-Asian vote in California—the choice, according to the *Washington Post*, of "practically the entire Congressional delegations from the Pacific Coast." Wheeler oversaw the western studies from a lush office he rented in San Francisco. The state of California was conducting its own study of the Japanese, but given "the present attitude of the Japanese people toward the state of California," Wheeler told Taft in 1909 that he seriously doubted anything the state could come up with would prove acceptable to the other country. In contrast, he thought, "data furnished by a federal body such as The Immigration Commission cannot but be accepted as authoritative."[36]

Like so many government projects, the Dillingham Commission's scope and scale expanded as it was implemented. Bartholdt's original resolution had proposed a brief investigation costing twenty thousand dollars, and Roosevelt had talked about twelve to eighteen months of work. But the final legislation put "no limit on the time the Commission shall consume . . . or on the expense it may incur," one newspaper reported. "The provisions of the law under which the commission will operate are broad." The commission considered using existing data, but this idea, its final reports explained, "was discarded in favor of an original investigation which, it was perfectly apparent, would necessarily be more far reaching and involve more work than any inquiry of a similar nature, except the census alone, that had ever been undertaken by the government."[37]

The 1907 law also gave the Dillingham Commission global reach to exercise its broad powers. It was "authorized to go anywhere in this country and abroad," the *Washington Post* noted, "or to send special commissioners to any foreign country to regulate by agreement the immigration of aliens and to do a number of other things." In May 1907 most of the commissioners, their wives, and several staff members set off on the SS *Canopic* for their four-month tour of port cities and migrant-sending communities. (The aristocratic Henry Cabot Lodge joined the others abroad, taking time out of his usual European holiday.) The steamship counted among its passengers 224 Italians returning to their homeland in steerage. The commission interviewed 108 of them to find out why they had left (about half said just to visit; three-fourths said they planned to return). The investigation included stops in "Italy, Austria,

Hungary, Russia, Finland, Greece, Turkey in Europe and Turkey in Asia, Roumania, Germany, Switzerland, Belgium, the Netherlands, Denmark, Sweden, Norway, France, England, Ireland, and Scotland." Press coverage was, inevitably, supplemented by editorials and quotations from Congressional speeches denouncing the "junketing." Senator Dillingham found time to attend a colleague's wedding at the U.S. embassy in Berlin.[38]

Daily reports document that the delegation conducted dozens of interviews and undertook many tours of gritty ports in between their official parties and sightseeing. One news report explained that the group "covered more ground than a pleasure traveler would care to undertake." They were not on "a pleasure jaunt, but on a business mission," wrote the sympathetic newsman. A report based on the tour analyzing emigration conditions in sending countries appeared in volume 4. The commission also considered, but nixed, a trip to Japan.[39]

A few other reports reflected international interests. William W. Husband, the commission's chief of staff, contributed a summary of the "Immigration Situation in Other Countries," which included a digest of federal laws in other white settler nations or receiving countries (vol. 40). The commission used the overseas work of two Bureau of Immigration agents, Marcus Braun (on sex trafficking and contract labor in Europe) and John Gruenberg (on labor recruitment in Europe). It also sent its own undercover agents, men and women, on overseas steamship travel. Jenks toured the U.S. sides of the Mexican and Canadian borders.[40]

In at least one area, the commission shrank from its originally international ambitions. In his 1906 address to Congress, Roosevelt proposed an international conference on immigration.[41] The 1907 law had also called for a conference to arrange what amounted to an international treaty on "the immigration of aliens to the United States" and on their inspection at American consulates overseas. Initial reaction was favorable. Similar endeavors, with names such as the "Universal Races Congress," were taking place around the globe. As late as 1909, newspapers across the country reported favorably on the measure. But enthusiasm cooled for a forum where the conversation could not be controlled. In the fall of 1908, Straus advised Roosevelt that it would be "very unwise . . . to call an international conference." It might, for one thing, "conflict with our policy of expatriation," codified in the 1907 law. In other words, it might spark another diplomatic crisis. Roosevelt, according to Straus, "entirely agreed," and the international commission never happened. In the end, most of the commission's reports focused on the domestic conditions and impact of new immigrants. But legacies of its origins in international diplomacy remained, especially in the disproportionate attention Japanese immigration received in the reports.[42]

The Japanese in the Reports

The title of volumes 23–25—"Japanese and Other Races in the Pacific Coast and Rocky Mountain States"—testified to the outsized impact of a group that represented fewer than 1 percent of the immigrants who arrived in the Progressive Era.[43] In April 1907, one newspaper had called the proposed research on Japan "likely to be the most important" because of potential "trouble with Japanese immigration . . . looming ahead." In private meetings, the commission described the volumes as "confined principally to a study of the Japanese and Hindus." The first of the three reports began with the statement that "special emphasis was placed on Japanese immigration." The data, the commission believed, was "superior to those collected for most other races" in the western states. Jenks met personally with U.S. Congressman E. A. Hayes, an ardent Asian exclusionist from San Jose, California, who had called Japanese immigration a "gigantic race problem, as ugly and dangerous as the negro question in the South" and who had told the Exclusion League, "If we are going to have war with Japan, let's have it right away!"[44]

The volumes on the West were among the most comprehensive of the commission's field studies. From 1907 to 1909, agents collected data on 13,307 Japanese (around 5 percent of their total U.S. population) and studied every industry in which the Japanese participated. The reports counted as many as five thousand Japanese-owned businesses in the western states—ranging from a sake brewery to a shingle mill. In Washington State, the commission investigated all but two of the eighteen canneries on the Columbia River, and nineteen of the twenty-three in Puget Sound. Some sections of Volume 25 analyzed industrial pursuits not unique to the West—the railroads, mining, smelting, coal and lumber—and these were structured like the eastern volumes overseen more closely by W. Jett Lauck, which compared races to each other within industry and used the same forms. The Japanese got the most attention—hundreds of pages, whereas the chapters on agriculture devoted a few pages each to Germans and Scandinavians, Portuguese, Italians, Armenians, and a group of settlers of German heritage who had emigrated through Russia. (The southern reports on agriculture were also organized by immigrant group.)[45]

This organizational method, and the fieldwork conducted with translators, produced a detailed picture of Japanese immigrant life. Its sweep of Japanese business ventures revealed their industriousness—they engaged in a wide variety of farm production and worked in businesses such as laundries, restaurants, barber shops, shoe repair, tailoring, and grocery stores. They also populated cannery districts and did coal mining. But a closer examination showed that this seemingly wide range of activities was actually quite proscribed: the farming was on leased land, and the business ventures were precisely the kind of low-capital, labor-intensive, retail-scale enterprises to which socially marginal peoples were often confined. These businesses, such as art or curio stores, bathhouses, and "billiard and pool halls and shooting galleries," showed the Japanese's confinement in lines of work, whose seamy reputation deepened prejudices against them. Still, the commission's special interest in the Japanese made possible a level of detail about their lives that went beyond what was evident in many other studies of particular groups.

The commission's close attention to the Japanese contrasted with its almost total lack of regard to Mexicans. Mexican immigrants—though far from the numbers they would reach after the Mexican Revolution—already outnumbered the Japanese by at least two to one in the United States. The Pacific Coast reports included Arizona, California, Colorado, and New Mexico. In three of these states, Mexicans were the most populous immigrant group—yet not a single listing in the five-page table of contents for the three volumes references Mexicans. In 1909, budget cuts spared studies of "Japanese and Hindus" but eliminated most plans to examine the Mexican population. Mexicans did not yet elicit the same interest—and, before the Mexican Revolution, they were not attached to any foreign-policy concerns. The federal Bureau of Immigration only began counting land-crossing migrants in

1908, and although Mexicans faced all kinds of discrimination, they were legally white and eligible for citizenship under U.S. law; the Japanese were neither.[46]

Overall, the Pacific Coast reports offered a sharply different portrait of Japanese immigrants than that produced by California's nativists. In 1914, Millis republished his Dillingham investigations for a Christian organization largely sympathetic to the Japanese. He favored their right to naturalization, believing that their ineligibility discouraged them from developing civic pride and committing to the broader community. His reports noted that Japanese immigrants learned English more quickly than Mexicans and other immigrants. This accomplishment was all the more impressive, according to the reports, because "they work together in 'gangs' of their own race very largely and come into little contact with English-speaking people," yet "make use of every opportunity" to learn the language. The Japanese expressed a desire to become citizens and kept more money in the United States than did many other immigrants.[47]

The four Japanese students from Stanford hired by Millis to undertake research and translate for the reports were part of a tiny cadre of Asian students across the United States (including several Chinese students recruited by Jenks to Cornell University). One of the Stanford undergraduates was Yamato Ichihashi. University president David Starr Jordan, a prominent eugenicist

Japanese graduates of Stanford University. These young men were likely working on the Dillingham Commission reports in rural California. One might be Yamato Ichihashi.

with a strong interest in Japan, had mentored Ichihashi and later hired him as a professor.[48]

Millis and Ichihashi's reports captured the daily lives and hopes of people who were otherwise bargaining chips in international diplomacy. The Japanese in the United States shared many aspirations with other immigrants but had fewer avenues to pursue them. Still, Japanese laborers, even in the harshest work situations, found ways to fight back. White farmers in California at first recruited Japanese to break strikes or simply because they assumed them to be compliant workers. Evidence from Hawaii might have warned them otherwise. Resistance and strikes by Japanese plantation workers there stretched back into the nineteenth century. In March 1907, after Roosevelt ordered that Japanese in Hawaii no longer come to the mainland, Japanese immigrants in Honolulu staged a mass protest, shouting, "It enslaves us permanently to Hawaii's capitalists!"[49]

Across the West, Japanese agricultural workers found strength in numbers as growers began to rely on them. One employer found the Japanese more likely than Mexicans to make "organized demands for higher wages and better conditions." Ichihashi and Millis's study of agriculture in Vaca Valley, California, documents how these assertions of rights developed over time and in relation to other immigrant laborers. Employers and commission agents alike held complicated views about the Japanese. Over the course of several seasons, Japanese workers eventually outnumbered Chinese and white competitors. To white ranchers' dismay, Japanese wages increased, in part because of workers' "well-ordered demands." Even without formal organizing, "concerted effort, occasional strikes, and regard for one another's 'jobs' have become almost as characteristic of the Japanese as laborers as of a trade union." As a result, their wages rose: "They are never paid less than the Chinese," and "usually" as much as whites. Whether it was a change in the "attitude" of the workers or their employers, "almost all of the ranchers find cause for complaint": The Japanese would "not do as much work as formerly"; they would "shirk and loaf" if paid by the day; they needed "much supervision"; and they were "arrogant and intractable," not to mention "dishonest." Ranchers who had once complimented Japanese "industry, quickness, adaptability, and eagerness to learn American ways" now complained about workers who had "become very independent and hard to deal with."[50]

Although the Japanese had a reputation for being the lowest-paid workers, the commission found that their wages ranged considerably from place to place. On one railroad line in Nevada and Utah, Italians made $1.50; the Japanese, just $1.10. But on two other railroads, the Japanese were paid "the same wages as all white men, $1.45 per day, and in one case more than the Mexicans." The investigators noticed that in the year or so after the Gentlemen's Agreement, the wage differential between Japanese and white workers began to diminish because of increased labor demand. Still, employers did not like workers who pushed for better wages; white competitors did not like when Japanese accepted lower wages and lowered the standard of living; and both groups used these facts to try to argue the Japanese were racially unacceptable. The Japanese, according to one employer, were "more alert, more progressive, and more temperate than the Mexicans, who, when of the peon class, are generally deficient in these qualities." These attributes were not necessarily desirable in unskilled immigrant labor.[51]

"Whatever the truth" of employers' complaints, the report continued, "it is true that the Japanese are ambitious" and "naturally shrewd." They "have made the most of the situation," and "the ranchers have come to feel that they are oppressed." From "the ranchers' point of view," the report continued, "the situation has been made worse" because many Japanese had leased their own farmland. The white landowner "now competed for laborers with these tenants," who had employed "almost any new race appearing in the community," including south Asians, largely Punjabis, about whom the commission was also concerned. Although the commission focused mainly on ethnic solidarity strikes, in 1903 Mexican and Japanese farmworkers in Oxnard, California, cooperated in a massive—and ultimately successful—strike.[52]

The reports also highlighted an isolated but intriguing example of cross-ethnic cooperation. In 1907, the United Mine Workers began organizing in the coal mines of Wyoming. Normally, Asian workers were the object of union opposition, but in this instance "a delegation of Japanese" attended the union convention in Denver "to present their side of the case." The union offered "a special dispensation" so that "the Chinese and Japanese who were on the ground were allowed to become members of the union on an equal footing with other races." As a result, the Japanese earned wages equal to all other workers: $3.10 per day for wage workers and equal piece rates for mining and loading. Japanese coal miners in Wyoming began making better wages than any of their fellow countrymen in the West. The vestiges of ancient Japanese caste distinctions, which reserved coal mining for the most undesirable social groups—"for criminals or the lowest of the low," as one migrant put it—made their wage successes and alliances with non-Japanese workers all the more meaningful.[53]

The Wyoming story had ended with some skepticism about Japanese workers' ability to be true "free laborers." "Though they are members of the union," the Wyoming passage noted, "individual Japanese are not masters of their own affairs." In most of Californian agriculture, white men were employed individually, whereas "Japanese 'bosses' were the most numerous labor agents." A gang system first introduced by the Chinese was adopted for Japanese workers, who received no board and got housing that whites refused. Some employers preferred this practice because they could negotiate directly with a contractor, who managed the workers and their room and board (which, unlike for most white workers, was almost never included in their wages). A Japanese contracting agency in New York City assigned them to the work, similar to the railroad and agricultural industries. According to the study, the " 'American' laborer comes to acquire a contempt for" any work done by the Japanese because "he regards it as too servile for an American to engage in"—"it is not regarded as 'white man's work.' "[54]

Some employers disliked the Japanese gang system, which they called "the evil of subcontracting." In Utah, sugar-beet growers and Japanese workers teamed up in trying to get rid of Japanese bosses. Investigations of the Japanese reflected concerns about the relationship between immigrants and the free-labor system that dated to the founding of the Republican Party (whose founding motto before the Civil War was "free labor, free soil, free men!"), and also colored the work of white unionists in the Democratic Party who opposed immigrant competition.[55]

Although many Japanese immigrants continued to work for wages, Ichihashi demonstrated that they leased land whenever and wherever they could, as in Vaca Valley.[56] They did so to escape exploitation from Japanese and white bosses alike, and perhaps to escape the vestiges of low status in Japan. In Washington State, an alien land law barred Japanese real-property ownership; passage of California's version was delayed until 1913 only because

Roosevelt had quashed earlier efforts. Unlike other immigrants, the Japanese and Chinese also could not file federal homestead claims, which were limited to people eligible for citizenship. So they rented land, often under unfavorable conditions, and with force behind their desires. "In their anxiety to obtain possession of land," they paid high prices, and "in several authenticated cases have made threats that if the land was not leased as desired," local Japanese workers would withhold their labor. Yet, "why," the report asked, "should the Japanese wish so strongly to lease land rather than to work for wages?" Then it answered: "Like other ambitious men," the Japanese immigrants "want the fullest opportunity to make money." Second, they took "a great deal of pride in controlling the land on which they work." Most had come from rural areas, where they had held their own property, so they had scant experience with a wage economy. Third, the Japanese, with "exaggerated ideas" about farming's profitability, had discounted "the element of risk, which, in its various forms, is very great." They were willing to be "speculative," and even the "disastrous year" after the Panic of 1907 had not dampened their enthusiasm for farming.[57]

The Japanese farmers lived and worked in ways that would have been a mark of good citizenship in native white Americans. They settled as family groups in rural areas at a time when leaders such as Theodore Roosevelt assailed the nation's increasing urbanization. The commission found almost 80 percent of Japanese women had arrived in the previous five years. (The Gentlemen's Agreement had made an exception for women, which launched concerns about "picture brides.") For reformers and immigrants alike, the patriarchal family was a key marker of assimilation. Escaping gang labor gave Japanese men a way to build a family life, and while the number of women in the Japanese American population remained tiny (only 867 Japanese women arrived in the United States in 1909), they were most likely to appear in farming families. In Oregon and Washington, "most of the laborers cannot secure tolerable conditions under which to live with their families, while the farmer and his family can lead a normal family life." As a result, Japanese were willing to pay high rents for agricultural land and had "displaced" other races—especially white farmers—in some regions. Overall, they did well: of 647 Japanese farmers interviewed in the Pacific Northwest, 432 had made a profit, and 101 had broken even.[58]

Women's presence was important because the school protests of 1906 had carried a sexual undercurrent about the largely male Japanese population. In San Francisco, pamphlets from the Native Sons of the Golden West asked, "Would you like your daughter to marry a Japanese? . . . If not, demand that your representative in the Legislature vote for segregation of whites and Asiatics in the public schools."[59] Activists complained about adult Japanese men crowding into primary schools to learn English. But the reports found that only a handful of students were above the appropriate age, and the two oldest among them were just twenty years old.[60]

The Japanese occupied an intermediate racial status—considered superior to other Asians because of their martial prowess and industrialization, yet inferior to white American workers. Ironically, as the commission's report on the mass meetings in San Francisco explained, critics wanted to exclude the Japanese "not only on the grounds set forth in the policy of Chinese exclusion but because . . . the assumed virtue of the Japanese—i.e., their partial adoption of American customs—makes them the more dangerous as competitors."[61] In short, it was a no-win situation.

Despite the prejudice they faced, the Japanese wanted to stay: "A comparatively large number of the farmers and business classes expressed a desire to become naturalized and expressed regret at the discrimination against persons who did not belong to some white race." Many Japanese had achieved financial independence, and "seldom have the Japanese become public charges or been charity patients at public hospitals"—in large part because their own fraternal organizations took care of the indigent.[62]

These sympathetic portrayals must have pleased Japanese diplomats. The consulate in San Francisco had offered the Dillingham Commission their "fullest cooperation" and "every assistance." Until the school board controversy, Japan and the United States had enjoyed good relations. Japanese officials no doubt believed that cooperation would demonstrate Japan's loyalty and friendship and help show Japanese immigrants in a positive light. Ichihashi and the other students literally translated the findings into their own words. The commission's Japanese translators were not members of the barred "laboring classes." They had the confidence and connections to study in the United States at the height of anti-Japanese agitation, and the translators themselves embodied and expressed the positive spirit of assimilation and progress. Or maybe they just needed the money: it was not cheap to live in the United States, and Asian students were barred from student housing. Ichihashi told David Jordan he was pleased with his job, because it would "help me financially."[63]

One report in particular reflected the influence of foreign relations and colonialism on treatment of the Japanese. A special report on "Immigration Conditions in Hawaii" appeared separate from the Pacific Coast volumes. Senator Dillingham traveled to Hawaii for research on it. Critics derided the Vermonter's trip to a tropical clime, but Dillingham's visit reflected his longtime interest in Hawaii as a member of the Senate Committee on Territories, and perhaps also his family connections—one of Hawaii's largest sugar barons was a Dillingham. Back in Washington, commission members also met with the governor of Hawaii while he was in town. Secretary Straus undertook his own investigation of Hawaii at the same time—a sign that the islands were important to the Bureau of Immigration as well as the commission.[64]

So, too, did the placement of the commission's sixteen-page Hawaii study, which appeared in the same widely read volume that contained abstracts of other reports. The Hawaii report's author, Victor Clark, a globe-trotting technocrat, mapped the close links between immigration and colonialism in the early twentieth century. Clark had been a high school teacher and administrator in his native Minnesota before earning a doctorate from Columbia University, while he served as a board of education official in Puerto Rico. Clark had also studied race and labor conditions in Australia, Cuba, Java, New Zealand, and the Philippines. "What ethnological range you evoke in my breast!," a friend wrote to Clark. "I wish we could have seen you to hear all about Javanese & Philippine doings, and the many amusing experiences you certainly have stored away for friends." Clark's career also linked external and internal colonialism. In 1908, he published an important field report on Mexican labor in the American Southwest for the Bureau of Labor for his close friend, Dillingham Commission member Charles Neill. Originally trained as a scholar of ancient languages and German, he may have also been the first U.S. government social scientist fluent in Spanish.[65]

In Hawaii, Clark served as the territorial commissioner of labor and then commissioner of immigration. His report for the Dillingham Commission portrayed Hawaii as another arena for struggle between Japan and Russia, here in the form of immigrant recruitment and settlement. Clark described a process of what the commission's "Immigrants in Industries" reports called the "racial displacement" of one immigrant group with another, this time the Japanese with Russians. Through the late nineteenth century, labor in Hawaii was predominantly contract peonage. "The system resulted," Clark explained, "in making the population of Hawaii predominantly oriental." Although contract labor was illegal in the United States, these laws did not apply to Hawaii prior to annexation. The joint resolution to annex Hawaii in 1898 forbade the continued importation of Chinese workers there but did not mention the Japanese.[66] American takeover ended penal contracts in Hawaii. And so, after 1905, as Japanese began to leave for the mainland United States in large numbers, Hawaiian employers attempted to recruit family groups from elsewhere. They tried Puerto Ricans and Filipinos, in part because as colonial subjects they did not count as "immigrants."

Plantation owners preferred what Clark called a "white immigration policy" designed to attract "a larger proportion of Caucasians" to Hawaii as permanent settlers. A 1909 scheme to bring Siberians to Hawaii promised the settlers supplies and property ownership. But the homesteads were too small to farm, the climate was hostile to subsistence farming, and the newcomers were homesick. The planter in charge also lied about the amenities. The Russians went on strike, and most left. As Clark observed, the "Caucasian population" leaves "almost as rapidly as it is recruited." Employers' next best hope, Clark wrote, was the impending completion of the Panama Canal, "through which European immigrants will reach Hawaii." Employers and territorial officials desperately wanted to replace the Japanese with "a home-owning domiciled citizenship population" from Europe. The shortage "of this population is the present immigration problem before the Territory."[67]

Whatever the overtures of friendship, the reality was that Japan and the United States were competitors, not allies, especially in the Pacific. In spite of public claims that the 1907 crisis was over, Roosevelt and his advisers were also secretly prepared for war with Japan. In San Francisco, riots broke out in the summer of 1907 over the Japanese segregation measure, and the California legislature continued to introduce discriminatory bills. By December, Roosevelt's

Great White Fleet had begun its round-the-world show of naval force. It docked at San Francisco in July of the following year, in the Philippines in early October, then in Yokohama, Japan, in October 1908. Cheering Japanese crowds greeted the fleet, eager to show their friendship with the United States, while back in the United States Millis and Ichihashi studied the immigrants who had generated such controversy.

Yet Yamato Ichihashi had begun his work with the Dillingham Commission optimistic about his new country and its government. He was "convinced," he wrote to Jordan in 1908, "that with a proper equipment I shall be able to help in bringing about a better understanding between the West and East. Such is the object of my life." Ichihashi went on to Harvard University for a PhD based on his research for the commission. At Harvard, he studied with early eugenicist William Z. Ripley and frontier historian Frederick Jackson Turner. He returned to his undergraduate alma mater to teach in 1913, in a position funded by "a group of Japanese friends of America" who wanted "one of their own scholars [to] interpret their civilization to Stanford University students." His early writings called for state and federal action to improve the lot of the Japanese in the United States. In 1913, Ichihashi published a pamphlet based in part on his research notes for the commission. In it, he lambasted the Asian Exclusion leagues and blamed the San Francisco schools controversy for "a great deal of unnecessary unpleasantness." Above all, he urged readers to accept the Japanese and support their naturalization. The two major obstacles to assimilation, he argued, were state laws banning Japanese-white intermarriage and federal laws barring their naturalization. "The students most familiar with the Japanese problem," he wrote, "unanimously favor removing all legal obstacles. . . . Japanese should be treated equally with other immigrant races." He ended his pamphlet with the exhortation that if the Japanese were allowed to naturalize, they would "make contributions to American civilization as its *loyal citizens*. Give them a chance." Ichihashi became a prominent scholar, in 1932 publishing a definitive history of Japanese immigration based in part on the Dillingham reports.[68]

After the attack on Pearl Harbor in 1941, Ichihashi—who remained ineligible for citizenship—supported the United States and bought Liberty Bonds to finance the American war effort. But in spring of 1942, the professor and his wife were interned, first at Santa Anita racetrack (where families were housed in horse stalls), and later in the desolate Tule Lake camp. Ichihashi kept diaries of his experience, but he became reclusive and never published again.[69]

In 1909, when Ichihashi and Millis interviewed Japanese American farmers and laborers and called for naturalization rights, no one could have predicted the internment of most of the Japanese American population of the United States three decades later. But scholars of World War II, in both Japan and the United States, have seen the controversies of 1906–1907 and the Gentlemen's Agreement as one source of the tensions between the two countries that would eventually erupt in war and internment. Japanese immigrants would not gain the right to U.S. citizenship until 1952. The Immigration Act of 1907 had quelled a short-term crisis but, in creating the commission, had concluded that the arrival of the Japanese was part of "the problem of immigration," in Ichihashi's own words.[70]

3

Hebrew or Jewish Is Simply a Religion

In 1907, the Japan crisis dominated press coverage of the immigration bill, but its role in the Dillingham Commission's creation quickly faded from public memory. By 1913, the nation's preeminent sociologist, the University of Wisconsin's Edward A. Ross, offered a new narrative. In his eugenicist manifesto, *The Old World in the New,* Ross described the commission not as a product of the "coolie bill," but as an outcome of Jewish influence. "Although theirs is but a seventh of our net immigration," he wrote, Jews "led the fight on the Immigration Commission's bill." This was no small claim in the era in which modern lobbying began.[1]

Ross highlighted the role of Jews in shaping the immigration bill because he was an anti-Semite. He twisted the commission's history, blaming "Hebrew money" and "subtle Hebrew brains" for all opposition to immigration restrictions. (In reality, German-language newspapers led the fight.) But not all his facts were wrong. He described the hundreds of letters and visits to Congress by American Jews, and their prominent role in seemingly nonsectarian lobbying organizations such as the National Liberal Immigration League, founded to fight restriction. The modern Jewish lobby developed out of the formative efforts from 1890 to 1914 first to influence the fate of Jews in Romania and Russia, and later to shape domestic immigration law. At the same time, Jews were negotiating their place in the American racial hierarchy—they were always white by law, but what that meant for their status and self-perceptions was undergoing dramatic, and often painful, change.[2]

One of the Jews to whom Ross referred had also been instrumental in Japan's victory in the Russo-Japanese War begun in 1904: financier and philanthropist Jacob Schiff. In 1906, alarmed at the escalating anti-Semitism of the Russian tsar, Schiff had issued bonds to fund a cash-strapped Japanese military. (Later, Jeremiah Jenks would claim the main reason Japan would never go to war against the United States was because it relied on "the Hebrew financiers of the Russo-Japanese War."[3]) Meanwhile, Schiff joined a handful of prominent Jews in New York City and Washington to lobby first for the creation of the Dillingham Commission instead of the literacy test, then to try to influence the investigations. In their own way, Jewish leaders endorsed greater federal power over immigration, even as they rebuffed proposals for new restrictions.

At the time, these behind-the-scenes machinations received little publicity. Activists wanted it that way. "It was not advisable," New York lawyer Louis Marshall told other Jewish leaders, "that opposition to the restriction of immigration should appear to emanate solely from Jews."[4] Organized Jewish activities carried with them a certain irony: even as their opposition to actual immigration restrictions grew, the measures Jewish lobbying groups did endorse—the Dillingham Commission itself, distribution of immigrants, civil rights for immigrants—all assumed a larger federal role in crafting immigration policy and shaping the lives of immigrants in the United States. At the same time, their access to the commission illustrated that it was not purely a nativist enterprise. These ironies shot through efforts to lobby for the Immigration Act of 1907, to protest the commission's use of "Hebrew" as a racial category in 1909, and to formulate policy recommendations for the commission in 1910. As a result, Jewish leaders played an ambivalent role in shaping future immigration policy. By endorsing more federal power, Jewish lobbyists handed valuable ammunition to those who ended up expanding restrictions. At the same time, Jews' own internal divisions—especially about whether Jews constituted a "race"—undermined their lobbying efforts.

The Jewish Lobby and the Immigration Act of 1907

Simon Wolf had the nickname "Lupus Washingtoniensis" because he was a true creature of Washington. Although he was neither famous nor wealthy, unlike New York financiers and merchants such as Schiff and Straus, the Washington attorney was nonetheless crucial to Jewish activism. One Washington judge called Wolf "the representative American Jew," and, in the Washington mold, he was more lobbyist than lawyer. Born in Bavaria, Wolf had come to Ohio with his grandparents during Germany's political upheavals in 1848. Like most of that cohort—known as "'48ers"—Wolf joined the Republican Party. He moved to Washington in 1862 and served as D.C. recorder of deeds under President Grant. By 1870, he was lobbying Congress on Jewish issues. In later life, he prided himself on knowing every president from Lincoln to Woodrow Wilson. Wolf belonged to both Jewish and German American organizations, and he served as president of the Washington Hebrew Congregation, founded by German Jews in 1852 as part of the Reform movement, known for modernizing its worship style and relaxing kosher food rules.[5]

Wolf made the debate over Jews' racial categorization his lifelong cause. In 1903, he lobbied the Bureau of Immigration to abandon the practice of classifying Jewish immigrants as "Hebrew" rather than by their nationality. In 1906, the seventy-year-old Wolf threw himself headlong into the debates over the immigration bill. In 1909, he managed to secure the only live hearing convened by the Dillingham Commission—mainly so he could protest the commission's continuation of the Bureau's use of "Hebrew" as a racial category.

Wolf's opposition to exclusion laws was not inevitable. In 1907, most prominent Jews belonged to a class of assimilated Germans who had arrived in the United States in the mid-nineteenth century. Much has been written, some of it exaggerated, about the suspicion and disdain that German Jews had for the new eastern European arrivals.[6] It is true, however, that many German Jews were middle class and assimilated. They practiced Reform Judaism and felt little in common with the eastern European newcomers, who tended to be poor, religiously Orthodox, and sometimes politically radical. Most of the old-line Jewish leaders were born in the mid-nineteenth century and had grown up in the United States.[7] Most were also longtime Republicans, alongside their '48er German gentile counterparts.

American Jews largely acquiesced to the Immigration Act of 1882's extension of federal control over immigration. The law focused on "quality," not quantity. The most controversial and important of the 1882 law's provisions was what became known as the "LPC" clause, which could exclude anyone "likely to become a public charge." Out of fear of being tainted by association with impoverished new immigrants, and perhaps because the LPC provision

Simon Wolf was a Washington lawyer, lobbyist, and Republican Party stalwart who devoted his life to challenging racial categorization and illegal exclusion from the United States.

disproportionately affected women traveling without husbands, most Jewish leaders acceded to the rule. (In contrast, several Jews opposed the companion Chinese Exclusion Act on civil rights grounds, figuring it did not affect them as an interest group, and they could therefore appear impartial in their opposition. Wolf testified against Chinese exclusion at a Congressional hearing, and New York lawyer Max Kohler defended Chinese immigrants in deportation cases, including in front of the U.S. Supreme Court.)[8]

But the world was changing. In March 1881, Russian tsar Alexander II was assassinated. The aftermath unleashed pogroms terrorizing Jews in the Russian Empire. The first large group of Jews fleeing Russia landed in New York, and so began the "new immigration" wave from southern and eastern Europe that would last for four decades. The impoverished and Orthodox arrivals troubled policy makers and government officials. Jewish leaders hoped in vain that the new immigrants would become farmers, not peddlers, and worried that any reliance on philanthropy would reflect poorly on all Jews. Schiff and Wolf were among the early activists who agreed to assist the 1881 immigrants as a one-time expediency. Their charity stemmed more from fear of being associated with the newcomers than from empathy. In 1882, when a similar group arrived, Wolf and Schiff, torn between distaste and duty, agreed again to help. It was only the beginning of a long struggle over how tightly bound American Jewry ought to be, or whether there even was such a thing as American Jewry.[9]

Either way, as immigrants continued to flee Russia's pogroms and poverty, Jewish leaders searched for a more systematic response. In 1890, wealthy Jewish German Baron de Hirsch established a fund to support the Russian exodus. American leaders were reticent to support it, fearing that a large influx would, in Straus's words, be "overwhelming and, to state it mildly, . . . a calamity and a misfortune not only for the emigrants, but for all American Jews." Straus, then a wealthy New York merchant and lawyer whose brothers owned Macy's department store, signed on to the cause but insisted that the fund should "in no way foster, encourage, or stimulate emigration to America."[10]

Growing exposure to the crisis of Russian Jewry changed Jewish American responses to federal immigration policy. The passage of a new U.S. immigration law in 1891 became a turning point. Appalled by the violence in Russia, Jewish leaders in both the United States and Europe began to accept that large-scale immigration was a civil rights and humanitarian necessity. In contrast to 1882, this time Jewish leaders openly opposed the new legislation, which made it easier to use the LPC clause to exclude men who, because of ill health or unemployment, might even briefly rely on public support. It also banned so-called assisted immigration—henceforth, anyone whose passage "had been paid by someone else" was to be detained. The rule was the product of a long history of agitation to protect "free labor" from unfree forms of foreign labor—stereotypically the Chinese, but also workers ensnared in debt peonage, indentured labor, and prostitution.[11]

In the hands of immigration inspectors hostile to Jewish immigration, the new clause threatened the ability of philanthropists to rescue Russian Jews: no laws specifically designed to aid refugees existed until after World War II. In his capacity as president of the United American Hebrew Congregation (UAHC), Wolf lobbied for a liberal interpretation of the 1891 law. Secretary of the Treasury Charles Foster (who oversaw the Bureau of Immigration) promised leniency for Russian Jews provided that "American Jewry undertake to disperse them to points other than the crowded industrial centers."[12] It was an open invitation for the de Hirsch fund and others to assist in resettling immigrant Jews.

Foster's response betrayed his belief that immigrant settlement and assimilation were mostly matters for private philanthropy. It spurred private efforts to distribute Jewish immigrants to Argentina, southern New Jersey, Connecticut, and even North Dakota.[13] Yet these actions already seemed inadequate as immigration politics became more restrictive. In 1897, Congress passed a literacy test for the first time (although it was vetoed by Grover Cleveland). Jews were at first ambivalent; most, after all, were literate in some language, which was all the law required.[14] A debate in Congress over whether Yiddish would count for the literacy requirement became a litmus test of anti-Semitism.

Jewish leaders responded in force. In addition to lobbying Congress, Wolf also contested deportation orders made by the Bureau of Immigration, especially those that separated families. This was painstaking work, but it was often effective. By the early twentieth century, Wolf and Kohler were working on dozens of individual cases of threatened debarment (removal at entry). These excruciatingly piecemeal challenges to unfair exclusion allowed as many as one hundred thousand Jews entry who might otherwise have been denied it. These Jewish activists became, in effect, the nation's first immigration lawyers.[15]

In 1902, Theodore Roosevelt appointed avowed restrictionist William Williams as commissioner of immigration at Ellis Island. Williams tightened administrative rules and, in 1904, instituted a new rule that allowed medical officers to exclude immigrants as LPC based on "low vitality or poor physique." This rule joined existing restriction laws based on public health that excluded people suffering with conditions such as epilepsy or carrying diseases such as the contagious eye disease trachoma or the scalp condition favus.[16]

The new clause's wording assumed new immigrants needed to be fit for manual labor. It was a perfect way to exclude Jews because many of them arrived at port underweight and malnourished from poverty, mistreatment, and the challenges of keeping kosher during their journey abroad (some steamship companies technically had kosher food, but it was often unavailable or inedible, or religious Jews did not trust it). By 1906, Williams's new "poor physique" rule was being used against Jews in large numbers, and Wolf and Kohler increased their efforts to stop debarments.[17]

By then, most old-line German Jewish leaders had overcome their initial reticence about the new immigrants. Led by Wolf's intercessions on behalf of individual immigrants, they had already been working on immigration policy for twenty-five years. Over time, attitudes and relationships among American Jews had changed. German Jewish leaders moved from cautious pessimism and a kind of defensive opposition to new immigration, to a dawning acceptance that fighting against further restriction was a civil rights issue—even one of self-preservation. In 1907, Roosevelt appointed Oscar Straus secretary of commerce and labor, making him the first Jewish member of the Cabinet. Straus threw out the poor physique rule in 1909. Even so, rank-and-file federal agents' anti-Semitism led to a rising number of exclusions of immigrants based on LPC and vitality charges, with the summer of 1909, to many Jewish activists, a crisis point.[18]

Men such as Schiff and Straus enjoyed personal success, but American Jewish leaders still lived in a world of precarious privilege. The discrimination they faced did not remotely approach that suffered by African Americans. The Ku Klux Klan had not yet reorganized to target Jews and Catholics alongside African Americans. No miscegenation laws barred Jews from marrying Gentiles. Jews, like all Europeans, were legally white, even if they were generally conceived of as a "race." They rarely faced violence, and they could vote. In the South and the West especially, Jews intermarried with Christians and often served in local political office. Greenville, Mississippi, had a Jewish mayor decades before New York City, as did Tombstone, Arizona.[19] Jews had more opportunity in the United States than anywhere in the world, and they treasured and celebrated it.

But elite Jews knew discrimination, too, even if they shrank from calling it anti-Semitism, a term more common in England. Cyrus Adler, who as head of the Smithsonian Institution was the nation's leading Jewish intellectual, wrote to Kohler, "I have very grave objections to importing the term 'anti-semitic' into our language, especially when dealing with the government here." He preferred "the word 'anti-Jewish.' 'Anti-semitic' has not been naturalized and I think it is bad policy for us to help make it a citizen."[20]

Whatever name you gave it, prejudice meant that even though Jacob Schiff was one of the richest men in America, he could still be refused service. Louis Marshall, who argued more cases in front of the U.S. Supreme Court than any other contemporary, built a summer enclave in Saranac Lake, New York, with other wealthy Jews because they were barred from other locations. Outside Washington, DC, Nevada Senator Francis Newlands was developing the tony suburb of Chevy Chase, Maryland, where restrictive covenants signed by homeowners excluded African Americans and Jews. Prestigious universities had tiny quotas for Jews (although most refused to admit African Americans at all).[21]

The desire for assimilation could create what later generations called the "self-hating Jew." In a talk he titled "Summer Hotels and Kindred Insanity," Wolf espoused a politics of respectability similar to that practiced by African American elites. As he told his audience, "There is no use disguising the fact that there are Jews whose company is not enviable." Their conduct is "more or less obnoxious." The bad behavior of a "Mr. John Smith" or "James Jones" reflected only on themselves, but "one loud Jew or Jewess in a hotel is enough to brand us all." "It is unjust," Wolf admitted, "but it is absolutely true [that] . . . *this cannot be changed except by ourselves.* The Jews who sit on porches without their coats and collars, smoking cigars and playing cards, and who are loud in their talk, naturally annoy, nay disgust, their surroundings. The Jewess who dresses in vulgar taste and comes to breakfast, bedecked with diamonds galore, and who talks in broken vernacular, is naturally an object of aversion, and stands unfortunately, as a symbol of the whole sex."[22]

Still, Wolf now accepted the new arrivals. "Not a Time to Despair," one headline declared. "Mr. Simon Wolf of Washington Is Apprehensive of the Large Immigration But It Cannot Be Stemmed: Influential Jews Must Help Us."[23] These were the tensions of the era: the possibility of opposition, the inevitability of change, and the role of Jewish leadership.

So, in 1906 and early 1907, while Roosevelt negotiated with San Francisco and Japan, Jewish leaders and their allies mobilized to shape the final bill.

Jewish groups perfected the mass meeting as a lobbying strategy, holding at least seventy public events in twenty-seven states across the country. In June 1906, just after the passage of the Senate version of the bill, 175 Jewish organizations hosted a rally at New York's Cooper Union against its restrictive measures. At the crowded meeting, Congressman William Bennet, who represented Jewish Harlem, singled out the literacy test ("That absurd piece of legislation," as Wolf called it) as especially loathsome. Jews also joined Irish, German, and Italian American leaders and prominent Protestants (including Woodrow Wilson and Charles W. Eliot, the president of Harvard University) to create the National Liberal Immigration League (NLIL). German American organizations and newspapers—whose membership and readers often included German Jews—prominently objected to new restriction laws. In this new style of demonstrations and pressure politics, German Jewish elites aligned themselves with working-class eastern European political activists.[24]

In the months that followed the 1906 Cooper Union meeting, almost every major Jewish leader wrote letters and made personal visits to members of the House and Senate immigration committees. Flanked by William Bennet, the NLIL, and other organizations, prominent Jews advocated "for strict enforcement of the existing immigration laws" instead of new restrictions. Laws already banned individuals based on character and condition—criminal background and health—as opposed to mass restrictions by quota or literacy test. They excluded on the basis of the "quality" of immigrants rather than their "quantity." The "quality" approach appealed to Wolf, Marshall, and Kohler, lawyers who embraced a model of individual rights under the Constitution borne from the same Enlightenment ideals that informed their Reform Judaism. They hoped that by accepting qualitative restrictions (but challenging individual cases that seemed motivated by bias) they could avoid wholesale limits. Their vision was at root individualistic: they rejected the idea of Jews as sharing in collective "group rights." That collective view would develop later, in the context of American Zionism and African American civil rights.[25]

Jewish leaders paid special attention to the proposal for an immigration commission. In mid-1906, encouraged by Roosevelt's secretary William Loeb (himself of Jewish descent), Wolf had written to the president suggesting its creation. Roosevelt had already thought of this idea and discussed it with Charles Neill, but he let Wolf feel he had been the inspiration. Marshall, who

REGULAR REPUBLICAN NOMINEE
For Assemblyman
21st ASSEMBLY DISTRICT, MANHATTAN.

WILLIAM S. BENNETSKY
(OVER)

Congressman William S. Bennet (R-NY). Bennet's district was largely Jewish. He opposed the literacy test and was the only Dillingham Commission member to write a dissent to the recommendations. This voting card from 1890, which was defaced, appears to be a slur associating him with his Jewish constituency and calling him a deceiver. William Stiles Bennet Papers, Scrapbook 1889–1890.

chaired New York's state immigration commission, lobbied for a federal version. Jewish leaders focused on getting yes votes from the New York and New Jersey delegations, especially from Benjamin Howell, who favored restrictions and chaired the House Committee on Immigration, and was then appointed to the Dillingham Commission.[26]

The 1907 law's passage proved a partial victory for Jewish leaders. It substituted the commission for the literacy test. Lobbyists also succeeded in eliminating a "low vitality" exclusion from the legislation. But Jewish leaders were nervous about the bill's expansion of executive power. "The so-called 'Japanese clause,'" as Cyrus Adler put it, "vest[ed] a large discretion in the President which may be used as an argument against us." In Great Britain, some anti-Semites were arguing that Jews could be defined as Asian and thus excluded. Schiff met with the president in person for reassurance on this issue. So far, the focus was only on Japan, but if that changed, Adler vowed, "we can fight."[27]

Next, "it was important to lobby for good appointees," Adler remarked: "much depends upon the report of the Commission." He and others hoped that Straus would give them access to the new commission. On the day the new law passed, officials from the NLIL and the Reform Jewish organization B'nai B'rith sent Straus letters, some marked "personal," urging the appointment of Jews to the commission. No one, wrote one Jewish leader, is more "interested in the investigation which is to be made by the Immigration Commission" than "our people." It would be "advisable," he wrote, for "the President [to] appoint one of our representative citizens who is intelligent, fearless and absolutely reliable." NLIL official Nathan Bijur recommended two women, Jane Addams and reformer Frances Kellor. Neither was Jewish, but both worked closely with Jewish immigrant welfare organizations.[28]

But the president did not want "the representative of any special interest," Straus replied to one query. That is to say, "he does not intend to take anyone to represent Jewish immigration, Italian immigration, or any of the streams of immigration." "An exception in one direction," Straus explained, would require more "in other directions." (In any case, there is no indication Straus had any say in the appointments.) Jewish leaders also tried to block prominent restrictionists from being nominated, but in the end, at least six of the eventual appointees were known supporters of the literacy test. William Bennet was the closest thing to a Jewish representative, given his close ties to the NLIL and his largely Jewish constituency in Harlem.[29] Jews were left to hope for the best, keeping a close eye on the commission's work and attending to their own efforts. Even as Jewish leaders lobbied the federal government, their private efforts expanded, which they saw as models for new public programs. In this way, Jewish lobbying matched the larger pattern of Progressive reforms, in which activists began with private philanthropy, then expanded toward calls for local, state, and federal policy solutions to social problems.[30]

This trajectory was most evident in Jewish lobbyists' enthusiasm for the small program in the 1907 law called the Division of Information, a recruiting agency for rural settlement. The Division's "duty," according to the law, was "to promote a beneficial distribution of aliens." It would be a clearinghouse for promotional "information regarding the resources, products, and physical characteristics of each State and Territory," available in several languages for new immigrants. "This so-called white immigration problem," Congressman Anthony Michalek (R-Ill.), an immigrant from Bohemia, told colleagues in 1906, was "a question largely of proper distribution," for which "a bureau of information . . . will accomplish its purpose."[31]

Distribution programs held broad appeal in the early twentieth century. Supporters hoped they might appease those restrictionists who complained that immigrants were destroying American cities but stopped short of essentialist (what would later be called eugenic) arguments that immigrants were inherently inferior. Jacob Riis's lurid 1890 photo essay about immigrant New York, *How the Other Half Lives,* became a kind of bible for Theodore Roosevelt and many urban reformers who saw immigrant slums as "hot beds of vice and seething pots of corruption,"[32] as one nativist tract put it. Anti-urbanism pervaded both houses of Congress, where rural areas were overrepresented. Distribution offered a palatable solution to the inseparable concerns about immigration and rapid urbanization, while also promising to solve labor shortages in the South and West.

Many rural places wanted immigrants. Before 1907, most southern states sponsored public immigration bureaus to recruit laborers and farmers. The 1907 law's ban on induced immigration effectively outlawed this practice and replaced the state offices with the federal Division of Information. Federal distribution efforts were popular in Congress because they appealed both to urban immigrant constituencies and to western and southern business interests. After being run briefly by former labor leader Terence Powderly, the Division's second director was Philip Cowen, the longtime editor of a Jewish newspaper who went on to work in several immigration-related federal posts.[33] Congress renewed the Division of Information's funding, even as it set aside most immigration legislation while the Dillingham Commission did its work.

Distribution fit reformers' faith in a rural revival that could forestall more urbanization. In private, the president told Schiff that he "viewed the large immigration settling to so great an extent in a few cities with the greatest alarm," especially during the Panic of 1907. In 1908, Roosevelt created the Country Life Commission to promote his rural vision. William Dillingham was another champion of distribution. In 1904, he had promoted a kiosk at Ellis Island encouraging rural settlement and, as governor of Vermont, had used state funds to recruit Swedes (the "purest type" and "ideal farmers"), but got just twenty-seven families. Most, if not all, of the commission's members endorsed distribution. The 1910 appointment of LeRoy Percy, as we shall see, brought someone who had even tried it—the Mississippi planter recruited Bohemians and Italians to replace African Americans on his Arkansas plantation.[34]

As Jewish leaders had hoped, their philanthropy became a model for federal distribution efforts. Baron de Hirsch funded agricultural colonies for Jews in the United States and Argentina. Others tried Africa and Palestine. Jewish organizations "have no greater problem to solve," and "no greater work," Wolf told an audience in 1908, "than how to dispose of the incoming immigration." But he reassured his audience: "There are still millions and millions of untilled acres in the South, West and on the Pacific slope." So "every effort should be made" by "every patriotic American citizen" to "divert the stream of immigration" toward western and southern ports, where "organized committees [can] help newcomers establish homes and roots."[35]

By 1906, New York's Jewish ghetto had become the main charitable cause of Jews across the United States. By Schiff's estimates, 60 percent of American Jews lived on the eastern seaboard, and fewer than 10 percent west of Chicago. Distribution, largely a defensive measure against prejudice fueled by disgust with urban overcrowding, was disliked by some. Early on, some had already foreseen a downside. Nativist groups such as the Immigration Restriction League (IRL) had never liked the idea—they opposed new immigrants, wherever they were. And during the Depression years of the early 1890s, some Jewish leaders wondered if distribution schemes, by exposing more Americans to impoverished, religious Jews, might actually exacerbate discrimination rather than relieve it.[36]

The personal histories of these men nurtured a romanticism about distribution. None had grown up in New York City, much less a ghetto. Wolf was raised outside Cleveland, Ohio; Marshall, in upstate New York; Kohler, in Detroit; Adler, in Van Buren, Arkansas; and Straus, in rural Georgia. In the nineteenth century, Cincinnati—not New York—was the center of Jewish life, which is to say German Jewish life. The Ohio city was home to the Reform movement's Hebrew Union College, as well as the United American Hebrew Congregations, which Wolf represented. The West and South were strongholds of B'nai B'rith. In 1899, a rabbi from Galveston, Texas, served as its president.[37]

In spite of their enthusiasm for rural distribution, most Jewish leaders had themselves long left small-town life behind. Schiff and Straus lived in New York mansions. In 1911, Adler visited his Arkansas hometown. He found the hotel's 5:30 p.m. supper hour uncouth, the meal "uneatable." After dinner he listened to "about 10 men of the country yokel stripe" engage in "a debate on the shortcomings of the Jews." "Think of it," he marveled to his wife. "The Jew question has never been raised before me in my life and I had to come back to my native town to get it." But he excused it, since "the Hotel was the poorest I have ever been in—I never met anything like it even in Africa."[38] If he saw the flaw in distribution schemes, though, he omitted mention of it.

Galveston was home to the most famous effort at Jewish distribution, whose funders included Schiff and Straus. The idea was not only, in Schiff's words, "to divert the stream" of immigrants from the East Coast south and west through Texas, but also, by doing so, "to promote a larger immigration than we now receive." In spite of great effort and much publicity, the southern Ellis Island failed to thrive. Infighting and political conflict hampered the efforts. Schiff ended the experiment in 1914. In eight years, only about ten thousand Jewish immigrants had taken the Galveston route.[39]

The Dillingham Commission's reports praised the experiments with rural resettlement that had emerged from the Dakotas to Utah to New Jersey. Few lasted more than a few years. Distribution appealed to elites and reformers, but for most recent Jewish immigrants, American rural life was utterly foreign. For centuries, Jews had been clustered by the Russians into the region known as the "Pale of Settlement," barred from landownership and forced to live in crowded shtetls, where their occupational opportunities were limited to peddling, tailoring, banking, and merchant trades. Orthodox Jews needed to be walking distance from places of worship, and to have a minyan (a quorum of ten men) to conduct services. Access to kosher food, especially a butcher, was also challenging in agricultural areas. Add to that the networks of friends and families in big cities, and rural life appealed to few eastern European Jews.[40]

Distribution was a resettlement program, but it reflected an assimilationist ideal that immersed Jews in the broader American culture. It stood in sharp contrast to the nascent Zionist cause, the campaign for an independent Jewish state. In the United States, Zionism was still a fringe movement to which most American Jewish leaders were openly hostile. Wolf believed that Jews belonged anywhere and everywhere, and on equal terms. He once corrected a Washington newspaper that described him as a Zionist, instead calling himself "an American citizen of Jewish faith, who looks upon the United States as the Palestine of his people." "The Jew," Wolf explained, "is the gulf stream, coursing through all the nations." He felt that "a separate autonomy would . . . be a calamity." As late as 1917, Schiff wrote to Wolf, "I have never said anything in favor of the foundation of a Jewish State." Not until after World War I and the conversion of Supreme Court Justice Louis Brandeis (and Schiff) to the Zionist cause would the movement become mainstream among American Jewry. In the meantime, distribution outside Palestine remained the main focus of efforts, just as other groups tried to relocate Italians, Bohemians, and other nationalities. Most Jewish leaders in the United States, however, saw distribution as an integrationist—not nationalist—project.[41]

The Division of Information gave federal dollars (if few) and federal backing to what had once been state programs or private philanthropic efforts. It collected data from states and offered pamphlets and connections to new migrants about western and southern settlement. Although it was largely ineffective, its supporters were effusive. By replacing state immigration bureaus, it federalized public distribution efforts. Substituting philanthropy and state-level efforts with a federal program expanded the government's role and reach. The failure of the private Jewish distribution efforts—and, for that matter, the Division of Information—is in a way beside the point. In promoting the Division of Information, Jewish leaders moved from defending against federal government's restriction of immigrants to endorsing an expansion of its role in integrating immigrants. By doing so, Jewish leaders were promoting a transition from private philanthropy to public welfare programs that reflected a larger pattern in the growth of the federal state.[42]

Internal Divisions and Racial Categories

Jewish lobbyists, calling on the federal government as a protector of immigrants' civil rights, lobbied for clear immigrant entry policies and funding for education and assimilation programs. They endorsed the proposal for an immigration commission because they believed objective findings would refute many of the negative stereotypes about immigrants. These combined lobbying efforts led Jewish leaders from philanthropy to lobbying and policy planning. In some arenas—distribution, for example—they argued for an expansive view of federal power. In others—restriction—they objected to it. In 1909, Wolf led a protest against the use of "Hebrew" as a racial category in the Dillingham Commission's reports. This incident highlighted the power of a democratically elected government to label and classify, and the dangers of social-science categories. It also unmasked the internal divisions among Jewish leaders.[43]

If Jewish leaders were sometimes inconsistent about federal power, in part this reflected the disagreements among themselves over strategy, religion, and identity. The lobbying successes of 1906 and 1907 had relied on a rare unanimity of effort among Jewish leaders and their organizations. Six months after the Immigration Act of 1907 passed, Wolf invited Cyrus Adler to lunch "to talk over . . . the immigration problem." We need "to act in concert," Wolf wrote, "or at least not act in opposition. The subject is too important to be handled indiscriminately or incoherently." Behind the efforts, however, were deep disagreements. American Jews have long disagreed over identity and religion.[44] These internal divisions limited Jews' influences on immigration policy (in spite of anti-Semitic characterizations such as E. A. Ross's of a Jewish conspiracy).[45]

Even as ties between German and eastern European Jews grew (Louis Marshall even learned Yiddish), tensions were simmering. Religious differences fueled conflict, symbolized by the fallout from the so-called trefa banquet in 1883 to celebrate the Reform movement's new Hebrew Union College in Cincinnati. The menu of shellfish, frogs, meat cooked in milk, and other non-kosher delicacies scandalized many Jews in attendance. In the historical memory of American Jews, the event became the decisive break that led the developing Conservative movement away from Reform Judaism.[46]

At the same time, the battle over immigration created the modern institutions that continue to shape Jewish life in the United States. The most important was the American Jewish Committee (AJC), originally called the Committee of Fifty. Focused at first on rescuing Jews in Russia, its prominent founders hoped to use pressure politics in place of the older, supplicant style of Wolf, whose dissembling and puffery grated on the New Yorkers. Oscar Straus thought Wolf "suffered from megalomania." "We in New York, such as Schiff, Cyrus Adler & others," Straus continued, think "Wolf had constituted himself as the spokesman for the Jews at the capital for his own advantage and glorification."[47]

Even if they did not like it, the uptown New York crowd knew they had to work with—not just on behalf of—the more than a million new immigrants downtown. In his insulated Washington world, Wolf was not so inclined. He refused to help the AJC, which he called "bungled and mismanaged," arguing that "the time has not yet come" for older "organizations to surrender their ground, [and] allow the immigrant element, which has scarcely risen to their environment," to control and dominate. "[W]hen a great crisis arises," such as restrictive legislation, "we can always unite for that specific purpose." But otherwise "there is too much divergence to expect harmony."[48]

Unlike Wolf, several of the New Yorkers recognized the danger of appearing elitist and top-down even as the growing Jewish community grew more diverse and less affluent. But it was difficult to avoid. Forward-thinking Louis Marshall had wanted the AJC to be an organization with a democratic structure to represent American Jews' diversity. But Straus and others wanted—and got—a handpicked executive committee of power players dominated by an "oligarchic triumvirate" of Jacob Schiff, *New York Times* publisher Cyrus Sulzberger, and Marshall himself. Adler hoped for an organization to protect the elite's interests from the inevitable challenge from newcomers: "[S]hall we wait until the Russians push us aside and speak for all American Jewry," he asked Marshall, "or shall the older people lead the movement and give it a sane and conservative tone? . . . This is the affair in a nutshell." They were smart, tough, powerful men, and several were very rich. This "circle," as Schiff's biographer points out, hewed to "the irony of insisting that new immigrants assimilate to American ways, while at the same time resisting their calls for democracy within the Jewish community."[49]

Too many egos and too many difficult issues: these men disagreed with each other even when they tried to get along. The question of Zionism and the idea of a Jewish people dogged their efforts to project a unified voice for American Jews. It was a wonder they could work together at all, but the urgency of the Dillingham Commission's work forced them. These were the hidden hurts and public priorities that fueled a lively debate at the end of 1909 between Wolf and Henry Cabot Lodge over whether Jews were a separate race.[50]

Is "Hebrew" a Race or a Religion?

On December 4, 1909, more than two years into its work, the Dillingham Commission held its only live hearing. Seven of the commission's nine members were in attendance, along with its secretary, William W. Husband, and five prominent Jewish lobbyists. It was a Saturday morning, still part of the Washington workday. The men's presence on the Jewish Sabbath, when work is forbidden for the religiously observant, indicated both the importance of the occasion and their assimilation.[51]

Wolf had asked Husband for the meeting "to bring to the attention of the Commission . . . the classification of [some] immigrants by faith." The commission used "Hebrew" as a category of "races or peoples" in its field reports, questionnaires, and statistics. In Wolf's view, however, "Hebrew" and "Jew" were religious, not racial, categories, and they had no place in government statistics. "The point we make is this," he explained. "A Jew coming from Russia is a Russian; from Roumania, a Roumanian; from France, a Frenchman; from England, an Englishman; and from Germany, a German; in other words," he continued, "Hebrew or Jewish is simply a religion." Wolf wanted neither Jews to be thought of as a race nor their religion recorded when other immigrants'

I. C. 79.

THE UNITED STATES IMMIGRATION COMMISSION, WASHINGTON, D. C.

CHECK OR PAY
No._____

1. What is your name? _____

2. Where do you live (street and number)? _____

3. Mark the race to which you belong with a cross (thus **X**):

_____American, white.	_____Finnish.	_____Lithuanian.	_____Russian.
_____American, negro.	_____French-Canadian.	_____Magyar.	_____Ruthenian.
_____Bohemian.	_____German.	_____Montenegrin.	_____Scotch.
_____Bulgarian.	_____Greek.	_____Moravian.	_____Servian.
_____Croatian.	_____Hebrew.	_____Norwegian.	_____Slovak.
_____Danish.	_____Irish.	_____Polish.	_____Slovenian.
_____Dutch.	_____Italian (north).	_____Portuguese.	_____Swedish.
_____English.	_____Italian (south).	_____Roumanian.	_____Syrian.

If of any other race, write name of race here_____

4. Occupation (what work do you do)?_____

5. What do you earn per day?_____ 6. What do you earn per week?_____

7. What work did you do before coming to the U. S.?_____

PLEASE ANSWER QUESTIONS ON BOTH SIDES OF THIS SLIP.

Interview Form, U.S. Immigration Commission. The form revealed the emphasis on "race" and the use of "Hebrew" as a category.

were not. Being singled out by religion, in Wolf's view, violated Jews' civil rights.[52]

It was very late to be asking for such a change—the commission had been at work for almost three years—but the matter was of grave importance for Wolf. Treating the category "Jew" as racial rather than religious violated his ideas about citizenship, assimilation, and civil rights. To Wolf, it smacked of the discrimination Jews faced in Russia.

Wolf's objection stood in opposition to the commission's effort—reflected in its *Dictionary of Races or Peoples*—to collect more specific information about new immigrants than had previous federal categories, which had listed only nation of origin. The commission had borrowed its list of races or peoples from the Bureau of Immigration, which began using the typology at Ellis Island in 1898 and had included it in its printed passenger lists in 1903. At the time, Wolf had objected to the then commissioner-general of immigration, Terence Powderly, who agreed to take statistics about religion out of his annual reports but kept a race question that used the "Hebrew" category in the Ellis Island intake forms.[53]

Wolf thought the "subject had ended then and there." But the inclusion of Jews in the list of races or peoples had reappeared at the Bureau of Immigration and was "also contemplated in the report of your honorable Commission." Wolf had raised the issue with William Husband at least a year earlier, but it had gone nowhere. In fact, earlier in the year, Husband and Dillingham had testified to the Senate Census Committee, urging the inclusion of the "race or people" category in the 1910 census for statistical comparisons with the commission's findings. Lobbying by Wolf, with the support of committee member Senator Simon Guggenheim of Colorado, a German Jew and AJC member, had scuttled the proposal.[54]

Perhaps emboldened by his success on the census question, Wolf, who came to the 1909 hearing representing B'nai B'rith, now hoped to stop the commission from making a "classification of immigrants by faith. That is what it amounts to as far as the Jewish immigration is concerned." The AJC, scrambling to make its own view heard at the hastily called meeting, asked Judge Julian Mack to speak on its behalf. Mack, the highest-ranking Jew in the federal judiciary, had grown up in the Reform world of Jewish Cincinnati and had built a career in law and social service in Chicago, where he worked with Jane Addams's famed Hull House settlement.

In spite of their own disagreements, Wolf, Mack, and other AJC members understood that the federal government's ability to label someone as belonging to a particular "race"—even if he or she remained legally white—represented an immense power to construct sociological categories and, with them, group and personal identities. Was the label "Hebrew" an equivalent to "south Italians," "Greeks," or "Mexicans"—or was it instead a religious group parallel to "Catholic," "Muslim," and "Hindoo"? The question was not just semantic: at the root of Wolf's fears was that such labels would encourage American Jews to see themselves as a race apart. In practice, the categories worked so that no Jewish person could use any label but "Hebrew." A Jew from Russia was not Russian but "Hebrew," as was one from Great Britain, France, or anywhere else. The labels would discourage assimilation, making it easier to ghettoize or even persecute Jews as a group, as in Russia.[55] The younger lawyer Kohler concurred with Wolf that labeling people by religion was unconstitutional; defenders of the "Hebrew" category claimed that it simply offered information on what the commission called "races or peoples" (and what we might today call "ethnicity"), and that it referred to race, not religion.

The question of how and whether to categorize Jews as a race was not new, nor has it ended. Christians had begun the debate, but Jewish scholars had participated since at least the 1880s. It was, in historian Mitchell B. Hart's words, "one element of a much broader debate about the identity of the Jews more generally, and the configuration of the modern nation-state, society, and culture." Studies of Jews and race proliferated in the United States and Europe (including that of Franz Boas for the Commission itself), and the men who appeared at the hearing were versed in these.[56]

The commission's Saturday morning hearing quickly devolved into a meandering debate between Wolf and Henry Cabot Lodge. The fellow Republicans held a long and mutual disregard. In 1895, Wolf had told a New Orleans rabbi, "Everyone knows what an anti-Semite . . . Senator Lodge is." Likewise, Lodge had no patience for Wolf, and, with the senator's PhD in history from Harvard University, he considered himself an expert on race. Lodge belonged firmly in the Jews-are-a-race camp, and he loved a good fight, which "kindled the forces of his brain and heated his blood," as one admirer said, and he could "strike his opponent dumb with one slash."[57] In other words, Lodge was prepared for the debate.

So Lodge did not mince words when he asked Wolf, "Do you mean to deny that the word 'Jew' is a racial term?" Could Wolf accept the statement about Benjamin Disraeli, who had served as British prime minister: "He was baptized as a Christian. He then ceased to be a Jew?" "Yes," Wolf replied, "Religiously he ceased to be a Jew." Lodge: "Ah! Religiously. He was very proud of the fact that he was born of a Jew, and always spoke of himself that way. Did the fact that he changed his religion alter his race?"

Wolf took the bait: "It did not change the fact that he was a Jew; not at all." He went on: "I know the Jewish people throughout the world have claimed him, and other converts," for their fame and talent. "But they ceased to be Jews from the standpoint of religion." "Undoubtedly," said Lodge, but "what I want to get at is whether the word 'Jew' or 'Hebrew' is not a correct racial term?" Wolf demurred: "The position we have broadly taken is that in the classification of immigrants the word 'Jew' is entirely uncalled for."[58]

Wolf allowed that some Jews called themselves a race. Zionists "cling to the idea of returning to Palestine and founding a Jewish state; and I am not speaking for that portion of the Jewish people." Wolf represented "the [R]eform element in the United States and throughout the world." Some eastern European Jews, Wolf felt, "proclaim themselves a race, in part because they have never known what it is to be an equal citizen." Jews were not of one mind, and Wolf came very close to saying that Jews who considered themselves a race suffered from false consciousness.[59] He did blame their "living in Russia and Roumania under medieval conditions" for their failure to see things from what he saw as a quintessentially American point of view.[60]

During his battle with the Bureau of Immigration in 1903, Wolf had surveyed other prominent Jews for their opinions about the "race question." The results did not go as he had hoped. Some people bluntly disagreed with Wolf. Even some Reform Jews used race talk. One elderly Reform rabbi called the government "perfectly correct in considering the Jewish people as a race." But Reform Jews had a very different view of the category of "race" than nationalist Zionists because Reform Jews believed that a person could "withdraw" from Judaism. Cyrus Adler thought all racial classification was absurd, and Wolf blamed Zionism itself for Jews who called themselves a race.[61]

B'nai B'rith's president, Rabbi Leo Levi, offered the best summary of what he called "one of the most vexing questions of controversy among Jews." On the one hand, "leading Reform rabbis of this country utterly repudiate the race doctrine and assent that the Jews are simply a religious community." On the other, for "many others, and especially the Zionists . . . the Jews constitute a race." This was an "academic question," warned Levi, and a "Pandora's box." Levi's own view was that Jews should be able to call Jews a race, but the government should not: "It is to the best interests of the Immigrants and the country," Levi continued, "that as speedily as possible he should become an American in every respect. It is therefore illogical for the country to classify the Jews in a way which in effect declares 'we receive you to be with us but not of us.'"[62]

At the 1909 hearing, Wolf told Lodge—not entirely truthfully—that none of his 1903 survey respondents thought Jews were a race. Lodge countered by quoting the preface of the recently published *Jewish Encyclopedia*. In it, a statement signed by Cyrus Adler, among others, explained that "the present work deals with Jews as a race," and thus "it was found impossible to exclude those who were of that race, whatever their religious affiliations may have been."[63] Even converts to Christianity, in other words, were included.

Then Lodge held forth on "scientific" versus "historical" race. "As you all know, there are what are called the scientific races—that is, the races which are defined by physical peculiarities—the great divisions, like the Mongol, the Negro, the North American Indian, the Aryan, the Semitic . . . where the difference in the skulls and so on have all been retained." In Europe, he conceded, "there has been a great mixture of races and the scientific divisions have largely disappeared," but the categories were still useful. The Immigration Bureau, from which the commission had borrowed its system, uses a "classification made . . . on the basis of historic races." These were the "peoples which have been formed gradually, as the English, the German, in which there is a great mixture of blood, but which are historically racial." The *Dictionary of Races or Peoples* used a similar argument.[64]

William Wheeler jumped in: "I must say that I never understood the word 'Jew' or the word 'Hebrew' to describe a religion." He knew "half a dozen prominent Jewish families in San Francisco who attend Christian churches. But we know them all as Jews." At this point, Wolf was swimming in deep water: "You know them as a class," he said, "but we would not recognize them as Jews." Take Judah Benjamin, the secretary of war for the Confederacy in the Civil War. He was born a Jew but became an Episcopalian. "There are any number of Jews who have become converted or who have married Christians."[65]

"Do they cease thereby to be Jews? Does 'Jew' become a wrong description?" pressed Lodge. Wolf, now contradicting his earlier claims about Disraeli, insisted, "They certainly cease to be Jews." Lodge: "Is no man a Jew unless he is of the Jewish faith?"[66] Wolf's desire to sing the accomplishments of Jews doomed him. To show "the genius inherent in the Jew as such," he conceded, "a great many claim Disraeli, Heine, Borne, Mendelssohn, Bartholdi, and other great celebrities. But in reality, from the Jewish standpoint, they ceased to be Jews when they became Christians." Wolf did not want the federal government to classify them as Jews, yet he wanted to claim them as Jewish. It was not so different than Rabbi Leo Levi's desire to use the term "Jewish race" even as he denied the government the right to do so.

At stake was the power to label and classify, a point made by the more intellectual AJC leader, Julian Mack. Should that power belong to the government? "If Disraeli had come to this country," Mack stated, "he certainly would have said, in answer to the question asked him at port, that he came as an Englishman." But, Lodge pointed out, "He would have been classified racially as a Jew." Mack asked, "Would some officer at the port have that power?"

Mack, the lawyer and judge, made a point to describe racial classification as a power held over the person—or group—being classified; Lodge couched it as simple fact. "It is not a question as to where a man happens to live or what his allegiance is," Lodge continued.[67] "If we were to classify men according to their allegiance, we would classify them in a manner which would be useless." The government chose what race people were, not the people themselves. That is why it was power. Yet here, Lodge fudged because evidence suggested that other immigrant groups did get to choose their ethnicity: William W. Husband claimed, "it came to be perfectly natural in canvassing among immigrants to ask their race. . . . Several races were found in that way of which we had never heard, and which were not in the bureau classification; but still the persons interviewed insisted they were of that race and objected to being classified as anything else."[68] Presumably, "Hebrews" were not afforded that option.

"I do not recognize the Jewish race," Mack replied. "There are Jews who do. I do not." Mack and Wolf tried to substitute ideas such as people, citizen, and nation. But none was a good fit. So Mack conceded that there was division between men such as himself and "the newer element of Jews in this country, who largely are not yet American citizens." The newcomers "claim there is a Jewish race—that it is historical—and they want to re-create it as a nation. They really claim the Jewish *nation* rather than the Jewish *race* [emphasis added]." Most American Jews disagreed. "I am very sure a majority of Jews *who are American citizens* [note his distancing from new immigrants] care nothing about the reestablishment of the Jewish nation as a nation and therefore do not feel themselves nationally Jews." And because of that, "they certainly do not feel themselves racially Jews. . . . They are proud of their Jewish ancestry, but in no other sense."

Lodge tried again: "They are proud of their race, and justly so." But Mack pushed back, "They are proud of their people." The commission, too, used this language rather interchangeably. The dictionary, after all, was of "races or peoples," and William Husband had used the words synonymously in his own statement. "What we want to do," Mack continued, "is nationalize the

Jew as an American citizen, independent of every other consideration. What he is religiously or by faith or by nonfaith is his business. That is a right guaranteed to him by the Constitution."

Wolf's goal for the hearing was made clear when William Wheeler brought up prejudice against Catholics: "There is no question of the existence, among some narrow-minded people, of a feeling which may be called anti-Romanism." True, said Mack, "but you do not classify Christians as Protestants or Roman Catholics" in your statistics. The result, Mack explained, was that Jews were "strangers." "There always was prejudice against the stranger, and you emphasize the fact that the Jew here, as a Jew, is like those of foreign nations—strangers to our land. That is the thing we resent." William Dillingham finally cut off the debate, telling Wolf, "I think we understand the position which has been taken upon this matter." The debate was over.[69]

Mack had tried to salvage the debate, but Wolf had been outmatched by Lodge. Adler, worried anew that Jews would be defined as Asians, proposed that questions of race in federal studies be referred to his own Smithsonian Institution for review. That idea went nowhere, but not long after, an Asian exclusion bill in Congress specified that it did not include Jews, Syrians, or Armenians.[70]

The exchange resolved nothing, but it exposed the nearly unresolvable muddle of racial meanings in the early twentieth-century United States. Wolf rejected the idea that Jews were a race and objected to collecting data about religion. Lodge believed Jews were a race. The two men disagreed with and disliked each other. Meanwhile, though, the Dillingham Commission was faced with a challenge. None of the words available—"race," "people," "nation," "ethnicity"—was fully effective, but the commission had to use something. Any choice would make someone of the Wolf or Lodge camp angry. When categories and labels were so freighted with different implications for different people, and when even professional social scientists differed on their meanings or significance, objectivity was impossible. This problem was, in some ways, the point that Jenks had made in his 1909 address on racial problems.

In the end, the commission acknowledged Wolf's and Mack's protests but did not act on them. The introduction to its final reports explained that "while appreciating the motive" of the Jews who "protest against the designation of the Hebrews as a race or people, the Commission is convinced that such usage is entirely justified. Unfortunately, both the terms in question are used interchangeably to designate a religion as well as a race or people but the Commission has employed them only in the latter sense." It also pointed out that Jews were the only group to complain (a point that simultaneously furthered stereotypes and revealed their high level of access to the commission). Then, the commission stated what was so painful for Wolf to admit: "As a matter of fact, the terms 'Jewish race' and 'Hebrew race' are in common and constant use, even among Hebrews themselves."[71]

The commission was not wrong. Within days of the 1909 hearing, some Jews had publicly criticized Wolf's and Mack's remarks. The AJC's secretary, Herbert Friedenwald, who had attended the meeting, called Wolf's arguments "very general and not very convincing," and when the AJC publicized the hearings, it omitted Wolf's role entirely. Friedenwald was dismayed: "The Yiddish press has been very condemnatory of Judge Mack's and Mr. Wolf's opposition to the classification of Hebrews among other races." One AJC board member demanded that the organization disclaim "the statements made by Judge Mack to the fact that the Jews are not a race." Some new immigrants called themselves "race Jews" to differentiate from the "faith Jews" of the Reform movement. A Zionist society in Baltimore applauded the commission's position "that the Jews are a strongly identified race."[72]

The last thing leaders wanted was a public dispute among Jews, which would only distract from their campaigns against restriction. Within a few weeks, the AJC's executive committee "resolved that it is unwise to make any further attempt to have the classification 'Hebrews' altered, as no good purpose can at this time be served by further agitation of the subject."[73]

Without a convincing argument against the "Hebrew" label, Jewish lobbyists ceded ground to future eugenics arguments for restriction that could now rely on government statistics organized by race. American Jews' internal debates undermined their ability to shape the commission's data collection, which in turn shaped its recommendations for restriction. Even if Jewish leaders had been more united in their opposition to designating Jews as a race, it would have been difficult to stanch the rising power of race thinking promoted by people such as Lodge.

Organizational Détente and the Statement for Volume 41

Jewish lobbyists were not yet done with the Dillingham Commission. A year later, as its work neared an end, the commission solicited policy recommendations—by invitation only—from labor, philanthropic, and patriotic organizations. Once again, Jewish leaders put aside their differences to craft a strong statement against restriction and in favor of a broader role for the federal government in welcoming immigrants to the United States.

The policy recommendations appeared in Volume 41, the commission's final report. Its list of contributors underscored the intensity of Jewish efforts to shape the immigration issue. Six of the fourteen statements in the volume came from Jewish organizations, and no other immigrant or ethnic organizations were included, although the nativist Junior Order of Mechanics and the IRL were. To show a united front, the leaders of the AJC, UAHC, and B'nai B'rith decided to issue a joint statement (so that in total, eight Jewish organizations were represented in the volume). At 17 pages, with another 130 pages in appendices, theirs was the longest entry. Eventually, twenty men signed it.[74]

Crafting this joint statement was an impressive achievement in sublimating conflict. In 1908, not long after the bitter divisions over the creation of the AJC, Wolf had given his speech calling immigration policy the most important issue for Jewish activists. Wolf insisted that rather than any "spirit of rivalry," there was "a concordant feeling of harmony among the organizations." Two years later, Wolf wrote to Kohler that he thought it "important for many reasons to submit our views forcibly and fully to the Immigration Commission." Public sentiment toward new immigrants was souring, and the commission's findings were "likely to shape our Immigration policy for a number of years." Louis Marshall was also "heartily in favor of the plan" to send a joint statement from Jewish groups "of national standing."[75]

The statement came together quickly and championed federal power. Kohler wrote the first draft, and Marshall made early edits. The young lawyers, who had tried immigration cases and defended deportation cases, including those against Chinese immigrants, heavily emphasized civil rights. Marshall's editing notes made clear that he rejected the emerging paradigm that immigration itself was a policy problem, instead calling it a "question," a "subject," and even "a desirability." He praised the status quo: current laws were, with a few exceptions, "satisfactory" and had even "been productive of great good." He suggested "a concise statement" explaining "the desirability of immigration," and even "the duty which this country owes to the immigrant," not the other way around. He inserted a line into the draft that called immigration a positive good, not a policy problem.[76]

Above all, Marshall wanted "no ambiguity." "Otherwise we would have no hope of success and would be traveling from the frying pan into the fire. Our definitions should be exact and scientific." He endorsed the exclusion of anyone "whose presence here could be fairly criticized," such as criminals and prostitutes. He also affirmed the current practice of selecting immigrants on the basis of quality, not quantity or national origin (what Jeremiah Jenks called "on an individualistic basis"). As Marshall wrote to one colleague, "We should not lay ourselves open to the attack that we favor indiscriminate immigration, without regard to the welfare of our country."[77]

Marshall guided the group in crafting a closely worded legal brief for their final statement. It asserted the legitimacy of federal power even as it recommended against further restrictive laws. It traced how Jewish organizations' role in immigration policy had transformed from reticent charity work to well-funded, organized philanthropy, and finally to sophisticated lobbying for new federal laws and protections. It validated the power the federal government already had but argued for the legislative status quo. Its main point was that the current laws worked, and that "no immigration law of the United States [except, it conceded, for Chinese exclusion] has ever been restrictive . . . but always regulative. . . ." Even "the head tax was not designed as a restrictive measure" but as a funding mechanism for the federal Immigration Service "to meet the cost of regulating immigration and caring for the immigrant." The United States had a long history of policies to "encourage immigration," and there was no reason to change.[78]

The statement also articulated Jews' nascent civil rights agenda. Lawyers Marshall and Kohler insisted that immigrants were entitled to due process, and that laws (such as the 1891 Immigration Act) that did not allow judicial review of immigration decisions should be abolished: "No other class of cases is beyond judicial review, yet personal liberty is even more precious than property rights," which dominated legal disputes. Even today, although immigrants facing deportation have a right to counsel, the government does not provide public defenders, or alert immigrants to these rights.[79]

Their statement also called for what would, by World War II, be called refugee policy. In unstated reference to the Galveston work, it pointed out that the rules against assisted immigration were not supposed to ban every kind of help: "Such statutes, reasonably construed, do not forbid even the part payment of passage money of self-supporting persons overwhelmed by some sudden calamity," that is, the kinds "of persecution as led to the Puritan settlement of New England, the Catholic settlement of Maryland, the Quaker settlement of Pennsylvania, or the Huguenot emigration to South Carolina." Here was a clever bit of politicking, for it made Lodge's Puritan forebears part of the American immigrant tradition that brought Jews from the shtetl.[80]

The statement endorsed federal statutory powers but objected to federal employees acquiring unlegislated power. It criticized arbitrary administrative procedures that hampered immigrants' entry rights, such as William Williams's rule at Ellis Island that anyone carrying less than twenty-five dollars was excluded as a likely public charge. The Jewish leaders also reiterated long-standing objections to the authority given to physicians to bar people with "trivial defects, such as the arbitrary estimate of 3 pounds underweight and . . . sweeping generalizations unjustified in fact, like 'lack of physical development,' [or] 'lack of muscular development.'" These rules "wholly ignore the physical and mental vigor of the immigrant from eastern Europe whose slight physique often is misleading to superficial observation."[81] These objections suggested that the decisions of individual immigration agents imperiled the civil rights of potential Americans no less—and perhaps even more—than bureaucratic classifications as "Hebrews."

It is worth noting that the questionnaire the commission sent to philanthropic organizations was itself a template for a broad view of federal power, a view that Jewish leaders eagerly shared. Consider the question, "What can the National Government do to promote the assimilation or Americanization of immigrants"? (This work was left entirely to private organizations.) In response, the AJC, UAHC, and B'nai B'rith statement offered up Jewish philanthropy such as the Baron de Hirsch Fund as a model for "the Americanization of children and adults." But, claiming that "the admirable results accomplished are not, however, as widely known as they should be," it suggested that it was well "within the province of the Government to pro-mote such work by disseminating information concerning it."[82]

Their statement envisioned a federal immigration policy focused on fos-tering immigrants' entry into U.S. society rather than hindering it. It argued that Jewish and other private associations were doing, in their words, "quasi-public" work. The statement called for "increasing the scope of the Government's own Information Division," as well as state and charitable and local ver-sions, to "encourage immigrants to go to districts where they are most likely to prosper, and thus be judiciously distributed throughout the country." The "Government should also cooperate with various quasi-public charitable organizations" who help immigrants settle. "Such disinterested benevolent agencies are entitled to assistance and encouragement from the Government, as they render at their own expense quasi-governmental service." The Galveston Jewish Immigrants' Information Bureau was one example. Another, the Industrial Removal Office, had resettled "over 50,000 Jewish immigrants since 1901, and made them self-supporting workers . . . in the interior of sub-stantially every State of the Union" rather than in "the congested districts" of the "seacoast" states.[83] Places that wanted immigrants were less likely to com-plain about the costs associated with them.

A separate brief, written by Julian Mack for the Immigrants Protective League (IPL), even more adamantly endorsed private reform as a conduit for federal funds and a model for federal programs. Mack was an officer for the Chicago organization, founded in 1908 by women reformers including Jane Addams and Grace Abbott. The IPL, created in part to combat the IRL, offered immigrants social services, education, and advocacy. It included many Jewish members and, of course, recipients. Mack's statement for the IPL emphasized that the federal government had the power—and the moral obligation—to let private charities know about incoming immigrants in order to connect them to services. Mack also called for a federal project modeled on the IPL to create a public "protective, not detective" agency to monitor immigrants' well-being, not as part of the punitive deportation investigations of the Bureau of Immigration. As he stated elsewhere, "Private citizens al-ways have to lead the way and then turn the task over to the public." Mack's statement concluded by reiterating its "opposition to sundry restrictive bills" before Congress.[84]

A broad range of Jewish leadership affirmed the federal government's power to regulate, promote, acculturate, and protect immigrants' civil rights. These men offered a decidedly positive assertion of federal power and used their own organizations as models for public programs. As it happened, the Dillingham Commission also embraced a broad view of federal power—but to restrict immigrants, not to protect them and promote their rights.

These briefs did not, it should be noted, convince the commission. Its final recommendations encouraged assimilation but noted, "It does not appear that the Federal Government can directly assist in this work, but where possible effort should be made to promote the activities of these [private] organizations."[85] This hesitation reflected the U.S. government's reticence for funding immigrant integration efforts, which continues, in contrast to many other receiving nations, to this day.[86]

Jewish leaders who lived through the massive transformation of American Jewry had moved from reluctant almsgivers and reformers to full-fledged lobbyists for civil rights and broad federal power to facilitate mass migration of Jews and others. Their advocacy had turned from Jacob Schiff's monetary support for Japan's defeat of Russia and monitoring U.S. relations with Russia, to immigration legislation, mirroring the larger trend of expanding federal powers from foreign policy to domestic immigration. Their new policy demands, it should be noted, applied to all immigrants, and they self-consciously did the work as "citizens." Wolf wanted one thing "distinctly understood" in their statement: "that whatever we ask we ask as citizens and not as Jews. Immigration laws are made for all and not for any particular class."[87]

In their lobbying, Wolf and the New Yorkers tried to couch their efforts in the universal language of individual rights. At the same time, though, as Wolf's and Mack's arguments with Lodge revealed, they could not avoid debates—both among themselves and with others—about their status as a unique and separate people. The only complaints about classification, according to the Dillingham Commission, had come from Jews. In the end, Jewish leaders abandoned their challenge to the "Hebrew" terminology, even accepting a compromise "mother tongue" question in the 1910 census, formulated in part by Daniel Folkmar, the author of the commission's *Dictionary of Races or Peoples.*

Wolf's and Mack's failure to convince the commission to abort the "races or peoples" question had enormous consequences. It appeared everywhere in the reports. To give one of hundreds of examples, the instructions for agents studying immigrants in school read, "The country of birth will in many cases indicate the race, but not always. For instance, special care should be exercised not to report as Russian any persons except those whose native language is Russian. The persons born in Russia now resident in the United States are Russian by *nationality,* but very few of them are Russian by *race.* Almost all belong to three races, Poles, Lithuanians, and Hebrews." Each of the commission's forty-one volumes would be organized around the race categories, and the issue would continue to haunt Jewish leaders.[88]

Two years after the Dillingham Commission reports were released, sociologist Edward Ross published *Old World in the New,* which accused Jews of controlling immigration policy. Among other things, the book gave scholarly imprimatur to the nation's increasing bent for eugenic thinking: it included sections on "evading the degrading competition by race suicide" and on "how immigration will affect good looks in this country." Equally significant, though, was Ross's singling out of "the endeavor of the Jews to control the immigration policy of the United States." His version of the passage of the 1907 immigration act emphasized "the power of the million Jews in the Metropolis [that] lined up the Congressional delegation from New York in solid opposition to the literacy test." "The systematic campaign in newspapers and magazines to break down all arguments for restriction and to calm nativist fears," he insisted, "is waged by and for one race. Hebrew money is behind the National Liberal Immigration League and its numerous publications."[89] By 1913, eugenic talk was becoming more fully developed in the United States (heard in Ross's snide phrase "subtle Hebrew brains") than it was during the Dillingham Commission's work. But the idea that Jews played an important role in immigration policy was not a new one. It had, indeed, been the motivation behind Jewish leaders' frequent comments to one another that they couch their efforts in the universal terms of citizenship. For all the talk of Jewish power, though, efforts to influence the commission had produced few tangible results.

4

The Vanishing American Wage Earner

Jewish lobbyists failed at altering the reports, so they made a final attempt at shaping public reception of them. In 1911, the American Jewish Committee hired government economist Isaac Hourwich to prepare a point-by-point rebuttal of the twenty volumes on immigrants in industry reports. Commission secretary William Husband, in a gesture of tremendous generosity, let Hourwich look at them before publication. Hourwich, a Jewish émigré who had trained as an attorney in Vilna, Lithuania, before emigrating, had earned a PhD in economics from Columbia University. He became a statistician for the U.S. Census Bureau and a specialist in the mining industry, as well as a political activist. He published *Immigration and Labor,* his five-hundred-page response, in 1912. It became the first critique of the Dillingham Commission reports, and it remains the most comprehensive. In it, Hourwich criticized the organization by race and nationality (based on the forms Wolf had protested) and the failure to compare "old" and "new" immigrants who had lived in the United States for the same amount of time.[1] He did, however, praise the reports for using an economic, rather than cultural or racial, analysis for immigrants' impact, even if he disagreed with the conclusions of the reports' chief architect, W. Jett Lauck.

The immigrants in industry investigation was a colossal undertaking. Twenty volumes covered an extensive array of American mining and manufacture: agricultural implements, glove making, meatpacking, silk spinning, glassblowing, cigar rolling, oil refining, typewriter assembly, zinc smelting, and rope, twine, and hemp production. From Buffalo to Butte to Birmingham, dozens of agents canvassed workers and their families, recording workers from ninety-three nationalities or "races." They collected original data from nearly every major industry and from one in seven members of the nation's manufacturing and mining work force.[2]

The young man overseeing this massive study—fully half of the commission's work—was W. Jett Lauck, a twenty-eight-year-old graduate-school dropout. Lauck was working as an adjunct instructor at his undergraduate alma mater when, in early 1907, he was hired as a field agent by the commission. Within a year, he had been promoted to agent-in-charge of the industrial series.[3]

In spite of the scale of his work and a lifetime's interest in workers and wages, Lauck spent his career behind the scenes. He was never famous—or defamed, for that matter. But he was as important to conceptualizing the "immigrant problem" as anyone in the United States. His reports amassed a colossal amount of data, cited and debated by scholars ever since, which convinced Lauck of the need for immigration restriction. The importance of Lauck's work made this obscure bureaucrat an essential figure in the commission's articulation of an "immigration problem," the title of the book he coauthored with his mentor, Jeremiah Jenks.

Lauck's project gathered its huge body of evidence in the service of crafting an immigration policy around domestic labor concerns rather than the dictates of international diplomacy. His broad plan of work for the industrial reports ensured that the immigrants' economic impact—not their culture or "race"—would be the primary evidence on which the commission would base its recommendations.[4] This emphasis was evident at nearly every turn of the reports' pages, especially in their final recommendations: "Further general legislation concerning the admission of aliens," stated the second of the commission's eight recommendations, "should be based primarily upon economic or business considerations touching the prosperity and well-being of our people."[5]

Lauck called this prosperity and well-being the "American standard of living." His focus on domestic labor conditions made him keenly attuned to the economic and cultural results of class difference, which would guide the rest of his career. Lauck and others promoted the American standard of living—supported by what economists, reformers, and labor leaders termed a "living wage"—as an objective, scientific standard. In actuality, it was anything but. The "American standard of living" metric relied on assumptions about culture, men and women, family life, and race that invariably cast new immigrants in a negative light. Lauck was not hesitant to criticize local governments and corporate elites for poor conditions, sometimes more than he blamed the immigrants. He did not think newcomers from eastern and southern Europe were inherently—or biologically—inferior. He was not a eugenicist. But it was easier to suggest restricting new immigrants than to demand reforming how local elites and government officials treated them. As a result, this untested and class-conscious young man built a framework for studying immigrants that would encourage restrictionist policy for decades to come.

A Young Economist in a Young Profession

Jett Lauck's perspective was deeply American. Born in 1879 the second of eight children, and the oldest to survive to adulthood, Lauck grew up on the Maryland border in Mineral County, West Virginia. His hometown, Keyser, was itself a product of the Industrial Revolution, when it became a stop on the nation's first railroad, the Baltimore & Ohio, in 1852. The railroad's arrival transformed a rural settlement into an industrial town and gave Lauck's father, William Blandford Lauck, his livelihood as an agent for the railroad-shipping company U.S. Express. William served on the town council and, in 1903, was elected mayor.[6]

The family, like many in the region, was German American and Protestant, with roots in the United States that dated to 1750. When Jett Lauck was born, less than 6 percent of Mineral County's population was foreign-born, almost all of them from Great Britain and Germany. A single Italian immigrant represented its entire southern and eastern European population. Old-stock, respectable, middling status: this was Lauck's upbringing and perspective. His college sweetheart, Eleanor Moore Dunlap, whom he married in 1908, was of solid Scots-Irish heritage. Together, Jett and Eleanor Lauck's ancestors belonged to the oldest and most revered of settlement stories, predating even the "old immigrants" of the nineteenth century.[7]

Lauck's old-stock background and his new education in the social sciences made him the quintessential product of the Progressive Era. He was almost certainly the first in his family to attend college, at the venerable Washington

& Lee University in Lexington, Virginia, where he was a debater and orator and served as president of the literary society and the press club. With a major in economics, his courses included some on business, socialism, American industry and foreign trade, and one on the economic significance of colonization. Most important, he encountered two young and ambitious assistant professors of economics, H. Parker Willis and Robert F. Hoxie, who had both trained at the prestigious University of Chicago. Only a few years older than Lauck, Willis was already moonlighting as a fiscal-policy consultant in the Philippines and elsewhere. He would soon leave Washington & Lee for government work, later serving as the editorial adviser at the Dillingham Commission; he is best known for coauthoring the Federal Reserve Act with Congressman Carter Glass in 1914.[8]

Willis became the first of several important mentors to Lauck. In 1903, Willis secured Lauck a graduate fellowship at the University of Chicago with the man who had been his own adviser: monetary-policy expert J. Laurence Laughlin. Laughlin introduced the German-style seminar to the University of Chicago, where he cofounded a practical school of economics that would become the business school.[9]

The political economy department at the University of Chicago was a heady place for a small-town West Virginian in 1903. It was still a half-century before the creation of the neoclassical Chicago School of Milton Friedman, but the upstart institution founded by John D. Rockefeller in 1890 was already an incubator for "all shades of opinion," as one of Lauck's classmates put it. In 1903, Lauck joined three dozen graduate students in the department, many of whom would go on to have prestigious careers.[10]

At a time when economists were increasingly attracted to Progressive reform, Laughlin was a conservative iconoclast who enjoyed diverse points of view. He was also farsighted in organizing the university's political economy department into introductory, theoretical, and practical subjects, with the latter "devoted mainly to the collection of facts, the weighing of evidence, and an examination of questions bearing on the immediate welfare of our people." Lauck took Laughlin's course on money and practical economics, which examined the theoretical and historical aspects of what it called "the Important Questions of the Day." The department included a laboratory for statistical research work, designed for students intending to join government agencies. Problems needed solutions, which required experts trained at places such as the University of Chicago.[11]

Laughlin was willing to hire colleagues who were his ideological opposites, most prominently the "naked revolutionary" Thorstein Veblen. Veblen's *The Theory of the Leisure Class: An Economic Study of Institutions* (1899) offered a trenchant critique of what would later be called the consumer economy. In the department, Veblen taught courses in political economy; Laughlin, in labor and capital, and finance, and also the economics seminar.[12]

Laughlin was also a strong supporter of female graduate students, even when their interests in reform fell far afield of his own conservative commitments. Lauck held one of only three fellowships in political economy at the same time as fellow Laughlin student Edith Abbott, who finished a doctoral dissertation on women's labor and went on to live and work at Jane Addams's famous social settlement Hull House. She was a much more prominent immigration expert than Lauck. The coeducational graduate experience at the University of Chicago was still rare, but it was good preparation for the Dillingham Commission, where Lauck, Jenks, and chief statistician Frederick Croxton hired many women with graduate degrees.[13]

The University of Chicago made a big impression on Lauck, but he made less of one on it. He got As in his courses on Labor and Capital, Economics of Working Men, and the Process of Legislation, a lot of Bs, and a C in Economic Factors of Civilization, Theory of Value, and Railway Rate Regulation. In a prize-winning essay that hewed closely to his adviser's specialty in monetary policy, Lauck argued that wavering international commitment to the gold standard had led to the Panic of 1893. Lauck published his essay as a book, but it was not a graduate thesis—he left the university in 1905, without finishing his degree, to fill in for Parker Willis as a visiting professor of economics back at Washington & Lee University.[14]

By the early twentieth century, with the growth of the federal government and its insatiable need for expertise, things looked better for "practical economists" such as Lauck than they had even a decade earlier. Still, taking a job at the Dillingham Commission was risky. Being a public expert—a technocrat—had little job stability. Unlike an academic, Lauck could not rely on the backstop of tenure in lean years. By leaving the University of Chicago without a graduate degree and committing himself to policy work and private consulting,

Lauck staked his career on recommendations, connections, appointments—even loans—from his mentors. It is almost certain Parker Willis recommended Lauck for the Dillingham Commission job, with the support of the gentlemanly Laughlin, whom Lauck peppered with obsequious requests. Laughlin also published Lauck's progress report on the industrial investigations in a journal he edited. Jeremiah Jenks, who hired Lauck at the commission, became a lifetime adviser, collaborator, and financial supporter.[15]

Lauck exerted great influence on the Dillingham Commission's work in part because he got in early, perhaps only the third staff member hired. First assigned to Jenks's subcommittee on statistics, he quickly moved up the commission's ranks. The following spring, he was asked to create an outline for what he called the "general investigation in the North, Middle West, and New England." (Probably because of the sensitivity about the Japanese issue, the western reports were managed separately.) Chief statistician Frederick Croxton and commission member Charles Neill, who did similar work at the Bureau of Labor, had already outlined an initial "general industrial survey." Lauck reworked it into a full-scale "economic investigation" that would become "the basis of all the other investigations." The industry studies and "special work," like the ongoing studies of immigrant homes and banking, would report to the same supervisor and use the same methodology—canvasses of homes and business places, as well as personal interviews.[16]

The commission adopted Lauck's proposal. Lauck worked with existing material—such as the interview and canvassing schedules—created by Croxton, but he altered these to his own vision, added more economic questions, and reorganized the hierarchy of collecting and collating data. Lauck's proposal suggested that the same person oversee the "field work of both the economic and general investigation." This chief agent would also "pick out the communities in which work would be done" and, in consultation with Husband and Croxton, "write the economic report when the work was finished."[17] Lauck was writing his own job description: by the summer, he was officially in charge of half the commission's reports. His salary doubled, and he assumed titles ranging from "superintendent of agents" to "industrial expert" to "expert in charge of general industrial investigation."[18]

Lauck's new job was a lofty one for someone of his age and modest credentials. The investigations in the eastern United States were consolidated and placed under his supervision; the Pacific Coast studies were parceled out first to one Stanford University professor then to another.[19] The other superintendent of agents was Roland P. Falkner, an old hand in Washington and in colonial administration, most recently as the commissioner of education in Puerto Rico. Lauck made the same salary as these more accomplished men, all of whom had PhDs.[20]

In lieu of an advanced degree, Lauck brought organizational skills, enthusiasm, and connections. His new plan was underway in September 1907, and he committed himself utterly to the task. To choose study sites, he and his staff scoured census reports on population and industrial growth, as well as ship manifests on destinations of new immigrants. After that, Lauck spent much of his time in the field. He proposed to take "the community as a basis from which to work." He visited dozens of the sites for preliminary reports modeled on the social survey model currently in vogue among reformers.[21]

He was on the road for weeks at a time. Lauck's son remembered about his father, "All he did was work." The pattern began early. "The amount of work which he can do is astonishing," Croxton observed, as was "the rapidity with which he can gain a general survey of any locality." "In many respects," Croxton went on, "he is better adapted to work of that character than anyone with whom I have ever been thrown into contact." As Charles Neill observed, "I question if there is another man in the country who has seen, personally, the labor conditions of so many wage-earners."[22]

Fieldwork began in August 1908, with twenty new agents, along with an appropriation of fifty thousand dollars, and lasted about eighteen months. Lauck began from home, in the coal and iron industry radiating from western Pennsylvania into Maryland, Virginia, and West Virginia. He was one of several agents who spent the second half of 1908 exclusively in "two steel and two coal communities—one bituminous and one anthracite" of Appalachia and western Pennsylvania. Newly wed, Lauck was absent from his wife, Ellen, but "the work is fascinating," he wrote to her, "and I have reason to be very proud."[23]

Johnstown, U.S.A.

As government experts, Lauck's mentors Jeremiah Jenks and Parker Willis traveled the world. Lauck climbed on the Baltimore & Ohio railroad to steel country. "I miss you all dreadfully now," he wrote on a postcard from Johnstown, Pennsylvania, to Ellen. "But I won't leave." It was just after Thanksgiving 1908, a raw time of year in a raw part of the country. The iron and steel town was best known for the flood two decades earlier that had killed 2,200 people. Johnstown had rebuilt, Lauck explained to his new wife, but it was not a cheery place. Poor, crowded, "dirty with dust and soot," in the words of one immigrant newcomer, Johnstown was as divided by class and ethnicity as anywhere in the United States. The dam whose 1889 failure had flooded the working-class town had belonged to a reservoir owned by a private rod and gun club whose members included Andrew Carnegie, Henry Clay Frick, and Andrew Mellon. The larger region was wracked with labor conflict—most famously the 1892 Homestead Strike against the Carnegie Steel Company.[24]

No place or industry epitomized the transformation of the U.S. economy—or its population—more than the iron and steel country of western Pennsylvania. Stretching "as far north as Sharon, Pa., to the east as far as Johnstown, to Youngstown, Ohio on the west, and to Wheeling and Morgantown, West Virginia, on the south," the region was a mountainous expanse of "blast surfaces, steel works, and rolling mills," and—beneath the surface—coal and iron mines spreading in all directions from Andrew Carnegie's Pittsburgh. Lauck began in this region, spent the most time there, and used it as a model for other reports. As a result, the most thorough of the industry reports were volumes 6–7 on bituminous coal mining and 8–9 on iron and steel manufacturing.[25]

Iron and coal mining had existed in western Pennsylvania since the early nineteenth century, but investment in the region's industry had quintupled over the preceding twenty-five years. The Carnegie Steel Company and others swallowed up smaller firms, so that more men worked for fewer and fewer companies. By 1905, investment in Pennsylvanian iron and steel totaled $473 million, and the industry employed 125,000 workers in that state alone—not counting the tens of thousands in coal mining. New immigrants comprised most of those workers. More than half the iron- and steelworkers in the region had been in the United States for less than five years, 80 percent for less than a decade. It was the first industry and region in the country to employ Slavs in large numbers. Where the Irish and Welsh had once predominated, now Magyars, Poles, Slovaks, Lithuanians, Italians, Russians, Croatians, Bohemians, Scandinavians, Greeks, Ruthenians, and Serbians were everywhere.

The Slavs, derisively nicknamed "Hunkies" in coal country, gained particular attention and opposition.[26]

On the back of a postcard with a view of the Susquehanna River from aptly named Steelton, Pennsylvania, Lauck wrote to his wife that the card's photo would give her "an idea of what Steelton looks like in general—without its horrors."[27] Housing conditions were often worse in such places, with new immigrants crowded into duplexes and apartment buildings, than they were in urban centers such as New York and Philadelphia.[28] The small-town West Virginian Lauck did not countenance these landscapes with ease. Here, in the charmless hamlets of industrial America, in his first job in public service, the young economist found his mission in life: to study and save the American workingman.

The region proved popular for economic and social research. The best-known study was the Pittsburgh Survey, undertaken simultaneous to the Dillingham Commission's work, in 1907. Social surveys performed by political and reform groups had a prodigious history in France and Great Britain. In the twentieth century, these investigations became the domain of "experts," especially in the United States. The Pittsburgh Survey was funded by the newly founded Russell Sage Foundation "for the improvement of social and living conditions in the United States." Paul U. Kellogg, editor of the influential social reform journal *Survey,* served as director. The famous study comprised six volumes and was illustrated by documentary photographer Lewis Hine (whose pictures were later borrowed by *Survey* to illustrate articles about the Dillingham Commission as well).[29]

The authors of the Pittsburgh Survey and the staff of the Dillingham Commission shared similar backgrounds and training. But the former were self-consciously reformers, whereas the commission's work aspired to scientific objectivity. By and large, the reformers who undertook the Pittsburgh Survey were "environmentalists," in the parlance of the day, which meant they did not blame immigrants for their poor living and working conditions. Yet even this overtly sympathetic approach drew criticism from some defenders of new immigrants. Prominent industrial reformer and Hull House resident Florence Kelley, whose father William "Pig Iron" Kelley had represented Pennsylvania as a Republican in Congress for decades, complained that the Pittsburgh Survey described horrible conditions but did nothing to change them.[30]

Lauck's own case study of Johnstown, Pennsylvania, set the template for the Dillingham Commission's industry reports and established his methods, priorities, and focus on the "American standard of living." He used the city as an example in his proposal to the Dillingham Commission membership. Johnstown appealed to Lauck as a case study because of his familiarity with its industry and its proximity to his hometown and to Washington, DC. He spent many weeks in Johnstown in 1908 and featured the town—labeled "Community A" in the official reports—in his published articles showcasing the commission's work.[31]

Johnstown was one of the oldest coal, iron, and steelmaking centers in the United States, situated among dozens of similar communities. Dominated by the Cambria Steel Corporation, the city's population increased by more than half between 1900 and 1910. More than one in five residents were eastern European.[32] Newcomers were often taken aback by their new surroundings. New Polish immigrant Anthony Cyburt thought he had arrived at Johnstown on a foggy morning. "Later I learned it was not fog but smoke. When I stepped my foot on Johnstown streets I was astonished what I saw there[—]dirty with dust and soot and small almost black homes and some large buildings which had very tall chimneys which were shooting black smoke. Yes, this was the America I saw." Bethlehem Steel Corporation founder Charles Schwab saw fire: "Along toward dusk, tongues of flame would shoot up in the pall around Johnstown," he wrote. "When some furnace door was opened, the evening turned red. . . . And the murk was always present, the smell of the foundry. It gets into your hair, your clothes, even your blood."[33]

Here were two men on opposite sides of Johnstown's world. The physical division of newcomer and native, and the noxious environment the former inhabited, fascinated Jett Lauck. The volume on Johnstown, unlike later reports, included extensive maps of the region's divided social geography. In his 1910 article for *Survey* about the region, Lauck sounded a theme he would often repeat: "The term 'American miner,' so far as the western Pennsylvania field is concerned, is largely a misnomer." (Or, as he put it in a later article, "the so-called American wage-earner does not exist.") This, Lauck emphasized, was the first thing to know about the region's workers.[34]

The "second fundamental condition" of the Pennsylvania coal miner was his location in "detached and, in many cases, isolated villages and communities"

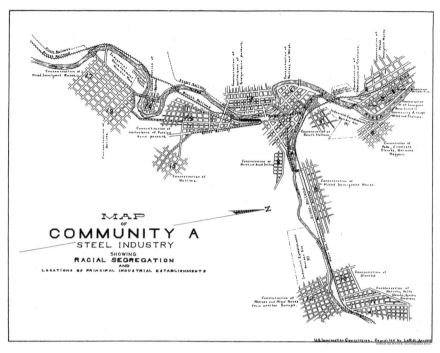

Map of Johnstown, Pennsylvania, emphasizing geographical segregation. Lauck used his study of Johnstown as a model for the twenty reports on immigrants in industries.

strung along the railroads that radiated from Pittsburgh. "Throughout this territory," Lauck wrote, "were larger cities or towns" such as Latrobe, Johnstown, and Uniontown—"diminutive Pittsburghs" of clerical workers, mine offices, and "so far as possible the American part" of the work force. New immigrants filled the smaller "camps and villages" nearby. On Saturdays and paydays, "a heterogeneous collection of races and tongues" crowded the "stores, amusement places, saloons, and even the principal streets of the urban centers."[35] The rest of the week, the two groups stood apart.

"The coal and coke villages surrounding the larger urban centers," Lauck wrote, "are much alike," with "fifty to one hundred red or gray square frame dwellings of uniform style and cheap material." Main Street ran from a company store on one end to a school and churches on the other. Some places had sidewalks of "coke, ashes, or slate," others just raw boards. "Open drainage is everywhere," he noted, with fetid gutters and "rubbish, household garbage and other discarded articles" scattered about. Some places were even worse—with almost no drainage, so that "the houses lower down are flooded and uninhabitable in rainy weather, and receive the refuse and waste water from those above." The coke ovens, he observed, "destroy all vegetation," exacerbating erosion.[36] "Old cans, broken boxes, discarded household articles, ashes, garbage, and refuse usually cover the yards" of company tenements. "The mining companies," he complained, "seem either unable or unwilling to keep their villages in the condition which American standards of life demand."[37]

The public health implications were obvious, but Lauck saw other dangers in the isolation of these villages: it bred hopelessness in immigrants. The "sparsely settled districts" led to a "lack of contact with American life and institutions, the absence of the educational status of labor organizations, the discouragement of thrift and permanent settlement, the necessity of living in company houses, and the impossibility of acquiring a home."[38] Lauck was listing all the "should-haves" of American life—unattainable by immigrant "have-nots."

None of these deficits, Lauck noted, were the immigrants' fault. Lauck offered an environmentalist analysis of immigration not unlike that of the Pittsburgh Survey staff.[39] These analyses differ in important ways from the hard eugenicism that emerged by the 1920s—indeed, in 1921, economist Irving Fisher, a leading eugenist, complained, "The core of the problem of immigration is one of race and eugenics, despite the fact that in the eighteen volumes [*sic*] of the [industrial] report[s] of the Immigration Commission scarcely any attention is given to this aspect of the immigration problem."[40]

To understand Lauck's different approach requires a detour into the field of eugenics, still in its infancy in 1907. It is easy to assume—as many scholars have—that eugenics played a pervasive role in the commission's research and findings. One scholar has called the commission's members "part of a well-defined group of nativists" and argued that their conclusions were made "under the sway of the theory of eugenics." (Nativism and eugenics are not the same thing.) Another scholar asserts that the commission was "deeply informed by racial theories," tying Jeremiah Jenks closer to eugenics than the evidence supports. Another, in a study of race and immigration in the United States, devotes an entire chapter to the "importance of eugenic and anthropological research" in the Dillingham Commission. "The connection between scientific arguments about race and patrician alarm about the new 'hordes' received its first explicit formulation in the 1911 Dillingham Commission," according to the account. The patricians were the Immigration Restriction League (IRL). But in fact IRL officials complained about the lack of eugenics in the reports.[41]

Critical analyses are often based on selective readings of the reports, and some Dillingham Commission volumes were clearly more influenced by eugenics than others. The methodology and racial classifications, as well as studies such as those of immigrant women's fecundity and immigration and crime, reflected some influence of the nascent eugenics movement. One scholar quotes the commission calling new immigrants "as a class . . . far less intelligent than the old" and "racially . . . for the most part essentially unlike the British, German, and other" old immigrants. But the statements come from the summary first volume, where the commission's recommendations were, which was more restrictionist in tone than most of the supporting research volumes. In 1956, an historian of the IRL accurately observed that the commission was "seemingly restrained in its ethnic judgments," but that it nevertheless "fulfilled the restrictionist tradition" because "intellectuals and reformers associated ethnic and economic liabilities of the latest immigrants so loosely that the one set of impressions inevitably suggested and complemented the other." In fact, "many humanitarian observers did not recognize the racial discrimination in the discrete phases of the Commission" and hoped that its findings might lead to a living-wage movement for all workers.[42]

Lauck's reports were the most important, the largest, the most expensive, and the most comprehensive that the commission produced. And by the standards of the day—and certainly by the standards of a few years later—Lauck's reports were hardly based on eugenics at all. The commission's views on the racial fitness of immigrants were equivocal, as evidenced in their general enthusiasm for distribution, and in Jett Lauck's insistence that emphasis be on the economic—not racial or cultural—impact of large numbers of new immigrants, not on their personal qualities. Even his concern about racial segregation (evident in the map of Johnstown) contained within it an implicit endorsement of integration.

Proponents of eugenics invoked Charles Darwin's naturalist work as their inspiration, but the field's real roots were in the social Darwinist work of

Darwin's less famous cousin, English biologist Sir Francis Galton, who coined the word "eugenics" in 1883. Eugenics was popularized earlier in Europe than in the United States. Galton's American protégé Charles Davenport opened his Station for Experimental Evolution in Cold Spring Harbor, New York, in 1904. Yale sociologist William Graham Sumner's influential social Darwinist tract *Folkways* was published in 1907, just as the Dillingham Commission got under way. Starting with Indiana in 1907, states began passing laws mandating sterilization for "feeble-minded" mothers. A bibliography of eugenics journalism revealed hundreds of articles in popular magazines as well as scientific journals throughout 1907 to 1911.[43]

As early as 1906, the IRL tried to inject eugenics into the immigration debate, with limited success. Even before the commission was created, IRL secretary Joseph Lee complained that it was too "easy to pile up a lot of figures about wages" and labor shortages, or "about crime and pauperism," and then to leave out the most important issues, such as "the more important subject of political capacity." As if he were writing about Lauck's not-yet-written reports, Lee worried that "the facts collected" in an investigation "are apt to be those which are easiest to collect and put into tables rather than those which have most bearing on the question. . . . The main question of immigration is whether the substitution of these new races in the former American race will be beneficial or harmful to the future of this country as a democracy."[44]

Lee's racial taxonomy was borrowed from the work of MIT economist William Z. Ripley. In 1899 Ripley had published *The Races of Europe,* identifying three major "races": Teutonic, Alpine, and Mediterranean. Lee, like Ripley, saw fitness for democracy as an inherited, not learned, quality. A few months after the commission began its work, Lee tried to convince the Russell Sage Foundation to sponsor a eugenics study of immigrants: "We have an opportunity . . . of (as it were) selecting our own ancestors, or at least selecting the ancestors of our own descendants. In selecting our immigrants we are, as it were, selecting the wives of our grandsons and the husbands of our granddaughters."[45]

In spite of Lee's efforts, the eugenicists of the IRL made little headway with the actual fieldwork of the Dillingham Commission, although Ripley's work did appear in the *Dictionary,* including his maps of racial groups in Europe. Climatologist Robert DeCourcy Ward's "National Eugenics in Relation to

Immigration," published in the widely read *North American Review* in July 1910 (when the commission's work was basically complete), relied on Francis Galton's work and other British publications. "The admirable work now being done in England along the lines of National Eugenics deserves far more attention than it has yet received in the United States," Ward complained. Given its high number of new immigrants, he suggested that "the United States, rather than England should be the center of eugenic propaganda. Yet so far, our people are practically silent on this question." He directly implicated the commission: "Most of the discussions of the immigration problem in the past have been concerned with its economic side." Too much time and energy had been spent on improving immigrants' living conditions, health, and public schools, when "it is race, not environment, which is with them the fundamental consideration."[46] In fact, Lauck's reports worked on the exact opposite principle.

Ward pointed out something many later scholars missed: the Dillingham Commission was too early—and too cautious—to be a full-blown eugenicist project. Harry Laughlin, who would become the Congressional Committee on Immigration's eugenics expert in 1920, and whose testimony was instrumental in the passage of the Emergency Quota Act of 1921 and the Johnson-Reed Act of 1924, had just begun his career at the Eugenics Records Office. Charles Davenport's influential text, *Heredity in Relation to Eugenics,* was published in 1911—too late to impact the commission's work.[47]

In all forty-one volumes and twenty-nine thousand pages of the Dillingham Commission's reports, I found the term "eugenic" only once—and that is from the IRL's contribution to the last volume's compilation of recommendations from outside groups. IRL president Prescott Hall called for the necessity of immigration restriction from a social, moral, economic and "eugenic standpoint." "Recent investigations in biology," Hall wrote, "show that heredity is a far more important factor in the progress of any species than environment." So in his view, immigration restriction of "undesirables" was essential. The noun "genetics" was coined only in 1905. The older adjective, "genetic," appears only once in the commission volumes, in the introduction to the *Dictionary of Races and Peoples.* No reports mention Galton. Eugenicist and statistician Karl Pearson is cited only once, in a footnote to Franz Boas's craniometry study.[48]

Even members of the IRL did not unanimously endorse eugenics arguments for restriction. Boston financier Richards M. Bradley, an IRL stalwart,
thought it was "a tactical mistake, and a serious one, for Hall to make a race
issue out of the present aspects of the immigration question." Bradley approved of Lauck's approach: "The Immigration Commission, who have put
the thing on economic and sociological grounds, other than the race issue,"
had taken a tack "which seems to me much better for all purposes, including
fighting purposes. I think we are likely to alienate many such if we make it a
race question, which becomes a personal question to the races involved, and
this affects their friends as well as themselves."[49] Isaac Hourwich praised
Lauck for sticking to an economic analysis: "Our statesmen in Washington
[at the Dillingham Commission] took scant notice of the academic disquisi-
tions in the domains of anthropology, ethnology, sociology, eugenics and
political science, which presented the old arguments of the Know-Nothings
dressed up in modern scientific garb."[50]

Hourwich noticed this absence because eugenics arguments were rapidly
growing in influence. By the end of 1911—after the Dillingham Commission
reports were published—IRL secretary Joseph Lee observed, "The general
tendency to talk eugenics is going to help us." He continued, "I wish the ami-
able philanthropists who see only the side of the immigrant would open their
eyes a little to the fact that his coming means the passing of the American. It
is all very well to sympathize with the cholera bug, but how about the human?"
Imagery of immigrants as a plague or a flood would proliferate in the years
that followed.[51]

Some of the Dillingham Commission reports do display nascent eugenic
thinking. Concern over the nation's "racial stock" (a term, in contrast to "eugenics," that already appeared frequently in this era) was one of the express
reasons for creating the commission in the first place. Some staff members
were open proponents. Economist Alexander Cance, who authored the reports on immigrants in agriculture, was unquestionably a eugenicist, although
his studies praised distribution policy. Scholars who emphasize the influence
of eugenics on the commission often point to demographer Joseph Hill's study
on the fecundity of women, which voiced concerns over the higher reproduc-
tive rates of immigrant women. Hill was later hired by Congress to formulate

the national-origins system to implement the 1924 quota laws. Elnora Folkmar, a holder of a PhD and a medical doctor who coauthored the *Dictionary of Races or Peoples* with her husband, later gave public lectures on eugenics, helped found the Society for Social Hygiene, in Washington, DC, and served as an officer of the Eugenics Committee of the American Breeders Association. Henry Cabot Lodge was closely allied with the IRL (although its leaders mistrusted him). Starting in 1914, he served for more than a decade on the board of the Carnegie Institution, which funded the Eugenics Records Office.[52]

Jett Lauck had no apparent connection to the eugenics movement, although Jenks, his mentor, had joined up with the IRL by 1915. It is possible to cherry-pick quotations that sound like racial slurs from Lauck's abundant reports and from Jenks and Lauck's *The Immigration Problem,* like a section remarking on the "tractability and lack of aggressiveness of the southern and eastern Europeans." But these bits and pieces were different than a full-blown racial justification for restriction. Economic historian Thomas C. Leonard concedes that Jenks and Lauck "used somewhat less contemptuous language to describe immigrants targeted for exclusion than did some other restrictionists." Exclusion, in Lauck and Jenks's words, should carry "no implication of inferiority," but rather of practicality. Some staff members believed in "innate" racial differences; others, including Lauck, did not. Lumping them together, as several scholars have done, oversimplifies restrictionist sentiments. That makes it easier to dismiss the commission simply as racist. Lauck's argument for restriction was about the overwhelming numbers of immigrants arriving, overpowering their ability to assimilate, not their biological capacity to do so.[53]

If anything, Lauck was harder on "Americans" than he was on the immigrants. In general, he complained, people in receiving communities "are treating the newcomers with aloofness and indifference" to immigrants' "welfare and progress." If individuals or institutions would "undertake this task" of Americanization, it would "not only benefit the immigrant mine worker" but also "contribute in a valuable way to the permanence of American standards and institutions." Otherwise, instead of uplift and good examples, the new immigrants would only "take on the more vicious habits of the Americans," such as drinking hard liquor instead of beer and drifting from one job to another without building new skills.[54]

A section in the Johnstown report on "local prejudice" concluded that the "general" attitude of Americans to new immigrants was "indifference."[55] "The native population knows practically nothing about these immigrants beyond what they read in the daily newspapers about crimes, etc., committed on the foreign section" and the "little contact they have with . . . servants, washer-women, etc." As a result, without exposure to native-born Americans, the new immigrants rarely became naturalized, and "as a general rule they do not understand American government or politics, and have no conception of civic responsibility." Role models for such values were lacking. Lauck accused Johnstown's city government of callous disregard and predatory taxation and assailed "unscrupulous 'interpreters' . . . who act with the municipal officers." As a result, the new immigrants "suffer from a constant attitude of contempt toward them." Police ignored public health laws in immigrant slums, where infant mortality was high, but then vigorously enforced public drinking and blue laws against Croatians who had no idea their traditional Sunday gatherings were illegal. The town's largest department store, owned by the steel company, paid a hundred dollar local license tax; an Italian storekeeper with only fifty dollars in sales per year paid ten dollars. Those immigrants who went to the trouble and expense of becoming citizens had to pay a poll tax, like blacks in the Jim Crow South. In Lauck's list of conditions "opposing Americanization," his Johnstown report listed isolation from natives and "indifference toward immigrants" above criticisms of immigrant culture itself.[56]

Lauck scrupulously documented Johnstown. But his lingering there short-changed other studies. Large-scale collection of data only began in January 1909, and thousands of survey cards were only filled out months later. In March 1909, twenty additional fieldworkers were approved for Lauck and Falkner, half of them transferred from the aliens in cities investigation; forty additional "tabulating clerks" were hired to handle the crush of incoming data in Washington. The agents were told they had until July 1, 1909, to complete their work, although some continued until December. The short time frame meant that, in Lauck's words, "the collection of all detailed and descriptive matter which was not absolutely necessary" was "abandoned," in place of information that was "susceptible of presentation in tabulated form"—numbers, in other words. Lauck decided to prioritize "purely statistical data" over the rich and time-consuming qualitative reports that he had originally begun.[57]

Already in July, Lauck's agents had more data than they could handle, and the largely female "calculator" staff spent the stifling Washington summer crunching numbers on tabulating machines borrowed from the Census Bureau. The last funds were gone by December, and layoffs began.[58]

Even with this truncated time frame, Lauck and his agents collected an astonishing range of information. Altogether, Lauck estimated they had gathered extensive data on "between one and two hundred immigrant communities," as well as "more or less detailed information" from "several hundred others." The first volume alone, on iron and steel manufacturing, contained "detailed information" on 11,908 individuals, including 4,693 women. More general data in the volume described another 86,089 male employees out of a total of 210,211 employed in the metals industry nationally.[59]

Lauck used at least eight forms to collect data. Some, such as the "individual nationality slip," were borrowed from the Department of Labor. Others were custom-made. Commission member William Bennet claimed that the commission collected more than 750,000 individual schedules and 23,000 family schedules, 85 percent of these from immigrants. Lauck guessed they had gathered original data from almost 15 percent of the nation's manufacturing and mining work force, and as many as 1 in 4 workers in some industries, like the Pittsburgh district's bituminous coal industry.[60] This figure excluded the additional data acquired from the U.S. Census and Department of Labor.

Field agents' interviews with workers were extensive, even intrusive, and sometimes required coercion. Agents consulted local clergy, interpreters, and town leaders for advice on "securing addresses of families of the various races to be studied." (This instruction indicates that the sample of people studied was predetermined by the commission's desire to study new immigrants in particular.) Agents were given "instructions to secure the consent of the industrial establishments" to take "a census of their employees," but they were not asked to obtain the consent of the workers themselves. Lauck praised the "co-operation of employers of labor," who with "scarcely an exception" and "with more or less inconvenience or expense" agreed to work with the commission. Many of the nation's largest corporations used their own employees for "the securing of the cards," which required "the outlay of money by the corporation, and a corresponding saving to the commission." Instructions dictated that "paymasters, foremen, and others" query their employees with questions about their national origin, earnings, family, and so on. These surveys took place in the midst of several workers' strikes, as well as a long recession—a chilling backdrop for answering more than two dozen questions asked by your foreman, on behalf of the federal government.[61]

The family questionnaires were even more daunting. Lauck expanded Croxton's original family schedule from 125 questions to 152, many of them with multiple subcategories. The questions were given to "carefully selected representative families," though the selection method is unclear. Besides the obvious inquiries about nationality, number of children, quality of housing, and work history, agents asked about lodgers, length of residence, schooling, money sent abroad, savings, grocery bills, prior occupations, indoor plumbing, and "living-room arrangements."[62]

A government agent, college-educated, possibly female, almost certainly native-born, would have knocked on a tenement apartment door in a smoggy, slapdash neighborhood, and proceeded—politely but firmly, and almost certainly in English—to ask these questions. An immigrant householder might not have wanted to be honest about his marital status, "affiliations with organizations," the newspapers he read, whether his wife worked, his female relatives' "attitude toward domestic service," or his savings accounts. He might not have wanted to answer whether he had insurance and what kinds, whether he had a chronic illness, or what his reasons were for leaving his home country. He might have thought it was no one's business whether he was interested in moving to a "smaller city," or to a "farm as laborer," or to "farm for self." He might not have understood the questions. Yet Lauck reported little resistance. Perhaps he shaded the truth, or maybe those surveyed felt compelled or intimidated into answering these questions.[63] The young man from West Virginia had become responsible for probing into thousands of lives and for producing half of a government survey second only in size to (and more intrusive than) the U.S. Census.

The American Standard of Living

For Lauck, "the immigration problem" implied neither that new immigrants were inherently racially inferior nor that they could not assimilate. In his solo publications, he underscored these points, arguing that limiting immigration was only necessary—and possibly only temporary—so that the current population could "be absorbed and elevated" to "demand proper wages and working conditions." In contrast, the IRL's Prescott Hall complained that new immigrants infected the United States with "instincts and habits" that were "matters of race and inheritance," not material conditions.[64]

In Lauck's view, the new immigrants' chief impact was not cultural or political, but economic. This rationale—not the eugenics arguments of Joseph Hill about women's fecundity, or Folkmar's racial typologies—became the basis for the Dillingham Commission's recommendations for restriction. In late 1911, Lauck summarized the commission's findings in his local newspaper, the *Richmond Times-Dispatch*. Recent debates have put "undue importance," he began, "upon the social and political effects of immigration." "Persons who have had little data at their possession," he complained, have blamed new immigrants for "crime, vice, insanity, or pauperism." But the commission's exhaustive studies, he wrote, "do not justify these contentions": crime among new immigrants was no higher than among other groups, and existing exclusion laws effectively kept out criminals and other "undesirables."[65]

"Despite this favorable condition of affairs, however," the Dillingham Commission had "emphatically and unequivocally" endorsed restriction. The reason, he wrote, was not the "social or political effects" of new immigrants, but the "disastrous effect upon the American wage-earners of the competition of the Southern and Eastern Europeans who have found employment in such large numbers in our mines and factories." Like other commission members and staff, Lauck advocated distribution policy, and he wrote favorably about Italian and Bohemian farm settlements. But in his view, the sheer numbers of new immigrants made it impossible for them to assimilate quickly enough to reduce their impact on prevailing wages, and thus on the American standard of living.[66]

Lauck presented the American "standard of living" as an objective metric. In reality, it rested on slippery assumptions about gender, class, and culture. It was at once immutable and protean, and its very suppleness allowed it to be deployed by both economic and eugenics-minded proponents of restriction. Columbia University economist Richard Mayo-Smith, a member of the IRL, argued that the American standard of living enjoyed a tacit acceptance among both employers and employees. As one of the first statisticians in the United States, Mayo-Smith had early exposure to eugenics arguments imported from Great Britain through Francis Galton, who invented modern statistics to calculate correlations and regression. Mayo-Smith was also one of the first American economists to argue for immigration restriction on "racial" grounds, beginning with a series of articles in 1888 warning about "the infusion of so much alien blood" into the American polity. "Most economists and statesmen now acknowledge that competition in the labor market should take place only on a certain plane of living," he wrote. Since new immigrants did not share that "plane," in his reasoning, they should be restricted. Far from a laissez-faire argument, Mayo-Smith and other Progressive Era economists acknowledged that wages could be determined by something outside the market itself—the "standard of living."[67] Cultural values were therefore embedded in the most fundamental economic analyses of the domestic wage economy.

Early twentieth-century economists were eager to establish their work as a science, and those efforts frame Lauck's work. Economists wielded a disproportionate influence at the Dillingham Commission. Jeremiah Jenks and Charles Neill were economists, as were several high-ranking staff, including all the supervisors of industry and agriculture reports. Given the economic bent and pressures from labor unions about restriction, there was no question that immigrants in industries would dominate the commission's investigations. That made Lauck's job extremely important. So did Lauck's decision to subordinate topical studies such as those on immigrant banking and charities to the economic studies under his purview. Much of his work used sociological categories (such as housing quality and family formation) to define the scientific variable of "standard of living" in his study.[68]

Lauck's outline had announced his intentions to create "a study of the immigration problem as viewed from the standpoint of the working man" rather than from, say, families, heads of households, neighborhoods, corporations, or even the general citizenry. Among the "principal points covered" would be "the races which and the races which do not lower the standard of living." Lauck presupposed that this determination could be according to race rather than, perhaps, marital status or duration of settlement in the United States. In a telling passage from an article he published in 1912, Lauck claimed that his "recent and exhaustive industrial investigation [had] attempted, with great care . . . to discover a purely American industrial community," like the one he had grown up in. He "was forced to acknowledge the effort a failure. No manufacturing or mining locality of any importance could be found which did not have its immigrant colony of industrial workers from southern and eastern Europe." It was one thing to survey immigrant workers, another for a study on immigrants to take as its special mission an attempt to find a "purely American" community, a goal that reflected Lauck's already anachronistic ideal. According to the commission's figures, the percentage of foreign-born workers in twenty-one industries ranged from 27 percent in shoemaking to 85 percent in sugar refining.[69]

Lauck identified with "American workers," which shaped his view of what the standard of living was and needed to be. He began with his conclusion already established: "Our industrial system has become saturated with an alien unskilled labor force of low standards, which so far has been impossible to assimilate industrially, socially, or politically, and which has broken down American standards of work and compensation." He described these newcomers as a "menace" that would destroy the American standard of living. Lauck's evaluations of immigrants deployed concepts such as "assimilation," "adaptability," "tractability," and "progressiveness" but failed to define what they meant. His outline also stated that all the "results should be presented as races," without evaluating whether this was the appropriate mode of analysis. It could have been by duration of settlement, education, literacy, age, marital status, or something else. The focus on the well-being of American workers reflected the commission's commitment that its study would be "chiefly" an economic one. As Paul Kellogg summarized the general view of the reports, "It is not the cultural deficit of a husky country lad of Croatia that threatens American standards. It is the fact that he sells his working day for less money than a family can live on."[70]

Lauck's use of the American standard of living as the centerpiece of the industry reports gave the concept a "scientific" sheen. Yet Lauck's use of "American standard of living" was in step with organized labor's recent turn from a utopian rejection of the wage system in the 1870s to a "bread and butter" unionism that sought binding wage contracts and concrete improvements in wages and conditions. That approach reflected union acquiescence to capitalism, in which crafts unions fought for a fair part of the corporate order, not its abolition. This tactic stood in contrast to socialist and syndicalist unions such as the Industrial Workers of the World (the IWW or "Wobblies"), who challenged capitalists and whom Lauck opposed—and blamed on immigrants—throughout his career.[71]

The economic discussion of an "American standard of living," or what others called a "living wage," was not new, nor was its relationship to ideas about men, women, and the family. The concept had existed since at least the era of Jacksonian workingman's democracy in the 1830s, and it remained popular in the labor movement. It meant generally that a workingman could support a wife, children, and home ownership on one income.[72] The Catholic Church called for a "just payment" in 1891, and in 1906, labor activist and priest Father John Ryan published a treatise on the subject, *A Living Wage*. There was a gendered component to the definition: in practice, it meant the ability of a man to support a family on his wage, without paid labor by his wife.[73]

Like many economic concepts, the "American standard of living" paradigm sounded scientific—it sounded like a real thing—but it was constructed out of opinion and assumption. It hid assumptions about women's and men's roles, housing choice, consumer culture, and morality and ethics. Like other reformers, Lauck identified women—especially mothers—as culture bearers. Americanization reformers often targeted immigrant women, assuming that converting them to American ways would bring the rest of the family along with them.[74]

Following Lauck's lead, the Dillingham Commission's industrial reports offered a gendered criticism of immigrants' cultural isolation and economic privation: "The status of the immigrant housewife from the south and east of Europe," Lauck informed *Survey* readers, "is deplorable." Most took in boarders to bring in extra household income, which invited impropriety: "When the men return from work it is a part of her duties to help them in their ablutions by scrubbing their backs"—an intimate task rife with moral risk. In addition to the boarders, the immigrant woman had "numerous children to care for and scores of other tasks demanding her attention."[75] Lauck, however, did not blame these women for "the marked untidiness of the immigrant households." After all, "so many things have to be done by the

A SIDE LIGHT ON CITIZENSHIP.
A Croatian housewife protesting against the payment of a dog-license tax.

Lauck and his agents used family structure and women's paid labor to evaluate the "fitness" of immigrants for American life. This picture was likely taken by a Dillingham Commission agent, perhaps Lauck himself.

immigrant women that they have little time for matters which may be neglected." In crowded homes with dirty coal miners, "any attempts at cleanliness" were "futile." In fact, Lauck's Johnstown report praised some immigrant women, especially the "Polish, Slovak, and Magyar" domestic workers, whose employers called them "quick to learn, capable, and industrious" and credited their "efficiency" (a favorite word of the Progressive Era) with "creating a better sentiment toward immigrants of their races."[76]

Lauck's work outline also reflected his particular interest in the relationship between trade unions and new immigrants. His initial proposal to the Dillingham Commission suggested "a study of the methods adopted by trade unions to prevent competition of immigrants" and a survey of "the stand taken by the organizations of wage workers," such as "whether aliens are admitted to the union . . . and union membership by race.[77] His outline proposed a study on the impact of language conflict on coal-mine disasters that sounded as if it had been lifted directly from an AFL playbook. It was the only part of Lauck's outline rejected by the commission's members.[78]

By personally identifying with crafts union members who were "old immigrants" or "Americans," Lauck took the side of the kinds of unions welcome in the influential National Civic Federation, with which he later worked, and those particularly associated with coal mining and railroads. In 1912 and 1913, Lauck wrote a regular column in the *Richmond Times-Dispatch* drawing on his Dillingham Commission research. Several articles outlined the threat new immigrants represented to old-stock union members: "The American workmen in general, and trades unionists in particular, have made one very serious mistake in their attitude. . . . [T]hey have failed to take into account . . . that the unskilled immigrant has been a potential competitor" and was "becoming an active one." "The influx of the Southern and Eastern Europeans," Lauck continued, "has been too rapid to permit" their inclusion in existing "labor organizations," which in many industries have "been completely overwhelmed and disrupted" by the newcomers.[79] Here again, he blamed the unions but adopted a policy stance—restriction—that punished new immigrants.

Lauck's Reports and Their Critics

Isaac Hourwich's 1912 analysis of the Dillingham Commission's reports was the first of many to argue that the evidence did not justify the commission's recommendations for restriction. According to Hourwich's critique, organizing the studies around race predetermined the findings, and an overreliance on quantitative data exacerbated the problem at a time when the definitions of race were, in one critic's words, a "muddle." Lauck's narrative descriptions were nuanced. But after lingering for months in western Pennsylvania, the agents rushed to complete the other volumes, and Lauck ordered them to focus on quantitative data organized by race, without considering whether that was the best method. Their volumes listed the numbers of each race, the percentage to naturalize by race, the proportion married by race, income by race, and so on, into dozens of categories. As Hourwich pointed out, even Lauck's mentor, H. Parker Willis, called the mass of data "still undigested."[80]

In his outlines, Lauck underscored the importance of categorization by race, for which he used a preexisting form: "Owing to the diversity of races in various countries, The Immigration Commission in its investigations particularly desires to secure all data by *race* (or people) as well as by *country of birth,*" the form explained. "Question 3 [on race] is the most important on the card," according to the instructions for "paymasters, foremen, and others in charge of filling out individual cards." "Take special care," it continued, to answer that question "definitely and correctly. No mere general answer, such as White, Austrian, or Slavish [*sic*], is sufficient. Get what the employee calls himself, *e.g.,* Irish, Slovak, Magyar, etc."[81] The form listed ninety-three "races" arranged under thirty-two country groupings: Austria-Hungary had eighteen subcategories, England five (English, Hebrew, Irish, Scotch, Welsh).[82] The instructions did add, "The list is not complete . . . , but it is sufficiently comprehensive to guide those using it. *Other countries* and *other races* should be enumerated when such other countries and races are reported."[83]

Although the *Dictionary of Races or Peoples* had been intended to aid agents in categorizing subjects, it was delayed too long for use in the field. Nevertheless, racial classifications were the lens through which the industry report data was organized. Lauck joined William Walter Husband and commission members in asserting that race was akin to "nationality" or "people," as the forms indicated, and did not imply immutable difference. The form for tabulators instructed, "All white persons born in the United States should be entered as 'American White.'" Indeed, all southern and eastern European immigrants were legally white, unlike African Americans and Asians.

The Dillingham Commission assumed that "race" was central to what was effectively a primer for Congress on which immigrants were more or less desirable, even if other factors (such as duration of settlement) may have been more relevant. The table of contents of the report on the bituminous coal mining industry in Pennsylvania in the sixth volume, which was the model for all subsequent industry reports, illustrated this emphasis on racial comparisons. An opening chapter on "racial displacements" (a regional history of the succession of migrants from different countries) was followed by ones on economic status, working conditions, housing and living conditions, general cost and standard of living, industrial progress and efficiency, and so on. The volumes concluded with a chapter on general progress and assimilation, measured by home ownership, school attendance, citizenship, and English language fluency. All were organized by race.[84]

Lauck's industrial reports found four economic impacts of new immigration: weakened unions, displaced American-born workers, low wages and standards of living, and unsafe and unclean conditions. But he lacked the intellectual or methodological tools to make his case about the harms inflicted by new immigrants. His biographer, Carmen Grayson, criticizes him for a "serious lack of proportion" in his zeal to gather data that could never be digested, noting that the methods needed to prove his points were yet to be invented. The field of statistics was still in its infancy. Sampling techniques did not yet exist, and social scientists favored quantity of data over quality. But Lauck failed to use even the statistical methods that were available to him, such as regression. Funding cuts to the commission in 1909 heightened the quantitative overload. Lauck abandoned qualitative studies in favor of amassing statistics, but he then lacked the time or funds to interpret them. The two volumes on the iron and steel industries illustrate his more-is-more approach. In the Midwest, agents gathered data on slightly more than one-fifth of industry workers; in the East, "nearly one-half"; and in the South, "over three-fourths."[85] Yet there was no discernible method for the collection of the numbers.

Grayson finds Lauck's assertion that immigrants reduced unionization to be unfounded, arguing that he failed to understand the "problem" of "displacement" of old immigrants by new. Lauck's undergraduate mentor, H. Parker Willis, publicly stated that displacement had actually been positive for many other members of the labor force: the arrival of new immigrants allowed more experienced workers, older immigrants, and native-born Americans to advance to higher-paid positions in an expanding industrial economy. Contemporaneous and later critics observed that Lauck never proved that immigrants were responsible for declining wages or poor working conditions.[86] But his findings did help validate that the working class was segmented along lines of nationality, which diminished union activism; in effect, he showed correlation (without the math), but not causation.

Even with the crush of numbers, hometown nostalgia peeked through Lauck's "scientific" analysis. A *New York Evening Post* writer critiqued Lauck's 1912 *Atlantic Magazine* article, "The Vanishing American Wage Earner" (based on his Dillingham Commission work): "When the critics of the 'new' immigration speak of the American standard of living there seems to be vaguely

present in their minds a picture of the America of seventy-five years ago, with
its industries located in the small manufacturing towns, and its population of
independent, native workingmen living in their own homes, and moving, out
of shop hours, on a basis of democratic equality with their employers." The
nostalgic tableau contrasted unfavorably with "what they describe as industrial serfdom under which the foreign mill-worker or miners lives to-day."
Lauck wanted to see the "immigration problem . . . from the standpoint of the
working man." But which workingman? The *New York Evening Post* complained that his idealized American villager of yesteryear had no parallel in
the "Bohunk" coal miner of today, who should have been compared with the
Germans and the Irish still coming to the United States.[87]

By using statistical data from the reports themselves, Isaac Hourwich made
the same critique more systematically. His study pointed out the rushed nature of the huge industries project and the unmanageable scope of subject
matter left to one or two individuals—no one could have come close to di-
gesting it all. Hourwich interpreted the data differently from Lauck, arguing
that when "duration of settlement" was taken into account, "new" immigrants
from southern and eastern Europe fared just as well as those from northern
and western Europe. Most important, Hourwich rejected Lauck's argument
that new immigrants reduced the American standard of living. Lauck's framework was "racial displacement," but Hourwich argued that new immigrants'
willingness to take unskilled jobs in a growing industrial economy allowed
more experienced native-born or "old immigrant" workers to climb the economic ladder.[88]

Lauck did not invent the American standard of living as an economic measure. But he did make it the centerpiece of the largest set of data ever amassed
to justify immigration restriction. The economic paradigm Lauck employed
had an impact that has lasted to today. As historian of statistics and quantification Theodore Porter observes, "Numbers turn people into objects to be
manipulated." He notes the formidable "authority of statistical and behavioral
norms. . . . Those who fail to conform are stigmatized." For Lauck, those
norms were old immigrants, the American workingman, and the American
standard of living. In their summary volume, *The Immigration Problem,* Jenks
and Lauck "laid special emphasis upon the economic influence of immigration as affecting the standard of living" but did not try "to analyze fully the

physical, mental and moral effects" of this change. The standard of living, they wrote, was "possibly the most fundamental factor in determining the quality of the country's civilization," and was "a preliminary that is absolutely necessary to better things."[89]

But their analysis could never be purely economic. If a native-born American man's household—a "wife and children supported by the earnings of the husband"—was the "normal form of family life," as Lauck wrote in a 1912 article, anything outside this model was aberrant.[90] So immigrant women's paid labor became a pathology, no matter how practical or prosaic.

Jeremiah Jenks came at the immigration problem from the perspective of international diplomacy and stamping out corruption; Lauck, his protégé, looked at new immigration from the standpoint of the "vanishing American wage earner" and the American standard of living. These remained themes in his own writings long after the Dillingham Commission reports were done. In 1912, workers in the textile mill town of Lawrence, Massachusetts, called a general strike after a cut in hours that reduced their pay. Organized by the radical IWW, the textile hands represented fifty-one countries and were mostly young women. After two months on the picket line, Lawrence strikers earned a 20 percent increase in wages. The strikers' nationalities, femininity, and youth shocked the nation. Yet what "the American people have not yet grasped," Lauck told readers of the *North American Review,* "is that the situation at Lawrence is not unique. It is typical." "All our important industrial centers" were dominated by immigrants. Without directly mentioning the predominance of women among the strikers, Lauck observed conditions in the Lawrence strike typical of industrial communities: low wages for married men led to wives and children needing to work, families taking boarders and lodgers in order to supplement the earnings of husbands, and "poor housing facilities and the highly congested living conditions." Unless something was done about immigration, Lauck warned his readers, Lawrence would be just the beginning.[91]

Lauck brought preconceptions to his work at the Dillingham Commission, but he also emerged from it a changed man. The poverty and inequality he encountered in his research undid his youthful academic conservatism. When he began his work on the commission as a young man, he belonged, in his words, to "the sect of conservatism and thought America was the land of great opportunities, but my impression from visiting these districts led me to think that . . . our democracy was pretty much of a failure." He questioned whether republicanism could work in a country with such a stark and growing divide between rich and poor. Under the right circumstances, he believed that immigrants could be "absorbed and educated to American standards of work and living," but their unprecedented numbers overwhelmed any ability to assimilate them into the American wage system, culture, and politics.[92] He bore no antipathy toward immigrants per se, nor did he believe in their inherent inferiority. His main argument for immigration restriction was that it was a means to raise what he saw as unfairly low wages in industries whose managers and corporations were making millions.[93] His beef was really with capitalists: the presence of new immigrants made it too easy for robber barons to continue to rob.

Lauck also supported legislative measures he hoped would diminish what he called "industrial autocracy" (in contrast to the "industrial democracy" that unions had been seeking). His commitment to improving American wages through labor organization strengthened throughout his career. In a series of articles in popular magazines in 1912 and 1913 (the one on Lawrence among them), Lauck assailed the low wages of industrial workers by blaming both competition from new immigrants and also the intransigence of employers. In each article, he recited his mantra about the vanishing American. The Dillingham Commission had found that only 5 percent of "the wage-earners in our mines and factories" were native-born American workers. As he wrote in several articles, "the so-called American wage earner does not exist," is a "real myth," and "has largely disappeared." In *Atlantic Monthly,* Lauck attacked industrial leaders who used the retread argument that protective tariffs helped industrial workers; on the contrary, Lauck argued, tariffs on imported goods increased company profits but meant that workers' wages—and purchasing power—stagnated.[94]

Lauck's own résumé increasingly reflected his interest in wages and American workers. After working briefly for the U.S. Tariff Board, he sent fifty employment inquiries and a recommendation from Jenks to the U.S. Commission on Industrial Relations, where he was finally hired as its first staff director. He modeled his work there on the Dillingham Commission, avoiding public hearings and hiring six former staff members (among them Husband and Croxton), and continued to push for the family wage.[95]

In 1918, Lauck was named secretary to the National War Labor Board (NWLB) by its chair, former president William H. Taft. The NWLB's command economy tactics gave Lauck an opportunity to refine his demands for a living wage, and he argued that wage scales should "not give particular attention to the supply and demand of labor." Rather, they should ensure the ability of workers to support their families and pay for their children's education. At a time when women made far less than men, Lauck proposed the same wages for both sexes. As his reform vision grew, he also criticized the "abstract economics" of academia. Later work came from the railway labor boards and from a nativist union, the Brotherhood of Locomotive Firemen. "I consider Lauck one of the best men in the country," Lauck's mentor Jenks wrote to a colleague in 1926. "Perhaps," Jenks conceded, Lauck was "rather sympathetic with the labor element, but I still think that he is very fair-minded and recognizes the weakness and sometimes the unfairness of the labor people as well as any well-informed person whom I know." Jenks was praising Lauck for acting as an expert rather than as an advocate.[96]

But Lauck was becoming an advocate. In 1921, he was still publicly calling for immigration restriction, but he called the open-shop movement (the anti-union campaign of large corporations)—not immigrants—"the greatest danger to the public."[97] In the midst of the conservative 1920s, Lauck published *Political and Industrial Democracy, 1776–1926*. The book called for unionization, labor laws, and popular democratic measures in the face of industrial autocracy of "stupendous" corporations with "no contact, as in former years, between the owners of an industry and its employees." Like his earlier searches for an "American" industrial community, this analysis was shot through with nostalgia about the economy and democracy.[98]

By the 1920s, Lauck's commitment to the working class included the very immigrants whose countrymen he had once recommended to be restricted. His campaigns for unionization and a "living wage" took on national significance when he became the closest adviser to John L. Lewis, the outspoken president of the United Mine Workers (UMW) and "father of the CIO." Lewis was one of Franklin Roosevelt's most important critics—it was Lauck who convinced the union leader to make a living-wage campaign one of the UMW's highest priorities. (By then, the UMW had long represented large numbers of southern and eastern Europeans.) As Lewis's chief aide, Lauck helped author Section 7(a) of the landmark Wagner Act of 1935, which legalized the right to organize unions. In 1937, Lauck also ran the American Association for Economic Freedom, a group of middle-class professionals, clergy, and intellectuals publicly in favor of unionization. Lauck's commitment to the living-wage ideal, according to labor historian Leon Fink, "helped to transform the political discourse of the New Deal era." In 1936, the *Christian Science Monitor* called him "a one-man brain trust."[99]

By the end of his life, Lauck had become what one might call a Christian syndicalist. Increasingly, he couched his interest in wages in a language of Christian morals and criticized the field of economics for abandoning its roots in moral philosophy. The Russian Revolution of 1917 intrigued him. His personal papers were full of notations about how Communism might be improved with Christian principles. If the Protestant Bible were presented to Russians, he wrote on one scrap, "with the dominance of the Bible in the Russian situation it would then easily become Christian Communism in a modern form, and, as such would gradually throughout the world substitute itself for our present capitalistic system." On another slip of paper he wrote out his personal "Code: Love-Faith-Truth-Hope," which was filed alongside his increasingly desperate notes to himself to "economize everywhere" and to "invest as to get appreciation in stock market values."[100]

The man so deeply concerned about the American standard of living and Christian socialism became preoccupied with savings after living for years beyond his means. In addition to an expensive office downtown, in later years Lauck kept a large home and domestic help in Chevy Chase, Maryland, as well as a country home on an island in Virginia's Rappahannock River. He collaborated with Jenks on several editions of *The Immigration Problem*, as well as on a number of other endeavors, but he also enticed Jenks to invest in one of his own ill-fated ventures, a mail-order publishing house. By 1926, the year he published *Political and Industrial Democracy*, Lauck was asking Jenks and other friends to lend him money "on moral risk" and "without security" to fund his "short-term obligations." Lauck's debtors struggled to get repaid; Jenks's secretary was asking Lauck (in vain) for repayment even as Jenks lay dying in his bed. After Jenks died, his estate lawyers continued for years to hound Lauck for what he owed. Constantly scrambling for money, Lauck lost his Chevy Chase home in the Depression, and had parted with "The Island" by 1948.[101]

Lauck harbored deeply American contradictions: he was at once practical and idealistic, scientific and moralistic, utopian and prosaic, prejudiced and compassionate. He remained concerned about the larger division between rich and poor, the preservation of small-town America, the fate of Christianity, the obligation of the rich to the poor, and the achievements of the "old immigrants" like his ancestors. He tied immigration policy explicitly to questions about wages, culture, and pessimistic ideas about class difference. By the time of the Dillingham Commission, the United States would never again look like his childhood hometown in West Virginia. Still, Lauck developed new tools to see the world and new ideas about how to fix it—immigration restriction and living-wage laws. Others may have looked to his industrial reports to bolster eugenical arguments against immigrants, but Lauck, through John Lewis, made the campaign for a living wage for workers, both native and foreign-born, a major component of Depression Era politics.

In some ways, Lauck outgrew his work for the Dillingham Commission, but the commission long outlived him. With its thousands of pages of statistics and data, it seemed scientific, factual, and irrefutable (even as it had already been refuted). The twenty reports remain a remarkable chronicle of the largest generation of immigrants and the largest industrial revolution the world had ever seen. But Lauck's preoccupation with the American worker undermined the objectivity he believed that quantitative data represented.

5

⁓⁓⁓

Women's Power and Knowledge

While Jett Lauck scoured the factory yards and tenements of industrial America, fellow Dillingham Commission agent Anna Herkner was donning peasant clothing and boarding a steamship in Myslowitz, Germany (now Poland), for a secret investigation of steerage-class conditions. It was unpleasant work. "There was no sight before which the eye did not prefer to close," and "everything was dirty, sticky, and disagreeable to the touch. Every impression was offensive." Born in 1878, Herkner grew up with her immigrant parents in a Bohemian enclave in Cedar Rapids, Iowa. In 1905, she graduated from the University of California with a degree in Slavic languages, then spent more than a year touring eastern and central Europe. She spoke Bohemian (Czech), German, Russian, Croatian, Polish, and English. Before being hired by the Dillingham Commission, she moved to Baltimore to work at Ann Street Settlement, also known as the "Polish Coffeehouse." Under Herkner's direction, several undercover agents—both men and women—made nine trips in third-class steerage across the Atlantic; Herkner herself undertook three such trips.[1]

Scores of women such as Anna Herkner found opportunity in the Dillingham Commission, job opportunity, above all. Historians have overlooked the prominent role the commission played in advancing women's federal work opportunities, but male supervisors at the time were well aware of it. From the very beginning, the commission deployed an army of young female college graduates, from Milwaukee to Philadelphia to Boston, interviewing immigrants and canvassing neighborhoods for several studies. Physician Elnora Cuddeback Folkmar collaborated with her anthropologist husband Daniel

This photo is likely of Anna Herkner, who
headed the steamship conditions study. She and
her agents crossed the Atlantic several times,
impersonating immigrants in steerage.

Folkmar on the commission's influential fifth volume, *Dictionary of Races or
Peoples.* Other women took on the commission's most dangerous work: attorney Mary Philbrook and her largely female staff went undercover in a dozen
cities, scouring the underworlds of procurement, prostitution, and sex
trafficking—then known as white slavery.

Back in the commission's Washington offices, dozens of women crunched
data on tight deadlines. Women supervised men, and vice versa. From cleaning
women to clerks to field supervisors, and from undercover investigators to report authors, women—mostly young, and both single and married—worked
in all but the commission's very highest levels. Some held jobs where their
femininity was assumed to be an asset, studying other women and children,
for example, or doing the "practical" work of tabulation (though even this role
had only recently opened to female federal employees). Others did work rarely,

if ever, offered to women in the federal government—supervising men. All told, more than half the commission's employees were women.

Jobs were not the only opportunities the Dillingham Commission offered women: it also allowed women employees to transform their perspectives—usually marked by their gender—into objective "facts." Women who worked at the commission produced knowledge that masked the gendered nature—or not—of their own work. This was true both of women who did typically "female"-gendered work and also of those who did not. The statistical tables they produced did not jump out as "women's perspective" but were instead embedded in the reports' larger maze of figures and numbers. Their reports were presented as objective, just as the men's were, even though some brought feminist perspectives (for example, on what we would now call sex work, sexual harassment, and violence). Of course, men also brought their own perspectives on their work (most notably—but certainly not exclusively—on standards of living and a disdain for immigrant women's paid labor), but no one understood these to be gendered. To put a sharper point on it, female commission employees were prohibited by their sex from voting to elect the very same government whose apparently objective knowledge they were producing.

The laundering of gendered interpretations into modern facts for these women was all the more notable given that they unapologetically represented the full spectrum of women's politics—electoral or otherwise—in the era. Their diversity of opinions reflected larger tensions that would eventually cause the "big tent" of Progressivism to collapse into the conservatism of the 1920s. Many harbored political perspectives at odds with the commission's reformist, Republican male establishment; like Jett Lauck, some women found their beliefs shattered by their work there.

Together, women's work and recommendations for the commission embedded gendered perspectives into government facts and strengthened their own power, as well as ratified federal power both over individual lives and also over local and state laws. Their contributions to the arguments over immigration were shaped by the opportunities federal regulation offered them. Women at the commission gained authority and "objectivity" by studying immigrants for the federal government, which linked their professional interests to the idea of an immigration problem that only federal policy could solve.

Among other things, women's work at the commission was instrumental to the passage of the Mann Act, which regulated interstate travel of prostitutes, and a companion law that banned overseas procurement of prostitutes. The enforcement of these laws increased government surveillance and made permanent the agency that would become the FBI. In many ways, then, middle-class women's work at the commission allowed them to transcend the limitations of sexual inequality by advancing the authority of "facts" and federal power over immigrants.

Women Pioneers in the Federal Government

Buried in the archival papers of obscure bureaucrats is concrete evidence that the Dillingham Commission was one of the first federal agencies to employ women in professional positions. This decision grew out of collaboration with the Census Bureau, close connections with the Bureau of Labor Statistics (BLS), and the support of key male supervisors and mentors—especially that of commission member Charles Neill and staff statistician Frederick Croxton. "During the period from 1906," Croxton later recalled in an unpublished memoir, "came real progress for those of the gentler sex in Federal employment. Prior to that period women had seldom been assigned to supervisory or policy making positions." The commission shared office space with the women and child labor studies conducted by the Bureau of Labor (run by Neill). The Census Bureau, from whom Neill and Croxton borrowed many staff, also employed large numbers of women, whom one study found to be 50 percent more efficient than their male coworkers.[2]

Charles Neill ran the BLS, which employed many women and provided the model for the commission's Immigrants in Cities studies as well as administering the family questionnaires. Along with the Census Bureau and the BLS, the Dillingham Commission became a major employer of women during its four-year existence. Croxton hired a "large staff of tabulators . . . organized in sections each with about two clerks," overseen by "a young lady whom we designated as 'working supervisor.'" Both the office tabulators and the female fieldworkers, according to Croxton, were "excellent."[3]

Approximately two hundred women were employed by the Dillingham Commission. In comparison, existing records list at most 172 men on the payrolls. To put these figures into context, in 1910, women constituted about 21 percent of the total U.S. workforce (up from 15 percent forty years earlier). In the executive branch, as early as 1903, more than a quarter of the staff were women. At the commission, women were employed at every level except as actual appointees (although Jewish activists did recommend two women for nomination). Three women headed investigations and were the sole authors of reports (Anne Herkner on steerage conditions, Mary Philbrook on white slavery, and Martha Dodson on immigrant homes and aid societies). Five other women were named on title pages as collaborators, annotators, or coauthors.[4]

The women working at the Dillingham Commission were among thousands of new women seizing new opportunities in the Progressive Era. Between 1890 and 1909, the number of women receiving college degrees more than tripled.[5] The women hired by the commission were exceptionally well educated. They held undergraduate and graduate degrees from the University of California, Berkeley (Anna Herkner and Mary Simonds), Ohio State University (Nellie F. Sheets and Mary Louise Mark), Columbia University (Mark again), the University of Minnesota (Mary Mills West), the University of Wisconsin (Emma O. Lundberg), and Barnard College, the London School of Economics, and Oxford University (Juliet Stewart Points). At least two were medical doctors (Kate Barrett and Elnora Folkmar). Mary Philbrook was a lawyer. Aside from women's colleges such as Barnard, most of the women attended public universities with early sociology, social work, and economics departments. All these universities had admitted women for a long time, or since their founding.

Many staff earned the same wages regardless of gender, usually seventy dollars per month for clerks and a hundred dollars per month for special agents. A few made $125, but these were disproportionately men. Before being hired by the Dillingham Commission, Anna Herkner had turned down a job at the Bureau of Immigration because she was told only men could be "inspectors"; women served as "matrons," which paid a lower salary. Top administrators—all men—made much more. Still, women earned decent salaries. As a comparison, at the Department of Treasury, about 57 percent of women made more than $1,000 per year, and in 1910, the average schoolteacher—male or female—made only about $518 per year.[6]

Nevertheless, many women at the Dillingham Commission made less than men in the same jobs. In May 1908, for example, the commissioners approved the hiring of two women to the congestion in cities study at a monthly salary of $100, but at the same time authorized a future "appointment of one man . . . in the same work at a salary not to exceed $125 per month."[7] In another case, commission members approved a smaller raise for a female agent than her male supervisor had recommended (although the increase did lower the disparity between her pay and that of her male coworkers).[8] Women's median salaries were much lower than men's, since women were clustered in the lowest-paid positions, such as charwoman and tabulating clerk.

The highest-paid woman was Mary Philbrook. In the middle of her investigation, she received a competing job offer that yielded her a raise from $1,500 to $2,500 per year, with a salary equivalent to many male staff members.[9] Then again, she had a law degree. In the early twentieth century, such examples of gender parity in salaries were rare.

The number of women employed by the commission, and their presence in supervisory and sometimes dangerous positions, evidenced their perseverance. But it also reflected mentorship and support from male supervisors such as Croxton and Neill—and Jenks, who taught at one of the oldest coeducational universities in the country and whose wife had a college degree. H. Parker Willis, whose mother, Olympia Brown, was a famous suffragist, presumably also approved. Jenks wrote a glowing graduate-school recommendation to University of Wisconsin economist Richard Ely for one female employee, Oberlin College graduate Alice Durand, in which he praised her "mental acumen, readiness to work, and untiring enthusiasm, balanced by good judgment." "She would do exceedingly well," he promised, in "either economics, politics or sociology"—indeed, "distinctly better than do most graduate students," which, he did not add, would have been mostly men.[10]

The Dillingham Commission even employed several married women (some of whom had spouses who appear to have also worked for the commission). Mary Mills West, a field and office worker who was later an expert on prenatal and child care for the federal Children's Bureau, was a married mother of five. At the time, only about 10 percent of married women worked in wage labor, and many employers refused to hire married women. Charles Neill was not among them. He wrote a glowing report on Mary Simonds, who was married, reporting that she had to take a civil service exam for "statistical clerks," and finished "at the head of the list" of the thirty out of over three hundred who passed the exam. She did "difficult statistical work" for the commission, wrote and edited the school reports, and was one of a handful of employees retained until the end of the commission's work. Neill's own wife, Esther Waggaman Neill, was a professional writer (as was her mother) whose work appeared in several popular magazines.[11] And contrary to the stereotype of women's rights supporters as Protestant reformers, Neill was a devout Catholic.

Women did not take these new opportunities for granted. Married women in particular were subject both to the lingering effects of the legal doctrine of coverture, which limited married women's legal rights, and also to strong cultural and structural biases against their paid labor. "There is a good deal of feeling against married women's being employed by the government," BLS employee Mrs. Daisy Worthington Worcester wrote to Neill in 1908. She was concerned whether "anything other than the quality and quantity of my work was being taken into consideration." She had several relatives to support, so needed the job even though her husband also worked for the bureau. Neill urged her not to "give yourself any concern in regard to the objection to married women's remaining in the Government service." "Some of the Departments" might oppose married women's work, and he admitted that it had been the policy of the previous secretary of commerce and labor. "However, I, personally," Neill explained, "do not share this view at all," nor did his boss, Oscar Straus. "As long as I remain here," Neill went on, "I shall insist that no consideration of this kind be given any weight in determining the employment or retention of an agent in the Bureau." Worcester was lucky to be able to combine career and family. Half of her generation of college-educated women never married.[12]

While single women were more common in the labor force, their opportunities at the commission were unusual. Most college-educated women were channeled into teaching and nursing. But many yearned for "a broader world and other opportunities," as commission agent Mary Louise Mark's male undergraduate adviser put it. Mark's correspondence traces the career trajectory of a pioneering female social scientist. The letters of this Ohio minister's daughter illuminate what professional women thought about their work, how their mentors helped, and how they moved between government, academic, and philanthropic work.[13]

In the summer of 1907, Mark was hired fresh from graduate school as one of the Dillingham Commission's first field agents for the study on congestion in cities. She worked her way up, became a supervisor, and eventually coauthored the study's two volumes. Her report called urban overcrowding "one of the most unfavorable features of the modern problem of immigration." The eighteen-month study examined "10,206 households, comprising 51,006 individuals," about half of them in the two largest cities, New York and Chicago. The rest were in Philadelphia, Boston, Cleveland, Buffalo, and Milwaukee. Jeremiah Jenks oversaw the project, which was headed by E. A. Goldenweiser, who had just finished his economics PhD at Columbia University. (The graduate schools of both Jenks's Cornell University and Goldenweiser's Columbia University were coeducational.) Mark and Goldenweiser coauthored the city reports, which were listed as being annotated by a fellow female Ohio State University graduate, Nellie Sheets (whose 1911 wedding announcement described her as "one of the most expert women statisticians in the service of the government").[14]

A letter of recommendation traced the shift in Mark's career aspirations from typically female teaching to sociological fieldwork. Women's government employment generally reflected a common belief that they were better suited for practical, on-the-ground work than the more prestigious theoretical work of academia reserved mostly for men. After college, Mark's adviser wrote a generic recommendation letter for her, in which he emphasized "both theoretical and practical work" in her sociology courses. He highlighted the published research she had done on juvenile delinquency and also noted that she "has had some experience teaching."[15]

Mark's first job was in West Virginia, but she soon moved to Manhattan for graduate school (probably a master's degree) at the New York School of Philanthropy, which was affiliated with Columbia University. Mark was part of a growing trend: from 1890 to 1900, women rose from 15 to 30 percent of graduate students in the social sciences, even as many fellowships remained closed to them. In those years, Columbia University, the largest university in the country, generated a remarkable crop of young female master's students and PhDs. Mark studied with Edward Devine, a professor of social work (a vocation invented in the Progressive Era). Devine was a prominent expert on philanthropy, the founder of a settlement house, and a champion of child-labor laws. He served as a consultant to the Dillingham Commission.[16]

With prestigious credentials, relevant experience, and an influential adviser, Mark's career blossomed. In 1907, she was hired as a special agent for the commission, at a hundred dollars per month. "It's a great satisfaction," Devine wrote to her upon her appointment, "to give those who are prepared for it a chance to show what good work they can do." Mark's undergraduate adviser at Ohio State University offered his own thoughts: "I want to congratulate you on your success," he wrote about her new job. "I feel that you will never regret abandoning teaching," he encouraged her. Every year "will open up to you a broader world and other opportunities if you care to accept them. After all, our greatest pleasure consists in adapting ourselves to the world so that we can get the most out of things and give back to the world the greatest good." But "don't do yourself up from over work," he warned.[17]

Here was the Progressive creed in a nutshell, tailored specifically to a young woman with promise and drive, but with a warning about her capacity. The central dilemma of this first generation of college women was how to fulfill both the desire to help others and also the need to help themselves. In an 1892 essay, "The Subjective Necessity for Social Settlements," Jane Addams, the founder of Chicago's famous Hull House settlement, had examined this not entirely altruistic impulse. Women reformers, she explained, needed their work as much as—maybe more than—the "reformed" did. Society wants "to give a girl pleasure and freedom from care." But young women are also "besotted with innocent little ambitions." Addams called this desire to do good a universal one, but one the first generation of educated women felt intensely. "There is a heritage of noble obligation which young people accept and long to perpetuate. The desire for action, the wish to right wrong and alleviate suffering haunts them daily." Addams was writing about herself, and about women such as Mary Louise Mark. Devine, Mark's well-connected graduate adviser, even wrote Mark a letter of introduction to the famous Addams.[18]

Whether or not she met Addams, the Dillingham Commission fulfilled this "subjective necessity" in Mark, and her career advanced rapidly during her year and a half in its employ. At the age of twenty-six, she was, according to

Jeremiah Jenks, the "first special investigator" for the congestion in cities project in New York City. She was well prepared—part of her graduate-school training had required a survey of twenty-five homes in an immigrant-heavy area of New York's Upper East Side. She performed nearly identical work for the commission, with a year of "house to house canvassing," during which she compiled statistics on, among other things, number of rooms in dwellings, years of residence, number of children, naturalization rates, family income, and indoor plumbing. "She showed so much good judgment and skill" in New York, according to Jenks, that "she was made a supervisor of the same work in Chicago."[19]

Letters of introduction on Dillingham Commission letterhead presented Mark as a "confidential agent," who was "authorized to ask what questions are necessary to enable her to report on conditions." These letters empowered Mark and other agents to extract sensitive and personal information. Their "official" status reflected the increasingly coercive nature of government experts. At the same time, the letters promised confidentiality about all material collected—they were meant to both coerce and reassure. In graduate school, when Mark did her housing study of the Upper East Side, she spent a great deal of time explaining and justifying her survey. Three people outright refused her queries, she reported, and "a larger number" exhibited "good-natured contempt for so impractical a use of my time," but "foreigners newly arrived" yielded with "an unquestioning submission to my inquiries as a matter of course."[20]

After her stints in New York and Chicago, Mark transferred to the Washington office. There, because of "her knowledge of field work and of her tact and good judgment," she supervised twelve clerks and served as Croxton's direct assistant. She was, in Croxton's words, "not only a good asset, but an exceptionally valuable one," with an "unusually wide experience both in the field and office work of the Commission." "In every place we have tried her," Jenks concurred, "she has shown the same qualities of carefulness, good judgment, tact and ability to get work done."[21]

But these were not, it should be noted, gender-neutral assessments. In a recommendation letter to the U.S. Census Bureau, Jenks called Mark "among the very best women that we hav[e] had working for us. If you wish to appoint women for special work, I hav[e] no doubt you would [find] Miss Mark very satisfactory." It is unclear whether she got the Census job, but in early 1912 she was hired at the Department of Labor at a respectable salary of $1,400 per year. Mark would eventually become a professor of sociology and social work at her undergraduate alma mater, Ohio State University. In the 1920s, she did extensive fieldwork as a staff member of the U.S. Survey of Indian Affairs. Like most female academics, including her own sister, who was a geologist, Mark never married. The two were buried side by side in a cemetery outside Columbus, Ohio.[22]

Women and Undercover Work

It took resolve to do what Mary Mark did—to knock on tenement doors, convince new immigrants of one's authority, and ask intrusive questions across divides of language, class, and culture. "After a time," Jenks wrote, Mark's "health broke down for a few months," and she was given a summer to recuperate. But this work paled in comparison to that of undercover agents who explored transatlantic steerage and the sex-trafficking industry. Both investigations put women agents in considerable danger, where they showed courage, even as they wrote about their female subjects as vulnerable creatures in need of protection. It was a hallmark of the Progressive Era that some women's power came at the expense of other women, yet could also help both. This was the intractable paradox of women's reform work and the class divide it could exacerbate.[23]

In May 1908, six people were appointed to the Dillingham Commission's investigation of steerage conditions, under Jenks's direction, at the salary of $100 per month (though this was raised for several by 1909 to $140). At least two of them—Anna Herkner and Elizabeth Goodnow—were women, with Herkner in charge of the investigation.[24] Her reports garnered attention from the public and from Congress, which used them to justify new regulations of steamship travel that expanded federal power beyond U.S. borders.

Herkner's reports trafficked in vivid detail—bordering on voyeurism. In fifty pages, she offered up a sometimes measured but often lurid travelogue of new immigration. The steamship industry was in the midst of a transition— "vile" older ships still served the majority of migrants, but "new-style" ships with better steerage conditions were slowly replacing them.[25] Herkner and her fellow agents found that the worst "old-type" steerage conditions were "so injurious to health and morals that there is nothing on land to equal it." The trips were harrowing. Vomit was rarely cleaned up, and those who suffered from seasickness lay "in their berths in a sort of stupor." The hardier passengers crowded the mess hall. "If the steerage passengers act like cattle at meals," Herkner defended, "it is undoubtedly because they are treated as such." It was amazing anyone could eat. "Only the fresh breeze from the sea overcame the sickening odors. The vile language of the men, the screams of the women defending themselves, the crying of children, wretched because of their surroundings, and practically every sound that reached the ear, irritated beyond endurance." A twelve-day voyage offered "abundant opportunity to weaken the body and emplant there germs of disease to develop later. . . . Surely it is not the introduction to American institutions" likely to garner "respect." This was muckraking exposé, not the dry prose and droning statistics of the commission's other volumes. Gritty undercover reports became a popular genre among journalists and reformers of the era, including women. It was no accident that women were assigned to this covert operation in spite of the dangers. Women were already doing undercover work for philanthropic organizations researching prostitution.[26]

Reformers and restrictionists alike worried about the vulnerability of young women, especially those traveling alone. Real safety concerns overlaid ugly stereotypes about lascivious male immigrants and conniving ship workers. Sexual harassment (a term that did not yet exist)—and rape—appeared to be endemic. "The atmosphere was one of general lawlessness and total disrespect for women," Herkner reported. Women were forced to undress under the leering gaze of male stewards, one of whom "began his offenses even before we left port." Every day, she found him "annoying some women, especially in the wash rooms." On deck, "the manner with which the sailors, stewards, firemen, and others mingled with the women passengers was thoroughly revolting."

Herkner concluded that "not one young woman in the steerage escaped attack," including herself. In her case, she had delivered "a hard, unexpected blow in the offender's face," but she recognized not all immigrants would have had that courage. "Two more refined and very determined Polish girls fought the men with pins and teeth, but even they weakened under this continued warfare. . . . There was no one to whom they might appeal." Several crew members told her that "many of them marry girls from the steerage." Wondering how they had "become well enough acquainted to marry," she found that "the acquaintance had already gone so far that marriage was imperative."[27]

When Herkner's report was released, the *New York Times* praised its uncovering of sexual improprieties but suggested that Herkner's middle-class sensibilities about dirt and privacy had caused her to exaggerate the impact of steerage's conditions on "very poor" immigrants who were used to being "crowded together in the tenements of European or American slums."[28] The *New York Times*'s critique held both truth and callousness—Herkner could not help but see through her own eyes, but just because people lived in dirt and poverty did not mean they were indifferent to it.

Herkner and her staff's investigations of ships sailing under foreign flags marked an assertion of federal power outside of the nation's boundaries, but it was not an entirely new one. The federal government had regulated various aspects of ocean travel since 1819, and the topic appeared in both Herkner's report and a separate review, of steamship law, by the Dillingham Commission. Support for the commission's steerage study included many constituencies. Henry Cabot Lodge and William Bennet—who usually found themselves on opposite sides of the immigration debate—had worked together to shoehorn into the Immigration Act of 1907 an increase in the minimum airspace per passenger required on transatlantic vessels, which went into effect at the beginning of 1909. Though couched in humanitarian and public-health language, the measure also served to reduce immigration by cutting the passenger capacity of steamships, thus raising ticket prices. Bennet, who generally opposed restrictions, agreed to the rule as a sop to labor (because the guidelines would reduce immigration capacity) without conceding to quotas or other quantitative limits. Other proponents of Herkner's investigation sought to learn how well European steamship companies were enforcing U.S. laws that required health inspections and assurances that passengers would not become public charges. Public health concerns were among the earliest and most enduring justifications for immigration restriction.[29]

Herkner's recommendations pointed the way toward greater federal power exercised both within and beyond the nation's borders. To protect immigrant women, Herkner wanted the federal government's protective arm to reach across the ocean. Herkner referenced precedents dating to the federal Passenger Act of 1819, which had established maximum passenger limits, had required minimum water and provisions, and had mandated accurate manifests and passenger lists. The law, though largely ignored, became an important precedent for federal regulation not just of immigration but also of corporations. Along the same lines, Herkner recommended regular surveillance of steamships by undercover American agents such as herself. She called for more immigration inspectors at foreign ports and for the United States' laws to be rigorously applied on foreign steamship lines. "The welfare of the immigrant is left entirely to the companies," she noted. "If the line is humane and progressive, the immigrants are well treated. If it is not, the immigrants suffer accordingly." Even "the enforcement of existing statutes" would help. These recommendations—"the system inaugurated by the Commission of sending investigators in the steerage in the guise of immigrants"—were included in the commission's final report, and the expansion of immigrant inspection overseas became a key feature of new enforcement measures in the 1920s.[30]

Anna Herkner was not the only woman agent calling for the government to flex its muscles. An international campaign against white slavery, coupled with stereotypes about immigrant women's sexual propriety, inspired the Dillingham Commission to produce an extensive report on the topic, "Importation and harboring of women for immoral purposes," in Volume 37. "White slavery" referred to international sex trafficking, which was widely blamed on immigrants—especially Jews and the French—and which was typically depicted as a vast global ring of forced prostitution. The term "white slavery" made the racial status of immigrants even more ambiguous—they were legally white, even as federal statistics categorized them as belonging to the "Italian" or "Hebrew" races. The term "white slavery" had originally been used by male labor activists, who compared debt peonage or low wages to the conditions of chattel slavery. But by the 1890s, it had been stamped female; "the prostitute," social critic Brand Whitlock remarked, had "become the white slave, a shanghaied innocent." Although evidence of the size of the problem was scant, the global campaign against white slavery served multiple political and psychological needs of the era. Around the world, reformers spearheaded dozens of investigations. By December 1909, when Mary Philbrook released her report, the campaign against white slavery was an international phenomenon that encompassed Argentina, continental Europe, and the United States.[31]

The Dillingham Commission's white slavery report spurred the passage of the Mann Act of 1910, which used the interstate commerce clause to ban the trafficking of women—whether or not they were immigrants—over state lines. A lesser-known but equally important companion law, named in part for its sponsor, William Bennet, banned the importation to the United States of women for immoral purposes. The Mann Act's reach was much larger than prostitution. The search for white slavery violations spurred the growth of the U.S. Bureau of Investigation (the precursor to the FBI), which was created in 1908, and with it, controversy about the expanding reach of federal law enforcement. One historian has called the Mann Act "the law which opened the way for the FBI to become a national crime-fighting organization." This, after serious opposition from Congress a few years earlier about creating a domestic "spy system." And so, a report on prostitution, written anonymously by suffragist and attorney Mary Philbrook, led indirectly to J. Edgar Hoover's surveillance empire. It is reasonable to argue that Philbrook's study had, over time, the largest impact on federal power of any of the Dillingham Commission's reports.[32]

Prostitutes brought by procurers had been ineligible for admission since the Page Act of 1875, which had targeted Chinese women. Ellis Island's female officers were supposed to identify prostitutes, but the system was imperfect at best. In 1903, the Women's Christian Temperance Union lobbied the Secretary of the Treasury to allow female immigration inspectors to board incoming vessels in search of prostitutes. But the women's inexperience, their feminist uniform of "bloomers and long skirts," and the resistance of male agents in the federal immigration service got "the project off to a very bad start." Ellis Island's commissioner was skeptical that the women could identify immoral behavior, one matron made a falsely suspected prostitute cry hysterically, and the program only lasted three months. But that same year, a new law made all prostitutes excludable, not just those "trafficked," or procured, and the Bureau of Immigration added new "boarding matrons" employed under civil service rules, who acted in an "advisory capacity only" to male "boarding inspectors."[33]

Mary Philbrook, c. 1915. Philbrook was a pioneering
lawyer and suffragist who anonymously headed the
Dillingham Commission's white slavery investigation.
She was a lifelong member of the Republican Party and
National Woman's Party.

The Immigration Act of 1907 increased the penalty for importation—
already a felony—and made prostitutes as well as their procurers "subject to
deportation" within three years of arrival. Another statute strengthening the
provision passed that July. The deportation rule's expanded reach drew a legal
challenge before the U.S. Supreme Court. It upheld the statute but limited
the government's ability to hold people accused of procurement. To enforce
these new, wider prohibitions, Ellis Island commissioner Robert Watchorn
hired a special woman immigration inspector, and investigators trolled the nation's largest cities to find deportable members of the sex trades. A black-
market trade quickly emerged selling documents "proving" residence of
greater than three years.[34]

Around the country, and especially in Chicago, religious reformers wrote titillating tracts and sermons against white slavery. Many were tinged with anti-Semitism. The victims, often Jewish, were called "white slaves," but the procurers, also Jews, were denigrated in racially marked ways. Meanwhile, women reformers, including Jane Addams, took up the cause as a symbol of male oppression.[35] In 1902, an international conference was held on the topic; in 1904, European nations (but not the United States) signed an international agreement. In 1908, with President Roosevelt's approval, the United States finally signed onto the international agreement, which required the creation of agencies to monitor and, if necessary, repatriate suspected trafficking victims.

That January, the Dillingham Commission authorized Jeremiah Jenks to cooperate with the mayor of New York and to purchase the research notes from a private white slavery investigation overseen by Jewish philanthropist Henry Morgenthau and women's trade union leader Mary Dreier, whom Jenks knew from New York reform circles. In addition, the commission (probably Jenks himself) hired Mary Philbrook and her staff to investigate "the excluded classes," especially prostitutes. The Justice Department undertook its own inquiry at the same time. Just after the commission completed its work, a vice commission in New York headed by John D. Rockefeller, Jr., held widely publicized grand-jury hearings to investigate suspicions of a large vice-trade monopoly, but failed to produce indictments. Jenks advised Rockefeller privately and was one of several experts called to testify.[36]

The anti-white slavery movement gained strength not from the actual size of the problem but from its ability to bring together diverse—sometimes opposed—interests and constituencies. In New York, Republican opponents of the Democratic Tammany Hall political machine formed a civic group called the Committee of Fourteen to root out corruption connected with the sex trades. William Bennet was a founding, if not particularly active, member. The group, which included several women reformers, performed undercover investigations of prostitution that Jenks used as a model for the Dillingham Commission.[37]

Proponents of immigration restriction saw white slavery as proof that immigrants—especially Jews—posed a threat to American morality. The mission of the leading organization fighting white slavery, the American Vigilance

Association, included "promot[ing] the highest standard of public and private morals." Crusading politicians such as New York police chief Charles Bingham saw the issue as a ticket to acclaim and reelection. Bingham, a blue-blooded reform Republican, famously—and speciously—claimed that half the criminals in New York were Jews.[38]

Historians have long debated the extent of the actual problem (compared to the hype, which by the 1910s reached the burgeoning motion-picture industry with films such as *Traffic in Souls, Inside the White Slave Traffic,* and *Smashing the Vice Trust*). Estimates of the number of prostitutes in New York City ranged from six thousand to thirty thousand. Yet when New York's Chief Bingham conducted a citywide sweep of the white slavery trade with the assistance of the Dillingham Commission's investigators, his reports showed only fifty-eight alien prostitutes and nineteen alien pimps arrested. These were hard people to catch, but clearly the problem was not as big as the hype.[39]

Mary Philbrook's investigation lasted throughout 1908 and 1909, at the height of the national and international mania over white slavery.[40] Because of the subject's sensitive nature, her report was written anonymously. She came at the topic as an active Republican, as a suffragist, and as a legal reformer. But in contrast to the outraged exposés by activists and politicians, Philbrook adopted a more measured tone. She called white slavery an "evil," but she also warned that the "subject is especially liable to sensational exploitation." She played up the menace of the industry when she pointed out that her agents—not to mention her subjects—often faced grave danger: "One woman agent was attacked and beaten," for example, "escaping serious injury, if not murder, only with the greatest difficulty," but "went cheerfully back to her work," albeit in a new location, the following day.[41]

On at least two key points, however, Philbrook's report departed from conventional wisdom. First, she argued that the industry was not a true monopoly or "vice trust": There was no "great monopolistic corporation" of traffickers, contrary to press reports. As she insisted, "The belief that a single corporation is largely controlling this traffic in the United States is doubtless a mistake." No one group, in other words, was importing women en masse, although Philbrook pointed to two New York-based organizations—one Jewish and one French—that did specialize in the work. The Jews, she claimed, even organized a "benevolent association," offering legal advice, insurance, and cemetery plots to its members. But Philbrook's reports described a "network," not a monopoly. Philbrook also reported that a relatively small number of people were barred entry or deported for the crime. In contrast to many of the Dillingham Commission's other agents, she found it "impossible to secure figures," so aimed to be qualitative rather than quantitative.[42]

Second, Philbrook offered a corrective to the movement's worst gender biases. She rejected the "victimhood" narrative by conceding that some women chose prostitution voluntarily in the United States or back in Europe. Like other immigrants, some prostitutes in eastern Europe or France had moved to America to make more money. In fact, "the much greater number of women" came to the United States already in the trade, "usually willingly," and were not becoming "innocent" victims after their arrival.[43] "The work is strictly foreign commerce for profit." If this claim horrified some reformers, it also affirmed women's capacity for cool-eyed rationalism. Nor did it deny the reality that some innocent women were "recruited . . . with a cruelty at times fiendish in its calculating coldness and brutality," which "exploit[ed] their attractions to the utmost" and could involve "intoxication and drugging." These women, she observed, were discussed as if they were goods or livestock. "The only remedy," Philbrook argued, was through "eternal vigilance and by the vigorous prosecution of the cases found."[44]

But more than that, Philbrook recognized that understanding sex work required a nuanced understanding of gender and sexuality. She and a few other investigators recognized that women were not the only victims of procurement, and that men were not the only procurers. A law had recently been passed to make the language gender-neutral: both traffickers and the trafficked could be either male or female. Citing recent reports by investigator Marcus Braun, who had gone overseas to explore white slavery both for the Dillingham Commission and for the Bureau of Immigration, Philbrook wrote, "There is a beginning . . . of a traffic in boys and men for immoral purposes." These were among "the vilest practices" infiltrating the United States from "continental Europe," home to "the most bestial refinements of depravity." These facts, she argued, meant that laws and crackdowns should be "applied with even more rigidity, if possible, in the case of men." Federal law should protect against decadent European immorality, homosexuality, and the menace of pedophilia.[45]

Morality's role as a justification for the Mann Act became more pronounced over time. After 1912, former Dillingham Commission agent Kate Barrett worked for the Bureau of Immigration to enforce the Mann Act. Barrett, a rare Southerner among women reformers, was a widowed mother of six and a physician. She headed the National Florence Crittenton Mission, a national charity devoted to reforming prostitutes and providing group homes for unwed pregnant women. She was eager to hold men to the same standards as women; in her charitable work with unwed mothers and prostitutes, she had held the same views. No patriotic American, she claimed, "can think of the fate of many of the immigrant girls in our country without a blush of shame. Thousands of them, every year, are sacrificed to commercialism and vice because of indifference and the lack of protection and proper care." The new law, Barrett argued, emphasized "the value and the standardizing of moral character, that has never been attempted by any government." She called prostitution "the festering cancer that has hitherto eaten the life out of every civilization" and pronounced that "the enforcement of a single standard of morality is the greatest advance that has ever been attempted."[46] The single standard represented a feminist argument for equality under the law.

Europeans were appalled by the crusade. In a visit overseas, Barrett "found that nothing so much excited the interest of Europeans" as the Americans' moral war on prostitution. Europeans "viewed the effort as absolutely quixotic and one of the leading men of Europe said to me, 'You don't mean that if a man in every other way except his moral character was suited for a high office that his moral peccadillo would keep him from it?'" That would, in fact, become an operating ethos in American politics.[47]

Mary Philbrook wanted to enforce morality by extending federal law into the personal lives of immigrants and native-born citizens. She called for new laws that allowed "special agents" with arresting powers to be stationed at overseas U.S. embassies to look for suspected white slaves. She also called for federal power to deport people for keeping disorderly houses (that is, houses of prostitution), which were "ordinarily matters of state legislation." She suggested that states pass laws "requiring the detention of every alien woman" suspected of trafficking or prostitution. Suspects would be guilty until proven innocent, since the burden of proof was on the landing alien, not the government, and, as the Page Act had demonstrated with Chinese women, it is difficult to prove a negative. In the supposed defense of women came a massive expansion of federal power into personal lives and international affairs.[48]

Philbrook's report had an immediate impact. She submitted her preliminary report, the "Importation and Harboring of Women for Immoral Purposes," to Congress in 1909, at the same time as an ancillary report by Illinois congressman James Mann. The two reports spurred Congress to amend the 1907 legislation to remove the three-year limit for deportations and increase sentences for procurers and madams to ten years. This law, known as the Howell-Bennet Act, had implications far beyond its technicalities. Anyone who could be considered part of the sex trades, whether voluntarily or not, could be deported. These laws increased the federal capacity to probe people's private lives and make assumptions based on race and gender.[49]

The more famous Mann Act, officially the White-Slave Traffic Act, was passed in July 1910 as a companion to the Howell-Bennet Act. While the Howell-Bennet Act was designed to prevent the immigration of people in the sex trades, the Mann Act forbade their passage over state lines—a federal crackdown on prostitution framed to secure its constitutionality through the interstate commerce clause. In this way, too, their anti-prostitution legislation could fit into the legal framework of antitrust law. Jenks was an expert on antitrust law, and Mann specialized in legislation that used the commerce clause, including the Pure Food and Drug Act of 1906. The otherwise rigidly conservative Supreme Court had allowed some leeway under the interstate commerce clause, as long as there was no abuse of local police power.[50]

The United States had finally signed the international agreement to curb white slavery in 1908, and the justification for the Mann Act's interruption of international sex traffic was the Senate's power to enforce treaties. Section 6 of the Mann Act enjoined the U.S. commissioner-general of immigration "to receive and centralize information concerning the procuration of alien women and girls with a view to their debauchery." The Supreme Court later ruled that "debauchery" did not need to include sexual intercourse, which opened the door to a broad reading that allowed the Mann Act to be used against women traveling over state lines with a man, even when the travel—or sex—was consensual. Over time, the law became a popular way to prosecute interracial sex and child pornography. From 1910 to 1912, federal agents tried to ensnare African American boxer Jack Johnson in the Mann Act, eventually arresting him for allegedly transporting a white prostitute from Pittsburgh to Chicago. This incident highlighted how easily the Mann Act could be turned to other purposes—in this case, policing interracial sex. The Mann Act marked a dramatic expansion in federal government and a decline in privacy. Because FBI agents often shared information with city and state law enforcement to encourage them to pursue their own prosecutions, the law extended the reach of the federal government from the international sex trade into domestic law enforcement.[51]

Women Agents and the Politics of Equality and Difference

As investigators, policy makers, and enforcement officers, women agents expanded their power in tandem with the state's. But what about their own political commitments? Their personal politics reflected the era's immense ferment over women's access to public life. Evidence suggests that the women who worked for the Dillingham Commission were more radical in their politics than their male coworkers. The Republican Party, which dominated the commission, was generally more supportive of woman suffrage than the Democrats. Still, both Dillingham and Lodge opposed suffrage. Jeremiah Jenks almost certainly trained female graduate students, and several supervisors clearly supported the right of women—including married ones—to work. Jenks appeared largely (but not wholly) sympathetic to women's suffrage, although the National Civic Federation was officially opposed. H. Parker Willis's mother, Olympia Brown, a suffragist and the first female ordained minister in the United States, must surely have schooled him on women's equality.[52]

In contrast to these moderate and conservative Republicans, several women who worked for the commission were current or future suffrage radicals and self-proclaimed feminists. At least one, cities investigator Juliet Points, became a Communist. As an undergraduate at Barnard College, Points cofounded a women's suffrage society, helping revive the organization after she graduated. Mary Philbrook had been a suffrage activist in New Jersey since the 1890s, when she became the first woman lawyer in the state (an achievement that had required legal action). Dr. Elnora Cuddeback Folkmar was also an outspoken supporter of women's suffrage—in addition to her work on eugenics—in the 1910s and 1920s.

It is not surprising that these well-educated, professional women were suffragists. Many came from the reform world that leaned toward "maternalism," that is, the advocacy of social policies that protected women and children, and the sense that women brought a special perspective to these issues. Much of their work for the Dillingham Commission concerned women and children: on schools, on white slavery, on steerage conditions, and on immigrant homes. At least one commission employee, Mary Mills West, went on to work for the Hull House alumna Julia Lathrop at the U.S. Children's Bureau, the federal citadel of maternalism. Elnora Folkmar had begun her career in the child-study and kindergarten movements. These were classic examples of women's activism that led incrementally toward advocacy of women's suffrage on the principle that women would bring a reforming zeal to politics and "clean up" society—an approach known as "social housekeeping." It was also the basis for the long-fought campaign for protective labor legislation—such as maximum-hour and minimum-wage laws—whose application only to women and children later feminists, including Ruth Bader Ginsburg, would reject.[53]

Many male and female reformers supported women's suffrage for practical reasons: they believed women voters would support causes such as temperance, child-labor laws, and protective labor legislation for female industrial workers. Other women, especially elite, native-born white women—not least Elizabeth Cady Stanton—argued that their superiority to lower-class immigrant and black men was another reason to grant women the vote.

In other words, by the turn of the century, many proponents of women's suffrage argued for their cause on the basis of women's difference from men rather than of their equality with them. They were willing to pursue political equality at the cost of conceding social difference, as well as economic equality. In 1908, advocates of protective labor legislation for women rejoiced in the Supreme Court ruling *Muller v. Oregon,* which upheld a state maximum-hours law for women in an Oregon bakery. Labor reformer Florence Kelley had recruited prominent corporate attorney (and future Supreme Court justice) Louis Brandeis to write a brief using sociological and medical expertise to argue that women's unique vulnerabilities and status as current or future mothers provided a rationale for gender-specific legislation.[54] Reformers such as Kelley rejoiced in their victory and the new legal license to protect the most vulnerable women workers.

Several women who worked for the Dillingham Commission, however, adhered to a more radical school of thought, one that advocated for women's strict equality and opposed special laws protecting women. They were the earliest group to call themselves "feminists." Herkner, Philbrook, Barrett, and Folkmar all became members of the National Woman's Party (NWP), founded in 1916. The NWP grew out of the Congressional Union for Woman Suffrage (CU), a federal lobbying arm of the staid and venerable National American Woman Suffrage Association. But by 1916, the CU's leaders, Lucy Burns and Alice Paul, frustrated by the slow pace of the campaign, broke free from its parent group. Inspired by British suffragettes, the NWP used direct action, lobbied Congress, held suffrage parades, picketed the White House during World War I, and staged hunger strikes in prison. In 1919, the Dillingham Commission's former steerage investigator, Anna Herkner, who later became a child-labor reformer and a statistician for the state of Maryland, was arrested along with Paul and Burns for picketing for suffrage in front of the White House. (To put her actions into context, at the same time, her former boss Jeremiah Jenks was negotiating fiscal policy at the Paris Peace Conference.) In 1922 and 1923, Herkner was in Russia with the American Friends Service Committee, founded by Quaker conscientious objectors in 1917 to provide food during the famine there.[55]

The NWP called for women's strict equality with men, without special favors. Their views stood in dramatic contrast to those women reformers who had worked within the system for decades to pass protective labor legislation for women and children. By the 1920s, the schism between the branches of the women's movement would turn ugly. After women's suffrage was achieved with the Nineteenth Amendment, the NWP drafted the Equal Rights Amendment (ERA), which it introduced to Congress for the next fifty years. Florence Kelley, initially allied with the NWP, parted ways when it became clear the ERA endangered special labor laws for women. Protective labor laws were designed to protect women in dangerous industrial work, not lawyers like Philbrook. Major female figures in the federal government, such as Mary Anderson, who headed the Women's Bureau in the Department of Labor, condemned the ERA because it threatened protective labor legislation. The split between NWP members and other women reformers was damaging, deep, and enduring.[56]

Mary Philbrook belonged to the NWP, which might help explain her earlier view that prostitution was not a story of exclusively female victimhood. She was a pioneer in many respects. Her mother and grandmother were both suffragists. Her maternal aunt was a Vassar College graduate and medical doctor. Mentored by her lawyer father, Philbrook had been, in 1894, the first woman to apply for the bar in New Jersey. Initially rejected, she sought and received legislative redress that made other women eligible as well.[57]

Philbrook rejected "special treatment." As early as 1897, she argued that "the custom of privileging a woman in some matters and restraining her in others" because of "pity for her bodily weakness and presumed mental incapacity . . . should be abolished." Her "theory would be to give neither sex more privileges than the other. Place them on the same footing, and by thus establishing this equality both man and woman will be better able to work intelligently in the business and professional world."[58]

Throughout a long career that spanned from the 1890s to the 1940s, Philbrook called for women's complete equality—in industrial workplaces as well as in law firms. After receiving her membership to the bar, Philbrook became legal counsel for the New Jersey suffragists, helped found the first organization for women lawyers in that state, and worked for the second legal aid society in the United States. She served as counsel for the State Board of Children's Guardians and advocated the creation of a separate juvenile court. In 1903, after exposing corruption in the Essex County probation office in Newark, she was appointed county probation officer. She often took home children who had no other place to stay. This kind of work garnered condescension from male attorneys who did not share her beliefs about equality. In an article discussing her probation work, the *New Jersey Law Journal* conceded, "a woman may perform certain classes of work of a semi-legal, semi-philanthropic character which men cannot do as well." The same article made veiled references to her sexual preferences by describing her as "fond of outdoor exercise, inclusive of bicycling and golfing."[59]

In 1904, Philbrook became involved with the work that would lead to her appointment on the white slavery report. While serving on a state commission on female incarceration, she discovered the parole case of a woman who had served thirty-five years for murdering her pimp. After other pardon attempts based on what Philbrook called "undue sentimentality" about the injustice of a woman serving such a long sentence, she secured the woman's release with a sound legal argument about parole guidelines that had nothing to do with gender.

In 1906, Philbrook cultivated contacts with "people in the underworld" while helping the Essex County sheriff with an anti-prostitution roundup. Soon after, she was appointed to the Dillingham Commission's white slavery investigation, perhaps at the suggestion of commission member Benjamin Howell, who represented nearby Middlesex County in Congress.[60]

In the 1920s, the NWP committed itself to lobbying for legal reforms that removed all sex discrimination from state and federal laws. Over the next twenty years, half of the six hundred pieces of legislation the NWP wrote were enacted into law. Among these efforts was a state-by-state campaign to make laws and prosecution pertaining to prostitution gender-neutral—that is, to arrest johns and pimps as well as prostitutes. In New York, the feminist NWP allied with the Committee of Fourteen, a more traditional defender of moral purity. This campaign matched Philbrook's sensibilities honed during her vice work in Newark. Later in her career, Philbrook would help create the NWP's historical archive, and she continued fighting for women's causes until the 1940s. For all her personal political bravery, Philbrook worked within the system as a loyal Republican and government appointee. (Membership in the NWP did not preclude membership in another political party.) Likewise, Kate Barrett was an active Democrat as well as an NWP member, and part of the Washington-area "establishment."[61]

More dramatic is the biography of Barnard College graduate Juliet Stuart Points, who became a Soviet spy. Some women, like Mary Louise Mark, experienced their fieldwork as a trajectory toward professional social science, but Juliet Points was baptized into class solidarity and radicalism. From a middle-class background in Omaha, Points became a suffrage activist, debater, and star student at Barnard College, where she was valedictorian of the class of 1907. In her commencement address, Points urged her classmates to see the world as it really was, to "see Truth unabashed and unafraid. . . . Let us seek for happiness; yes, but not a contented unintelligent happiness, but rather that which comes from the joy of striving[,] whether the goal be won or lost."[62]

Points realized these ambitions in her work for the Dillingham Commission, which hired her just after she graduated. Working as a field agent for the

Juliet Stuart Points, Jersey City, N.J.

" At her command the palace learned to rise. ''

Juliet Stuart Points (later Poyntz). One of more than 150 women to work for the Dillingham Commission, Barnard College valedictorian Points was a suffragist and feminist who identified with immigrants and helped found the Communist Party of America. She disappeared in 1937, presumed murdered by the Soviet secret police.

congestion in cities study and a study on seasonal unemployment, she stayed through 1909.[63] She is the only woman whose own thoughts about the commission have survived. In a Barnard College alumni yearbook published in 1912, Points wrote about her time with the commission as "the glad two years or less when I broke away from the respectable middle classes and found my proper level in the slums with the lowest of the low delightful immigrants."[64]

Her sense of connection was inseparable from her condescension. As a special agent for the Dillingham Commission, she told her classmates, she had "charge of this work in various cities of the U.S., Chicago, Milwaukee, Philadelphia, Utica, Lawrence [Massachusetts], etc. etc." Whereas a young Jett Lauck had been repulsed and saddened by what he found in immigrant colonies and villages, Points felt enlivened. Afterward, Points augmented her "practical" experience at the commission with academic work, teaching at the University of Chicago and Barnard College, and then studying "economics, sociology, anthropology, etc." at the London School of Economics and

Oxford, and traveling throughout Europe. In 1912, Points was, in her own words, "still . . . a woman's suffragist or worse still a Feminist and also a Socialist." (Her use of the term "feminist" was itself striking, as it had only just emerged in the United States, mainly among Greenwich Village bohemians who called themselves the Heterodoxy Society—perhaps she was a member.) By 1914, as a sign of solidarity, or to fit in with her new radical crowd, Points had changed the spelling of her last name to the more exotic and eastern European "Poyntz."[65]

Two years later, in 1914, Poyntz offered Barnard College women a short historical essay on suffrage's relationship to feminism and other causes, while also gently chastising her bourgeois classmates. In her senior year, "seven short years ago," the few "suffragettes" on campus had been "regarded as 'queer,' as lacking in balance and altogether abnormal," and—worst of all—as "being deficient in a sense of humor." Women could hide their "cleverness" in front of men, she explained, but "suffrage, like murder, would out, and cover its protagonists with confusion in the delectable world of 'men.'" (By the time she wrote this, Poyntz had married a radical German activist, who presumably supported her causes.) Since Poyntz's graduation, however, suffrage and feminism had become more popular, although Barnard College undergraduates had "never responded" as they "should to the claims of a movement" offering "the most cherished liberties and opportunities." Barnard College women did not understand what Poyntz called, using the Socialist Party's preferred terminology, the "woman question," or why it should be "a matter of primary interest" for them. Poyntz explained that many undergraduates had not yet embraced suffrage and feminism because they did "not yet [have] enough contacts with the realities of life to understand why it should center about the purely political demand for the franchise." Barnard College, she argued, should introduce courses in what would now be called women's studies and women's history. In the short term, this education need was fulfilled, "at least to some degree," by her help in turning Barnard College's newly revived suffrage club into a "feminist club without abandoning suffrage interests." The club would "concern itself not merely with the political question of suffrage but with the whole problem of the economic, social and moral advance of women." It would foster "the development of feeling of independence and responsibility in all women and the creation of wider opportunities for women in the economic, social and political field." She urged every "Barnard girl" to "join the great advance army of her sex in its march upward and onward."[66]

The following year Poyntz descended back to her "proper level" among immigrants, although she still used her elite education, becoming the founding director of the educational department for New York's International Ladies Garment Workers Union (ILGWU). The ILGWU, comprised almost entirely of eastern European Jewish and Italian women, had conducted the massive 1909 shirtwaist makers strike, known as the Uprising of the 20,000, and was an incubator for female leaders such as Fannia Cohn and Clara Lemlich. In spite of her idealism and experience, Poyntz—as a native-born Protestant with an elite education—faced resistance from her Jewish immigrant coworkers.[67] Yet in creating a social and educational space for young immigrant women workers, which the ILGWU called the Unity movement, Poyntz believed she could create a collective consciousness "geared not to individual mobility as the public schools were but to help female members understand their collective position in industry and society and giving them the skills to challenge it."[68]

Poyntz's idealism and radical principles—as well as her encounters with immigrants while at the commission—drew her to help found the Communist Party USA (CPUSA) in 1919, for which she would work and organize into the 1920s and 1930s. Left-leaning members of the Socialist Party founded the new party after the Bolshevik Revolution. One of their motivations was that the entrenched Socialist leadership had not paid enough attention to immigrants. In the years to follow, Poyntz would become a major figure in the CPUSA, as well as a Soviet spy. But a visit to the Soviet Union in 1936 so disillusioned her that, upon her return to the United States, she repudiated the party. In 1937, after walking out of her apartment, she was never seen again. She is widely assumed to have been assassinated by the Soviet secret police.[69]

It is not news that women worked for the federal government in the Progressive Era. Much of what we know about women federal workers, however, is in either menial jobs or in explicitly gendered sectors of the Women's Bureau, the Children's Bureau, or the Indian Service. The stories of Mary Louise Mark, Anna Herkner, Mary Philbrook, and Juliet Points show something important. Each of these women, and over a hundred more, not only contributed to the Dillingham Commission but also burnished their own credentials as professionals at a time when this heady experience was reserved for only a few people.

Women's advocacy of the federal government's surveillance, regulation, interstate policing, and broad powers of deportation—indeed, the very existence of a large workforce of professional social scientists in the government—all contributed to the growth of federal power. At the same time, these women brought a female perspective to the production of knowledge about immigration and policy. Protecting women on steamships was a new assertion of federal power, as was the employment of female immigration agents. The Mann Act expanded government power in new and dramatic ways, legislating morality and spurring the growth of the FBI. Histories of the Mann Act acknowledge its role in controlling women but pay less attention to the role of women—especially the anonymous Mary Philbrook—in the campaign for its passage. In steamship evaluations, in housing investigations, and in white slavery studies, women's work and recommendations for the Dillingham Commission presupposed that immigration was a problem to be solved by an exhaustive, Progressive federal state, staffed with both men and women. The radical Louise Points underwent a political epiphany in favor of government growth, not in opposition to it. Like other Progressive reforms, the commission's recommendations augmented some women's power (federal workers and investigators) but undermined others (women who were objects of surveillance and prosecution). As a result, even at its more radical edge, women's work for the commission strengthened the power of federal agents over some of the United States' most vulnerable residents, especially women, even as it strengthened the power of the women who did the work.

6

The American Type

The Dillingham Commission's most famous report is an outlier because it was a defense of immigrants. In the spring of 1908, commission members voted to hire Columbia University anthropologist Franz Boas to measure the heads and bodies of immigrants and those of their children to examine "the physical assimilation of immigrant races." Using the accepted scientific standards of the day, Boas hoped to determine whether the American environment changed newcomers—especially children—for the better or the worse.[1] Most Dillingham Commission reports concerned the question, "Were immigrants good for the United States?" Boas asked whether the United States was good for immigrants. In short, which was more powerful: nature or nurture?

After a year of fieldwork, Boas's study of craniometry (head proportions) and anthropometry (body measurements and types) examined 118,000 immigrants and their first-generation schoolchildren, which appeared in Volume 38. Craniometry was not the popular parlor-trick phrenology of the nineteenth century that purported to link shape of head to character traits, but a serious field of anthropological inquiry that used specialized instruments and was conducted by university experts. After a year of fieldwork, Boas concluded that among several groups, the largest of them eastern European Jews, all but Sicilian children showed remarkable physical progress and adaptation in the United States. Although Boas was friendly with eugenicists, his findings were a direct refutation of their central assumption: that heredity was destiny, and that racial characteristics were immutable.[2]

Boas's study for the commission would become some of his most famous and enduring work. He never gave up on it, and in 1928 he published a full version of his original, handwritten data, with the hope that other scholars would use it. In 2003, anthropology's flagship journal, *American Anthropologist,* published a special volume revisiting Boas's reports. In the main, the authors upheld his findings about the physical changes of immigrants, although scholars have continued to debate their larger implications.[3]

Boas's work for the commission has always been an enigma. He was the most prominent academic it employed—a man who would gain a "gargantuan stature in American intellectual history," as one biographer put it—and his volume was the most famous and well-publicized one.[4] But how did this life-long critic of immigration quotas and racism fit in with the commission's larger project, which was critical of immigrants and recommended their restriction?

Long before 1908, Boas believed in the adaptability of immigrants to the United States. As early as 1890, he suspected bodily change was possible, even while other scientists believed that race predetermined the cephalic index—the "ratio of head breadth to length." In 1894, in a lecture to fellow scientists on "Human Faculty as Determined by Race," Boas argued that culture, which was malleable and shaped by outside forces, explained apparent differences between the races. Since white "civilization is higher . . . we assume that the *aptitude* for civilization is also higher," he explained. An "inference is drawn that the white race represents the highest type of perfection," but—he argued—"the achievement and the *aptitude* for an achievement have been confounded." The problem, Boas explained, was that the study of races was never actually objective: "A race is always defined as the lower [one] the more fundamentally it differs from the white race." Boas had studied Native Americans, and he was already deeply immersed in debates about the racial characteristics of African Americans. He was a friend and ally of W. E. B. Du Bois. But his point had a parallel in the Dillingham Commission's assumption of difference between "old" and "new" immigrants, and in Jett Lauck's American standard of living.[5]

The 1894 lecture became an early statement of the cultural relativism made famous by Boas's *The Mind of Primitive Man* (1911), published the same year he completed his studies for the commission. As his preeminent biographer George Stocking has explained, Boas launched "an attack on prevailing classificatory and typological assumptions, whether these were the 'rigid abstractions' of the three European races," of theories linking race and language, "or of the evolutionary states of savagery, barbarism, and civilization." All of these seemingly fixed categories, Boas argued, were in fact malleable and developed in concert with "historical processes" and environment.[6]

Where Boas did find common ground with other Dillingham Commission researchers was in his passionate belief in scientific data and objectivity. This confidence in evidence allowed him to use the same tools as his critics—measurements of bodies, a key feature of eugenics—in order to refute them. Beating the restrictionists at their own game was clever, but it also reflected a shared sensibility that Boas's subsequent lionization as an antiracist has obscured. Boas was a participant in the developing field of eugenics, years before it had taken on its reputation as pure racism. For Boas, the "science of racial improvement"—if it was really a science—would subject its assumptions to proof. He felt he was doing just that. Boas was confident that immigrants' health depended on their environment. Using the body to measure the fitness of southern and eastern Europeans for American society shared some tools from the eugenics toolbox, but, at least in his view, did not predetermine the outcomes of his studies.

Boas's work was controversial and had important implications. Many of the immigration restrictions that did exist were based on physical fitness, which biased immigration agents tended to use to keep out Jews. At the same time Boas was doing his work, Jewish lobbyists—with whom he was in conversation—were feverishly working to forestall immigration restrictions based on physical health. Boas was not immune to the larger pressures of culture and politics: a large portion of his Dillingham Commission study concerned Jews, and as his colleague Maurice Fishberg observed in 1911, "the whole world is interested in the subject of the Jews as a race. . . . [T]he perennial problem, whether it is possible to assimilate the vast number of Southern and Eastern immigrants to the United States and British colonies, has been applied more to the Jews than to any other white people."[7]

Boas and other commission researchers shared an unwavering certitude in their own objectivity. Perhaps that was why Boas agreed to work for the commission. He had already spent two decades defending and developing anthropology as a real science, in which he had insisted that observation and data collection must trump and precede theory. That is not to say the professor lacked opinions: Boas saw himself as a friend of the immigrant—indeed he was an immigrant himself—and he was eager to refute claims of immigrants' inferiority. But his own investment in the certitude of professional expertise, objective social science, and inductive reasoning meant that his actions and methods differed little from many of the men he saw as his adversaries.[8] By using his federally funded studies of young immigrants' bodies and skulls to "prove" objective truths, Boas brought the power of the state to bear on his subjects and took liberties with the rights of the subjects he claimed to be trying to help. He strengthened the power of the expert, even as he offered a dissenting expert opinion. In this, Boas's own work—however subversive or revelatory in its intentions and conclusions—enhanced the coercive power of the state over individual people, even as it offered scientific evidence to refute claims of their inferiority.

Making Anthropology into a Science

In 1908, Franz Boas was nearing fifty years old and had been chair of the Department of Anthropology at Columbia University for over a decade. He had already published nearly four hundred articles and several books. But his real fame came later, when his graduate students—among them Margaret Mead, Ruth Benedict, Zora Neale Hurston, Manuel Gamio, and Ashley Montagu—rose to acclaim. "Boasian anthropology" would become synonymous with antiracism and cultural relativism. In the decade before his death in 1942, the German-born secular Jew would become a hero to the anti-Nazi movement. Grizzled and a bit wild-eyed in his late seventies, he graced the cover of *Time Magazine* in 1936.[9]

In 1908, that international acclaim outside academia still lay in the future. Boas was already revered in academic circles as the inventor of modern anthropology in the United States, and in 1906 he was the subject of a festschrift by colleagues and former students honoring his work. He was, in Margaret Mead's words, "the man who made anthropology into a science." She did not mean that he had one way of doing things—"There is no Boas school," she insisted—but rather that he believed in examining data without preconceived theoretical notions. He thought of himself first and foremost as a scientist, and he was wedded to the inductive method. His parents were secular Jews who had encouraged his education (his mother had founded a kindergarten), and

Franz Boas, c. 1915. By 1907, Boas was already famous in
academic circles but was not yet known for his antiracism work.

his religious grandparents gave him insight into the eastern European Jews
he would study.[10]

As a young boy growing up in Bavaria, Boas was fascinated with the
outdoors. He "had come to learning through nature," as one biographer explains. Even as a small boy, he showed an interest in observation and historical
change, and his studies concentrated on the physical sciences. Eventually, his
education and curiosity led him away from his initial training. "The objec-
tives of my studies," he wrote to an uncle in 1882, "shifted quite a bit during
my university years." He first thought of "mathematics and physics as the
final goal," but natural science brought to him new queries that led him to
geography. Although his doctoral dissertation at the University of Kiel in 1881
concerned the color of seawater and was technically in physics, he also studied

geography, and his interests soon moved to more human concerns. He found his "previous materialistic *Weltanschauung* [world view]—for a physicist a very understandable one—was untenable." Instead, he embraced "the importance of studying the interaction between the organic and the inorganic, above all between the life of a people and their physical environment." After a year of mandatory military service in Germany, in June 1883, he left for a research trip to the Arctic Circle to study the environment and the native peoples. During the frigid evenings, he read Immanuel Kant by firelight. His mentor at the time was physician and anthropologist Rudolf Virchow, who was skeptical of Darwin's evolution theory but pioneered cell theory and analysis of hair, eye, and skin color as a critique of Aryan race theories. Virchow was, by the standards of the late nineteenth century, a race "liberal." In Boas's formative years, the late nineteenth century, German anthropology looked very different from the Nazi-justifying field it would become after its "rapprochement" with German colonialism and social Darwinian theory in later decades.[11]

Boas did his work with Inuit people on Baffin Island, Canada, in the 1880s not as an anthropologist but as a geographer and, even then, he claimed to be interested in what he called "psychophysics." His "chief aim" on Baffin Island, he explained, was to learn "about the knowledge peoples have of the local geography, which will be followed by a psychological study about the causes for the limitation of the spreading of peoples." Even as his curiosity about "physiological and psychological mechanisms" for cultural and biological change led him toward physical and cultural anthropology, Boas's intense interest in the impact of environment revealed the lingering influence of the field of geography. He wanted to redirect his inclination for method and observation to a focus on culture. In 1887, after conducting his first of many studies in the Pacific Northwest, he relocated permanently to the United States to work as an editor at *Science*. From there he did a stint at the Smithsonian's Museum of Natural History, secured an academic position that bridged anthropology and psychology at Clark University, and by 1899, had landed at Columbia's anthropology department.[12]

Throughout his career, Boas worked tirelessly to transform anthropology from the domain of dilettantes, armchair theorizing, and voyeurism into a respectable academic science based on observation and study. One former student recalled that Boas "brought into anthropology a sense of definiteness of problem, of exact rigor of method, and of highly critical objectivity." Boas eulogized his mentor Virchow, a pioneer in medical pathology, by explaining that "sound" science "requires of us to be clear at every moment, what elements in the system of science are hypothetical and what are the limits of that knowledge which is obtained by exact observation." Few people "possess that cold enthusiasm for truth," which can keep a "sharp line between attractive theory and the observation that has been secured by hard and earnest work." In 1920, he described the field of American anthropology as one engaged in "a mass of detailed investigations" not for their own sake but for what they might reveal about "human civilization." "We do not hope," he explained, "to be able to solve an intricate historical problem by a formula."[13]

Boas's early work focused more on physical anthropology than on the cultural theory for which he later became famous. In 1908, he was still interested in quantitative bodily measurements. In his commitment to objectivity, Boas was a good fit for the Dillingham Commission—at least methodologically. Boas believed in data, but he was suspicious of theory. He subscribed to something he called "historical particularism," which was less historical than it was particular. He wanted anthropologists to pay attention to the situation at hand rather than to lay totalizing theory on it, whether that meant a strong preconception about the commonalities of culture, the superiority of white Europeans, or anything else. This is not to say he rejected hypotheses: he began his study for the commission with some skepticism about the permanence of body and head shape, based on earlier studies in Germany and the work of physician Maurice Fishberg. The field was in flux—until recently the conventional wisdom had held that craniometric measures were among the most stable of the physical attributes.[14]

In retrospect, Boas might seem less an interpreter than a data collector (in this, too, he shared a dominant commission trait). One critic called his method "inductive to the point of self-destruction." Boas often pursued scientific objectivity by avoiding the imposition of any filtering or interpretive mechanism on his data. He put more than ten thousand pages of data about American Indians of the Northwest Coast into print, for instance, much of it, as one anthropologist has explained, "without commentary, without the bare information that would be needed to render it intelligible to the reader." Maybe this was objectivity, but it was the objectivity of the grocery list, not the reasoned intellectual. Boas's commission study, too, would contain "so vast an accumulation of material" that he admitted it was "quite impossible for me to handle it." In an era before sampling methods had been developed, Boas was constantly asking for more workers to process massive amounts of raw data. Like Jett Lauck, Boas piled up research material in far greater amounts than he could ever digest. It was practical, in the sense that it was collected for observation in advance of abstract theory, but it was impractical for turning out reasoned analysis. There was a fine line between "objective" and "undigested."[15]

Boas took the Dillingham Commission job amidst a rancorous debate among social scientists about the primacy of "pure" versus "applied" knowledge. Jeremiah Jenks was responsible for hiring Boas, whose work he almost certainly encountered through Albert Jenks (likely his cousin), a physical anthropologist in the Philippines who had known Boas since at least 1902.[16] Jeremiah Jenks and Boas shared a commitment to producing knowledge useful to social policy. Boas's emphasis on applied knowledge was evident in his commission report's introduction, which pointed out that *"from a practical point of view* [emphasis added] it seemed all-important to know" the impact of the American environment on immigrants.[17] His was not just idle curiosity, but work with a public purpose.

There was also a guild-keeping aspect to Boas's work. He wanted to purge the profession of amateurs, to mark anthropology as a distinct discipline, and to move it "toward university-based credentialing," as one historian of the field has put it. Ruth Benedict recalled that Boas "found anthropology a collection of wild guesses and a happy hunting ground for the romantic lovers of primitive things; he left it a discipline in which theories could be tested." He helped found the American Anthropological Association (AAA) in 1900 and to revamp its professional journal.[18]

At the turn of the century, all the academic disciplines included dilettante hobbyists, but no field more so than anthropology. The independently wealthy and curious often funded excavations and collections of native artifacts. Well-known anthropologist Daniel Brinton, for example, whose *The American Race* (1891) provided the basis for the commission's *Dictionary of Races or Peoples,* was an army surgeon who had only turned full-time to his lay interest in American Indian ethnology at age fifty. Boas also followed a peripatetic, if more academic, route to anthropology.[19]

When Boas entered anthropology, it was perfectly acceptable for the president of the AAA to claim, for instance, that "possibly the Anglo-Saxon blood is more potent than that of other races" and that "the Anglo-Saxon language is the simplest, most perfectly and simply symbolic that the world has ever seen." In 1896, Brinton gave a presidential address for the American Association for the Advancement of Science in which he stated, "The black, the brown and the red races differ anatomically so much from the white, especially in their splanchnic [internal] organs, that even with equal cerebral capacity, they could never rival its results by equal efforts."[20]

Boas harbored views quite distinct from Brinton's racial typologies borrowed for the *Dictionary of Races or Peoples*. Dillingham Commission staff respected his expertise on race and periodically consulted him on several reports. William Husband consulted Boas about the feasibility of the dictionary and sent him drafts of the "Hebrew" and "Ruthenian" entries to vet. In early 1909, Husband and Boas discussed the category for "descent" used in the blanks filled out by immigrant subjects for the field reports. Boas wanted a finer division for Italians than simply "north" and "south," for his study, presumably because he focused on Sicilians. But he lumped together all Scandinavians, whereas the commission distinguished them as "Norwegian, Swedish or Danish," because, as Husband explained to Boas, "some of the Scandinavians were proud of their particular country and desired to be recorded as Norwegians or Swedes." This was merely a nicety: "Of course this makes no particular difference," Husband continued, as, without doubt, they will be classed as Scandinavians in the Commission's reports." It was a rare glimpse of how the subjects shaped the study. But it also demonstrated the commission's lack of fixed standards or authorities on race.[21]

Boas's participation in early eugenics is less an indictment of him than evidence of the movement's centrality in scientific developments of the era. Since its adoption by Nazism, eugenics has become synonymous with "pseudo-science." But in the early twentieth century, it was "science," full stop. It had not yet reached its full influence, but it was a serious branch of inquiry among serious scientists (it is, after all, the forerunner of genetics), though it was not without its critics. So Boas's joining the eugenicists did not mean he was joining some racial cult (which is how it seems in retrospect). Rather, it indicates that he was engaged in the professional life of a physical scientist. More interesting is how he used its tools—physical measurements, statistics—to undermine its foundations.

Boas's interest in race and eugenics—and "type"—took a different direction from most Dillingham Commission staff. He "insisted on the conceptual distinction of race, language, and culture" at a time when others, including politicians such as Lodge and Roosevelt (who spoke of the "English-speaking races") blended the two in deeply deterministic ways. "If the Germans, the French, and the Americans were called races," George Stocking writes, "It was not simply a confusion of terminology. To some, they were races in the making. To others, including Lodge, they were already races in the sense that 'race' had meaning: as a community of 'sentiments, models of thought, an unconscious inheritance from their ancestors'—a community that was ultimately cultural, but whose essence had been infused by a biosocial Lamarckian heredity into the very 'blood' of its members." In other words, as Stocking continues, "to appreciate the significance of race around 1900, we must start with the understanding that there was a body of assumption that many environmentalists shared with quite extreme hereditarians." "Boas did not reject race altogether," a recent study of bodies and race in anthropology notes. "But neither did he believe in biological essentialism that promiscuously linked apparent physical difference to moral or intellectual traits, nor did he regard physical differences as any kind of marker of inferiority." In 1911, Boas reviewed extant race theories in *Mind of Primitive Man,* only to show that they offered nothing but "utter confusion and contradiction," so that "we are led to the conclusion that type, language and type of culture are not closely and permanently connected."[22]

Boas used the word "type" with "an amazing frequency," in the words of scholar Yu Xie. But Boas meant something different by the term than did most other scholars of the era, who claimed to group types by "biological principles," which were in reality based on "subjective attitudes" rather than on rigorous testing. His use of the word was informed more by the field of statistics than by anthropology. For Boas, the concept of "types" was an imperfect shorthand for classifying groups and comparing them to individuals: "The group," Boas wrote, "is the center of interest for the anthropologist," and the

"individual appears important only as a member of a racial or social group."
As a result, he believed in the idea not of a representative individual type but
rather of averages for a group type.[23]

This comparative work required statistics. And not just statistics, but the
particular methods developed by the leading scientific minds in the field of
eugenics. In the late nineteenth century, British eugenicist Sir Francis Galton
(Charles Darwin's cousin) dramatically advanced the field of statistics by developing the concepts of regression and correlation to do generational studies
of breeding and heritable traits.[24] Ironically, it was through Franz Boas that
eugenics made its biggest mark in the Dillingham Commission's reports.

Physical anthropology was the first academic field to use statistical correlations, and Boas was an early adopter. He assigned Galton's work to his students at Clark University, where he taught from 1889 to 1892, and developed
a series of lectures, later published, on "The Application of Statistics to Anthropology." To Boas, statistics helped make anthropology a science. At Columbia University, he required his graduate students to take his statistics
course, which most had to complete twice before passing.[25]

Boas especially admired the work of Karl Pearson, Galton's protégé. Boas
shared Pearson's view that statistics "must be taken out of the hands of the
dilettanti" and hoped that the "science" of anthropology could eventually sur-
pass the mathematical innovations of eugenicists. In June 1895, Galton introduced Boas and Pearson to each other. Pearson was interested in studying
human skulls, and Galton told him that Boas would be a "real catch for you"
because he had "heaps" of data about whites and North American Indians.
As it turned out, Pearson shared Boas's belief that cranial measurements did
not determine intelligence. For the Dillingham Commission reports, Boas
used statistical methods borrowed from charts in Pearson's journal of statistics, *Biometrika* (later renamed *Genetics*). Boas liked Pearson's advancements
in calculating correlations and called the cephalic index "a simple proof of
Pearson's methods."[26]

Boas's interest in correlation had developed from his early efforts to develop anthropometry. Boas first used anthropometric studies on his second
trip to the Pacific Northwest, in 1886, and began serious research on mathematical models for it at Clark University. He was able to take his ideas much

further at Columbia University, which had become an incubator for new social science statistical methods.[27]

Galton and Pearson had developed the methods to compare parents and offspring that Boas hoped to test in his Dillingham Commission study. His appears to have been the only commission report to use correlations. In his correspondence with commission staff, Boas "demanded training in theory of statistics" for new clerks and asked for a relaxation of nepotism rules to hire his son Ernst, because of the shortage of people who knew statistics.[28]

Despite his opposition to many of the goals of the nascent eugenics movement, Boas had a practical reason to maintain ties with its leaders: they had well-heeled benefactors, and he needed their money (just like he needed the commission's). As Boas began his commission study, he lobbied Charles Davenport, the most prominent eugenicist in America, and his Eugenics Records Office for more funding. It is worth noting that the British eugenics movement was more "scientific" and quantitative than the far more politicized and racialist branch headed by Davenport in the United States; Davenport rarely used biometry (statistics) in his work. In 1910, when Boas sought funds from the Smithsonian Institution's Bureau of American Ethnology (where he had previously worked) to continue his body-and-skull studies, he emphasized the relevance of his research to the field of eugenics. The head of the bureau declined because he thought the project might excite "race feeling" and thus do "much harm" politically.[29]

If the Smithsonian Institution was controversy-averse, Boas was not. He was not afraid of a fight: in college, he had participated in at least five duels, some in response to anti-Semitism. His face boasted scars from "saber cuts and slashes" that "would make a jailbird turn green with envy," as one newspaper put it. Boas often took up combat in print with his critics. Later, in the 1930s, when he became a prominent critic of the Nazis, the regime burned his books at the University of Kiel, his alma mater.[30]

Two decades earlier, during his tenure with the Dillingham Commission, Boas did not shy from publicly criticizing restriction-minded eugenicists. In 1909, he attacked William Z. Ripley's *Atlantic Monthly,* December 1908 article, "Races in the United States." Ripley used craniometry and anthropometry to make his claims about the three main "races," but he argued that the racial features of mind and body were permanent and hereditary rather than changeable, as Boas believed. Ripley invoked fears of "race suicide," the belief that Anglo-Saxons' low birthrate would lead to their extinction. In March 1909, Boas published a rebuttal in *Science* magazine. The thrust of Boas's argument was that the question of the American people's racial future could not be answered based on "many of the generally accepted assumptions" about new immigrants. Rather, it needed "the most painstaking and unbiased investigation" of careful scientific query." "Speculation" by alarmists such as Ripley "is as easy as accurate studies are difficult." One reader wrote a fan letter, telling Boas, "You are entirely right that these fears of deteriorating the American races are groundless, and I write to thank you for your stand."[31]

Boas may have disagreed with the outcomes of most eugenicists' studies, but he did so as a participant in their scientific zeitgeist. He was named to the first immigration subcommittee of the influential Committee on Eugenics of the American Breeders Association (ABA) (renamed the American Genetics Association in 1914). This organization launched and funded the eugenics movement in the United States. Alongside Boas on the commission were at least two officers of the Immigration Restriction League—Robert Ward and its president, Prescott Hall. Boas and Hall got along well enough for Boas to recommend Hall as a conference speaker to his colleague Maurice Fishberg. Boas also regularly interacted with Davenport, Pearson's American acolyte.[32]

On the other hand, Boas appears to have attended the immigration committee meetings only irregularly, and by 1912 his differences with eugenics leaders were apparent. Alexander Cance, who had overseen the Dillingham Commission's agriculture reports, served as secretary of the ABA's immigration committee. He asked an unimpressed Boas for feedback on a draft report of their meeting. Boas told Cance that he might start to attend the meetings "if a serious report is to be drawn up." Cance did "not think it is very courteous" for Boas "to imply that that is not a serious report." Still, a year later, Boas was soliciting Davenport for funding from the Eugenics Records Office.[33]

As Boas's complicated relationship with eugenics underscores, the meaning of race as a static scientific category remained unresolved. Boas interacted with eugenicists, even as he pursued research he hoped would show the mutability of racial characteristics. The field of eugenics remained inchoate in the United States, as did its factions. This lack of certitude helps explain the variety of depictions of race across the Dillingham Commission's reports—static, mutable, heritable, cultural, or all of the above. An introductory section of the *Dictionary of Races or Peoples* contained a table comparing the different terms theorists used for the same groups. As the Folkmars explained in the introduction to the *Dictionary*, "The sciences of anthropology and ethnology are not far enough advanced to be in agreement upon many questions that arise in such a study."[34]

The Commission, Coercion, and Costs

In 1908, Boas's intellectual infrastructure included a devotion to scientific certainty, a nascent cultural relativism, sympathy for new immigrants, and an interest in eugenics. Boas may have impressed the Dillingham Commission with his scientific objectivity, but his complicated and expensive project was a hard sell. Even by the commission's standards, his initial proposal to examine "the physical assimilation of immigrant races" was ambitious. It promised to investigate whether they began to conform to a "type" (that is, whether their measurements began to match those of native-born Americans), whether they developed more quickly in the United States, and whether their development "improved." Boas's goal was to study "about five racial types" of immigrants, by which he meant the "most important types of Europe"—north, west, central, south "(particularly Italians of the region south of Rome)," and, "as a fifth group should be added [perhaps] . . . Russian Jews. . . ." His study "could require the taking of three head-measurements" and the recording of eye and hair color, eruption of teeth, time of puberty, and overall physical condition, as well as "stature, weight, circumference of chest, [and] strength of muscle." "For older individuals, observations will have to be taken upon signs of beginning senility." He proposed to study subjects at four stages: as outbound emigrants, as just-arrived immigrants, at some point "after their arrival here," and their native-born children. He proposed a sample of 200 individuals in each of the four stages for each sex, in 15 age groups, and 5 races, for a total of 120,000 subjects. He asked for a staff of twenty "observers"—maybe thirty—but if this was too much, he offered to cut the study by using three racial groups instead of five, although he warned that the reduction would undermine the findings.[35]

Boas proposed a "practical carrying-out of this plan" ("practical" was one of his favorite words) that would require male and female agents collecting data at Ellis Island among both immigrants to the United States and emigrants leaving the country, as well as measurements of both adults and children. All of it, he figured, could be done in New York City (although as late as summer of 1909, he was hoping to add data on the Polish in Chicago or Milwaukee, children in Toronto and Milwaukee, and perhaps the quite different environment of San Diego). He was "reasonably certain" his "plan could be carried out" with "the powers granted to the Immigration Commission," the help of New York City officials, "and of a number of settlements." In March, the two professional academics on the commission, Jenks and Neill, discussed bringing it to the rest of the commission for a vote.[36]

The commission liked the proposal, but as Jenks pointed out to Boas, it was a "rather large expenditure." He had proposed a big, wishful budget of $19,510. Boas lobbied the commission about the value of physical data. "The problem before us," he explained, "is essentially in how far the different races that come to our country are being assimilated." The commission's research "will be much enhanced in practical value when it is supplemented by a physical examination in which the actual effect of the new environment upon the physique of the immigrants is tested." Children in Europe and in the United States developed differently, but he wanted to know if it was the varied "social and physical conditions of the two continents" that accounted for the difference. "We have evidence that even under the same conditions children of different races develop in a different manner."[37]

Two weeks later, the commission voted on Boas's proposal. An initial tally was tied 4–4. Jenks told Boas that the "no" voters were concerned about cost and about whether "the measurements taken would be accurate," since "in the present stage of anthropological science, there would be so much dispute over the significance of the figures that the results probably would be considered barren and would not be of any special credit to the Commission." Those who voted against Boas's proposal viewed physical anthropology as less scientific than sociological and economic research. Jenks assured Boas, however, that this was not his personal view. When the ninth member showed up, the vote went in Boas's favor, and he received a small initial appropriation of a thousand dollars to work up a more detailed plan.[38]

William Bennet and Henry Cabot Lodge were "strongly favorable to" hiring Boas. Lodge's support seems odd given his vocal support for immigration restrictions. But Lodge also had a PhD and may have accepted more readily than others the opinion of an academic expert. In fact, when Boas began to despair about funding to complete his study, he lobbied Lodge for money. Perhaps Lodge knew Boas through eugenics circles. In any case, Lodge devoted little time to the commission. It was Jenks's support that mattered most, and it is almost certain his cousin Albert had vouched for Boas. Albert, a sociologist-turned-anthropologist, studied the Bontoc Igorot of the Philippines, whom he brought to the St. Louis World's Fair in 1904. Jenks's own work in China and the Philippines may also have heightened his interest in anthropology.[39]

Other commissioners had their own reasons to support Boas. They shared his interest, if not his assumptions, about southern and eastern Europeans. Most previous anthropometric work (including Boas's own) had focused on American Indians or northern Europeans. "Instead of the tall blond northwestern type of Europe," wrote Boas (himself a short, dark Jewish immigrant), "masses of people belonging to the east, central, and south European types are pouring into our country." He wanted to know "whether this change of physical type will influence the marvelous power of amalgamation that our nation has exhibited for so long a time. The importance of this question can rarely be overestimated." Boas promised results: "The development of modern anthropological methods makes it perfectly feasible to give a definite answer."[40]

Boas both raised the vexing racial question—what would happen to Anglo-Saxons?—and soothed with the promise of objective science. "The essential question," as he saw it, was how to understand immigration as a process of "selection," a choice of vocabulary that tied his study to evolution and, by implication, to eugenics. But it also reflected current federal policies that used quality, not quantity, to regulate immigrant arrivals. Boas wanted to document "the modifications that develop in the children of the immigrants born abroad," the changes in those born in the United States, "and the effect of intermarriages in this country"—although in the end he scuttled this last point as too controversial for the commission. Finally, Boas wanted to compare subjects in the United States and Europe. "On the whole," he believed, "the American develops more rapidly and more favorably than the European." He wanted to know whether eastern and southern Europeans could match "the power of assimilation of the northeast European type."[41]

Boas's focus on physicality reflected the larger context of immigrant life and policy. In an era of infectious disease and malnutrition, poor physical health was one of the few attributes that could bar immigrants from entry. The few existing federal restrictions on immigration focused on political, physical, and mental fitness—which could be directed toward specific groups, such as eastern European Jews, with the "low vitality clause." The vague "likely to become a public charge" (LPC) could exclude people with "abnormal" bodies. Interest in the topic reflected the raw reality of poverty in Europe and in poor immigrant neighborhoods of the United States. (Indeed, Boas's study found delayed bodily development in the United States during the privation that followed the financial panics of 1893 and 1907.) Boas was interested in whether immigrants grew and developed bodies that were literally more "American." How did those who were immigrants and those who stayed in the old country "differ . . . in regard to physical development and racial character?" Were the migrants who decided to return to Europe "in any way different" from those who stayed? Did children born and raised "in the United States differ from the development of the immigrant race?" Did these tendencies persist in the next generation of American-born children?—that is, "do they tend to become similar to the American type?" The answers could shape the course of immigration policy and racial science.[42]

Boas's belief in his work's importance fueled certainty about his own authority, at the price of full disclosure to subjects. A look at medical science in the era is revealing: today's ideas about informed consent did not yet exist, and the term itself was decades from being coined. The debate over consent for medical and scientific research had barely begun. One early twentieth-century doctor recalled using what he called "the usual system of benevolent lying" in communicating with his patients. Physicians grappled with the ethics of informing patients about their care, and whether they should be forced to "comply," if not consent, to treatment. In the early twentieth century, the American Medical Association was "almost wholly consumed" with ethical questions that shaped public image.[43]

Cases pertaining to medical patients' consent to surgery appeared in U.S. courts as early as 1904. Even without formal consent protocols, medicine was decades ahead of science and social science on this issue. Widespread use of indigent or institutionalized peoples for such research went largely unquestioned. The National Institutes of Health's timeline of laws for the protection of human subjects lists nothing between antiquity (the Hippocratic Oath) and the 1938 Food and Drug Act. The U.S. Department of Health and Human Services only created an institutional review board process in 1966, almost sixty years after Boas sought research subjects.[44]

People—even uneducated or young immigrants—do not need formal institutional review boards and signed waivers to be wary of being subjects for government study. Archival evidence of pushback against Boas's work might even constitute the beginnings of a "bottom-up" history of informed consent. In part because of this resistance, the Dillingham Commission took care to establish its fieldworkers as legitimate agents of the government. These men and women were government agents whom immigrants ought to respect or even fear: the agents carried official papers and wore badges, and they had the right to ask intrusive questions, as the industrial and city studies showed. The tug of war between democracy and coercion was always at the heart of both Progressive reform and the social science from which it was inseparable.[45]

In the name of objective science, commission agents interfered in the lives of vulnerable people. Boas's study was invasive. He did seek some version of consent, but he also resisted constraints on his authority. Boas called his agents "observers," an innocuous title for people who entered people's homes and schools, demanded their family history, and measured their skulls and weight. Touching and evaluating people's bodies was an intimate act. Adult strangers presumed to measure the length of a thigh, the width of a head, or the pubic development of young immigrants. Boas did not hide this requirement from commission members. He used the word "consent." His initial proposal called for "extended series of measurements of whole families" in "house-to-house canvases." He noted this process would be slow, "since these would presumably require the consent of the individuals measured, unlike the basic measurements in schools." Permission might be difficult, so he expanded his original request of twenty agents to thirty, "in case a considerable amount of explanation should be necessary to get consent to be measured." Indeed, he noted, the amount of work he could complete depended "largely on the powers of the Commission" because its authority to cajole, even coerce, would greatly affect the "rate of work that may be accomplished by the observers," which was as yet "an unknown quantity."[46]

Sensibilities were different then than now, but Boas knew that this kind of work was controversial and that access to research subjects, especially children, was a delicate matter. In 1892, he altered a study of intermarriage between American Indians and white Americans after subjects refused to submit to some measurements, including those that required them to disrobe. Later, at Clark University, Boas started a study of children with the approval of the school board in Worcester, a once-Waspy enclave whose population was now half immigrants. Boas used permission slips, but a local newspaper caught wind of the scheme, and its editor warned readers that the board had given "the open sesame to the anatomies of the public school children of the city." Readers must not stand idle, the editor railed, "while their children at school have their anatomies felt of and the various portions of their bodies measured for no reason established in science." Did parents want "the hero of German duels feeling their sons' and daughters' heads and bodies over, just as he did those of the Eskimaux?"[47]

The broadside against Boas reflected a deeper suspicion about elitist, academic expertise that threatened populist democracy. The author of these opinions, newspaper editor Austin P. Cristy, had been waging an attack on Clark University and social science for years, and it was only in part about Boas. Cristy sponsored a local vote on whether to approve Boas's studies on schoolchildren, in which he claimed to receive 15,116 opposing votes and only 345 in favor. Yet 80 percent of the permission slips were signed and returned. Some teenagers who got measured found it fun, Cristy confessed, even though a reporter found that many had themselves voted against the plan.[48]

Needless to say, the vote in Worcester was not a valid referendum on Boas's methods. It does show that Boas knew perfectly well that his methods could meet resistance. His attempts to avoid individual consent for the Dillingham Commission's reports relied on his abiding belief that his work was for the immigrants' own good, in the name of science. In his concluding report for the commission he acknowledged, "a considerable amount of opposition was offered to observers," and he was grateful for "the assistance of the Italian, Jewish, and Bohemian newspapers" for encouraging readers to "submit to testing."[49]

Some reform types refused to participate because they did not want the taint of association with Boas's coercive methods. An umbrella organization of settlement house workers demurred because "it would probably be very difficult to get many of our friends to consent to having such work done." To ease the consent process, Boas asked William Husband for letterhead with "the names of the [commission] members, [and] 'United States Senate and House of Representatives' . . . printed in full." He would not be able to "take up work in private schools until I have the letter." But "with a letter of this kind," he thought, "there will be no difficulty in getting the consent of the people I need." The people he needed to convince were not those tested, but the school officials. Most private schools proved to be a dead-end: few kept the kinds of records he desired, and their administrations did not want to antagonize parents or risk controversy. At the prestigious Horace Mann School, an administrator wrote that, "since this is a private school, . . . parents are rather inclined to be sensitive about any matters of this sort."[50]

At least one parent formally protested. "My children," wrote Martin Beck to a school administrator, "have handed me the circular letter from Professor Franz Boas. . . . The observation blank does not appeal to me in its make-up," Beck explained. "I have considered it best not to file the same." In particular, he did not like the section asking for "descent." "To my mind," the father wrote, "it is erroneous to class the Hebrew as a nationality; he should be classed as a religion, same as any other. I am sorry to say that I think, by filling out the blanks no purpose is served." Here, Boas got caught up in the controversy Simon Wolf had flared over Jews' racial status.[51]

Students at Boas's own Columbia University also resisted participating. An attempt to have students fill out family histories garnered "considerable reluctance, and in some cases positive refusal," according to the university registrar. If Boas made another attempt, he would only "summon . . . again a very rigorous, and partly justified protest." In spite of resistance, though, the university did manage to get four thousand cards.[52]

Boas was especially eager to garner participation from public school systems because schoolchildren, like institutional wards of the state subjected to medical research, had little right of refusal. Boas relied heavily on the New York public schools, whose public health officer, Dr. Ward Crampton, he put on his payroll and thanked in his report. Crampton worked to secure children at the YMCA for the study as well but found few other institutions who were "making any arrangements or care to assist in any way," although at one point Chicago's school board expressed interest in the study. Even with Crampton's aid, Boas complained about "a lot of discussion, committee meetings, and Heaven knows what all, before I could get permission to go ahead." These permissions were from administrators, not the parents of the children who were weighed "without clothing" and on whom "observations were made on pubescence as a means of determining the approximate physiological development." Boas also got home addresses from at least one public school to interview and measure students' families.[53]

Perhaps the most vulnerable subjects were immigrants who had just arrived at Ellis Island. Language barriers and foreignness afforded them little sense of their rights or the limits of government power. For this work, Boas drafted a special letter explaining his intention "to secure some definite opinions regarding the physical characteristics of different races." He promised "the details regarding individuals which may be secured by agents of the Commission, are strictly confidential, [and] the reports will simply show totals," not names or identifiable characteristics. He continued, "Inasmuch as the inquiry is of so great importance, I request that every person who is asked to give assistance in this investigation will do so freely and cheerfully, feeling that he is thereby not merely assisting the Commission but also rendering a genuine service to the public." Jenks, who drafted the letter for Boas, trusted that it would be "of service in securing the co-operation of those whom you approach."[54] Jenks's letter underscores the shared sense of authority among these two social scientists from different disciplines.

As it turns out, Boas's confidence, both about how much he could get done and how easy consent would be, proved unfounded. When his study began to run behind schedule, getting quick consents became imperative. His efforts to secure the consents documented suspicion of and opposition to his work. Because Jenks wanted the fieldwork done by the beginning of July, Boas told his agents they would "have to hustle as much as possible among the families."

A few weeks later, he asked for help from the New York commissioner of police, to whom he explained, "The agents are instructed in every case to get consent of the people whom they measure, which is generally willingly given. Sometimes, however, cases arise where an irascible person thinks that they are trying to infringe upon his rights; and if he is a person of some standing in his neighborhood, the work is seriously impeded." It was "a great help" in these cases "if an official of recognized standing, particularly a police officer, should be willing to explain that the object of the investigation is purely for the benefit of the immigrants, that agents are authorized to carry on this work for the United States Immigration Commission, and that they desire the co-operation of the people." Of course, he conceded, "each individual person who chooses not to co-operate is at liberty to do so," but "he should not interfere with others who may be willing." It would be enormously helpful, Boas concluded, "if you could authorize officers under your jurisdiction to give such assistance in this matter as the law may permit." When Boas's agents went out without badges, they had "some difficulty because of the absence of credentials."[55]

Even the police, it seems, had been previously skeptical of Boas's staff. (It hardly seems a surprise that the mainly Irish New York City police force of 1908 was hesitant to aid a Jewish anthropologist from Columbia.) Husband eventually sent Boas "the customary credential for each person," a badge, which he hoped "may be found of value." A month later, Boas asked for "eight more badges" because "we have had a good deal of trouble during the past week, and the badges seem to work wonders with people and with the police." Boas also requested additional copies of his preliminary reports because they were "of great help in convincing people of the necessity of submitting to measurements."[56] This last action, at least, demonstrated transparency and disclosure.

Boas tried whenever possible to use influential go-betweens to bring in subjects. In the summer of 1909, he contacted the Caledonia Club, the Celtic Society, and other ethnic organizations to recruit subjects. "On Wednesday evening," he wrote to one agent, "ask for Mr. W. M. Brittain, who will give you details in regard to the [Celtic] picnic." Even with these inroads, Boas's frank focus on children raised the suspicions of immigrant families. Boas struggled to find people to survey the Italian community because, he acknowledged, the work was "of course a delicate matter" that required "somebody familiar with the region to introduce the observers."[57]

His fellow Jews were easier, but not by much. In a letter to the wealthy financier Felix Warburg, head of the Educational Alliance, a philanthropic organization on the Lower East Side, Boas called himself "particularly anxious" to get the measurements of teenaged "Russian Hebrews who have been in this country only a very short time." These young adolescents, who had escaped from tsarist Russia to a crowded and impoverished tenement district, had little context for understanding Boas's work but may well have been terrified by his intrusive measures. In fact, Boas's strong language appears to have put off the philanthropists whose aid he requested. The Educational Alliance's board at first vetoed any "measurements taken at the building, as, in that supersensitive neighborhood, this might start all kinds of discussion. . . . [R]esearch of this kind might create too much sensation." Yet the powerful Warburg was interested in the study, and connected Boas with doctors at Mount Sinai Hospital and a public-school nurse. Warburg also showed a predilection for deceit. He inquired to the superintendent of the Educational Alliance whether the gym teacher might be able to take the measurements "as part of a medical examination, *without giving any further explanation to the boys, and without exciting any comment* [emphasis added]." That last line could have affirmed any immigrant's worst fears about the power that reformers hoped to hold over them—all in the name of "their own good."[58]

Boas praised Warburg's subterfuge. He sent "many thanks for your kind letter" and agreed that "work of this kind can be done very readily in connection with Gymnasium work, and that the boys rather like it. . . . As you suggest in your note to Mr. Fleischmann, it is always easiest to do so by placing myself entirely under the gymnasium teacher, so as to avoid the appearance of a foreign agency coming in."[59]

The term "foreign agency" was oddly apt because Boas's study employed many immigrants, the majority of whom worked for the commission. Boas, of course, was an immigrant, too, who kept up a steady mail correspondence in German with his elderly mother, sometimes on commission letterhead, during the years of the study. Among Boas's immigrant assistants, two deserve special notice. Maurice Fishberg had emigrated as a teenager from what is now western Ukraine. He was a medical doctor whose own research anticipated Boas's. In 1905, Fishberg published *Jews, Race, and Environment,* in which he argued that Jews were not a distinct race, but rather were fully intermixed with the populations with whom they lived (that was why, according to Fishberg, German Jews looked distinct from Russian or Alsatian Jews). The *New York Times* praised the book but noted, perhaps with caution, that Fishberg's evidence suggested he was "anxious to make his own people as commonplace as possible and to rob them of all claim to the title of a peculiar people." A more clearly eugenicist employee was Boas's assistant Osiah Schwarz, who ran Boas's study while Boas was abroad in the summer of 1908. (Boas called him a "very faithful worker, not exactly brilliant.") In 1916, Schwarz articulated his own eugenic views in *General Types of Superior Men,* which included a preface by the eugenicist, socialist, and popular author Jack London.[60]

Like the rest of the Dillingham Commission, Boas also employed several women as "computers" (number crunchers), medical doctors, and experts. Particularly because he needed family measurements, female agents were essential. He hired a "young woman physician" and asked Jenks to recommend "a girl connected with your work who speaks Italian."[61] That Boas was so willing to hire women should not be surprising—many of his graduate students were women.

Boas's request for a woman who spoke Italian came out of the difficult time he had staffing the Italian portion of the study. He sought suggestions from several Italian academics, including a Columbia University colleague. Employees on the Italian study continued to be unsatisfactory, perhaps because the community resisted their efforts. They may well have been suspicious of head measurers: the world's most influential criminal anthropologist was Cesare Lombroso, an Italian Jew whose own work on craniometry had created the scientific arguments for southern Italians' inferiority. Although most southern Italians had little education, they may well have heard of Lombroso. He was a prominent lecturer, he opened a museum in Turin, and his theories played a central role in Italian state consolidation efforts and public arguments that southern Italians suffered from "inferior civilization" and a "criminality of blood." Boas tried to convince three different Italian American newspapers to promote his study. One (non-Italian) supervisor told Boas, "My Italian [agent] refused to go downtown for reasons he refused to give. This annoyed me and I attempted to get someone else which attempt proved fruitless." He then tried to measure some more Italians, but street parades for a *feste* for St. Maria meant no one was home. "This is the tale of misfortune," Boas's assistant wrote, "which while it does not help you any has depressed me much."[62]

For its part, the Dillingham Commission was mostly concerned with the study's expense. Budget debates had delayed a final approval for Boas, and he would continue to pepper the commission with funding requests for such things as comparisons with European data, access to newborns' measurements, and dental studies. After his initial one thousand dollar budget allocation, the commission approved a hefty twenty-five thousand dollars for his study. But his appeals for money escalated even as the commission was staving off criticism and budget cuts from Congress. He made unfulfilled requests for expensive color plates in his final reports and complained that the commission was starving his valuable work. He claimed he was not even sure exactly what his budget was or how much he had spent. "It seems to my mind," he wrote to Jenks in March 1909, "that the results so far obtained are so fundamental and far-reaching" that he was "justified" in receiving another five thousand dollars. "I ought not," he insisted, "feel the necessity of being over-economical." He also wanted more time because "the statistics are so involved, and the results so radically opposed to all our present theories" that he needed to "eliminate every possible source of error which might serve as the basis of an attack on the validity of our results."[63]

By December 1909, Boas was requesting sixteen thousand dollars a year for three years and was asking Jenks for advice on whom he ought to lobby for it. He pestered Jenks and Lodge, Smithsonian Institution official Cyrus Adler, and several wealthy philanthropists and institutions (among them Jewish philanthropists Henry Cabot Lodge and Charles Davenport) for both public and private funds. Indifferent to other demands on the federal budget, he complained, "The whole attitude of Congress is very discouraging, and one might almost despair of having serious scientific work" get "appreciated in this country." The remark ignored the generous appropriation and scope the commission had already given him as Congress grew skeptical of its costs. Still, Boas ran his project on a shoestring compared to the copious funds

to give an impression of the change in proportions.   It does not represent the head forms in other directions in detail.

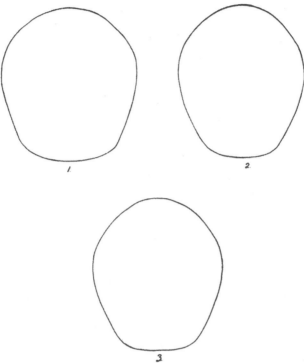

Fig. 3.—Sketches of head forms.

Showing (1) the average form of the head of the foreign-born Hebrew; (2) the average form of the head of the foreign-born Sicilian; (3) the average form of the head of the American-born Hebrew and Sicilian born more than ten years after the arrival of the mother in America.   These sketches are intended only to give an impression of the change in proportions.   They do not represent the head forms in detail.

MEASUREMENTS OF DISTINCT TYPES.

In the following pages a condensed tabulation and graphical representation of the measurements of various types are given.   (Tables 3–6, figs. 4–33).   In the figures, Bohemians, Hungarians, Slovaks, and Poles are combined into one group.   The numerical values of the hair-colors will be found explained on p. 98.   The full tabulations will be found in the Appendix, Tables I–XVI, pp. 169–369.

Sketches of Head Forms. Boas oversaw the measurement of thousands of skulls and bodies for his anthropometric study.

Chicago industrialists would later offer social scientists such as W. I. Thomas for their studies of immigrants.[64]

In the end, although the study that Boas called "very intoxicating" was much smaller than his original vision, it was no less bold. In place of the 15 divisions and 120,000 subjects he had hoped to study, Boas and his 13 researchers eventually narrowed the final research mainly to men in three groups: central Europeans, Hebrews and the "two south Italian divisions" in Brooklyn, Manhattan, and Yonkers. The three categories matched the hierarchies of most prominent race theorists. In addition, a very small sample of Scots stayed in the final version. Unedited appendices contained additional data that could not be assimilated into the textual analysis.[65]

Even with budget cuts and undigested numbers, Boas and the Dillingham Commission touted his work as a major breakthrough. The abstract in Volume 1 called Boas's findings a "discovery in anthropological science that is fundamental in importance." The first generation born in the United States, it announced, "changes his type . . . almost entirely." Most striking was the alteration in head shape, because it "has always been considered one of the most permanent hereditary features." Boas called this movement toward a norm "cranial assimilation." That the children of (most) immigrants appeared to "differ in type essentially from their foreign parents" was an "entirely unexpected result" (yet one Boas had hoped to show). Its significance was that "even those characteristics which modern science has led us to consider as most stable seem to be subject to thorough changes under the new environment." Another way of saying this was that the data suggested that "even racial physical characteristics do not survive under the new social and climatic environment of America."[66]

Boas's language in the full report was even more effusive, befitting a major finding. His research had found a "far-reaching change in type," and this "adaptability of the immigrant seems to be very much greater than we had a right to suppose." The implications were vast: if immigrants were so adaptable, then perhaps immigration restriction was unnecessary. "For instance, the east European Hebrew, who has a very round head, becomes more longheaded; the south Italian, who in Italy has an exceedingly long head, becomes more short-headed; so that in this country both approach a uniform type, as far as the roundness of the head is concerned." In short, whereas scientists once thought that "human types are stable, all the evidence is now in favor of a great plasticity of human types." "Permanence," it appeared, was "the exception," not the rule. To make such a claim on behalf of a government body packed with restrictionists was bold, even shocking.[67]

Boas was least optimistic about Sicilians, the largest immigrant group to the United States, and arguably the most reviled. Because they seemed to progress the least in New York, Boas concluded, *"We can now say with great certainty to the Sicilians that they should stay away from New York* [emphasis in original]." The findings reaffirmed Boas's emphasis on the impact of environment: Summaries sent to the press stated that "removal from Europe to New York has had a beneficial effect upon the physiques of East-European Hebrews. But the result has been just the opposite upon the Sicilians, the conclusion being that, bad as they are, the surroundings in New York are better for the Jews than in their city homes in the Old World, while cramped quarters which the Sicilians occupy in New York City are not so desirable as their rural surroundings in Southern Italy." This finding would have pleased distribution advocates. But perhaps most interesting, the remarks Boas made about Italians' slow development were made not in the reports but in private correspondence with Jeremiah Jenks and in the press release. The reports included the data from which these tentative conclusions were drawn but did not spell out Boas's view. All he announced there was "an unexpectedly wide range of variability of types." He was not willing to pinpoint the exact cause of this variability.[68]

Boas extrapolated from his physical data that immigrants' minds might also improve as their skulls changed. In an era in which rating intelligence by both race and skull size was commonplace, this was a bold assertion. Intelligence tests were just being developed. But as Boas explained to Jewish philanthropist Jacob Schiff, "There can be no stability in mental traits of the races, such as is so often assumed." "The startling change in head shapes," Boas claimed, "compelled me to conclude that . . . the whole bodily *and mental* make-up of the immigrants may change." Boas admitted he did not have evidence for this conjecture: "It is true that this is a conclusion by inference; but if we have succeeded in proving changes in the form of the body, the burden of proof will rest on those who, notwithstanding these changes, continue to claim the absolute permanence of other forms and functions of the body." His conclusion was now for others to disprove.[69]

Boas grumbled to Jenks that he was "constantly bothered by reporters," but this was a convenient complaint in a letter asking for more funds. The copies of his full report, Volume 38, disappeared quickly because of interest from the press, policy makers, and scientists. Boas, annoyed that the Senate would not consent to printing more copies, made repeated requests. An article in the popular magazine *McClure's* in the spring of 1910 "brought in again a flood of requests for copies." Columbia University Press published an expanded version in 1912. Boas's report received significant publicity. "Aliens Change in America," announced a typical headline in the *Baltimore Sun*. Boas claimed he found the "newspaper notoriety" garnered by his preliminary report in 1909 to be "rather embarrassing," though that seems like dissembling.[70]

The media was particularly interested in the concept of the "American type." In an editing discussion about the final report, Boas had wanted to add "of the Hebrews" after a line that mentioned "the American type." "The newspapers make such a fuss about the 'American type' that I should like to avoid the possibility of any misunderstanding of my meaning." "This talk about the American type is nonsense," he told the *New York Times,* "because in a country of this size there are probably many types. In my report to Congress I had said not one thing about the American type." Nevertheless, this idea of one general "American type" was exactly how people interpreted his findings. One news article opened with the proclamation that "[Playwright Israel] Zangwill's idea of America as a 'great melting pot' . . . seems actually to have received the indorsement of anthropological science."[71]

"Is there a distinctive American type?" asked *Leslie's Weekly* in March 1916. "Scientists for years past have been quarreling over the question. Professor Franz Boas, of Columbia University, holds that while there may not be a type distinctively American, we are rapidly approaching a uniform fusion of the races that seem at home in this land of freedom. He has shown that the children of alien races born in this country show a very marked physical and mental change, and that the amalgamation of these races is producing a uniform type of offspring."[72] But the question remained: Did this "amalgamation" amount to something that Americans hoped for, or feared?

The idea of an "American type" could be deployed by more than one side of the immigration debate. Eugenicist Robert Ward had asked in 1910, "Will the new American type be a superior one or an inferior one?" While men such as Theodore Roosevelt worried about the impact of new immigrants in the United States, the president was also inclined to wax eloquent—and optimistic—about the possibility of "amalgamation" of a new American race (although his rhetoric was meant as much to exclude African Americans as it was to include new immigrants). The idea of evolution to a new "American type" tapped into both hopes and fears about the impact of new immigration. For his part, Boas had wanted a study of intermarriage of "types" and race for precisely this reason, but it did not make it into his final version for the Dillingham Commission reports.[73]

In 1916, Boas published an article entitled simply "Eugenics" in *Scientific Monthly*. It was one of the earliest critiques of eugenics in the United States. Boas acknowledged the enormous appeal of a field that promised an end to human suffering through the breeding of a better human race. The hitch was figuring out what breeding could really yield: "It would seem the first obligation of the eugenicist ought to be to determine what traits are truly inherited and which ones are not." Boas objected to the tendency of eugenicists to take for granted that "traits were inherited" when this "was, of course, the point to be proven in the first place," as biologist Garland Allen has explained. As Boas put it, " 'Nature not nurture,' has been raised to the rank of a dogma" by eugenicists, "and the environmental conditions that make and unmake man, physically and mentally, have been relegated to the background." For eugenics to be a science, "in each and every case the hereditary character of a trait must be established before it can be assumed to exist." That has not been the strategy pursued. In contrast to eugenicists, "the anthropologist is "the student of human society," who has shown that "we must assume that all complex activities are socially determined, and not hereditary." "Eugenics," he concluded, "is not a panacea that will cure human ills, it is rather a dangerous sword that may turn its edge against those who rely on its strength." It would destroy, rather than improve, human society.[74]

In spite of Boas's protests, the eugenics movement gathered steam in the 1920s. After the initial burst of interest, his Dillingham Commission study only gained popular and scholarly purchase in the 1930s. In 1936, at the high-water mark of eugenics thought, two researchers with close connections to Pearson assessed Boas and Fishberg's measurements of Jews in New York. They concluded that the evidence was not clear enough to indicate that head shapes and bodily form had really changed. In the same volume, Pearson himself published a short piece claiming that a high rate of Jewish-Gentile intermarriage shaped cephalic indices, not "improvement" of type, as Boas would have had it. Yet the work of new researchers in the 1930s and 1940s, especially anthropologist (and prominent eugenicist) Harry Shapiro, began to draw new attention to Boas's indictment of racial "types" that lumped physical and cultural characteristics.[75]

In 2003, careful studies by two teams of researchers again reexamined Boas's data and calculations. These scholars concluded that the most important thing that Boas did was to demonstrate that the physical measurement most anthropologists of the era assumed to be the most static—the head—was actually capable of change. A stable craniometric measure, wrote one historian of anthropology, was the "central tabernacle of the doctrine" of the field, so Boas's entire hypothesis would have been heretical in his time in the United States, although German anthropologists had already grown skeptical of craniometry. One set of researchers concluded, "Given the prevailing faith in the absolute permanence of cranial form, Boas' demonstration of change—*any* change—in the cephalic index within a single generation was nothing short of revolutionary." Another explained, "His demonstration of plasticity in head form 'laid to rest, forever, the belief that body characteristics were . . . only under hereditary control.' The old notion of race has been slow to die out, but Boas' study of immigrants and their children was a crucial step toward the development of the modern anthropological concept of race."[76]

Boas's impact on the immigration debate is more equivocal. The Dillingham Commission, giving his study a positive summary (written by Boas himself) in the widely read volume of abstracts, declared that his provocative findings deserved further research. These striking findings "awakened the liveliest interest in academic circles here and abroad." The commission called for more funding, "either private or public," so that the "work may be continued." Despite this endorsement of immigrants' inherent assimilability, the commission went on to recommend a panoply of restrictions. Boas continued to try to influence immigration legislation. He sought funds to finish his Dillingham Commission research and participated in policy discussions. In May 1917, Jenks invited him to dinner to discuss legislation that would become the literacy test.[77]

The Dillingham Commission's decision to hire Franz Boas to measure immigrant bodies shaped attitudes not just about immigrants but also about the very ideas of race and culture for decades to come. That Boas used coercive methods to prove his point that immigrants could make good Americans—that they were culturally malleable rather than racially static—reflected a sensibility about authority and expertise shared by other social scientists on the commission.

Boas's *The Mind of Primitive Man,* published just after the commission reports, became his manifesto in favor of cultural relativism. For the most part, Boas's legacy has been anchored to his later work. Yet it built on the statistical reports he did for a government agency whose most powerful members favored immigration restriction—at least some of them on grounds Boas would have considered racist. Boas used and advanced eugenicists' methods to counter their claims, while other Dillingham Commission researchers used data to "confirm" the ideas they already had—exactly the approach Boas hoped to vanquish in the field of anthropology. Boas used data to debate and challenge. His work for the commission engaged the question of immigrants' suitability for the nation, even as it presented an optimistic answer. Boas believed in using physical characteristics to evaluate immigrants, and his allegiance to the authority of the expert was at least as strong as that of Jenks, Lauck, and the rest of the commission.

7

⊶∞∞⊷

Not a Question of Too Many Immigrants

"In the opinion of many the Italians of the [Mississippi] Delta region have pointed a way to the solution of some of the labor difficulties of the South." Italian immigrants "can endure the climate, withstand fever, and produce better crops of cotton than the average negro." In the Dillingham Commission's southern reports came at last significant enthusiasm for immigration—but only as a substitute for African Americans. The American South attracted a surprising amount of attention from the commission, given that, by its own admission, immigration to the region was "not only recent, but numerically insignificant." Because the South never succeeded in attracting mass immigration, it has barely figured in histories of the "immigration problem" of the early twentieth century. But like many people in the American West, the South's business and political leaders clung to the dream of distribution as a way to populate their underdeveloped region, solve the "race problem," and stave off new expansions of federal power.[1]

The South had an outsized influence in Congress. Small states were overrepresented in the Senate, and apportionments for House seats were based on total population (even though Jim Crow had disenfranchised African Americans). Three of the nine seats on the commission belonged to southerners. Charles Neill was from Texas and considered himself a southerner; John Burnett, who later chaired the House Immigration Committee, was from Alabama; a third spot was reserved for the succession of three southern senators, the first of these South Carolina's Asbury Latimer.[2]

So the South appears frequently in the reports. Lauck's industrial reports covered several southern locations, including Burnett's Birmingham. The

South featured prominently in a digest of state immigration laws, which were compiled by Alexander Cance, the head of the South studies. Southern cities were included in the reports on charities and schools.[3]

The region received the most sustained attention, however, in Volumes 21 and 22, on recent immigrants in agriculture. Alexander Cance headed the project while finishing his doctorate in economics at the University of Wisconsin, Madison. His reports gave voice to southern leaders who were more interested in attracting immigrants than restricting them. To promoters, the impact of experimental colonization efforts rippled well beyond the South: if immigrants could flourish outside industrial towns and cities, then they could demonstrate the potential of distribution schemes. Italians received the most attention. Cance's reports dedicated 150 pages to rural Italian settlements in the South. The largest section, which ran to approximately twenty-five pages, concerned the Sunnyside Plantation on the Arkansas side of the Mississippi Delta. Run by prominent planter LeRoy Percy, the plantation served as a feeder colony, or "mother," for other rural Italian communities in the South—mostly in the Delta, but as far away as Missouri. In the debates on the House floor over the immigration bill in 1906, William Bennet had praised Percy by name.[4]

The plantation attracted close scrutiny both from foreign leaders and from the federal government. It received lavish praise in the national press. But in 1907, at the behest of Italian diplomats and the Vatican, it became part of a large Department of Justice investigation into suspected debt peonage. Crusading justice department lawyer Mary Grace Quackenbos led an inquiry that yielded a federal indictment—but not conviction—of one of the plantation's business partners, O. O. Crittenden. Even without convictions, her findings were highly unflattering.

Southern politicians were outraged by Quackenbos's critical investigations, and in March 1908, Congress called on the Dillingham Commission to conduct a separate, nationwide inquiry into debt peonage. So now the plantation was the subject of two commission inquiries: Cance's on agriculture, and the new one on peonage. By early 1910, both southern senators on the commission, Latimer and his replacement, Mississippi's Anselm McLaurin, had died in office. In February 1910, the Mississippi legislature appointed his successor. It was none other than LeRoy Percy, a resident of Greenville just over the Mississippi River from Sunnyside.[5] A month later, Percy had been tapped to fill the vacancy on the Dillingham Commission as well.

By then, most of the major decisions about the scope and direction of the commission's work had been taken. It was almost—but not entirely—too late for Percy to influence the reports. Unlike his predecessors Latimer and McLaurin, who had done relatively little for the commission, Percy had a deep-seated connection to the topic. "Unfortunately," he wrote to his son Will, "[John] Elder, the young lawyer who was sent to Greenville to investigate Delta conditions [for the peonage reports], is an ass, and his report not only unfavorable but extremely stupid. Whether I can induce the commission to modify it or throw it out I don't know. It is scarcely capable of modification."[6] Cance's agriculture reports described the Sunnyside Plantation in terms more fitting for a travel brochure than a federal document. After months of study by at least six agents and a budget that swelled to perhaps fifteen thousand dollars, the peonage report, in contrast, was short and perfunctory, and mentioned neither the plantation nor Percy.

The Dillingham Commission's complicated relationship to the South is essential to understanding the path toward restriction. Percy's last-minute appointment to the Dillingham Commission showed the continued interest in distribution policy, and, it is fair to say, altered the outcome and content of the commission's highly politicized peonage investigations. The final version of Cance's reports was so favorable to Percy's point of view that John Burnett, who opposed immigrant recruitment, vocally objected to the reports' "statements relative to the peaceableness of Southern Italians in rural communities."[7] The commission's internal debates over immigration to the South once again revealed the variety of views still coursing through policy makers' minds. Although the immigration experiment there ultimately failed, the Sunnyside Plantation was a lightning rod for differing ideas about immigrant distribution and policy, particularly about ideas on labor and race.

In its broad endorsement of the Sunnyside Plantation, the Dillingham Commission took the side of Percy and New South employers over widely publicized concerns about debt peonage and unfree labor. The commission grasped at the slender reed of distribution as a viable solution to the immigration "problem" but also revealed an ongoing unease about immigrants' place in the free-labor system. Modern "facts" and age-old inequalities were irreconcilable in the messy boundary between free and unfree labor, the South's racial apartheid, and the challenges faced by Italians there.

Promoters' zeal for distribution schemes, in short, collided—and colluded—with the ugly reality of American race relations and with tensions over the meaning of free labor for immigrants and African Americans alike. In 1907, LeRoy Percy had been one of the nation's most prominent defenders of immigrants. To Percy, "It [was] . . . not a question of too many immigrants, but of improper distribution of them."[8] But by the end of 1910 Percy had joined the rest of the Dillingham Commission (save William Bennet) in recommending immigration restrictions.

The South's transformation from the region most opposed to restriction—and thus to federal immigration laws—to the one most enthusiastic about it was the last straw in an increasingly feeble bulwark against this particular expansion of federal power. By the time the Dillingham Commission had finished its work, southerners had become Congress's most reliable restrictionists.[9] When even stalwart supporters of states' rights ideology and immigrant recruitment such as Percy stopped opposing federal restriction laws, the political calculus for passing restriction laws changed forever. In the Sunnyside Plantation investigations, the production of propaganda about immigration collided with the production of knowledge.

Immigrants and the South

The dream of an immigrant South was not entirely new. In the chaos of Reconstruction, New South businessmen and planters had come up with the idea of replacing black sharecroppers with immigrants. In the 1870s, various schemes brought Chinese to the sugarcane fields; later, planters tried bringing Bohemians, Swedes, Danes, and Mexicans to cotton country. From the end of the Civil War until after 1907, most (though not all) southern leaders opposed restrictive laws against immigrants. The xenophobia of the Ku Klux Klan in the 1920s has obscured this earlier history of the New South. In 1898, only three southern senators voted for the literacy test (even as southern states were crafting similar tests restricting African Americans from the vote), and southerners in Congress usually opposed immigration restrictions. A few discussed repealing the Chinese Exclusion Act. In 1902 the Immigration

Restriction League (IRL) compiled a list of pro-restriction newspapers around the country. Out of 110, only 10 were in the South. During the debate over the immigration bill in 1906, a Southern Immigration Commission lobbied President Roosevelt and House Speaker Joe Cannon against any "further restrictive laws."[10]

The South's race problems were always the backdrop for other dramas. While the Dillingham Commission studied the "immigration problem," southern lawmakers and business leaders such as LeRoy Percy focused instead on what they referred to as the "race problem," the "labor problem," or the "Negro question." The New South's aspirations for new commerce and industry demanded cheap labor, but many African Americans resisted working at slave pace, for pitiful wages, or in constant indebtedness. African Americans were just beginning the Great Migration (first to southern cities and, eventually, to the North). Employers hoped immigrants could solve their labor shortages. But the nature of southern labor arrangements remained a point of contention. What did free labor mean in the shadow of slavery and sharecropping?

Elite proponents of a New South of revived agriculture and commercial growth wanted to attract new workers to replace African Americans, as well as poor whites. As one small-town newsman wrote, "Every time an [*sic*] European settles in Alabama we grow that much whiter, get farther away from the negro incubus, that hangs like a pall over the South." These voices also drew on the South's long-standing suspicion of federal power—which new restrictive immigration laws unquestionably required. In the Congressional debates over the Immigration Act of 1907, southerners had compared the Japanese "race problem" in California to the "Negro problem" in the American South.[11]

Several southern states, otherwise parsimonious in their use of public money, had funded immigrant recruitment bureaus and pamphlets since Reconstruction. Percy's predecessor at the Dillingham Commission, South Carolina's Asbury Latimer, was typical. He had opposed the literacy test and had thought the United States should consider "regulating the destination of these new citizens" and allowing every state to have "a special Commissioner of Immigration." By 1906, however, the federal Bureau of Immigration was monitoring labor agents, "especially representatives from southern states," for violations of contract labor laws. The Division of Information, created by the Immigration Act of 1907, federalized recruitment efforts and banned state efforts as "induced" immigration. But southern businessmen, LeRoy Percy included, continued to lobby for permission to recruit immigrants.[12]

In any case, the South's recruitment efforts were largely futile. In 1910, only one in fifty southerners were immigrants (about a half million people), compared to almost one in five of the rest of the country, or thirteen million. Most of the immigrants in the South lived in urban industrial centers (for example, New Orleans and Birmingham). Boosters for the region such as LeRoy Percy placed great hope in immigrant colonies, but these colonies remained tiny. The Dillingham Commission found about thirty-five Italian farm settlements across the South, a dozen of them, with about four hundred families, in the Mississippi Delta region. All told, the southern communities amounted to about 1,500 families, or 8,600 people. To put these numbers in context, in the year 1907 alone, almost three hundred thousand Italian immigrants came to the United States.[13]

LeRoy Percy and the Sunnyside Plantation

No southern immigrant community was more celebrated and promoted than the Sunnyside Plantation. Investors, journalists, politicians, federal officials, clergy, and foreign diplomats were curious about its residents, labor practices, and sustainability. Some brimmed with enthusiasm; others expressed suspicion. The plantation garnered extensive media attention, praise from politicians, and a 25-page section of the 150-page report in Volume 22 on Italians in southern states.

The Dillingham Commission's final report about the Sunnyside Plantation read like a promotional advertisement for Little-Italy-in-Dixie. Peasant women in head shawls baked bread at a communal oven. The rafters of their little cabins were laden with "strings of peppers, onions, dried butter beans, okra, and other garden projects." Corn dried on sunny verandas. Chickens squabbled in side yards. A plantation store offered the usual fare of salt pork and cornmeal, but also macaroni and other "articles of Italian diet." Men worked in the fields and at the sawmill, and a private train hauled the cotton crops into town. The plantation was encircled by eyebrow-shaped Lake Chicot (which had once been part of the Mississippi River), where the men fished and the women cooled off and did laundry. The train, and a ferry on the lake, offered rides into town. On Sundays, a Catholic priest presided over a church built by the Sunnyside Company, and there was a public school.

The plantation's residents, according to the report, combined southern hospitality with Italian sociability. "Occasionally one of the Italians gives a large barbeque" for friends and overseers. "Roast lamb, roast pig, and roast chickens are cooked in large quantities after approved southern methods, with the necessary vegetables. Italian pastry and wines complete the menu, and great merriment is customary at these gatherings." "This form of festivity," the author observed, "is interesting as an adaptation or an Italian adoption of an old southern custom."

Still, darkness dwelled at the plantation, too. Few children, for example, actually attended the school. The adults learned "a little English" but had little interest in citizenship, landownership, or education. "It is said," the report concluded, "that many intend to go back to Italy when they have saved a sufficient amount of money." The quaint little homes were, in the report's words, "crowded with children and so encumbered with household utensils" that housekeeping was nearly impossible. The "Italian housewife," as it turned out, was no housewife at all: "[H]er time is occupied in the cotton field and the matter of housekeeping is only secondary." "Many of the women," the report noted, "can manage a mule and guide a plow as well as the men," and the small boys and girls each had their own hoes to help with the cotton. In addition to working family plots like other sharecropping women, many Italian women were also paid as fieldworkers.[14] In the Johnstown reports, immigrant women's paid labor was a mark against them, but not at the Sunnyside Plantation. The Italian immigrant, according to the report, "is the solution of the labor problem of the South; secure him, interest him in buying land and making a home for himself, and the cotton belt will increase in prosperity with wonderful rapidity."[15]

Even before his appointment to the Dillingham Commission, LeRoy Percy's prominence and vigorous promotion of his plantation had heavily influenced its report. Percy joined the commission just in time to read, edit, and approve the draft and final reports. There were striking parallels between the Dillingham Commission's report and the version Percy had promoted in the years before its publication. It bore the marks of Percy's editorial hand, as did the conspicuous absence of the plantation—or anywhere in the American South—in the final peonage study.

To understand Percy's role at the Sunnyside Plantation, and his influence on the final report, requires accounting for the man himself. Percy's family, in the Delta nearly a century, towered over its history. "The building of legend about the Percy name," family biographer Bertram Wyatt-Brown notes, helped put the family at the top of the South's social registers, and its influence spread well past the South. LeRoy's father, Colonel William Alexander Percy, was educated at Princeton University (the "southern Ivy," the prized finishing school for the young planter class, and the last of the elite schools to admit Jews and African Americans). The elder Percy was a Confederate hero who came home to enter politics just long enough to create a fusion ticket of Bourbon Democrats and cooperative African Americans to overthrow Republican "Black Reconstruction." LeRoy Percy settled into Greenville as a small-town corporate lawyer, married a French Catholic woman from New Orleans, hunted big game in Alaska and Canada, toured Europe, collected fine wine and liquor, and associated with famous men from North and South. LeRoy Percy's nephew and adopted son, novelist Walker Percy, recalled an upbringing steeped in "the Southern honor code, chivalry, grace about doing right, [and] treating women with respect." But this code also required that "if somebody insults you, then fight." Percy's son William, also a noted writer, commissioned a statue of a medieval knight at his father's tomb in the Greenville cemetery. The monument is engraved with a poem about honor, and the inscription "PATRIOT."[16]

The Percy family symbolized the Delta culture and economy, with its combination of southern noblesse oblige and unapologetic capitalism. "[LeRoy] Percy's chief object," Wyatt-Brown points out, "was making money." Generations of Percys, who had been Whigs, "helped to create the Deep South—not just as slaveholding frontiersmen but as agents of change in the post-Civil War years." The Percys "belonged as much to the New South of heavy industry and plantation agribusiness as to the Old South" of land wealth and slavery.[17]

LeRoy Percy's nomination to the Dillingham Commission had surprised close observers, including the officers of the IRL, who had wagered on other candidates for the job. From President Taft's perspective, though, the pick

LeRoy Percy, c. 1910. The wealthy planter in the
Mississippi Delta was appointed to the U.S. Senate and
to the Dillingham Commission in 1910. He was investi-
gated for debt peonage in his efforts to replace African
American sharecroppers with Italian immigrants at
Sunnyside Plantation, Arkansas.

made perfect sense. (Although the nomination technically came from Vice
President James Sherman, it seems likely Taft weighed in.) He needed a
southerner. Percy was a Democrat, but of the "Bourbon" variety, the capitalist-
minded southerners who had allied with northerners and some African Americans during Reconstruction and who believed in political reform. They
tended toward the aristocratic and were, by definition, anti-Populist. Taft's
mentor, Roosevelt, had hoped that patronage positions for Bourbons such
as Percy might lead them into the Republican Party. Percy was as close to a
southern ally as a northern Republican could hope to find. And Taft might

have owed him: Roosevelt and Percy were friends and hunting buddies. In fact, in 1902 Percy had hosted Roosevelt on the bear hunt in the Mississippi Delta when the president famously refused to shoot a bear cub tied to a tree. A New York toy store created a stuffed animal to honor the story.[18]

Suffice to say Percy's public career proved much shorter than the teddy bear's. After his 1910 interim appointment to the Senate, Percy lost the election to retain his seat. He later gained fame for challenging the Ku Klux Klan in the 1920s. In an era of populist xenophobia and demagogues he called "peanut politicians," Percy's frankly elite manner, corporate conservatism, and adopted Catholicism meant his influence remained largely outside electoral politics.[19]

Percy blamed anti-immigrant attitudes in the South on the men he called "demagogues," such as Mississippi governor James Vardaman, who was a racist populist par excellence. But other, less virulent types were also suspicious of immigration, not least the Dillingham Commission's John Burnett. "In his opinion," writes Burnett's biographer, "the people of southern Europe were 'mixed with the black races.'" Burnett's comments reflected his view of a common question: Were Italians white? Or, perhaps worse, did they blur the color line? Burnett claimed that neither southern whites nor African Americans wanted "dagos"—a term he pointed out African Americans also used. As Burnett asked, "Is it fair to the poor farmer, the blacksmith, or the mechanic to tax their little homes to educate the children of the dago, while our sons and daughters are growing up in ignorance?" He once announced in Congress, "My colleagues from the South, God knows we have illiterates enough of our own, both black and white, without scouring the scums of Europe and Asia for more."[20]

The South's preoccupation with distribution was always about race, just as racism had created the southern "labor shortage." Yet Burnett, who represented the most industrialized city in the South, was an anomaly. To its promoters, the beauty of immigration to the South was its ability to kill two birds with one stone: it was both a distribution scheme and a way to solve the "Negro problem." The South was the rare domestic venue where—not unlike Brazil, Cuba, and Argentina—immigration was framed as a solution, not a problem. In 1910, Jewish philanthropist Cyrus Sulzberger could maintain that distribution would make African Americans leave the South, because "the immigrant pushes away the less thrifty, [and] the less industrious." African Americans would "be scattered over the entire United States, and would become an infinitesimal percentage of the whole population," rather than be concentrated in a few areas. "It will solve the greatest problem our country has to deal with"—the "Negro problem."[21] Immigration reform, then as now, made strange bedfellows.

The Sunnyside Plantation dated to the 1820s, but its Italian phase lasted only from about 1895 to 1913, reaching its peak around 1907. The plantation had been farmed by slaves since at least the 1830s and, during Reconstruction, was the site of an experiment with black ownership. In 1886, New York businessman Austin Corbin took over the property. Both the Dillingham Commission's report and LeRoy Percy's writings began their histories of the plantation with Corbin's purchase.[22]

Much of the Delta relied on northern capital and southern Bourbon management, and the Sunnyside Plantation was no different. Contrary to its stereotype as backward and isolated, the Delta was corporate, capitalist, and infused with northern capital. In its labor and production practices, it served as a colonial outpost for the northern economy. In the late nineteenth century, new levees on the Mississippi River reclaimed river plain that became aggregated in massive lumber plantations as large as 100,000 acres. The Sunnyside Plantation had a lumber mill, but cotton was still king.[23]

Austin Corbin was a classic robber baron, earning ostentatious wealth from banking, investing in Coney Island hotels, and developing the Long Island railroad. His obituary called him "impetuous and brusque," and he was accused, among other things, of anti-Semitism and of stealing American Indian land on Long Island. His New Hampshire estate featured a game reserve that several presidents and the Prince of Wales visited. In Arkansas, he kept a large steamboat—the "Austin Corbin"—at Lake Chicot.[24]

Corbin mixed business with leisure, but the Sunnyside Plantation was mostly an investment. According to the Dillingham Commission report, Corbin had come to Italian labor only after exhausting other options: "He had failed with the negro [sharecropper], and he had tried convicts from the Arkansas penitentiary, but those were not satisfactory." In fact, Arkansas—unlike much of the South—had outlawed convict lease labor. So, in 1895, Corbin

hired Italians "as a last resort." Through a connection with an Italian information officer at Ellis Island, Corbin became "very well acquainted" with Prince
Emanuele Ruspoli, the then mayor of Rome, whom he invited to visit the plantation. Ruspoli recruited the first group of about five hundred people from the
Marche, Emilia, and Veneto regions of Italy. In Percy's words, Corbin "determined to import Italians from northern Italy, sell them land, and make independent farmers of them," though not all of them were northern Italians.[25]

In December 1895, the first families arrived at the Port of New Orleans, and
from there were ferried up the Mississippi River to the Sunnyside Plantation
(Italian settlements dotted the river). Corbin built houses for them, which were
"stocked," according to the Dillingham Commission's version of events, "with
sugar, flour, tea, and other necessities sufficient to last a family a month,
plenty of wood had been cut ready for use, and in the small sheds were the few
farming implements necessary. It seemed . . . that every need of the Italians
had been supplied," including three interpreters "to assist in acquainting
them with their new conditions."[26]

But Corbin had bad timing. The 1890s were years of calamitous depression, climaxing in the Panic of 1893. When cotton prices collapsed, the Italians
"became very dissatisfied," in LeRoy Percy's take. Corbin devised a new plan
to sell, rather than lease, land to the Italians, "hoping thereby to satisfy them."
But ownership could not change low cotton prices. "They were unable to pay
for the land," Percy noted, "and the property was very unproductive."[27]

In 1896 Corbin died in a carriage accident. Many residents fled the colony
to found a new colony in Arkansas called Tontitown. Corbin's heirs hired
a Greenville cotton factor (broker) to manage the property, with "entire control over it." As justice department attorney Mary Quackenbos later described
them, "The members of this firm are O. B. Crittenden a cotton broker, Le Roy
Percy an attorney and political leader of Mississippi, and Morris Rosenstock
a wealthy Hebrew." (In 1879, Corbin had cofounded an American Society for
the Suppression of the Jews in New York. The co-management of his property by Greenville's most prominent Jewish resident—and it had several, including its first mayor—was a rich irony.) The Crittenden Company raised
money, the Corbin heirs owned the real estate, and the plantation proceeds
would be split equally. By 1907, Percy and his partners had gotten perhaps
six thousand acres in cultivation, a third of them recently developed.[28]

Sunnyside Plantation, c. 1893.

In the years before his appointment to the Dillingham Commission, Percy's abundant correspondence talked up the merits of the plantation with old-school paternalism, eloquent bluster, and frank capitalism. He tried to recruit Danes, English cotton-mill workers, and Bohemians for his other properties. Only the last group tried the Delta, but they had no farm experience and left soon after. Percy had more success at the plantation. He used Italian recruiters, in Greenville and in New York, and touted the same amenities—a school, transportation, the priest—as the Dillingham Commission reports later did.[29]

Alongside the boosterism, Percy appears to have genuinely believed that the Sunnyside Plantation might become a model for immigration distribution and for solving the labor crises and race relations of the South. "The Delta is suffering semiparalysis from lack of labor," Percy wrote in early 1907. "My experience with the Italian colony at Sunny Side," Percy told an Italian investor in 1906, "satisfied me that if the right class of immigrants are secured, and proper treatment accorded them, great benefits will result both to the land owners here, and to the immigrants. . . . The Italian, in my opinion, is the only immigrant adapted to this climate. He is unaffected by the warm weather, and when he learns to use ordinary care, he is not seriously inconvenienced by malaria." The Delta's rich soil and "his industrious habits" can yield "remarkable returns for his labor." "A more prosperous agricultural colony," he insisted, "cannot be found." Percy promised, "What has been done at Sunny Side can be done all over the country, and a contented, intelligent citizenship can be built up."[30]

In the 1890s, local news stories about Corbin's plans for the plantation had initially complained about "Corbin's dagoes," but protest had died down upon word that they were not Sicilians. Percy credited the success of his recruits to the fact that "they are nearly all from Northern Italy." He insisted to labor recruiters that his workers "must be from Northern Italy, and they must be agriculturalists, desiring to earn a livelihood by cultivating the soil." Unlike earlier settlers, the plantation's Italians "have always been farmers and never resided in the cities." Darker-skinned Sicilians made up perhaps 80 percent of the Italian population of Louisiana, where they were often assumed to be mixed-race and were compared to African Americans. In 1891, eleven Sicilians acquitted of the New Orleans police chief's murder were dragged from jail and lynched. (A young congressman—Henry Cabot Lodge—wrote a prominent article using the event to grandstand for immigration restriction—in other words, to blame the victims.) In 1899 five Sicilians were killed in Talullah, Mississippi, just eighty miles from the plantation. These episodes were widely publicized in Italy and the United States.[31]

To Percy, all the talk from "labor agitators" and Congress about limiting immigration drowned out how badly the rural South needed population. In 1907, Percy complained to his son Will, "Anyone interested in the development of Mississippi is confronted with an awkward problem. The 'hot air' demagogues are circulating over the state proclaiming 'Mississippi for the Mississipians,' [but] . . . in fact, a large portion of the state is undeveloped, . . . Mississippians have no idea of doing any work [there] themselves and nobody else on God's green earth is thinking about coming there or can be made to contemplate such a dire possibility."[32] (The Sunnyside Plantation was just over the Mississippi River in Arkansas, but Percy lived and owned other properties in Mississippi.)

The early twentieth century was a transition period in the American South. The exodus of African Americans from the South was still small before 1910, but the southern labor force did not meet the demands of capitalist expansionists such as Percy. In some Delta counties, African Americans still accounted for more than half the landowners. They were understandably reluctant to work for whites, although they often did so, sometimes in lumbering, to make ends meet. In pockets of the Delta, local black office-holding persisted until the end of the nineteenth century. While immigrant workers saturated the industrial North and the Midwest, in 1910 more than 90 percent of Chicot County's workforce remained African American.[33]

The full "redemption" of the South by whites was under way, with the ratification of new "Jim Crow" state constitutions that enshrined discrimination in law. The first was Mississippi's in 1890. Soon southern blacks, including those in the Delta, were fleeing sharecropping, debt peonage, disenfranchisement, and the violence of white supremacy. Lynchings, which reached their peak in the 1890s (at least 230 nationally in 1892), remained common. In 1906 and 1907, at least 120 black men were lynched in the South (compared to 6 whites). By the height of the Jim Crow era, the South's supposed labor shortage was a direct consequence of African Americans moving North.[34]

In response, Percy emphasized the superiority of Italian workers to African Americans. The Sunnyside Plantation had had no "serious difficulty among the Italians, and between the Italian and negro tenants." There was no "real race hatred between the two, nor is there any race mixture," he promised a Memphis newspaperman. This last remark implicitly contrasted the plantation's Italians with New Orleans' Sicilians, many of whom socialized with African Americans. Moreover, the "Italian makes twice as much as the negro." The price was worth it because of their greater productivity.[35]

All in all, Percy painted a picture of a prosperous, growing settlement. "For the past few years the colony has increased naturally and gradually by Italians sending for their relatives." Their crops yielded "a premium in all cotton markets." He admitted that "very few of the colonists have ever been naturalized" as citizens, but this was because "they seem bent upon making money, and at this they are a great success. The next generation," he thought, might be more interested in "statesmanship." His immigrants were workers, not citizens. Percy was just as happy they did not want to involve themselves in politics (unlike African Americans, whose political power in the Delta Percy's father had helped blunt a generation earlier). In short, Percy claimed, "I do not believe there is a colony anywhere in the United States that can show as successful results.[36]

In 1907, a Memphis journalist asked Percy for information about the Sunnyside Plantation, "*most particularly* the comparisons in favor of the Italians over the negroes," which he thought "*will interest 5,000,000 readers.*" Percy pointed him toward an expert: "As to mere statistics showing what the Italian can do as a cotton grower and demonstrating his great superiority in this respect over the negro," he recommended A. H. Stone's recent national magazine article "Italian Growers in Arkansas." It offered "accurate data . . . which is absolutely reliable, by . . . a writer on the negro subject, of well earned reputation." Percy did not mention that Stone was a fellow cotton planter, a resident of Greenville, and an old friend, or that Stone had received much of his material from Percy himself.[37]

It is true that Alfred Stone was well-known. Mississippi congressman William Humphreys called Stone "perhaps the most profound student of the race question in this country to-day," and cited his work on the House floor. Stone was an autodidact whose personal library held thousands of books and pamphlets on African Americans. Under the mentorship of prominent academics, including Jeremiah Jenks's Cornell University colleague Walter F. Willcox, Stone gave scholarly papers at national conferences and corresponded with prestigious scientists and social scientists.[38]

Like Percy, Stone thought Italians might be the South's salvation because the inherited characteristics of "the Negro" made him guilty of "shiftlessness and improvidence." In contrast, "the Italian works more constantly than the Negro and, after one or two years' experience, cultivates more intelligently." Stone was bullish on the Sunnyside Plantation, which the title of one of his national articles called "a model Italian Colony in Arkansas."[39]

The Dillingham Commission's report on the Sunnyside Plantation drew heavily on Stone's work in a segment on the "Italian versus Negro." It evaluated the tilling methods and standards of living of African Americans and Italians, and tallied their family sizes, rent, and productivity. "Every comparison that can be drawn," according to the report, "points clearly to the superiority of the Italian." As the report acknowledged, in one way this finding matched conventional wisdom—Europeans, even Italians, were superior to "Negroes"—but in another it seemed to refute it: "The negro has always been associated with the growing of cotton," so much so that many Italians learned cotton cultivation from their African American neighbors and co-workers. "Yet after a few years the pupils so outdistance their teachers that the negroes can not be considered in anywise the equals of the Italian farmer." These comparisons were lifted almost directly from Stone's analyses.[40]

Given the timing of the research for the Dillingham Commission's agriculture reports, it seems unlikely that LeRoy Percy had anything to do with their initial drafting. But author Alexander Cance knew Alfred Stone from mutual work with the Carnegie Institution of Washington and at academic conferences. Several passages in the Dillingham Commission's reports matched Percy's claims and cited Stone's data. Stone found Italians increased production per acre by 120 percent over African Americans and worked more acres per capita. Given the commission's own point that Italians chose better land than African Americans (which was why they paid more to rent it), Stone's claim was questionable.[41]

Stone's longest publication about the Sunnyside Plantation began by calling it a "mental habit" and "popular fallacy" to assume African Americans tilled most of the South's cotton, when in fact white farmers had always been in the majority, even among sharecroppers. Stone went to great lengths to debunk a speech given by black abolitionist Frederick Douglass more than two decades earlier, claiming that "the dependence of the planter . . . upon the negro is nearly complete and perfect" and that "neither Chinamen, German, Norwegian, nor Swede can drive him" from his position. Those who tried to claim that the plantation was a "failure" were wrong. "In truth," Stone claimed, "it is outranked by few, if any, as a success." He concluded his article with a long quotation in broad dialect from a "gray-haired veteran" of the cotton fields, an African American man who called himself a "natchel-bawn cottonpicker." The man thought himself to be a hard worker, but one night, he "found dat Dago en his wife en fo' chillum wuz picking cotton by de moonlight." The point of the anecdote was clear: Italians succeeded because they worked harder than African Americans.[42]

Stone's broadsides attracted the attention of African American sociologist W. E. B. Du Bois. As early as 1903, the two kept up a lively correspondence, and Du Bois rebutted Stone's comparisons of Italian with African American labor. Du Bois refused to concede that African Americans were inferior workers, pointing out the miserable conditions and underpayment they received in most places across the South.[43]

The Dillingham Commission's reports concealed in the language of objectivity the goal that Stone himself admitted—to prove that African Americans were inferior workers to Italians. "From the figures previously given it has been plainly shown that in all respects the Italian is superior to the negro, whose place he has taken." The result was a remarkably different tone than Jett Lauck's industry reports. The report on Italians in agriculture sang with enthusiasm, while Lauck offered a long, sad dirge about the displacement of native white industrial workers by new immigrants. Unlike the criticism of low naturalization rates in Lauck's industrial reports, the Sunnyside Plantation report, like Percy's private letters, excused Italian disinterest in citizenship. Only 4 of 150 Italian men at the plantation had received their final citizenship papers, but "in this locality there is little to be gained by voting." "Many of them intend to return to Italy, and naturally do not wish to relinquish their allegiance" to the old country.[44]

The Dillingham Commission's report on the Italian colonies was completed on June 15, 1910, and approved in late November, after Percy was appointed. The Sunnyside Plantation section mentioned Percy as a manager but did not divulge his relationship with the commission. Still, the report echoed Percy's depiction of the plantation. Italians there had it pretty good, with their kitchen gardens, a church and clergy, a school, dances on Sunday, community cookouts, a train service and a ferry to town, generous terms at the plantation store, options for landownership, and a chance to better the lot of their children. If Percy and other promoters could just get Italians to the region, they could save themselves and save the South in one fell swoop.[45]

The Peonage Investigations

There was only one problem: after the initial group, the Italians did not seem to want to go to the Sunnyside Plantation. Two Dillingham Commission investigations had examined the plantation, but only one—Cance's—ended up in the final reports. The other was part of a highly politicized study of peonage labor. Some of the plantation's residents claimed conditions were unsafe and that their labor was forced. At the request of Italian diplomats, the Department of Justice had added the plantation to a large federal investigation into violation of peonage laws. O. O. Crittenden, Percy's business partner, was indicted (though not convicted). Yet these well-publicized facts never appeared in the commission report's own brief study of peonage immigrant labor.

The idea of "free labor" was central to Anglo-American political thought. But it was always more of an aspirational ideology—and a northern one at that—than any particular practice. The founding motto of the Republican Party had been "Free labor, free soil, free men." It was supposed to work like the fable of Abraham Lincoln's story—from wage earner and log-splitter to landowner and self-made man. That was not, however, the white South's version of the future of its labor force. African Americans in the South and immigrants under coercive labor contracts represented the greatest threats to the free-labor ideal. The laws surrounding peonage, especially for immigrants, remained murky. Since the indentured servants of the colonial era, immigrants had often come to the United States under conditions that were less than free. By the 1860s, this kind of unfree labor was associated primarily with the Chinese, and the federal government passed the so-called Anti-Coolie Act in 1862. The Peonage Act of 1867 augmented the Thirteenth Amendment's abolition of slavery by banning "voluntary servitude"—mostly debt peonage—for both immigrants and natives. Because the law was intended to protect vulnerable workers who had theoretically chosen their servitude, it reflected a rare appearance of paternalism in a common-law system that usually assumed the superiority and a priori equality of participants in free contract. For thirty-five years, however, the law remained unenforced.[46]

Immigrants were also governed by the 1885 Foran Act, or Alien Contract Labor Act, which banned any kind of "assisted" immigration. It forbade payment of passage by a boss, *padrone*, or business and voided any contracts made before arrival in the United States. In other words, by 1885, it was patently illegal to recruit immigrants as contract labor, also known as "induced immigration." But it still happened.

The prohibition on recruiting workers overseas rankled promoters such as Percy, who argued that labor shortages made these arrangements necessary. In late 1906, Percy had sought guidance from Secretary of Commerce and Labor Oscar Straus about how he might recruit Italians without violating contract labor laws.[47] Meanwhile, for African Americans and many poor whites in the South, debt peonage arrangements and the threat of violence from employers were endemic.

By the turn of the century, the practice of using indebtedness to extract labor in the South—mostly from African Americans, but also from immigrants—attracted the attention of prominent muckrakers such Ray Stannard Baker and NAACP cofounder Oswald Garrison Villard. From 1906 to 1908, the Department of Justice, aided by the Bureau of Immigration, oversaw an extensive investigation into the violation of contract labor laws and, for the first time, the federal law banning peonage.[48]

In 1905, a U.S. Supreme Court decision defined peonage as the "status or condition of compulsory service based on the indebtedness of the peon to the master. The basic fact is indebtedness." In addition, various state laws could either facilitate or reduce peonage. Some laws heavily favored employers by making employee contract violations a criminal offense; others actually helped indebted workers (like homestead laws that protected real property from debt seizure) or forbade convict labor, a reform white populists championed in the early twentieth century. But none of the state or federal laws accomplished much because they were almost impossible to administer.[49]

Although even northern, white free laborers might technically have contracts, in urban areas, these contracts were rarely enforced. This lax approach, according to legal scholar Robert Steinfeld, "was perfectly acceptable to [northern] employers." But the opposite was true in agricultural areas, where labor shortages were chronic, especially in the South: "The American South following the Civil War," Steinfeld notes, "is normally thought to have been the one major exception and a striking anomaly in the Anglo-American legal universe," in that it often involved elaborate contracts, indebted labor, and—most especially—physical coercion and violence.[50] Austin Corbin had used contracts.

Most southern states had broad laws governing breach of contract, some of them part of the post-Civil War "black codes" (whose coercive measures had spurred Radical Reconstruction in Congress and which the Peonage Act had tried to correct). The black codes were meant to trap poor blacks into involuntary labor arrangements. But they could also ensnare immigrants. One South Carolina state judge invalidated a state law that made breaching a contract a criminal charge. He argued that the law had been intended for black sharecroppers, but, at a time when South Carolina was using private and public money to recruit immigrants, it was "as economically unwise as it [was] constitutionally illegal." Recruitment would fail, the judge wrote, "so long as our statute books hold legislation tending to create a system of forced labor, which in its essentials is as degrading as that of slavery. Desirable immigrants from foreign lands look for a land of freedom, where labor is respected and protected." As a result, the law he invalidated "constitutes a menace surely calculated to repel the coming of white men."[51]

Federal prosecutors revived the Peonage Act at the same moment as LeRoy Percy and his partners were trying to revive the Sunnyside Plantation. The first federal peonage case was in 1898; the Supreme Court upheld the law in 1905. At that point, a hundred cases were under way, almost all of them in "a crescent from South Carolina to Mississippi through the Delta on both sides of the river."[52]

Most of the federal peonage inquiries involved African Americans, but well-publicized cases from Florida to Texas alleged the virtual enslavement of eastern European Jews, Slavs, and Bohemians in turpentine, lumber, and railroad camps. After years of puff pieces about Percy's Sunnyside Plantation, the national press began publishing exposés such as "Slavery in the South To-day." The article, which was about Florida, appeared in March 1907.[53]

Peonage was a fuzzy concept that could apply—or not—to diverse realities. Immigrants came to the United States anticipating a job, or by borrowing money, all the time. The question was evidence of coercion before or immobility afterward. Many cases involved collusion between southern employers and corrupt local justices of the peace who fined or jailed workers who escaped bad conditions. The association with slavery meant that discussions of peonage were always racialized. For reformers, the re-enslavement of African Americans was tragic, but the actual enslavement of white immigrants was unthinkable.[54] As a result, immigrant peons in the South were relatively few in number compared to African Americans, but they received disproportionate attention from reformers and journalists. In part, this was because they had advocates that African Americans did not: their home countries' governments.

By 1905 or 1906, the Italian consulate in New Orleans was hearing complaints about conditions from Sunnyside Plantation residents, perhaps encouraged by the Catholic priest LeRoy Percy himself had recruited. (Percy told his son, Will, that "without a priest, there is scarcely anything that could occur that would make any considerable number of the Italians leave Sunnyside." But "an improper use of his influence, [could] . . . practically depopulate the property within a year.") Whatever the cause, complaints were mushrooming. One recruiter told Percy that getting immigrants was "harder work than I thought, because the people are afraid to go." Immigration laws, contracts, agents, transatlantic passage, and yellow fever were all disincentives. The Italian consul devised a rule that immigrants who wanted to bring relatives over had to make a signed "affidavit to their relationship" in person at the New Orleans consulate. LeRoy Percy hated the rule, which was intended to quash the Sunnyside Company from circumventing contract labor laws by pretending its recruits were relatives of current colonists. Percy was sure he could get more people, "but for some reason the Italian government has taken a decidedly hostile stand against Mississippi, and the Delta in particular."[55]

The consulate had also heard complaints from Sunnyside Plantation farmers typical of sharecropping arrangements, particularly requiring them to sell their crops to the landlords and to patronize the plantation store. Percy insisted, "We never exercised the least coercion, moral pressure or influence to induce them to trade at the store." Of course, "When they have no money they are compelled" to shop there, "because they can get credit nowhere else." Percy tried to get the Italians' business "by catering to their wants, and by competing in prices with the Greenville merchants." As for the rule that the Italians had to sell their cotton to the company (which Percy elsewhere claimed was not the case), the Crittenden Company was, he claimed, doing the Italians a service: "In the first place they know nothing of the value of cotton, and will, to a certainty be fleeced in attempting to sell it," he wrote to the head of the Mississippi Board of Trade. If they "come to Greenville in order to sell it . . . this would necessitate a very considerable loss of time from their crops." Finally, "it would be out of the question to permit them to sell their cotton until their accounts with us were paid, as it would require a regiment of Pinkerton Detectives to keep them from stealing it. They are industrious, but no more honest than the negro, and much more enterprising."[56] But Percy relented on some of the consulate's complaints. "This year [we] prepared a contract with them [the Italian tenants], giving them the right to dispose of their cotton as they see fit, after settling with us."[57]

Percy grew increasingly concerned about the Italian government's complaints. In April 1907, he traveled to Washington. While there, the planter enjoyed a friendly lunch at the White House with "Teddy" (as Percy called the president) and his family, and met with the Italian ambassador trying to soften the New Orleans consulate's rules. He had also hoped to "secure a ruling" from the Bureau of Immigration "favorable to Alien agriculturalists: that is, differentiating them from contract laborers, the import of whom is prohibited by the government." It was a curious and telling aim, for he did not dispute that the Italians at the Sunnyside Plantation were contract laborers, only that they should not be treated the same as other immigrants, because "there is no labor" to do the work of developing Mississippi. Percy repeatedly used the word "induced" to describe the Italians' immigration. (In a 1907 letter he boasted, "Quite a number of them [northern Italians] have been induced to come here.")[58]

In Washington, Percy focused mainly on the ban on induced immigration, but he soon came under investigation for violations of the federal peonage laws. In early June 1907, Ambassador Des Planches asked Secretary of State Elihu Root to launch an investigation of the Sunnyside Plantation. The ambassador had heard "numerous complaints" about "insalubrity of the soil, disease, inadequacy of medical assistance, exorbitant cost of medicines . . . , low rates of wages, lack of drinkable waters and filters, [and] general bad conditions of the farm hands, who are more like beggars than tillers of the soil." The ambassador had heard of a "woman lawyer" from New York, Mary Grace Quackenbos, who was already conducting investigations in Florida and Alabama for the Department of Justice. Could she be the one to investigate the Sunnyside Plantation? To smooth diplomatic feathers, Attorney General Charles Bonaparte accepted this unorthodox request.[59]

Bonaparte was also looking to relocate a talented troublemaker. Quackenbos's previous boss was Henry Stimson, the future secretary of war who was then the U.S. Attorney for southern New York. Stimson thought she was a competent investigator but labeled "her judgment on both the facts and the law entirely untrustworthy" and compared her to a team of horses that had never been under harness. In September 1907, the president himself wrote to ask Bonaparte, "Is Mrs. Quackenbos still connected with the Department [of Justice]? What is she doing!" As Bonaparte put it, "She and Stimson were getting along rather badly in New York." Bonaparte told President Roosevelt that he thus "seized an opportunity" created by the ambassador's request.[60]

It would be hard to imagine a person less suited to LeRoy Percy's liking than Mary Quackenbos. She was a striking figure, "tall, slender, and girlish," with black hair, eyes, and attire. But she was also a quintessential New York feminist, a wealthy divorcée and heiress with a public interest law practice on Manhattan's Lower East Side called the "People's Law Firm." Her family had held deep ties to the antebellum antislavery movement. Recently appointed the nation's first female assistant U.S. attorney, she had already been working on peonage cases in the South. The *New York Times* praised her "vivacious manner, and a glance of keen penetration." Her colleague Charles Russell called her "an enthusiast & intelligent." Bonaparte explained that she "acted from 'philanthropic motives.'"[61]

These were not qualities that would endear her to southern planters. Bonaparte explained, "She observed great secrecy, at first," in her investigations, "and had various and very romantic plans for securing access to certain closely-guarded settlements." But soon she was blunt and inelegant and a bit conniving. Early on, she had gathered evidence against southern employers by using her maiden name, Winterton, and pretending to be a magazine writer. LeRoy Percy, on the other hand, was couth and masculine and deeply conservative. And he was right that Quackenbos did not "come as an impartial investigator, but, as she says, as an advocate of the poor" who cast her "womanly sympathies" on the Italians without, in his opinion, a whit of knowledge about the realities of cotton cultivation. For Quackenbos, sexism came with the job.[62]

Percy tried his southern charm on Quackenbos, but soon she was complaining that he "had endeavored to insult me several times," and she was shocked by his "ungentlemanly behavior." At one point, her notes and papers were stolen out of her room in Greenville, and it was clear that Percy's people had done it. She later complained, "Mississippi and Arkansas regard Percy as a 'hero,'" but in her view, "he is not on the square." He was "committing crimes against the government cleverly hid."[63]

In her southern investigation, Quackenbos reserved her greatest criticism for the labor agents who recruited Italians to the Sunnyside Plantation and to other plantations across the South. These men, some based in her native New York, misled vulnerable peasants and subverted immigration law. "The labor agents, steamship agents, and planters too, knew that a penniless Italian attempting to enter with pre-paid passage was a 'public charge' under our Federal law, and that a workman engaged to cultivate cotton or work as a cotton picker was an 'alien contract worker.'" Both categories were among "the 'excluded classes'" under the law. So "agents connived to deceive the Governments here and in Italy, and taught the immigrant his first impression of America by instructing him that it was necessary to make false statements to officials on either side of the water.[64]

Quackenbos offered several examples of this practice at the Sunnyside Plantation. Humbert Pierini, hired by the Crittenden Company, had begun as a worker on the colony, but he soon moved into the recruitment business as a steamship ticket agent. He returned to the plantation as the clerk of the plantation's store, where he "placed a sign at the entrance" advertising transatlantic tickets. Pierini "supplied all its labor and began by selling tickets to friends and relatives of Italians already there." Quackenbos claimed he had "imported about 150 families to Sunny Side and to other places as well, drawing many fees in addition to his salary." Tenants "desirous of the company's favor" offered names of potential recruits. Pierini then sent the recruits a set of instructions in Italian coaching them how to answer questions from immigration officials.

Are you bound by a labor contract? Have they written you to come to this country to work? NO. NO. You have to answer that you came to this country to find your relatives, but that regarding work you are at perfect liberty to go to work where you wish and where you may find more wages and better conditions. So far as work is concerned you are not engaged or bound to anybody.

Yet Pierini printed circulars that told the plantation's residents that if they lacked money for their relatives' tickets, "I have the possibility of making them come here, with the understanding that they will place themselves to where they are assigned; lands of the most fertile, and conditions the best." For other recruits, Quackenbos alleged, Pierini provided false names of relatives or listed names of relatives without their consent. The arrival of distant relatives from the old country "would occasion surprise and consternation." Worse, "Sometimes, if an imported laborer became dissatisfied and left, the relative would be charged with his transportation debt." The plantation's on-site manager, J. B. Ray, later fired Pierini.[65]

Quackenbos also relayed harrowing tales of residents who tried to escape. "There is a disposition on some plantations to terrorize the foreigners and keep them in a constant state of fear and dread. This is particularly so at Sunny Side." One tenant claimed he "was warned by Manager Wright and the Italian 'boss' Catalani" that if he left the plantation, the overseers " 'would blow his brains out.'" Angelo Casavecchia and Domenico Nobili amassed large debts in their two years at the plantation, where Nobili's child had also died. The two fled in April 1907, first by steamboat to Greenville, then by boarding a train for Birmingham, Alabama.

> While sitting in the [rail]car and before the train started O. B. Crittenden, their landlord, with several other men appeared, and ordered them to leave the car which they refused to do. Mr. Crittenden thereupon called Casavecchia out on the platform while a Greenville policeman took Nobili. Their railroad tickets were taken from them and they were searched. A Sicilian named Guarino was called to interpret for Mr. Crittenden. He then threatened these Italians with arrest and sentence to the chain gang [which he had no legal right to do] if they refused to return. Casavecchi said he would not allow himself to be arrested and would send for his consul. Mr. Crittenden, however, still threatening, escorted them to a gasoline boat which he hired and forced them to return to Sunny Side.

Another example relayed the story of two Italian families who tried to escape and "were later discovered" by a plantation manager, "who threatened them with arrest," dragged them into Crittenden's office, and "ordered them to return to Sunny Side to work out their debts. The women and children were crying, and in fear of the chain gang the families returned." The plantation's manager gave her a list of thirty families who had fled the colony. Father Galloni claimed that "more than 100 persons escaped from this locality" in the course of a year. Family stories handed down for a century corroborate these affidavits.[66]

Quackenbos depicted the plantation's managers as modern-day slave catchers. In other words, she saw the Italians at the plantation being treated like black people. Quackenbos shared a widespread tendency to see grievances against white immigrants as worse than those against African Americans. "Like a galvanic shock," a national article on peonage cases in Florida argued, "it undermines our self-importance to find this new form of slavery places white and black on a plane of perfect equality." The whites included "starving Jews, decrepit Poles, and mangy Scandinavians," and the motivation was capitalist greed.[67]

Quackenbos's own report on peonage painted a romanticized image of Italy as a paradise in contrast to Mississippi's humid hell for white people from Italy. "I found illness in nearly every home—and those that were working were yellow and lean and sickly," she wrote. "The conditions for agriculture there are wonderfully rich, but *for white human beings,* sadly deplorable. . . . Investigation shows that sickness comes to him more quickly and detrimentally than to native Americans of the South, white or colored, because the Italian is not accustomed to swamps [emphasis added]." Yet managers showed "little disposition to separate them from the negro race or differentiate them in their treatment." She even "found instances where Italians work for negroes."[68]

In October 1907, on Quackenbos's recommendation, a federal grand jury indicted Orlando B. Crittenden on peonage charges. (A month earlier Bonaparte had told Roosevelt that Quackenbos did not have evidence for these charges, but that the Sunnyside Company had likely violated contract labor laws.) LeRoy Percy believed the charge was revenge for his resistance to her inquiries. Her final report had been submitted a few weeks earlier. Percy shared a "great deal of concern" with his son, Will, about "the injustice, the studied perversion of truth accompanying the report, and the feeling of helplessness caused by finding the government apparently in all of its departments bent solely upon securing an indictment." Bonaparte's view was that Quackenbos could not understand that poverty did not necessarily make someone guilty of a crime: "Mrs. Quackenbos is unable to give the matter judicial consideration because of her earnest desire that all persons shall be relieved of poverty and because of her inability to understand that certain persons might be very comfortable and yet seem very miserable and squalid to her eyes."[69]

Percy was powerful enough to meet with President Roosevelt personally to discuss the case. Roosevelt was sympathetic but promised nothing. In the end, the case was doomed by being locally prosecuted. Percy served as Crittenden's attorney in a local jury selection for the federal court in Greenville. The local clerk of the court fashioned "a Grand Jury fairly drawn" (in Percy's view) and made up of "ten or twelve men well acquainted with conditions throughout the Delta" (sympathetic to planters, in other words) and "a friend of mine" as foreman. Percy spent a week "nursing . . . the Federal Grand jury . . . as tenderly as a mother ever nursed a stricken loved one," to help Crittenden escape conviction. Percy succeeded; no one on the jury believed he could be convicted in a local court.[70]

The backlash against Quackenbos was not over. Mississippi's William Humphreys, who represented Greenville in Congress, announced on the House floor that Quackenbos had "taken advantage of all the courtesies extended by a gracious people." The Sunnyside Plantation "was a model colony," yet Quackenbos had claimed to find "a system of bondage existing uniformly where Italians are employed. The so-called 'colonists,'" according to her, "are in reality, slaves, and are treated worse than the negroes." Congressman Frank Clark of Florida (home to Quackenbos's first and most extended peonage investigation) accused the attorney general of having neglected "the law business of the United States Government" in launching "a crusade in certain States to regulate sociological conditions." Bonaparte had sent a "lady . . . whose field of labor . . . was in the slums of the east side of dear old Manhattan isle" to a place she knew nothing about.[71]

Humphreys and Clark resolved to use the Dillingham Commission to refute Quackenbos's work. On March 2, 1908, the two sponsored a Congressional resolution "that the Immigration Commission be requested to make an investigation into the treatment and conditions of work of immigrants on the cotton plantations of the Mississippi Delta, in the States of Mississippi and

Arkansas, and to report thereon at the earliest possible date." This was the only direct interference by Congress into the commission's work during its four years of investigations.[72]

Initially, the South appears to have been an afterthought for the commission. Southerners John Burnett and Asbury Latimer were unpopular with their fellow commission members, and the two disagreed with each other about immigration restriction. In 1907, a subcommittee on immigration in the South seemed mainly a vehicle for Latimer's patronage. After Charles Neill worked up a general plan, in January 1908 the commission hired L. Martin Heard, Latimer's son-in-law, to serve as its superintendent. Latimer was an opponent of restriction, and Heard was a banker in Elberton, South Carolina, with no apparent experience of immigration or social science.[73]

But Latimer died three weeks after Heard was hired. In late February, Senator Anselm McLaurin of Mississippi replaced Latimer. In March, Humphreys and Williams made their resolution for the Dillingham Commission to do its own study of peonage. After Heard resigned, he was replaced by a seasoned civil servant, Major W. A. Rauch. Rauch endeavored to investigate "the immigration problem peculiar to that section," but the study was now under the control of the Dillingham Commission's Washington office and would not get a separate published volume. The southern study had suddenly gained unwanted attention.[74]

Clark and Humphrey's resolution accelerated the Dillingham Commission's work in the South. McLaurin became the head of a new subcommittee, which also included New Yorker William Bennet. Commission members authorized an additional five thousand dollars to investigate "the existence of, or the non-existence of, peonage in that community [the South]." In summer 1909, the peonage report received another five thousand dollars in appropriations. In a departure from its usual practices, the subcommittee on peonage could "subpoena witnesses, and hear their testimony, and report their findings, with the evidence, to the Commission."[75]

But none of this testimony, if it was ever collected, appeared in the final peonage report.[76] The commission's peonage study expanded from the South to the national level, with the implicit goal of de-emphasizing the region's role in the problem. At least two or three other agents worked on the investigation, including John Clifton Elder, a young lawyer from Georgia whose research took him from Mississippi to Maine. Something in his work did not please them, however; just months after giving him a raise, the commission tabled Elder's report on peonage in the state of Maine.[77]

After devoting at least fifteen thousand dollars and several field agents to the study, the final report on peonage was a perfunctory seven pages of generalities that reported only a fraction of the research conducted. True to the intentions of Congressmen Humphreys and Williams, it emphasized that conditions of peonage existed in all regions of the country, with "only sporadic instances" of peonage in the South. The brief summary shifted attention to the North: "In connection with the southern cases," it noted, "in nearly every instance brought to the attention of the Commission the laborers who were held in peonage had been sent south from New York City, the victims of gross misrepresentations," by corrupt labor agents. Although commission members had personally investigated several cases of peonage in the American West, they noted that none, as far as they could tell, had been prosecuted. The report did summarize violations in the Maine lumber industry uncovered by Elder, where the commission claimed that a new state statute had all but solved the problem. It concluded, "While from time to time sporadic cases of peonage have occurred in nearly all the states, there is no apparent general system of peonage and no sentiment supporting it anywhere. . . . The law as to peonage does not require any amendment, and its enforcement is reasonably sufficient" in states that have prosecuted it. In short, the report said, there was nothing to worry about.[78]

The Sunnyside Plantation did not appear in the peonage report at all. LeRoy Percy must have had a hand in that decision. In December 1910, as the commission was making final edits and approvals of the reports, Percy complained that "much of it is very interesting, but of course it is impossible for me to do more than hurriedly glance at it." He did, however, take time to read the topics dearest to him, such as the peonage report—and memorably called Elder an "ass." An unfavorable review of the plantation would hardly have matched the fulsome travelogue that appeared in Volume 22. For Percy personally, and for the credibility of the commission more generally, it made sense to avoid the Sunnyside Plantation controversies.[79]

Not coincidentally, in the same month that Percy was busy bowdlerizing the peonage report, Mary Quackenbos published an article in the popular magazine *Pearson's*, which stated that a "U.S. Senator from Mississippi" who served on the Immigration Commission "has been also a big importer of immigrants." Her article was so negative that the IRL ordered twenty thousand copies to distribute as a repudiation of distribution policy.[80]

In the end, the attorney general's various peonage investigations yielded a few convictions, as well as two U.S. Supreme Court cases, decided in 1911 and 1914. The legacy of these peonage cases was equivocal. Both cases involved black workers, and both upheld the constitutionality of the federal law against peonage. The rulings offered two rare victories for civil rights from a conservative court in the age of Jim Crow.[81]

Peonage persisted in the South until well into the twentieth century. The laws, as Mary Quackenbos had observed and Percy's interference in Crittenden's case had shown, were nearly impossible to enforce in southern courts. Moreover, the Supreme Court upheld the Peonage Act on the relatively narrow grounds of freedom of contract, rather than arguing that these arrangements violated the Thirteenth Amendment by constituting slavery, as some reformers had hoped they would.[82]

In the final analysis, the Dillingham Commission described the Sunnyside Plantation in glowing terms and whitewashed debt peonage. It was easy, then, for its final recommendations to include a long paragraph (twice as long as the one about Asian exclusion) expressing continued support of immigrant distribution policy. Distribution did not undermine the American standard of living, as defined by the desired wages of white native-born workers. The goal of experiments such as the Sunnyside Plantation was to put Italians in direct competition only with African Americans, not with other whites. As a result, the far more widespread abuse and debt peonage of African Americans remained unaddressed. For all the impediments to their success—poverty, isolation, illness, language barriers, the duplicity of employers—immigrants like those at the Sunnyside Plantation had advantages over their African American coworkers, not least their whiteness. Immigrants attracted notice from more successful compatriots and policy makers, were interesting and exotic, and—above all—had ambassadors and consuls who at least occasionally looked after their welfare. The zealous Mary Quackenbos had only gone to the Sunnyside Plantation after the Italian ambassador's complaint to Elihu Root and Charles Bonaparte. African Americans could (maybe) complain to their foremen, or to their ministers, or try to escape the plantation or the South. They had no foreign government to support them. Although immigration was increasingly the purview of domestic policy, foreign relations still mattered.[83]

The Italian colonies of the South never made a noticeable dent in national settlement patterns, although a small Italian presence in Mississippi and Arkansas persists. The Delta remained blacker than it did Italian, and distribution never solved the "immigration problem." The Great Migration of African Americans accelerated during World War I, only to deepen the labor shortages that had prompted planters to look to Europe for workers in the first place. But by then, most white southerners had turned sharply against immigrants and would in the 1920s build a new Ku Klux Klan that vilified Catholics and Jews—once the elite of Greenville—almost as much as African Americans.[84]

LeRoy Percy gave up on Italian labor. He had succeeded in influencing the Dillingham Commission's reports, but he was disillusioned. His partner had been indicted. The Sunnyside Plantation was an economic failure and a diplomatic nightmare. By the end of 1910, Percy had changed his mind about Italians and told the other commission members so. It was too hard to get them, they complained too much, and the people of his state did not want them. On November 8, the IRL's Joseph Lee claimed Percy "is really against us tooth and nail." Two weeks later, he reported that Percy had complained to his fellow southerner Burnett that "those Italians stole worse than the niggers."[85]

The Sunnyside Plantation experiment ended not long after the Dillingham Commission printed its reports. In 1912, the boll weevil and floods inundated Sunnyside, destroying what was left of the Italian colony's profitability. In 1907, the plantation had had more than 120 Italian families; by 1912, it had just 60. Some families moved to cities, others to more prosperous agricultural settlements, where they were better treated. In 1913, the Sunnyside Company sold the plantation. In 1918, the always resourceful Percy was looking into whether Germans paroled from World War I enemy alien camps could come to work in Mississippi, where he still ran plantations. During the New Deal, the plantation became an experimental camp for the federal Resettlement Administration.[86]

By the time of the Dillingham Commission's investigation of the Sunny-side Plantation, two narratives had emerged. Side by side, the two stories reveal competing visions and anxieties about the immigrants, race, and labor at the turn of the century. One story, the one articulated first by LeRoy Percy and echoed by the Dillingham Commission, depicted a noble experiment that might save what was best about the South. The other version, expressed in the skeptical reports of Italian diplomats and Mary Quackenbos, saw immigrants as hapless victims of colonial overlords first in the old country, then in the new. In 1913, Italian ambassador Des Planches wrote a treatise on Italian emigration in the United States. Like other critics, he blamed capitalism for the treatment of the South's newest class of peons. The Sunnyside Company, he wrote, "tries to obtain the maximum profit from its immigrants without reciprocating on their behalf. The Italian immigrant at Sunnyside is a human production machine. He is better off than the black man, more perfect than he is, but like the black man, still a machine."[87]

The authors of each version held fast to their truths: In Percy's version and the agriculture reports, the labor shortage was a fact that must be solved. In the version of the Italian diplomats and Mary Quackenbos, peonage and coercion were facts, as was Italians having been reduced to little better than black sharecroppers. For Percy, the failure to solve these problems would lead to the tragedy of the South's decline, to underdevelopment, and to personal financial loss. For the Italian officials and Quackenbos, the tragedy was one of taking predatory advantage of one nation's underclass, putting it at risk of becoming another country's underclass, and, indeed, at risk of losing—or of never gaining—the racial privilege this hard-working proletariat deserved.

Both versions hinged on a critique of the labor system as it was, accompanied by an idealized version of what it might be, and who stood to benefit. Should federal immigration policy benefit employers or workers? Should it benefit one region over another? Balancing those interests became the central challenge of deciding what conclusions the Dillingham Commission should ultimately make. Mary Quackenbos suggested a federal labor bureau to manage foreign immigrants' work, but this was one manifestation of federal power that the commission declined to recommend.

LeRoy Percy's own abandonment of the dream of immigrant distribution symbolized a larger southern acquiescence to federal power. It was a solution that avoided complexity. Many southerners had opposed the 1907 immigration bill because of its ban on state recruitment of immigrants, but also because it bestowed powers on the federal government. John Burnett had been one of the leaders of the opposition.[88] In the years hence, southerners grew more amenable to federal power, at least certain kinds. After *Plessy v. Ferguson* in 1896, the federal government shrank from preventing segregation. Jim Crow was firmly embedded in state constitutions and was only advancing.[89] In 1911, Percy lost his Senate seat to the unvarnished populist demagogue governor, James K. Vardaman. The South's growing zeal for nativism triumphed over any lingering concerns about the federal power invested in immigration restriction. Even if the final reports were ambivalent about the impact of immigrants, the Dillingham Commission's recommendations would not be.

The failure of distribution ventures such as the Sunnyside Plantation would become fodder for erstwhile supporters of restriction such as LeRoy Percy and William Dillingham to strengthen restriction. In 1914, Dillingham gave a speech on the Senate floor asking whether immigrants had "come with the purpose of making the United States their residence? . . . Have they brought their wives? Have they brought their children? Are they actuated by a desire to enter into our life and to find their development under American institutions? *In other words, have they sought the soil, or are they the denizens of the cities, belonging to a floating population, unrecognized by the permanent population except as so many labor units?*" The old immigrants, Dillingham said, "sought the soil and open[ed] up farms. What about the new?" According to the census, in 1909 "only nine-tenths of 1 per cent of these nationalities [were] operating farms in the United States, either as owners or as tenants. Think of it! After 30 years' inflow of these nationalities less than 1 per cent of the men could be found operating farms in the United States." Here, to Dillingham, was incontrovertible evidence of the new immigrants' inferiority.[90] Restriction seemed almost inevitable.

Epilogue

As 1910 drew to a close, the Dillingham Commission rushed to compile and edit the last reports and to write their conclusions and recommendations. It was not entirely clear what these would be. The commission, IRL secretary Joseph Lee observed, "was not made up altogether of friends of restriction, having about two or three good restrictionists, one or two dilutionists [distribution advocates], and the rest more or less open to public opinion." IRL officials fretted over Senator Dillingham's commitment, questioned even their stalwart Henry Cabot Lodge, and campaigned successfully against William Bennet and LeRoy Percy's reelections that November. Three of the men—Percy, Bennet, and New Jersey's Benjamin Howell—were lame ducks by the time they wrote their recommendations.[1]

Joseph Lee need not have worried. Behind the scenes, the commission members were indeed divided over the literacy test. But John Burnett, the strongest restrictionist in the group, eventually called for consensus. In the end, all but William Bennet—longtime ally of the Jewish lobby—concurred on the crucial points. Their opening statement maintained that immigration policy should consider both "quality and quantity." Their four pages of recommendations were uniformly restrictive. LeRoy Percy's conversion to pessimism about immigrants may well have swung a vote or two. The commission continued to recommend distribution, but it did so alongside new suggestions for federal laws that limited immigrant entry.[2]

The recommendations suggested that the existing exclusion of Chinese remain permanent and that the temporary ban on Japanese and Korean immigrants be maintained (although it recommended no new legislation). About European immigration, the commission concluded that the federal government needed to exclude enough people "to produce a marked effect" on the general "oversupply of unskilled labor." It recommended a "limitation of the number of each race arriving each year to a certain percentage of the average of that race arriving during a given period of years"—a quota. It also proposed "as far as possible" keeping out aliens who "by reason of their personal qualities or habits, would least readily be assimilated or would make the least desirable citizens."

Its chief recommendation was the literacy requirement. William Bennet issued a half-page dissent opposing the literacy rule, "a selective test for which no logical argument can be based on this report." Since the recommendations gathered a lot more attention than the rest of the volumes, Bennet's dissent was the only window most observers had on the internal inconsistencies, differences of opinion, and equivocal evidence in the reports.[3]

It was not inevitable that the commissioners would recommend these restrictions. The evidence presented in their own volumes did not support the weight of their conclusions. There were places in the text where they admitted as much. But the pressure to recommend decisive action was strong. A mandate by Congress to solve the "immigration problem" necessitated a clear response. Congress had put aside immigration legislation while the commission did its work. Calls for restrictions from other arenas grew louder, too. The Panic of 1907 had alarmed white labor leaders about unemployment and wavering standards of living. And the establishment of the Eugenics Records Office in 1910 by Charles Davenport had given an American home to eugenic ideas that had begun in Europe.

Above all, Dillingham Commission members held close ties to academia, the Republican Party, and organizations such as the National Civic Federation, all of which valued study, solution, and policy. They produced a particular kind of knowledge, accepted because it was quantitative and produced by experts. But they did not necessarily follow it to its nuanced and conflicting conclusions. They believed in federal power in general, and in federal power over immigration policy specifically. So too, did, the commission's rank-and-file employees, from the women who enjoyed rare career opportunities and personal authority to the technocrats who had worked in Puerto Rico and the Philippines. The burgeoning authority of social science and certitude in its modern facts encouraged statist solutions to social problems.

For most immigrants studied and interviewed by the Dillingham Commission, the experience was probably a fleeting annoyance, just another intrusion by reformers and government workers with little impact on their lives. Some might have had stronger feelings, a few with hopes that their participation might publicize their point of view (such as the Japanese farmers interviewed by Yakamoto Ichichashi) or might right wrongs (such as the prostitutes who shared information with undercover investigators for the white slavery reports). Others clearly resented the queries, such as the father who refused to let his children be measured for Boas. Some immigrants must have feared the work, especially those who had to endure being barraged with questions by interviewers who worked not for the commission but for their own employers.

Many of the Dillingham Commission's volumes were like other government reports, easily ignored or forgotten. Even the commissioner-general of the Bureau of Immigration, Charles Nagel, read only the abstracts, not the reports. "As to the forty volumes," he told Simon Wolf, "I feel constrained to consider my limited time and my obligations to my family."[4] Indeed, the commission's brief list of recommendations in the first volume had remarkable influence. With the exception of barring single men from entry, versions of all of its other recommendations were eventually incorporated into federal law. Few federal commissions—if any—have ever enjoyed such success.

By 1911, John Burnett and William Dillingham were now the chairs, respectively, of the House and Senate Immigration Committees, where they worked up bills based on the commission's conclusions. Drafting the bills took them longer than expected—the old tradition of immigration policy as diplomacy had not yet died out. Dillingham was still unconvinced about the literacy test, but, once again, pressure from Burnett and others convinced him to include it. In 1913, the Burnett-Dillingham bill passed both houses of Congress. It included a literacy test, an increased head tax, and the explicit exclusion of anyone ineligible for citizenship (in other words, the Japanese as well as the Chinese). Dillingham—who still subscribed to a diplomatic rather than legislative approach to Asian exclusion—had to be pressured into the last provision, which went beyond the commission's own prescription. In the end, President Taft vetoed the bill after William Bennet (who had won back a House seat) invited him to meet with immigrant leaders in his Manhattan Congressional district. In 1915 President Wilson vetoed another version of the bill, even after William Husband and Jeremiah Jenks met with him personally to urge him to sign it.[5]

A similar bill passed yet again in 1917. Its central feature was the literacy test, but it also created an "Asiatic barred zone" from India to China to New Guinea (though not Japan) that used geographical boundaries to codify racial exclusion, the head tax increase, and a new system of immigrant health inspections. President Woodrow Wilson used a pocket veto at the end of the session. But in the throes of World War I, this time a Democratically controlled Congress marshaled the votes to override the veto of a president from its own party. The literacy test was finally law.

As Taft's and Wilson's vetoes showed, the executive branch continued to resist an immigration policy driven by domestic concerns and prejudice. The Dillingham Commission had specifically recommended restriction on "economic, moral, and social considerations," not on racial, "ethnical," or eugenic ones. But in the intervening years, the diplomatic priorities of an earlier era had lost ground to increasing nativism and isolationism. Ironically, presidents who generally called for limited government—Warren G. Harding and Calvin Coolidge—were the custodians of this shift toward greater federal power over immigration policy, pushed by newly powerful West Coast anti-Asian activists. In surprising ways, the history of immigration policy is the history of states ceding power to the state—that is, the kind of power monopolized and exercised by the federal government.[6]

It is possible to explain the passage of the quota laws of 1921 and 1924 with an equation we could call the "Immigration Problem":

Dillingham Commission Reports + Red Scare + Eugenics =
Immigration Restriction

The commission's most important contribution to the equation was to define immigration as a "problem" in the first place. In January 1911, Max Kohler

and Jacob Schiff gave speeches on the "Immigration Question, with particular reference to the Jews of America." They were trying to maintain the
terminology of "question" instead of "problem," but it was not to last.
Jeremiah Jenks and W. Jett Lauck, rushing their summary of the commission's reports into press, called it *The Immigration Problem*. A question
needed answers; a problem, fixes. All the fixes Jenks and Lauck suggested
involved federal action.[7]

The terms of the equation are in chronological order. The commission's
reports were completed in early 1911, the Red Scare flamed fears of foreign
radicals in 1919, and the eugenics movement began to explode in popularity.
In 1913, the IRL's cofounder Robert D. Ward had called for "the application
of eugenics to the American immigration problem"—in other words, this
had not yet happened. That same year, Jeremiah Jenks gave a lecture in
which he called for immigration restrictions but emphasized that the reasons for these restrictions were purely economic and went "far beyond prejudice." Jenks's kind of argument was losing ground. Eugenics received an
official federal stamp of approval when the House Immigration Committee
appointed the Eugenic Records Office's Harry Laughlin as its "eugenics
expert" in 1920.[8]

The unreconstructed John Burnett died in 1919. Two years later, Congress
passed the Emergency Quota Act of 1921, which created the first numerical
restrictions (albeit relatively generous) on immigration in American history.[9]
Senator Dillingham, who had been a voice of moderation, especially on the
issue of legislative Asian exclusion, died in 1923. Henry Cabot Lodge—more
famous now for his obstruction of U.S. membership in the League of Nations
than for his association with immigration—lived to see the passage in May 1924
of the Johnson-Reed Act, and died six months later. The law created an annual quota of 2 percent of the total number of each nationality in the U.S. population according to the 1890 census. By using a baseline year that predated
the large-scale settlement of southern and eastern Europeans to the United
States, the Johnson-Reed Act effectively turned the clock back to the immigration patterns before 1880. The discriminatory quotas dictated that 82 percent of the slots go to western and northern Europe, and just 16 percent to
southern and eastern Europe. Dillingham Commission executive secretary
William Husband took credit for the quota system in his new capacity as
commissioner-general of immigration (1921–1924). Husband later remarked

that he preferred the quota over the literacy test as a restriction method because "it promised mathematical certainty instead of a theoretical result" based on estimating the number of illiterates.[10]

After World War I, Japan introduced an amendment to the Versailles Treaty calling for racial equality between nations. (And Yamato Ichihashi named his only son "Woodrow.") The Japanese amendment spoke to the troubled history of its relations with erstwhile allies such as the United States. The proposal was defeated. In the aftermath of the Versailles Treaty, immigration policy makers, increasingly insular, reverted to an insistently domestic policy. U.S. senator James D. Phelan offered perhaps the most emphatic example. His 1920 campaign posters proclaimed, "Keep California White." In 1924, he wrote, "You know, of course, that immigration is conceded to be a domestic question and is not a proper subject for international discussion, nor has the United States any treaty with any other nation affecting immigration. The so-called 'Gentlemen's Agreement' with Japan is wholly exceptional." The Immigration Act of 1924 went farther than the Asiatic Barred Zone of 1917 by legislating the ban on any "alien ineligible for naturalization" (which included the Japanese). Japanese newspapers called the day the law went into effect "National Humiliation Day"; the law's sponsor, Washington senator Albert Johnson, called it "America's Second Declaration of Independence." These measures were a direct repudiation of what the commission's own experts H. A. Millis and Yamato Ichihashi had recommended.[11]

Then, in 1929, a legislative tweak changed the baseline for the numerical limits to an arcane "national-origins quota system." A formula that was as sociological as it was mathematical was calculated by Census demographer Joseph Hill, who had written the Dillingham Commission's reports on immigrant occupations and female fecundity. Hill's methodology excluded people of African ancestry and overcounted western Europeans. Several countries, including Greece, Turkey, and Bulgaria, ended up with quotas under 400 people each; Germany's was 26,000. The law also implemented an overall cap of 150,000 immigrants for each year—regardless of whether a country's individual quota had filled. The cap was designed to reduce the total numbers of migrants, and thus the competition among unskilled laborers. The quota for Asians—from India to the South Pacific—was zero, a racist and inflammatory move that the late Senator Dillingham and his close adviser William Husband had spent years opposing.[12]

In 1927, Max Kohler blamed the quota laws in part on the commission's use of "race or people" as an organizing principle. In a private letter to William Husband, Kohler wrote, "I think the action of the Commission, in conducting all its investigations in terms of race, was most deplorable and greatly injured the position of millions of residents of our country." It was, he continued, "a great blow at true American ideals" because "it led logically to Quota Laws, based on racial distinctions and preferences, which I abhor." For his part, Simon Wolf would protest defining Jews as a race until the end of his days.[13]

As we have already seen, the Dillingham Commission all but ignored today's largest group of migrants. In 1911, Mexicans constituted only a tiny proportion of the immigration stream. Ten years later, it would be a different story. The Mexican Revolution and bad blood between the Wilson administration and Mexico made national headlines and drew the attention of foreign-policy expert Lodge. Between 1910 and 1920, the census count of Mexicans living in the United States (which was likely low because many Mexicans were seasonal workers) tripled. Although Burnett sought to restrict Mexicans in the 1917 law, Secretary of Labor William B. Wilson made temporary exceptions for Mexicans and Canadians due to wartime labor shortages. Burnett grudgingly acquiesced.[14] The secretary of labor's decision to let in temporary Mexican workers during World War I angered many labor-union interests and nativists. Thanks to the Mexican Revolution and the temporary exemptions from the head tax and literacy test, the number of Mexicans in the United States increased rapidly after the commission completed its report.

In the 1920s, once the quotas on eastern and southern Europeans choked off other migrant flows, Mexicans began to assume a greater real and symbolic importance in immigration debates. As eugenics rose in influence, racialized denunciation of Mexicans became more frequent. Nevertheless, Mexicans would not have a numerical limit until the Hart-Celler Act of 1965.[15]

In a radio interview in 1931, William Husband predicted, "It is very certain that the country will never return to the open door policy which prevailed before the adoption of the quota limit system."[16] Each of the restriction laws would change over time—in 1943 wartime diplomacy with China demanded a nominal end to the ban on Asian immigration, the unequal quotas and the literacy test ceased with the Hart-Celler Act of 1965, and Latin American immigration became a top priority in the form of border security. Yet the framework envisioned by the Dillingham Commission and implemented by Congress still shapes our federal immigration policy.

The Dillingham Commission emphasized problems, data, and exclusion in its recommendations; it avoided praise, alternative explanations, or the promotion of federal efforts at assimilating immigrants. To this day, the United States has a federal immigration policy, but no assimilation or integration policy. A version of the literacy tests survives in our citizenship exams, and our immigration system is still undergirded by a numerical quota system. Equally important, the economic impact of immigrants remains the predominant issue of political and public debate. Above all, the idea of immigration as a "problem" for the federal government to fix has become so obvious across the political spectrum that it is almost impossible to question.

The Dillingham Commission's work was both a product of its era and a lasting influence on contemporary immigration policy. Just because the Hart-Celler Act created "parity" in the quota system did not make it "fair"; the absurdity of giving neighboring Mexico the same quota as overseas nations has helped create the crisis over undocumented immigration.[17] The Dillingham Commission's quotas and economic conditions are historical artifacts of their time—one of fear of immigrants, boundless confidence in expertise, and optimism about the possibilities of government. Of these, only the first appears persistent in American culture and politics.

Almost everyone involved in the Dillingham Commission was dedicated to the ideal of objectivity. Their recommendation for a quota system looked bad even by the 1930s, when it cost the lives of thousands of European Jews trying to escape the Nazis, and it took decades to repair. The Dillingham Commission's reports and the particular ways they conceptualized immigration as a "problem" paved the way for a breathtaking expansion in the immigration bureaucracy and enforcement regime, and its quota recommendations still shape the demographics of the United States. The laws it recommended—though since modified—remain the shell from which modern immigration policy emerged. In this sense, the story of the Dillingham Commission is both a cautionary tale and a necessary history of the present.

Dillingham Commission Members and Selected Staff

Appointed Members

Unless otherwise stated, members' appointments ran from 1907 to 1911.

EXPERTS

Jeremiah Jenks. Professor of Political Economy, Cornell University.

Charles P. Neill. Professor of Economics, Catholic University, and U.S. Commissioner of Labor, 1905–1913.

William P. Wheeler. San Francisco wholesale hardware businessman, Assistant Secretary of Labor and Commerce, 1908–1911. Became president of the San Francisco Chamber of Commerce.

UNITED STATES HOUSE OF REPRESENTATIVES

William Bennet. Republican from New York.

John Burnett. Democrat from Alabama.

Benjamin Howell. Republican from New Jersey.

UNITED STATES SENATE

William P. Dillingham. Republican from Vermont.

Henry Cabot Lodge. Republican from Massachusetts.

Asbury Latimer, 1907–February 1908 (death). Democrat from South Carolina.

Anselm McLaurin, February 1908–December 1909 (death). Democrat from Mississippi.

LeRoy Percy, February 1910–1911. Democrat from Mississippi.

Notable Staff

Franz Boas. Anthropologist. Author, vol. 38.

Alexander E. Cance. Agricultural economist. Author, vols. 21–22.

Frederick Croxton. Chief statistician for Dillingham Commission. Author, vol. 3. Also worked on vols. 34–35.

Roland P. Falkner. Economist and Commissioner of Education of Puerto Rico, 1904–1907. Author, vols. 29–33. Left the Dillingham Commission to become financial representative of the Republic of Liberia.

Daniel Folkmar. Anthropologist. Lieutenant Governor, Philippine Civil Service, 1903–1907. Author, vol. 5.

Elnora Cuddeback Folkmar. Medical Doctor. Assistant, vol. 5. Became National Woman's Party activist and public speaker on eugenics.

E. A. Goldenweiser. Economist. Author, vols. 26–27. Later worked for the Department of Agriculture and Federal Reserve System.

Anna Herkner. Settlement House director and Slavic languages expert. Author, vol. 37, pt. 1. Later Assistant Chief of the Maryland Bureau of Statistics and Information, American Friends Service Committee volunteer in Russia, and member of the National Woman's Party.

Joseph Hill. Economist. Author, vol. 28. Became Chief Statistician, U.S. Census in 1909.

William W. Husband. Vermont newspaperman and public servant. Executive Secretary (Chief of Staff) of Dillingham Commission. Author, vol. 40. Former Chief of Staff, Sen. William P. Dillingham. Became U.S. commissioner-general of immigration, 1921–1924, where he implemented the national-origins quotas.

Yamato Ichihashi. Special agent, vols. 23–25. Japanese immigrant and Stanford University undergraduate and later professor. Interned at Santa Anita Racetrack, World War II.

W. Jett Lauck. Economist. Staffer for the Dillingham Commission. Directed vols. 6–20.

Mary Louise Mark. Social worker. Lead investigative agent, vols. 26–27. Later became a professor of social work at Ohio State University.

Henry A. Millis. Stanford University economist. Author, vols. 23–25. Served on the first National Labor Relations Board and chaired its second term.

Mary Philbrook. Republican lawyer and suffrage activist. Anonymous author, vol. 37, pt. 2. Joined National Woman's Party.

Juliet Stewart Poyntz (née Points). Feminist labor activist. Field agent, vols. 26–27. Later joined Communist Party of USA, and reportedly killed by Soviet Secret Police.

H. Parker Willis. Economist. Editorial adviser to the Immigration Commission. First secretary of the Federal Reserve System, 1914–1918. First president of the Philippine National Bank. Son of Olympia Brown, prominent suffragist and first female ordained minister in the United States.

Dillingham Commission Reports

Volume 1: *Abstracts of Reports of the Immigration Commission* (in two volumes: vol. I), *with Conclusions and Recommendations, and Views of Minority* [Serial set no. 5865, Senate document 747/1, session 61–3, session-date: 1910, 1911].

Volume 2: *Abstracts of Reports of the Immigration Commission* (in two volumes: vol. II) [Serial Set no. 5866, Senate document 747/3, session 61–3, session-date: 1910, 1911] p. 253–290: Immigrants in charity hospitals [Serial set no. 5866, Senate document 747/5, session 61–3, session-date: 1910, 1911].

Volume 3: *Statistical Review of Immigration, 1819–1910—Distribution of Immigrants 1850–1900* [Serial set no. 5878, Senate document 756/1, session 61–3, session-date: 1910, 1911].

Volume 4: *Emigration Conditions in Europe: General Survey; Italy; Russia; Austria-Hungary; Greece* [Serial set no. 5870, Senate document 748, session 61–3, session-date: 1910, 1911].

Volume 5: *Dictionary of Races or Peoples* [Serial set no. 5867, Senate document 662, session 61–3, session-date: 1910, 1911].

Volume 6: *Immigrants in Industries: Pt. 1, Bituminous Coal Mining, Vol. 1* [Serial set no. 5667, Senate document 633/1, session 61–2, session-date: 1909, 1910].

Volume 7: *Immigrants in Industries: Pt. 1, Bituminous Coal Mining, Vol. 2* [Serial set no. 5668, Senate document 633/2, session 61–2, session-date: 1909, 1910].

Volume 8: *Immigrants in Industries: Pt. 2, Iron and Steel Manufacturing, Vol. 1* [Serial set no. 5669, Senate document 633/3, session 61–2, session-date: 1909, 1910].

Volume 9: *Immigrants in Industries: Pt. 2, Iron and Steel Manufacturing, Vol. 2* [Serial set no. 5670, Senate document 633/4, session 61–2, session-date: 1909, 1910].

Volume 10: *Immigrants in Industries: Pt. 3, Cotton Goods Manufacturing in the North Atlantic States* [Serial set no. 5671, Senate document 633/5, session 61–2, session-date: 1909, 1910]
Pt. 4, p. 635, *Woolen and Worsted Goods Manufacturing* [Serial set no. 5671, Senate document 633/6, session 61–2, session-date: 1909, 1910].

Volume 11: *Immigrants in Industries: Pt. 5, Silk Goods Manufacturing and Dyeing* [Serial set no. 5672, Senate document 633/7, session 61–2, session-date: 1909, 1910]
Pt. 6, p. 253, *Clothing Manufacturing* [Serial set no. 5672, Senate document 633/8, session 61–2, session-date: 1909, 1910]
Pt. 7, p. 663, *Collar, Cuff, and Shirt Manufacturing* [Serial set no. 5672, Senate document 633/9, session 61–2, session-date: 1909, 1910].

Volume 12: *Immigrants in Industries: Pt. 8, Leather Manufacturing* [Serial set no. 5673, Senate document 633/10, session 61–2, session-date: 1909, 1910]
Pt. 9, p. 203, *Boot and Shoe Manufacturing* [Serial set no. 5673, Senate document 633/11, session 61–2, session-date: 1909, 1910]
Pt. 10, p. 773, *Glove Manufacturing* [Serial set no. 5673, Senate document 633/12, session 61–2, session-date: 1909, 1910].

Volume 13: *Immigrants in Industries: Pt. 11, Slaughtering and Meat Packing* [Serial set no. 5674, Senate document 633/13, session 61–2, session-date: 1909, 1910].

Volume 14: *Immigrants in Industries: Pt. 12, Glass Manufacturing* [Serial set no. 5675, Senate document 633/14, session 61–2, session-date: 1909, 1910]
Pt. 13, p. 395, *Agricultural Implement and Vehicle Manufacturing* [Serial set no. 5675, Senate document 633/15, session 61–2, session-date: 1909, 1910].

Volume 15: *Immigrants in Industries: Pt. 14, Cigar and Tobacco Manufacturing* [Serial set no. 5676, Senate document 633/16, session 61–2, session-date: 1909, 1910]
Pt. 15, p. 463, *Furniture Manufacturing* [Serial set no. 5676, Senate document 633/17, session 61–2, session-date: 1909, 1910]
Pt. 16, p. 605, *Sugar Refining* [Serial set no. 5676, Senate document 633/18, session 61–2, session-date: 1909, 1910].

Volume 16: *Immigrants in Industries: Pt. 17, Copper Mining and Smelting* [Serial set no. 5677, Senate document 633/19, session 61–2, session-date: 1909, 1910].

Pt. 18, p. 195, *Iron Ore Mining* [Serial set no. 5677, Senate document 633/20, session 61-2, session-date: 1909, 1910]

Pt. 19, p. 585, *Anthracite Coal Mining* [Serial set no. 5677, Senate document 633/21, session 61-2, session-date: 1909, 1910]

Pt. 20, p. 741, *Oil Refining* [Serial set no. 5677, Senate document 633/22, session 61-2, session-date: 1909, 1910].

Volume 17: *Immigrants in Industries: Pt. 21, Diversified Industries, Vol. 1* [Serial set no. 5678, Senate document 633/23, session 61-2, session-date: 1909, 1910].

Volume 18: *Immigrants in Industries: pt. 21, Diversified Industries, Vol. 2* [Serial set no. 5679, Senate document 633/24, session 61-2, session-date: 1909, 1910]

Pt. 22, The Floating Immigrant Labor Supply [Serial set no. 5679, Senate document 633/25, session 61-2, session-date: 1909, 1910].

Volume 19: *Immigrants in Industries: Pt. 23, Summary Report on Immigrants in Manufacturing and Mining, Vol. 1* [Serial set no. 5680, Senate document 633/26, session 61-2, session-date: 1909, 1910].

Volume 20: *Immigrants in Industries: Pt. 23, Summary Report on Immigrants in Manufacturing and Mining, Vol. 2* [Serial set no. 5681, Senate document 633/27, session 61-2, session-date: 1909, 1910].

Volume 21: *Immigrants in Industries: Pt. 24, Recent Immigrants in Agriculture, Vol. 1* [Serial set no. 5682, Senate document 633/28, session 61-2, session-date: 1909, 1910].

Volume 22: *Immigrants in Industries: Pt. 24, Recent Immigrants in Agriculture, Vol. 2* [Serial set no. 5683, Senate document 633/29, session 61-2, session-date: 1909, 1910].

Volume 23: *Immigrants in Industries: Pt. 25, Japanese and Other Immigrant Races in the Pacific Coast and Rocky Mountain States, Vol. 1.—Japanese and East Indians* [Serial set no. 5684-1, Senate document 633/30, session 61-2, session-date: 1909, 1910].

Volume 24: *Immigrants in Industries: Pt. 25, Japanese and Other Immigrant Races in the Pacific Coast and Rocky Mountain States, Vol. 2—Agriculture* [Serial set no. 5684-2, Senate document 633/31, session 61-2, session-date: 1909, 1910].

Volume 25: *Immigrants in Industries: Pt. 25, Japanese and Other Immigrant Races in Pacific Coast and Rocky Mountain States, Vol. 3—Diversified Industries* [Serial set no. 5684-3, Senate document 633/31, session 61-2, session-date: 1909, 1910].

Volume 26: *Immigrants in Cities, Study of Selected Districts in New York, Chicago, Philadelphia, Boston, Buffalo, Cleveland, and Milwaukee, with Statistics and Tables, Vol. 1* [Serial set no. 5665, Senate document 338, session 61–2, session-date: 1909, 1910].

Volume 27: *Immigrants in Cities, Study of Selected Districts in New York, Chicago, Philadelphia, Boston, Buffalo, Cleveland, and Milwaukee, with Statistics and Tables, Vol. 2* [Serial set no. 5666, Senate document 338, session 61–2, session-date: 1909, 1910].

Volume 28: *Pt. 1: Occupations of First and Second Generations of Immigrants in U.S.* [Serial set no. 5664, Senate document 282/1, session 61–2, session-date: 1909, 1910] *Pt. 2: Fecundity of Immigrant Women*, p. 731 [Serial set no. 5664, Senate document 282/2, session 61–2, session-date: 1909, 1910].

Volume 29: *Children of Immigrants in Schools, Vol. 1* [Serial set no. 5871, Senate document 749, session 61–3, session-date: 1910, 1911].

Volume 30: *Children of Immigrants in Schools, Vol. 2. General Tables—Baltimore, Bay City, Boston, Buffalo, Cedar Rapids, Chelsea, Chicago, Cincinnati, and Cleveland* [Serial set no. 5872, Senate document 749, session 61–3, session-date: 1910, 1911].

Volume 31: *Children of Immigrants in Schools, Vol. 3. General Tables—Detroit, Duluth, Fall River, Haverhill, Johnstown, Kansas City, Missouri, Los Angeles, Lowell, Lynn, Manchester, and Meridian* [Serial set no. 5873, Senate document 749, session 61–3, session-date: 1910, 1911].

Volume 32: *Children of Immigrants in Schools, Vol. 4. General Tables—Milwaukee, Minneapolis, Newark, New Bedford, New Britain, New Orleans, New York, and Philadelphia* [Serial set no. 5874, Senate document 749, session 61–3, session-date: 1910, 1911].

Volume 33: *Children of Immigrants in Schools, Vol. 5. General Tables—Pittsburgh, Providence, St. Louis, San Francisco, Scranton, Shenandoah, South Omaha, Worchester, Yonkers, and Higher Institutions* [Serial set no. 5875, Senate document 749, session 61–3, session-date: 1910, 1911].

Volume 34: *Immigrants as Charity Seekers, Vol. 1; General Summary, and Data for Cities of United States and Hawai* [Serial set no. 5868, Senate document 665, session 61–3, session-date: 1910, 1911].

Volume 35: *Immigrants as Charity Seekers, Vol. 2; General Tables and Summary* [Serial set no. 5869, Senate document 665, session 61–3, session-date: 1910, 1911].

Volume 36: *Immigration and Crime* [Serial set no. 5876, Senate document 750, session 61–3, session-date: 1910, 1911].

Volume 37: *Pt. 1: Steerage Conditions* [Serial set no. 5877, Senate document 753/1, session 61–3, session-date: 1910, 1911]
Pt. 2: Importation and Harboring of Women for Immoral Purposes, p. 53 [Serial set no. 5877, Senate document 753/2, session 61–3, session-date: 1910, 1911]
Pt. 3: Immigrant Homes and Aid Societies, p. 125 [Serial set no. 5877, Senate document 753/3, session 61–3, session-date: 1910, 1911]
Pt. 4: Immigrant Banks, p. 197 [Serial set no. 5877, Senate document 753/4, session 61–3, session-date: 1910, 1911].

Volume 38: *Changes in Bodily Form of Descendants of Immigrants* (final report) [Serial set no. 5663, Senate document 208, session 61–2, session-date: 1909, 1910].

Volume 39: *pt. 1: Federal Immigration Legislation* [Serial set no. 5879, Senate document 758/1, session 61–3, session-date: 1910, 1911]
Pt. 2: Digest of Immigration Decisions, p. 149 [Serial set no. 5879, Senate document 758/2, session 61–3, session-date: 1910, 1911]
Pt. 3: Steerage Legislation, p. 339 [Serial set no. 5879, Senate document 758/3, session 61–3, session-date: 1910, 1911]
Pt. 4: State Immigration and Alien Laws, p. 505 [Serial set no. 5879, Senate document 758/4, session 61–3, session-date: 1910, 1911].

Volume 40: *Immigration Situation in Other Countries: Canada, Australia, New Zealand, Argentina, Brazil* [Serial set no. 5880, Senate document 761, session 61–3, session-date: 1910, 1911].

Volume 41: *Statements and Recommendations Submitted by Societies and Organizations Interested in Immigration* [Serial set no. 5881, Senate document 764, session 61–3, session-date: 1910, 1911].

Volume 42: A planned index, never published.

Notes

Abbreviations

BIP   Bureau of Immigration Papers, National Archives and Records Administration, Washington, DC.

BP-APS   Franz Boas Papers, American Philosophical Society, Philadelphia, PA.

BP-LoC   Franz Boas Papers, Manuscript Division, Library of Congress, Washington, DC.

CAP   Cyrus Adler Papers, P-16, American Jewish Historical Society, New York, and Boston, MA.

CBP   Charles J. Bonaparte Papers, Manuscript Division, Library of Congress, Washington, DC.

DBP   W. E. B. Du Bois Papers, MS 312, Special Collections and University Archives, University of Massachusetts Amherst Libraries, http://credo .library.umass.edu/view/pageturn/mums312-b005-i152/#page/1/mode/1up.

DoJ-GR   General Records of the Department of Justice, National Archives and Records Administration, College Park, MD.

FCC   Oral History Transcript, Frederick C. Croxton Papers, Herbert Hoover Presidential Library, West Branch, IA.

HCLP   Henry Cabot Lodge Papers, Massachusetts Historical Society, Boston, MA.

HP   William Walter Husband Papers, 1891–1940, Chicago Historical Society, Chicago, IL.

IRLR   Immigration Restriction League (U.S.) Records, 1893–1921, MS Am 2245, Houghton Library, Harvard University, Cambridge, MA.

JLP   Joseph Lee Papers, Massachusetts Historical Society, Boston, MA.

KWB   Kate Waller Barrett Papers, Manuscript Division, Library of Congress, Washington, DC.

LLP   J. Laurence Laughlin Papers, Manuscript Division, Library of Congress, Washington, DC.

LMP   Louis Marshall Papers, P-24, American Jewish Historical Society, New York, and Boston, MA.

LP   William Jett Lauck Papers, Accession #4742-b, Special Collections, Albert and Shirley Small Special Collections Library, University of Virginia, Charlottesville.

MJKP   Max James Kohler Papers, P-7, American Jewish Historical Society, New York, and Boston, MA.

MP   Mary Louise Mark Papers, MSS 497, Ohio Historical Society, Columbus.

NCFP   National Civic Federation records, Manuscripts and Archives Division, the New York Public Library, Astor, Lenox, and Tilden Foundations.

NP-CUA   Charles Patrick Neill Papers, American Catholic History Research Center and University Archives, The Catholic University of America, Washington, DC.

NP-TRC   Charles Patrick Neill Papers, 2001M-78, Theodore Roosevelt Collection, Houghton Library, Harvard University, Cambridge, MA.

OSP   Oscar Straus Papers, Manuscript Division, Library of Congress, Washington, DC.

PP   LeRoy Percy and Family Papers, Mss. 3275, Louisiana and Lower Mississippi Valley Collections, LSU Libraries, Baton Rouge, LA.

SWP   Simon Wolf Papers, P-25, American Jewish Historical Society, New York, and Boston, MA.

UCL   Special Collections Research Center, University of Chicago Libraries.

USDS   File 6923, Reel 539, *Numerical and Minor Files of the Department of State, 1906–1910,* National Archives microfilm publication M362 (Washington, DC: National Archives and Records Service, 1972).

USHR   Record Group 233, Records of the United States House of Representatives, Center for Legislative Archives, National Archives and Records Administration, Washington, DC.

USIC   U.S. Immigration Commission, *Reports of the Immigration Commission . . . ,* 41 vols. (Washington, DC: Government Printing Office, 1911). For titles of volumes, see list in preceding section, "Dillingham Commission Reports."

Introduction

1. Henry Cabot Lodge to Professor Barrett Wendell, Harvard University, April 13, 1910, Reel 27, HCLP. On their friendship, see William Lawrence, *Henry Cabot Lodge: A Biographical Sketch* (New York: Houghton Mifflin, 1925), 106. The most important recent work to date that relates immigration and imperialism is Donna R. Gabaccia, *Foreign Relations: American Immigration in Global Perspective* (Princeton, NJ: Princeton University Press, 2012).

2. A planned forty-second volume (an index) was never published, although because it was listed in tables of contents, many secondary sources claim there are forty-two volumes.

3. The Magnuson Act of 1943 symbolically ended Chinese exclusion by allowing a tiny quota and naturalization to a few resident aliens in order to support a World War II ally, but it retained other Asian exclusion until the McCarran-Walter Act of 1952. On the impact of the Hart-Celler Act, see Mae M. Ngai, *Impossible Subjects: Illegal Aliens and the Making of Modern America* (Princeton, NJ: Princeton University Press, 2004), 265–268. For immigration figures, see Thomas C. Leonard, *Illiberal Reformers: Race, Eugenics, and American Economics in the Progressive Era* (Princeton, NJ: Princeton University Press, 2016), 142.

4. The Office of the Superintendent of Immigration, created in 1891, became the Bureau of Immigration in 1895, the Bureau of Immigration and Naturalization in 1906, the Bureau of Immigration in 1913, and the Immigration and Naturalization Service in 1933, before dividing into U.S. Customs and Immigration Services (USCIS), Immigration and Customs Enforcement (ICE), and Customs and Border Patrol (CBP) in 2003. See www.uscis.gov/history-and-genealogy/our-history/organizational-timeline.

5. On the relative harshness of the recommendations compared to the reports, see Handlin, "Old Immigration and New," and Karen Schoenewaldt Buchholz, "The Politics of Research: Social Scientists and the New Immigrant Labor, 1880–1924" (PhD diss., Temple University, 1992), 83. The photographs for the special issues of *Survey Magazine* about the commission appear to have been produced by the commission as well. My thanks to Chad Frazier for research on these photographs.

6. "Bannon Vows a Daily Fight for 'Deconstruction of the Administrative State,'" *Washington Post,* February 23, 2017.

7. On the modern state and expertise, see especially James C. Scott, *Seeing Like a State: How Certain Schemes to Improve the Human Condition Have Failed* (New Haven, CT: Yale University Press, 1998). On the history of "experts," see Peter Burke, *What Is the History of Knowledge?* (Cambridge, UK: Polity Press, 2016), 21, 31.

8. Even "liberals" on immigration see the federal government playing the dominant role in policy; the only sustained critique of this approach has come from libertarians, especially the Cato Institute. See e.g. Bryan Caplan, "Why Should We Restrict Immigration?," *Cato Journal* 32, no. 1 (2012): 5–24.

9. "Recommendations," USIC, 1:45–46.

10. Quotation from USIC, 1:15. Senator Latimer died in office, as did his successor Anselm McLaurin, who was replaced by LeRoy Percy.

11. "Nation Aroused: The Need of Exhaustive Investigation into Immigration Problem Recognized," *Berea (KY) Citizen,* April 25, 1907, 6.

12. Isaac Hourwich, *Immigration and Labor: The Economic Aspects of European Immigration to the United States* (New York: G. P. Putnam's Sons, 1912).

13. USIC, 1:14. Oscar Handlin named a revised version of his famous essay about the commission, "Old Immigrants and New," a replication of the framework the Dillingham

Commission made paradigmatic. Quotation from Thomas J. Archdeacon, *Becoming American: An Ethnic History* (New York: Free Press, 1983), table of contents, vii.

14. Roger Daniels, *Coming to America* (New York: Harper Collins, 1991; 2002), 121, 183 of the 2002 edition.

15. The exception is scholars who have focused on immigrants in the American West or on specific ethnic groups, such as the Japanese, although even most of these scholars have not used the commission's reports extensively, perhaps because of their association with European immigration. See especially Elliott Barkan, *From All Points: America's Immigrant West, 1870s–1952* (Bloomington: University of Indiana Press, 2007), chap. 12. On Mexicans in the Dillingham Commission and the analogy with overseas colonies, see Katherine Benton-Cohen, "Other Immigrants: Mexicans and the Dillingham Commission," *Journal of American Ethnic History* 30, no. 2 (2011): 33–57. See also Mae M. Ngai, "The Architecture of Race in American Immigration Law: A Reexamination of the Immigration Act of 1924," *Journal of American History* 86, no. 1 (1999): 67–92.

16. Daniel Folkmar, assisted by Elnora Folkmar, USIC, 5:8. Mark E. Pry, "Arizona and the Politics of Statehood, 1889–1912" (MA thesis, Arizona State University, 1995), 112.

17. Starting with Hourwich and Oscar Handlin, most scholars have replicated the commission's focus on eastern and southern Europeans. See Oscar Handlin, "Old Immigrants and New," chap. 5, in *Race and Nationality in American Life* (Boston: Little, Brown, 1957). The only other book on this subject, Robert F. Zeidel's otherwise thorough *Immigrants, Progressives, and Exclusion Politics: The Dillingham Commission, 1900–1927* (DeKalb: Northern Illinois University Press, 2004), has no index entries for "Mexico," "Mexicans," "Latinos," or "Hispanics." But see Gunther Peck, *Reinventing Free Labor: Padrones and Immigrant Workers in the North American West, 1880–1930* (New York: Cambridge University Press, 2000), esp. 96–98, and Ronald Takaki, *A Different Mirror: A History of Multicultural America* (Boston: Little, Brown, 1993), 187 n. 55. The omission of Mexicans can be seen, for example, in inter alia, U.S. Bureau of the Census, *Thirteenth Census of the United States: 1910, Vol. 3* (Washington, DC: Government Printing Office, 1911), New York City tables on 218–219. Quotation from USIC, 6, Pt. II, 11.

18. Lawrence Downes, "One Hundred Years of Multitude," *New York Times,* March 26, 2011. See "Dillingham Commission's Ranking of Immigrant Groups Affected Policy for Decades," *All Things Considered,* January 28, 2013, transcript at NPR.org, retrieved June 29, 2017.

19. Handlin's chapter was based on his memo for the President's Commission on Immigration and Naturalization, *Hearings* (Washington, 1952), 1189 ff. Quotation from Handlin, *Race and Nationality in American Life,* 81–82. And see Oscar Handlin, "Introduction to the Arno Press edition," in *Reports of the [Dillingham] Immigration Commission: Abstracts of the Reports of the Immigration Commission, 61st Cong., 3rd sess.,* edited by U.S. Senate (New York: Arno Press, 1970).

20. For other important treatments of the commission besides Handlin and Zeidel (and this list is not exhaustive), see also John Higham, *Strangers in the Land: Patterns of American Nativism, 1860–1925* (New Brunswick, NJ: Rutgers University Press, 1955); Archdeacon, *Becoming American*, esp. table of contents, vii; Desmond King, *Making Americans: Immigration, Race, and the Origins of the Diverse Democracy* (Cambridge, MA: Harvard University Press, 2000); Daniels, *Coming to America;* Roger Daniels, *Guarding the Golden Door* (New York: Hill and Wang, 2004); Herbert Klein, *Population History of the United States* (Cambridge: Cambridge University Press, 2004); Lawrence H. Fuchs, "Immigration Reform in 1911 and 1981: The Role of Select Commissions," *Journal of American Ethnic History* 3, no. 1 (1983): 58–89. At the time of press, a new book was appearing that focuses closely on the commission's racial categories: Joel Perlmann, *America Classifies the Immigrants: From Ellis Island to the 2020 Census* (Cambridge, MA: Harvard University Press, 2018), esp. chap. 4.

21. Scholars such as Gabaccia, Matthew Jacobson, Paul Kramer, and the late Aristide Zolberg have begun this work. As Gabaccia has noted, "Unlike histories that examine immigration restriction as a product of domestic racism, a history of American immigration from a global perspective situates the racism and xenophobia that drove immigration restriction within a century-long political strategy over American foreign policy and its governance." Gabaccia, *Foreign Relations,* 124.

22. See Leonard, *Illiberal Reformers,* 43.

23. Unless you count the Interstate Commerce Commission, created by statute in 1887.

24. Again, the most critical analysis of these claims of expertise is Leonard, *Illiberal Reformers,* whose book operates as a broadside against Progressive reform, especially in the field of economics, by linking it to eugenics and by disputing any notion of its objectivity. Although my longer citations on many of these topics appear in subsequent chapters, one major influence on my thinking about social categories and the state is Margot Canaday, *The Straight State: Sexuality and the State in Twentieth-Century America* (Princeton, NJ: Princeton University Press, 2009). See Simon Lassig, "The History of Knowledge and the Expansion of the Historical Research Agenda," *Bulletin of the German Historical Institute* 59 (2016): 29–58, quotation on 39; on immigration and history of knowledge, see 46; Burke, *What Is the History of Knowledge?*; and Mary Poovey, *A History of the Modern Fact: Problems of Knowledge in the Sciences of Wealth and Society* (Chicago: University of London Press, 1998).

25. Higham, *Strangers.* For more on this point see Katherine Benton-Cohen, "*Strangers in the Land:* A View from Western History" (forum on John Higham's *Strangers in the Land*), *Journal of Gilded Age and Progressive Era* 11, no. 2 (2012): 263–269. On region, though, see David J. Tichenor, *Dividing Lines: The Politics of Immigration Control in America* (Princeton, NJ: Princeton University Press, 2002). On Lodge, see Lawrence, *Henry Cabot Lodge,* 64–65, 134, 109. USIC, 3:405–583.

26. See Thomas F. Gossett, *Race: The History of an Idea in America* (New York: Oxford University Press, 1963; rev. ed. 1997).

27. See James R. Barrett and David Roediger, "Inbetween Peoples: Race, Nationality and the 'New Immigrant' Working Class," *Journal of American Ethnic History* 16, no. 3 (1997): 3–45. Although the term was popularized by Barrett and Roediger, it appeared first in Higham's *Strangers in the Land*.

28. Thomas A. Guglielmo, *White on Arrival: Italians, Race, Color, and Power in Chicago, 1890–1945* (New York: Oxford University Press, 2004). For an excellent distillation of the book's ideas, see "Affirmative Action for Immigrant Whites," Oxford University Press Blog, March 27, 2015. A useful defense of the field is David R. Roediger, "Whiteness and Its Complications," *Chronicle of Higher Education,* July 14, 2006, http://chronicle.com/article/WhitenessIts/21922/.

29. For examples of its influence on commission members and staffers, see e.g. Solomon, *Ancestors and Immigrants,* chap. 10; "Lectures in Eugenics," *Journal of Heredity* 6, no. 4 (1915): 162; and Warren Zimmermann, *First Great Triumph: How Five Americans Made Their Country a World Power* (New York: Farrar, Straus and Giroux, 2002), 459. On eugenics' chronology, see Matthew Frye Jacobson, *Barbarian Virtues: The United States Encounters Foreign Peoples at Home and Abroad* (New York: Hill and Wang, 2000), chap. 5, and Daniel E. Kevles, *In the Name of Eugenics: Genetics and the Uses of Human Heredity,* rev. ed. (Cambridge, MA: Harvard University Press, 1995), esp. 102–103; Handlin, *Race and Nationality in American Life,* 104–106. Lodge later served on the board of the Carnegie Institution, which funded much of American eugenics research.

30. Scott Nearing, *The Super Race: An American Problem* (New York: B. W. Huebsch, 1912), 31. Robert DeC. Ward, "National Eugenics in Relation to Immigration," *North American Review* 192, no. 656 (1910): 56. Ward also made what would become a common distinction between negative and positive eugenics: "the prevention of the unfit as well as the conscious attempt to produce the more fit." Immigration restriction, like sterilization, was negative—a way to keep the unfit out of the U.S. population.

31. "The Races That Go into the American Melting Pot," *New York Times,* May 21, 1911.

32. USIC, 5:3–4.

33. Kitty Calavita is more careful on this point than some, calling the commission reports "a forewarning of the influence that the eugenics movement and immigrant scapegoating were to have on immigration policy," but then says the volumes were published in 1912, and she only looked at the first volume. Kitty Calavita, *U.S. Immigration Law and the Control of Labor, 1820–1924* (London: Academic Press, 1984), 113–114.

34. Gary Gerstle, *American Crucible* (New York: Oxford University Press, 2001).

35. On state limitations on immigrants, see Hidetaka Hirota, "The Moment of Transition: State Officials, the Federal Government, and the Formation of American Immigration Policy," *Journal of American History* 99, no. 4 (2013): 1092–1108. Jason Silverman, "Lincoln's 'Forgotten' Act to Encourage Immigration," www.lincolncottage.org/lincolns-forgotten-act-to-encourage-immigration/.

36. In the early 1980s, Thomas J. Archdeacon's *Becoming American: An Ethnic History* discussed Asian exclusion but remained organized around European immigration. With the exception of a few early interventions by Roger Daniels, Alexander Saxton, and Ronald Takaki, the full reckoning of Asian exclusion in the formative "restriction era" emerged only at the turn of the twenty-first century. Lucy Salyer, Erika Lee, Adam McKeown, and Mae Ngai are among the scholars who have brought the full racial implications of Asian exclusion to the fore of our understanding of modern notions of "immigrant," "citizen," and "alien." Lucy Salyer, *Laws as Harsh as Tigers* (Chapel Hill: University of North Carolina Press, 1995); Erika Lee, *At America's Gates: Chinese Immigration during the Exclusion Era, 1882–1943* (Chapel Hill: University of North Carolina Press, 2003); Mae Ngai, *Impossible Subjects;* Adam McKeown, *Melancholy Order: Asian Migration and the Globalization of Borders* (New York: Columbia University Press, 2008).

37. See John Higham, "Instead of a Sequel, or How I Lost my Subjects," *Reviews in American History* 28, no. 2 (2000): 327–339.

38. Quotations from Prescott F. Hall, "IV.—The Immigration Situation in Congress in Congress," *The Outlook,* November 10, 1906, 611–615. The commission also called immigration before 1882 "largely unregulated." USIC, 1:26; *Chae Chan Ping v United States* 130 U.S. 581 (1889). Angel Island, for processing Asian immigrants, only opened in 1910. The Bureau of Immigration moved to the Department of Commerce and Labor in 1903, became the Bureau of Immigration and Naturalization in 1906, and its successors moved to the newly created Department of Labor in 1913, the Department of Justice in 1940, and to Homeland Security in 2003. See U.S. Citizenship and Immigration Services, "Our History," www.uscis.gov/about-us/our-history.

39. Vincent J. Cannato, *American Passage: The History of Ellis Island* (New York: Harper Perennial, 2009), 221.

40. USIC, 41:141.

41. Grover Cleveland, "Veto Message," March 2, 1897. Online by Gerhard Peters and John T. Woolley, *The American Presidency Project,* www.presidency.ucsb.edu/ws/?pid =70845.

42. Although there is much disagreement about the nineteenth-century state, more consensus seems possible about the growth of the early twentieth-century administrative state. The "classic" political historians of the Progressive Era, men such as Samuel Hays, Robert Wiebe, Alfred Chandler, and Morton Keller, shared an interest in what Julian Zelizer calls the "organizational synthesis" that saw a distinct break from the nineteenth century in the "consolidation of national political institutions, including the administrative state, the corporation, and the professions." Stephen Skowronek, in contrast, wanted to see how "reformers maneuvered around the institutions that were already in place." Julian E. Zelizer, "Stephen Skowronek's *Building a New American State* and the Origins of American Political Development," *Social Science History* 27, no. 3 (2003): 432. See also Elisabeth S. Clemens, "Rereading Skowronek: A Precocious Theory of Institutional

Change," *Social Science History* 27, no. 3 (2003): 446, and William J. Novak, "The Myth of the 'Weak' American State," *American Historical Review* 113, no. 3 (2008): 758. For more information on the state in the nineteenth-century United States, see Brian Balogh, *A Government Out of Sight: The Mystery of National Authority in Nineteenth-Century America* (New York: Cambridge University Press, 2009).

For almost a century before the commission met, intellectuals, technocrats, and politicians across the United States and Europe had written and thought about the "social question" and its ancillary questions—the Jewish question, the woman question, the race question, and so on. By the turn of the twentieth century, the focus on a question was switching to thinking about a "problem." See Holly Case, "The 'Social Question,' 1820–1920," *Modern Intellectual History*, April 2015, 25–28.

43. USIC, 1:39; Ngai, *Impossible Subjects*, 17–20.

44. Ferris Stovel, "Reference Report," General Services Administration, National Archives and Records Service, Washington, D.C., n.d. My thanks to Robert Zeidel for making a copy of this document available to me, and for his support of this project.

45. I am especially grateful to Robert Zeidel for finding many of these sources.

1. The Professor and the Commission

1. Beatrice Webb, "A Traveler's Sharp View of Ithaca, 1898," in *What They Wrote: 19th Century Documents from Tompkins County, New York,* ed. Carol Kammen (Ithaca, NY: Cornell Department of Manuscripts and University Archives, 1978), 142–143. For a different view of Jenks's wife, see Mr. Butts, Ann Arbor, Michigan, to My dear Beal, March 8, 1909, Folder: Candidacy of J. Jenks for Pres. Univ. of Michigan, Box 5, Walter H. Sawyer Papers, Bentley Historical Library, University of Michigan. The Webbs were also inveterate eugenicists; see Thomas C. Leonard, *Illiberal Reformers: Race, Eugenics, and American Economics in the Progressive Era* (Princeton, NJ: Princeton University Press, 2016).

2. B. P., "College Professors and the Public," *Atlantic Monthly*, February 1902, 282–288.

3. First quotation from Paul B. Cook, *Academicians in Government from Roosevelt to Roosevelt* (New York: Garland, 1982), 63; Mary O. Furner, *Advocacy and Objectivity: A Crisis in the Professionalization of American Social Science, 1865–1905* (Lexington: Published for the Organization of American Historians by the University Press of Kentucky, 1975), 161, 248. Other material here and below from W. F. Willcox, "The Teaching of Economics, Political and Social Science at Cornell University," n.d., unpublished manuscript, Box 6, Folder 8, Walter Francis Willcox Papers, #14-10-504, Division of Rare and Manuscript Collections, Cornell University Library. My thanks to Chad Frazier for acquiring this document for me. In 1900, Jenks drafted a "model companies law for New York" for Roosevelt when he was governor. John Howard Brown, "Jeremiah Jenks: A

Pioneer of Industrial Organization?," *Journal of the History of Economic Thought* 26, no. 1 (2004): 80. On concurrence about his importance to the commission, see David Michael Grossman, "Professors and Public Service, 1885–1925: A Chapter in the History of the Professionalization of the Social Sciences" (PhD diss., Washington University in St. Louis, 1973), 115.

4. The term comes from Elisabeth Clemens, "Rereading Skowronek: A Precocious Theory of Institutional Change," *Social Science History* 27, no. 3 (2003): 443–453. See also the assessment of Cook, *Academicians,* 64. Cornell University's economics department became so involved in government work that it struggled to staff its classes. See Furner, *Advocacy and Objectivity,* 241, 285. On Jenks's relative obscurity today, and on more attention granted to him by historians than economists, see Brown, "Jeremiah Jenks," 69–89. There is not a lot of work on Jenks, but another useful analysis of Jenks's career includes Jerry Israel, *Progressivism and the Open Door: America and China, 1905–1921* (Pittsburgh, PA: University of Pittsburgh Press, 1971).

5. See e.g., Minutes, 2, 6, 10, 13, 25, 54, HP.

6. Minutes, 1908, 68, 78, HP.

7. Alan Trachtenberg, *The Incorporation of America: Culture and Society in the Gilded Age* (New York: Hill and Wang, 1982). See, for example, Jeremiah Jenks, *Principles of Politics from the Viewpoint of the American Citizen* (New York: Columbia University Press, 1909), 120, 126.

8. The historiography of Progressivism is far too vast to summarize, but classic and recent treatments include Robert H. Wiebe, *The Search for Order, 1877–1920* (New York: Hill and Wang, 1967), whose "organization thesis" and emphasis on bureaucratization make a great deal of sense in the context of the commission, as does Alan Trachtenberg's argument in his *Incorporation of America.* See also Michael McGerr, *A Fierce Discontent: The Rise and Fall of the Progressive Movement in America* (New York: Oxford University Press, 2003); Maureen A. Flanagan, *America Reformed: Progressives and Progressivisms, 1890s–1920s* (New York: Oxford University Press, 2007). Excellent brief overviews include Arthur S. Link and Richard L. McCormick, *Progressivism* (Arlington Heights, IL: Harlan Davidson, 1983), and Daniel T. Rodgers, "In Search of Progressivism," *Reviews in American History* 10, no. 4 (1992): 113–132. On Mrs. Jenks's education, see Mr. Butts to My dear Beal. On Jenks's origins, see Sarah Hall Johnston, ed. and comp., *Lineage Book— National Society of the Daughters of the American Revolution* (Washington, DC: Daughters of the American Revolution, 1903), 43:54. Between 1900 and 1910, the federal budget grew by a quarter. Frank Hobbs and Nicole Stoops, *Democratic Trends in the 20th Century,* Census 2000 Special Reports (Washington, DC: U.S. Census Bureau, 2002), 4:11, 13.

9. U.S. Census Office, *Twelfth Census of the United States, Taken in the Year 1900. William R. Merriam, Director. Census Reports, Volume III. Vital Statistics, Part I: Analysis and Ratio Tables. Prepared under the Supervision of William A. King, Chief Statistician for Vital Statistics* (Washington, DC: United States Census Office, 1902), xlix–liii. This

phenomenon led to Theodore Roosevelt and others crying that white native-born women's declining birthrate would result in "race suicide." Death rates also fell. See ibid., lvi–lxiii.

10. Edward A. Ross, "The Causes of Racial Superiority," *Annals of the American Academy of Political and Social Science* (1901), 18:67–89. Roger Daniels, *Guarding the Golden Door: American Immigration Policy and Immigrants since 1882* (New York: Hill and Wang, 2004), 5. On twenty-first-century statistics, see Migration Policy Institute, "U.S. Immigrant Population and Share over Time, 1850–2014," www.migrationpolicy.org /programs/data-hub/us-immigration-trends. On the commission and "new immigrants" not staying, see for example, USIC, 1:24. A general discussion is in Mark Wyman, *Round-Trip to America: The Immigrants Return to Europe, 1880–1930* (Ithaca, NY: Cornell University Press, 2003).

11. Daniels, *Guarding the Golden Door,* 5–6. These numbers are based on the official totals of the Bureau of Immigration, one of the forerunners of the Immigration and Naturalization Service, which only began counting land migrants across the Canadian and Mexican borders in 1908. They are thus obviously incomplete. See U.S. Immigration and Naturalization Service, *Statistical Yearbook of the Immigration and Naturalization Service, 2001* (Washington, DC: Government Printing Office, 2003), 16. USIC, 1:13.

12. In the last three decades, scholars have focused intense interest on the origins and nature of the American state. Some—such as political scientist Theda Skocpol—have placed the U.S. bureaucratic state in its international context. Others have focused on internal debates about the nature and size of the American state. As Karen Merrill has observed, new studies of the state have largely ignored territoriality. See Karen R. Merrill, "In Search of the 'Federal Presence' in the American West," *Western Historical Quarterly* 30, no. 4 (1999): 449–473, esp. 452. The commission endorsed a spread of sovereignty to overseas steerage ships and even to ports of entry on foreign shores. What did this mean for territoriality? This point can be directly credited to Matthew Frye Jacobson, *Barbarian Virtues: The United States Encounters Foreign Peoples at Home and Abroad, 1876–1917* (New York: Hill and Wang, 2000), esp. 8. But see also Paul Kramer, "Power and Connection: Imperial Histories of the United States in the World," *American Historical Review* 116, no. 5 (2011): 1348–1391, and Donna Gabaccia, *Foreign Relations: American Immigration in Global Perspective* (Princeton, NJ: Princeton University Press, 2012). For an older view, see Robert W. Tucker, Charles B. Keely, and Linda Wrigley, eds., *Immigration and U.S. Foreign Policy* (Boulder, CO: Westview Press, 1990). For a regional study, see Christopher Mitchell, ed., *Western Hemisphere Immigration and United States Foreign Policy* (University Park: Pennsylvania State University Press, 1992). On Asian exclusion and transatlantic history see, inter alia, Adam McKeown, *Melancholy Order: Asian Migration and the Globalization of Borders* (New York: Columbia University Press, 2008).

13. H. Parker Willis, editor of the reports, was an economist who published *Our Philippine Problem: A Study of American Colonial Policy* with Henry Holt in 1905. Superintendent of agents Roland Faulkner served as education commissioner of Puerto

Rico. Victor Clark served in a similar capacity there and then as labor commissioner in Hawaii. He also worked in Cuba and elsewhere. For more, see Chapter 2.

14. Jeremiah W. Jenks, "The Philippine Islands under the American Government," in *Colonies of the World,* ed. Henry Cabot Lodge (Chicago: H. W. Shaw & Son, 1907), 20:354–394.

15. USIC, vol. 4.

16. USIC, vol. 40. Some historians argue that the push to harmonize other nations' immigration laws with those of the United States was itself a form of imperialism. See especially Erika Lee, "Enforcing the Borders: Chinese Exclusion along the U.S. Borders with Canada and Mexico, 1882–1924," *Journal of American History* 89, no. 1 (2002): 54–86.

17. Biography compiled from various sources, but see esp. "Personal Notes," *Annals of the American Academy of Political and Social Science* 2 (July 1891): 105–106. On Halle, see *Encyclopædia Britannica,* s.v., "Martin Luther University of Halle-Wittenberg," www .britannica.com/EBchecked/topic/252769/Martin-Luther-University-of-Halle -Wittenberg. On German influence on U.S. training, see Cook, *Academicians,* 23.

18. Grossman, "Professors and Public Service," 95.

19. As late as 1912, sociologists and economists, though belonging to different professional organizations, held a joint annual meeting in Washington, DC, where they discussed public policy at length. See T. N. Carver, "The American Economic Association," *The Survey* 27, no. 15 (1912): 1582–1584; Herbert N. Shenton, "The American Sociological Society," *The Survey* 27, no. 15 (1912): 1584–1585. On Cornell University's department, see Willcox, "The Teaching of Economics."

20. Francis A. Walker to Richard T. Ely, April 30, 1884, quoted in A. W. Coats, "The First Two Decades of the American Economic Association," *American Economic Review* 50, no. 4 (1960): 557. Although Adam Smith's name has become practically synonymous with laissez-faire theory, this shorthand leaves out his work's origins in moral philosophy and the Scottish Enlightenment. See Dorothy Ross, *The Origins of American Social Science* (New York: Cambridge University Press, 1992), chap. 2. See Theodore M. Porter, "Genres and Objects of Social Inquiry, from the Enlightenment to 1890," 30; Mary S. Morgan, "Economics," 275–305; and Dorothy Ross, "Changing Contours of the Social Science Disciplines," 203–237, all in *The Cambridge History of Science.* Vol. 7, *The Modern Social Sciences,* ed. Theodore M. Porter and Dorothy Ross (New York: Cambridge University Press, 2003). Cook, *Academicians,* 23–24. See also Edward T. Silva and Sheila A. Slaughter, *Serving Power: The Making of the Academic Social Science Expert* (Westport, CT: Greenwood Press, 1984), 12.

21. Axel R. Schäfer, *American Progressives and German Social Reform, 1875–1920: Social Ethics, Moral Control, and the Regulatory State in a Transatlantic Context* (Stuttgart: Franz Steiner Verlag, 2000), 89. Jeremiah W. Jenks, "Henry C. Carey as *Politickoekonom* [Political Economist]" (PhD diss., University of Halle, 1885). My thanks to Alexander Macartney for his translation skills.

22. Alexandra Oleson and John Voss, eds., *The Organization of Knowledge in Modern America, 1860–1920* (Baltimore, MD: Johns Hopkins University Press, 1979), x. Willcox, "The Teaching of Economics." Course titles culled from Cornell University Registers, 1902–1909, Cornell University Digital Archives, http://ebooks.library.cornell.edu/c /cuda/.

23. On "the social consequences of capitalist industrialization" as impetus, see Dietrich Rueschemeyer and Theda Skocpol, "Introduction," in *States, Social Knowledge, and the Origins of Modern Social Policies,* ed. Dietrich Rueschemeyer and Theda Skocpol (Princeton, NJ: Princeton University Press, 1996), 4.

24. In contrast, the AEA today lists no such goals. American Economic Association, "About the AEA: More Than 130 Years of Encouraging Economic Research," www.aeaweb .org/AboutAEA/gen_info.php; Coats, "The First Two Decades," 558; Jonathan S. Franklin, *A History of Professional Economists and Policymaking in the United States: Irrelevant Genius* (New York: Routledge, 2016); Clemens, "Rereading Skowronek," 446.

25. Jeremiah Jenks and W. Jett Lauck, *The Immigration Problem,* 2nd ed. (New York: Funk and Wagnalls, 1912), xv. For a reading quite different from mine, see Leonard, *Illiberal Reformers,* 149. Bjorn Wittrock and Peter Wagner, "Social Science and the Building of the Early Welfare State: Toward a Comparison of Statist and Non-Statist Western Societies," in Rueschemeyer and Skocpol, *States,* 106–107.

26. The most famous tenure and freedom of speech case involved economist E. A. Ross at Stanford University, who gave a fiery speech at an anti-Japanese rally while Jenks was a diplomat to East Asia. Jenks had worked briefly with Ross at Cornell University and did not come to his defense after the Stanford incident, unlike many other economists. Furner, *Advocacy and Objectivity,* 231, 247. See also Helene Silverberg, "Introduction: Toward a Gendered Social Science History," in *Gender and American Social Science: The Formative Years,* ed. Helene Silverberg (Princeton, NJ: Princeton University Press, 1998), 7. Jenks had commitments to the YMCA and Boy Scout movements, dating as far back as his time at Knox College in Illinois, a center of Protestant reform activity; John Lewis Recchiuti, *Civic Engagement: Social Science and Progressive-Era Reform in New York City* (Philadelphia: University of Pennsylvania Press, 2007), 27. The committee—with Jenks as chair—was credited by name on the page with the Scout Oath in the first edition of the *Boy Scout Handbook* (1912). For Jenks's quotes, see, for example, "The Teachings of Jesus as Factors in International Politics, with Especial Reference to Far Eastern Problems," in *Christianity and Problems of To-day: Lectures Delivered before Lake Forest College on the Foundation of the Late William Bross* (New York: Charles Scribner's Sons, 1922), 108–154. Hadley, quoted in Grossman, "Professors and Public Service," 141.

27. Ibid.; Jenks, *Principles of Politics,* 102; *Ithaca Journal,* August 26, 1929.

28. Jeremiah W. Jenks, "Some Difficulties in the Administration of Dependencies," in *Proceedings of the Twenty-Third Annual Meeting of the Lake Mohonk Conference of*

Friends of the Indian and Other Dependent Peoples, ed. Lillian D. Powers (Mohonk Lake, NY: The Conference, 1905), 80–113; Jenks, *Business and the Government* (New York: Alexander Hamilton Institute, 1921); Jenks, *Governmental Action and Social Welfare* (New York: Macmillan, 1910); and Jenks, "English Colonial Fiscal Systems in the Far East," in *Essays in Colonial Finance by Members of the American Economic Association.* (New York: Published for the American Economic Association by the Macmillan Company, 1900): 263–303.

29. Brown, "Jeremiah Jenks," 82; Willcox, "The Teaching of Economics"; Jeremiah W. Jenks, "The Japanese in Manchuria," *The Outlook,* March 11, 1911, 549; Silva and Slaughter, *Serving Power,* 150, 136–137; Cook, *Academicians,* 64, and L. S. Dudley, "Progressivism: Critiques and Contradictions," in *Handbook of Organizational Theory and Management: The Philosophical Approach,* ed. Thomas D. Lynch and Todd J. Dicker (New York: CRC Press, 1997), 237.

30. See for example Alfred W. McCoy and Francisco Scarano, eds., *Colonial Crucible: Empire in the Making of the Modern American State* (Madison: University of Wisconsin Press, 2009), and especially Paul Kramer, "Reflex Actions: Colonialism, Corruption and the Politics of Technocracy in the Early Twentieth Century United States," in *Challenging US Foreign Policy: America and the World in the Long Twentieth Century,* ed. Bevan Sewell and Scott Lucas (New York: Palgrave Macmillan, 2011), 14–35, esp. 23; Cook, *Academicians,* 54. On the AEA's Committee on Colonial Finance and pragmatic stance toward imperialism, see especially Silva and Slaughter, *Serving Power,* 133–138. For summaries of their work on the committee, see *Essays in Colonial Finance.* See also Grossman, "Professors and Public Service," 85–86.

31. Jenks, *Principles of Politics,* 161, 167–168, 164; Jeremiah W. Jenks, "How Congress May Control Trusts," *The Outlook,* December 13, 1902, 880. On colonies influencing the federal state at home, see McCoy and Scarano, *Colonial Crucible.*

32. Cook, *Academicians,* 64; Israel, *Progressivism and the Open Door,* 46.

33. Andrew Wender Cohen, "Smuggling, Globalization, and America's Outward State, 1870–1909," *Journal of American History* 97, no. 2 (2010): 371–398, quotation on 372. See also Brian Balogh, *A Government Out of Sight: The Mystery of National Authority in Nineteenth-Century America* (New York: Cambridge University Press, 2009), 151–218. Aristide L. Zolberg, *A Nation of Design: Immigration Policy in the Fashioning of America* (New York: Harvard University Press, 2006), 110–113.

34. Jenks, *Principles of Politics,* 1.

35. Jeremiah W. Jenks, "Money in Practical Politics," *Century Magazine,* October 1, 1892, 940–952; Recchiuti, *Civic Engagement,* 10, 99.

36. "Notes," in *University Extension,* ed. George F. James (Philadelphia: The American Society for the Extension of University Teaching, 1892), 1:27. See also "The Mission of the University," *The Outlook,* January 4, 1913, 11. The money-making efforts were a financial disaster. See correspondence between Lauck and Jenks, Box 38, LP.

37. On Jenks's views about free speech and the academy, see Edward Cary, "Making Good Citizens," *New York Times,* August 4, 1906, BR481, and Furner, *Advocacy and Objectivity,* 247. Jenks, "The Modern Standard of Business Honor," *Publications of the American Economic Association* 3rd Ser., 8 (1907): 22; Jenks, "The Principles of Government Control of Business," *American Economic Association Quarterly* 3rd ser., 9 (1908): 9, 20. See also Ross, *Origins,* 146. Some of his contemporaries saw Jenks's claims as self-promotion and pointless pablum, but a more sympathetic view of this era of practical economists appears in Joseph A. Schumpeter, *History of Economic Analysis,* with a new introduction by Mark Perlman (1954; repr., London: Routledge, 1997), 864; Coats, "The First Two Decades," 262. See also Karen Schoenewaldt Buchholz, "The Politics of Research: Social Scientists and the New Immigrant Labor" (PhD diss., Temple University, 1992).

38. For an extended discussion of special interests and scholarship, and on debates on whether economics is a "real" science, see Schumpeter, *History of Economic Analysis,* 10–11, and Alex Rosenberg and Tyler Curtain, "What Is Economics Good For?," *New York Times,* August 24, 2013, SR9, and Donald N. McCloskey, Review of *Economics: Mathematical Politics or Science of Diminishing Returns?,* by Alexander Rosenberg, *Isis* 84, no. 4 (1993): 838–839. The debate between Thomas Huxley and Matthew Arnold in Great Britain in the 1880s over the virtues of the arts over the sciences echoed throughout the social sciences in this period. See Guy Cortolano, "Introduction," in *The Two Cultures Controversy: Science, Literature and Cultural Politics in Postwar Britain* (Cambridge: Cambridge University Press, 2009), 1–27. My thanks to Kate de Luna for this point. For more critical views of Jenks, see Alvin Johnson, *Pioneer's Progress: An Autobiography* (New York: Viking Press, 1952), 220. Cornell University was one of the first places—if not the first—to teach statistics in the United States. An 1887 course in mathematics included "probabilities and least squares with sociologic applications, including some recent work of Galton," although there is no indication that Jenks knew the first thing about it. See Stephen M. Stigler, *The History of Statistics: The Measurement of Uncertainty before 1900* (Cambridge, MA: Belknap Press of Harvard University Press, 1986), 301. Jenks's quotation from his "The Racial Problem in Immigration," *Proceedings of the National Conference of Charities and Corrections* 36 (1909): 215.

39. For a negative view of government work by a former Immigration Commission employee, see Lucy Sprague Mitchell, *Two Lives: The Story of Wesley Clair Mitchell and Myself* (New York: Simon and Schuster, 1953), 184, quoted in Grossman, "Professors and Public Service," 57. According to Willcox, the first edition of Jenks and Lauck's *The Immigration Problem* was "so full of errors that it had to be withdrawn." Walter Francis Willcox to Alvin Johnson, February 5, 1932, Allyn A. Young Papers, Harvard University, quoted in Grossman, "Professors and Public Service," 57. A more positive view appears in Butts to Beal, March 8, 1909, and M. B. Fites, Ithaca, New York, to Mr. Butts, Ann Arbor, Michigan, March 3, 1909, Folder: Candidacy of J. Jenks for Pres. Univ. of Michigan, Box 5, Sawyer Papers.

40. Jenks, "Government Control of Business," 14–17.

41. Jeremiah Jenks, "The Urgent Immigration Problem," *World's Work* 22, no. 1 (1911): 14368–14374, and Jeremiah W. Jenks, "The Character and Influence of Recent Immigrants," in *Questions of Public Policy: Addresses Delivered in the Page Lecture Series, 1913, before the Senior Class of the Sheffield Scientific School, Yale University* (New Haven, CT: Yale University Press, 1913), 1–40. See Kramer, "Power and Connection," 1350.

42. Jenks, *Principles of Politics,* 40–60; USIC, 1:45–48.

43. Jenks, "Racial Problem in Immigration," 216. Daniel Tichenor claims, without evidence, that Jenks was "enamored with the earlier ethnic and racial theories of Walker and Mayo-Smith" and coauthored the *Dictionary of Races or Peoples.* He also cherry-picks quotations from the "Racial Problem" speech that greatly exaggerate Jenks's racism. Daniel Tichenor, *Dividing Lines: The Politics of Immigration Control in America* (Princeton, NJ: Princeton University Press, 2002), 129. See also Leonard, *Illiberal Reformers,* xiii, 149–150, which quotes Jenks from Tichenor, which suggests he did not consult the original.

44. Jenks, "Racial Problem in Immigration," 216–219, 222.

45. Jenks, "The Urgent Immigration Problem," 14370.

46. The book will continue to develop this point, but for a similar conclusion, see Ian Robert Bowdiggin, *Keeping America Sane: Psychiatry and Eugenics in the United States and Canada, 1880–1940* (Ithaca, NY: Cornell University Press, with a new preface, 2003), 209.

47. Thomas F. Gossett, *Race: The History of an Idea in America* (New York: Oxford University Press, 1963), 173–174.

48. Marguerite Green, *The National Civic Federation and the American Labor Movement, 1900–1925* (Washington, DC: Catholic University of America Press, 1956), 8.

49. Richard Salvato, "National Civic Federation Records, 1894–1949" (New York: Manuscripts and Archives Division, Humanities and Social Sciences Library, New York Public Library, 2001), 6–7. Jenks and fellow NCF member Charles Neill were even charter members of the American Association for Labor Legislation, which was founded at the 1905 AEA meeting. Recchiuti, *Civic Engagement,* 153. The NCF struggled to maintain corporate loyalty after the rise of the open-shop movement promoted by the National Association of Manufacturers. NCF leaders turned their energy toward welfare capitalist measures such as better factory conditions, libraries, and recreation centers for workers. On the NCF and labor relations, see Green, "The National Civic Federation," and David Montgomery, *Workers Control in America: Studies in the History of Work, Technology, and Labor Struggles* (Cambridge: Cambridge University Press, 1979), 48–90. In order to control women's influence at NCF, Gertrude Beeks Easley created a Ladies' Auxiliary designed to deter the growth of sentiment in favor of women's suffrage and protective labor legislation.

50. Silva and Slaughter, *Serving Power,* 192. Charles Neill served on NCF's child labor committee—a topic in which he would specialize when Roosevelt appointed him federal commissioner of labor. Silva and Slaughter, *Serving Power,* 195.

51. Jenks, Chairman of Committee on Legislation and Its Enforcement, to "Dear Sir," August 4, 1906, Reel 164, NCFP; Silva and Slaughter, *Serving Power,* 201; Martin J. Sklar, *The Corporate Reconstruction of American Capitalism, 1890–1916: The Market* (New York: Cambridge University Press, 1988), 228–229. The executive council "determined the social, economic, and political issues the NCF would study and the patriotic causes it would support." Salvato, "National Civic Federation Records," 22. Jenks also favored private ownership of public utilities, albeit regulated by the state. See James Weinstein, *Corporate Ideal in the Liberal State, 1900–1918* (Boston: Beacon Press, 1968). See also Jenks, *Great Fortunes: The Winning, the Using* (New York: McClure, Phillips, 1906), 268–270.

52. All quotations from correspondence in Reel 167, NCFP.

53. The immigration committee included more academics than any other NCF committee until 1913. Silva and Slaughter, *Serving Power,* table, 190. On the enforcement committee, see Minutes of Committee, September 24, 1906, Folder 1059, IRLR. See Reel 167, NCFP.

54. Secretary to Nathan Bjiur, September 14, 1906, Reel 163, NCFP. Someone, likely Jenks, reported that the bulk of time they considered the Korean issue, then would turn to the Japanese. He felt it likely that the question of labor at the Panama Canal, in addition to the availability of an easier route to the Pacific, would press the Chinese question on them. Secretary [Jenks? Easley?] to Professor Mary Coolidge, Stanford, California, n.d., Reel 163, NCFP.

55. On turning over the files, see pamphlet, n.d., in Folder 12: "Miscellany," Reel 167, NCFP. On discussion with Neill about the Bureau of Labor's study of immigration, before the creation of the commission, see Frank Julian Warne to Charles P. Neill, August 6, 1906, Reel 165, NCFP, and Neill to Warne, August 7, 1906, Reel 165, NCFP; Chairman Executive Council [Easley?] to Hon. Robert Adams, January 9, 1906, Reel 163, NCFP, emphasis added; Silva and Slaughter, *Serving Power,* 205. On conflict, see correspondence in Folder 18: Immigration Special Committee, Reel 182, NCFP. Whatever the NCF's faults, the IRL's proto-eugenics was not their main avenue of inquiry, and Jenks always disavowed any inherently racial considerations in his evaluation of immigration. See for example Joseph Lee (the IRL's president) to Jeremiah W. Jenks, March 20, 1906, and August 9, 1906, both Reel 164, NCFP. Jenks did maintain, however, that cultural and political differences might be an argument for restriction because of the difficulty of assimilation. See also Jenks to Industrial Removal Office, May 28, 1915, Records of the Industrial Removal Office, I-9, Box 91, Folder: Jeremiah Jenks, Reel 55, American Jewish Historical Society, New York City. See also Jenks, "The Racial Problem in Immigration." After the commission's work was complete, the NCF did create a new special committee on immigration, again

run by Jenks, who asked commission alumni William Bennet, William Walter Husband, and Jett Lauck to serve on it. Moreover, by 1915, Jenks had joined up with the IRL to write pamphlets lobbying for restriction. See Jeanne Petit, *The Men and Women We Want: Gender, Race, and the Progressive Era Literacy Test Debate* (Rochester, NY: University of Rochester Press, 2010), n.24, 160.

56. Secretary to Jenks, November 1, 1906, Reel 164, NCFP. On Jenks's responsibilities, see Immigration Commission Notebook, 64, 65, 68, 34, HP, and correspondence between Jenks and Warne, October 11, 1906, October 17, 1906, and November 1, 1906, Reel 164, NCFP. In addition, he oversaw the anthropological study by Franz Boas and a history of immigration legislation, and served on the committees on statistics both for the commission and for the federal government. Buchholz, "The Politics of Research," 68; Secretary to Nathan Bijur, September 14, 1906, Reel 163, NCFP; here, both the NCF and the commission made use of Jenks's legal background. On digest work, see Warne to Jenks, October 11, 1906, Reel 164, NCFP, and Jenks to Warne, October 17, 1906, Reel 164, NCFP. Jenks also compiled a similar list of state and federal trust legislation for NCF and for the 1908 committee that drafted early versions of the Hepburn Act; Immigration Commission Notebooks, January 18, 1908, 6–9, HP.

57. "Oriental side" in Easley to Franklin MacVeagh, July 29, 1907, Reel 167, NCFP; "Asiatic Phase" from Jenks to R. M. Easley, October 23, 1905, Reel 164, NCFP. While the NCF generally welcomed the commission's takeover of the immigration study, Ralph Easley tried to keep plans for "a friendly delegation of NCF officials" to Japan, the Pacific Coast, and the Philippines. But the federal government was tightening its hold on diplomacy; by the end of 1907 Jenks and Roosevelt had put the kibosh on Easley's plans. Chairman to Jeremiah W. Jenks, January 22, 1907, Reel 164, NCFP. Easley to Nicholas Murray Butler, August 9, 1907, Reel 167, NCFP. On Root's support see Telegram, Easley to Butler, August 16, 1907, Reel 167, NCFP. On Neill, see Easley to MacVeagh, September 8, 1907, Reel 167, NCFP. On the discussion of the Japanese investigation, see correspondence in Reel 167, NCFP. Reynolds to Easley, December 9, 1907, Reel 167, NCFP. And see the sarcastic response denigrating Taft in Easley[?] to Reynolds, December 12, 1907, Reel 167, NCFP. Asian affairs were a concern mainly on the Pacific Coast, so were also of interest to William Wheeler, who cooperated with Jenks on the investigations of Asian smuggling from within the Immigration Bureau, while he also served as assistant secretary of commerce and labor.

58. Jenks to Ralph M. Easley, December 11, 1905, Reel 164, NCFP. And see correspondence between Jenks and Easley, December 13, 18, and 23, 1906, Reel 164, NCFP. For more on Jenks's view and the issue more generally, see Jenks, "The Japanese in Manchuria," and Paul A. Kramer, "Empire against Exclusion in Early 20th Century Trans-Pacific History," *Nanzan Review of American Studies* 33 (2011): 13–32.

59. See Mae Ngai, *Impossible Subjects: Illegal Aliens and the Making of Modern America* (Princeton, NJ: Princeton University Press, 2004), and Erika Lee, *At America's Gates:*

Chinese Immigration during the Exclusion Era, 1882–1943 (Chapel Hill: University of North Carolina Press, 2003). A good administrative overview appears in Waverly B. Lowell, comp., *Chinese Immigration and the Chinese in the United States: Records in the Regional Archives of the National Archives and Records Administration* (Washington, DC: National Archives and Records Administration, 1996), www.archives.gov/research/chinese-americans /guide.html.

60. The IRL tried to influence the study through its third member, an IRL member and another NCF insider, Charles Bronson Reynolds. See DeWard to Lee, December 27, 1906, and Ward to Lee, January 4, 1907, File J. Lee IRL Correspondence, Jan.-Apr. 1907, JLP. On NCF wanting Reynolds as "third man" appointed to the commission with Jenks and Neill, see Rue East [Easley?], National Civic Federation, to Oscar Straus, March 13, 1907, Box 6, OSP. On white slavery, see Edward J. Bristow, *Prostitution and Prejudice: The Jewish Fight against White Slavery, 1870–1939* (New York: Schocken, 1983), 160–169, and Brian Donovan, *White Slave Crusades: Race, Gender, and Anti-Vice Activism, 1887– 1917* (Urbana: University of Illinois Press, 2006). On investigations on immigration by Reynolds et al., see Watchorn-Reynolds correspondence, Reel 164, NCFP. On Jenks's role on the Ellis Island Commission, see Hans P. Vought, *The Bully Pulpit and the Melting Pot: American Presidents and the Immigrant, 1897–1933* (Macon, GA: Mercer University Press, 2004), 62. On the millionaire Oliver Belmont, see Theodore Roosevelt to Jeremiah Jenks, enclosure, February 24, 1906, Folder 12, Reel 167, NCFP.

61. USIC, 1:9.

62. Ibid., 1:12.

63. The citations in this and subsequent notes are to digitized documents in the database Proquest History Vault, Series A: Subject Correspondence Files, Part 1: Asian Immigration and Exclusion, 1906–1913, RG 85, Records of the Immigration and Naturalization Service. The citations list page numbers in collections of downloaded case documents, as well as the file number, collection, and location. As part of this investigation, Jenks received documents from the Bureau of Immigration dating as far back as 1898. List of files obtained by Jenks, p. 14 of pdf, listing his acquisition of Miscellaneous Index File No. 436, Investigation by Oscar Greenhalgh, alleged corruption in Immigration Service, Folders 001738, 001738-019-0825, 001738-0825. Jenks received fifteen packages of documents from the Immigration Service. See Jenks to Herbert Knox Smith, January 31, 1908, and Jenks to Honorable Herbert Knox Smith, February 18, 1908, ibid. On 1898, see Daniel Keefe to Jenks, February 5, 1910, pdf, p. 3, ibid. See Immigration Commission Notebook, p. 75, HP. And see 00138-006-447, pdf p. 61.

64. See Commissioner-General to Secretary of Commerce and Labor, March 20, 1909, reiterating recommendation of May 14, 1908, p. 3 pdf. On Jenks's continued belief in Tuttle's guilt, see solicitor to the assistant secretary of Commerce and Labor [probably Wheeler], p. 5 pdf, both in 001738-007-0037, 001738-0037-000. On Tuttle's resignation, see November 23, 1909, p. 2 pdf, and on his self-defense, see Guy Tuttle to Commissioner-

General of Immigration, December 26, 1907, p. 21 pdf, 001738–007–0000, Date: Jan 01, 1907–Dec 31, 1908. In the interim, the commission's records have been destroyed, so Jenks's report does not survive. "Executive Committee Minutes" Notebook, January 10, 1908, 28, HP. A keyword search of "Chinese" in volumes 23–25 of the reports of the U.S. Immigration Commission, which discussed the Pacific Coast states, turned up no evidence. Nor did one of the volumes 1–2, in which the Dillingham Commission summarized its findings (although volume 1 might allude to the investigation very indirectly in saying that the commission made recommendations to city, state, and federal officials about the administration of Chinese exclusion laws). See USIC, *Abstracts,* 1:23. Volume 1 also notes that "no special investigation of Chinese immigration was planned" because they had long been excluded and because "the Chinese laborers were very suspicious of the motives of the Commission's agents." "The slight investigation made of Chinese immigration was, therefore, purely incidental to the investigation of industries in which they are or have been employed." USIC, *Abstracts,* 1:625–626. NCF also kept a file on the U.S. attorney embroiled in the case. Report entitled "OSCAR LAWLER," Reel 167, NCFP. Meanwhile, the IRL's secretary, J. H. Patten, believed that Mr. North, the critic of Jenks's investigation, was also corrupt. J. H. Patten to Joseph Lee, May 21, 1910, Carton 1, JLP; Undated, unsigned report, sometime after 1912, Reel 167, NCFP.

2. The Gentlemen's Agreement

1. Millis had replaced fellow Stanford University economist Wesley Clark Mitchell, originally head of the agricultural studies and the Japanese studies for the reports, who resigned in July 1908. Notebook, "U.S. Immigration Commission Records 1907–1910," July 10, 1908, 66, HP. Letter, Ichihashi to Jordan, n.d. [1908], Folder 578, Box 60, David Starr Jordan Papers (SC0058), Department of Special Collections and University Archives, Stanford University Libraries, Stanford, CA. Harry A. Millis, "Population and Immigration—Discussion," *Bulletin of the American Economic Association* 4th ser., no. 2 (1911): 246–247; USIC, 23:3.

2. "Senate Passes Coolie Measure," *New York Times,* February 17, 1907, 1; John Lund, "Boundaries of Restriction: The Dillingham Commission," *University of Vermont History Review* 6 (1994), www.uvm.edu/~hag/histreview/vol6/lund.html; Daniel J. Tichenor, *Dividing Lines: The Politics of Immigration Control in America* (Princeton, NJ: Princeton University Press, 2002), 128–132. For the centrality of the passport measure to Congressional debates, see "Restriction of Immigration," Cong. Rec.59th Cong., 2nd sess., 1907, vol. 41, pt. 4, esp. 3083–3099; USIC, 23:1, 4. I found their names in payroll records in HP.

3. See also Paul Kramer, "Outside Agitators: Civilization, Empire, and the San Francisco School Crisis of 1906–7" (unpublished paper in author's possession); we share a similar argument about the relationship between foreign policy and immigration in this incident, although his work is unrelated to the formation of the commission.

4. Raymond A. Esthus, *Theodore Roosevelt and Japan* (Seattle: University of Washington Press, 1967), 133. Charles Scawthorn, John Eidinger, and Anshel Schiff, eds., *Fire Following Earthquake* (Reston, VA: American Society of Civil Engineers, 2005); numerical data from "Casualties and Damage after the 1906 Earthquake," United States Geological Survey, http://earthquake.usgs.gov/regional/nca/1906/18april/casualties.php.

5. USIC, 25:191. The Japanese population increased from 1,781 in 1900 to 11,380 in 1907, while the city's total numbers increased perhaps only 15 percent, based on estimates by the U.S. Census. "San Francisco Earthquake of 1906: Census Facts. Comparing 1906 to More Recent Times," *Infoplease,* www.infoplease.com/spot/sanfranearthquakecensus .html. The commission's own statistics claimed that the overall U.S. population of Japanese had increased by four times from 1900 to 1909. USIC, 23:5. I have not calculated whether the increase in violence was proportional to the population increase. Esthus, *Theodore Roosevelt and Japan,* 133. In contrast, the San Francisco fire was somewhat of a boon for the Chinese community. Most of the birth records were destroyed, allowing Chinese to claim "paper sons," children of legal Chinese immigrants. These children were technically U.S. citizens, and so fraudulent "birth certificates" became a way to immigrate to the United States and / or become a citizen, by claiming a father who was a legal resident. See Ronald T. Takaki, *Strangers from a Different Shore: A History of Asian Americans,* rev. ed. (New York: Little, Brown, 1998), 234–237.

6. It was a pattern that would repeat itself with each successive restriction law. Filipino and Mexican migration increased after the restrictions on European immigration in 1921, 1924, and 1927. Although the commission and the Bureau of Immigration would both study Japanese who smuggled across the Mexican and Canadian borders (early "illegal immigrants"), these represented less than 5 percent of the total. USIC, 23:15. Marcus Braun, an agent for the Bureau of Immigration, undertook a report on the subject. See Gunther Peck, *Reinventing Free Labor: Padrones and Immigrant Workers in the North American West, 1880–1930* (New York: Cambridge University Press, 2000), 102. USIC, 23:6, 13; Esthus, *Theodore Roosevelt and Japan,* 146; see also Letter, Oscar Straus to Mr. Secretary (Elihu Root), December 22, 1906, Box 20, OSP; "American fever" quoted in Takaki, *Strangers,* 147; USIC, 23:21–22. The Japanese never exceeded 9 percent of the population of any county. Yamato Ichihashi, *Japanese Immigration: Its Status in California* (San Francisco, CA: Marshall Press, 1915), 19; William S. Rossiter, Willard Long Thorp, and LeVerne Beales, *Increase of Population in the United States, 1910–1920: A Study of Changes in the Population of Divisions, States, Counties, and Rural and Urban Areas, and in Sex, Color, and Nativity, at the Fourteenth Census* (Washington, DC: Government Printing Office, 1922), 175–176.

7. Esthus, *Theodore Roosevelt and Japan,* 134; USIC, 23:167; Examples of the petitions can be found in HR59A-H8.1, Committee on Immigration and Naturalization / Chinese Immigration, Box 404, Record Group 233, Records of United States House of Representatives, Center for Legislative Archives, NADC; See, for example, Letter, John

P. Irish, U.S. Customs Service, Port of San Francisco, CA, to Secretary of Commerce and Labor Oscar Straus, March 29, 1907, Box 6, OSP. On the crisis's roots in leftist San Francisco politics, see Michael Kazin, *Barons of Labor: The San Francisco Building Trades and Union Power in the Progressive Era* (Urbana: University of Illinois Press, 1987), 162–169.

8. Kiyo Sue Inui, "The Gentlemen's Agreement: How It Has Functioned," *Annals of the American Academy of Political and Social Science* 122, The Far East (1925): 188–198, quotation on 188; Eldon R. Penrose, *California Nativism: Organized Opposition to the Japanese, 1890–1913* (San Francisco, CA: R and E Research Associates, 1974), 27; Gilbert P. Gia, "States' Rights, T.R., and Japanese Children, 1907," *Historic Bakesfield & Kern County, California,* 2012, 2–3; USIC, 23:162; Esthus, *Theodore Roosevelt and Japan,* 144. The solicitor general made an ominous comparison: "What happened to the Fourteenth Amendment may well happen to the Treaty of 1894." It was a veiled reference to the *Plessy v. Ferguson* case of a decade earlier, when the Supreme Court had gutted the Fourteenth Amendment's promise of equal protection by arguing it was consistent with "separate but equal" accommodations for African Americans. Coming from a Republican lawyer, Scott's statement was not one of praise. For two views, see "Olney Disagrees with Roosevelt over Japan," *New York Times,* February 6, 1907, 1, and Elihu Root, "The Real Questions under the Japanese Treaty and the San Francisco School Board Resolution. Presidential Address at the First Annual Meeting of the American Society of International Law, Washington, DC, April 19, 1907," in Elihu Root, *Addresses on International Subjects,* ed. Robert Bacon and James Brown Scott (1916; repr., Freeport, NY: Books for Libraries, 1969), 274–286.

9. See Esthus, *Theodore Roosevelt and Japan,* 76–96, 106; Ichihashi, *Japanese Immigration,* 46; Kramer, "Outside Agitators"; Michael R. Auslin, *Pacific Cosmopolitans: A Cultural History of U.S.-Japan Relations* (Cambridge, MA: Harvard University Press, 2011), 87.

10. Roosevelt quoted in Esthus, *Theodore Roosevelt and Japan,* 128, also see preface. On Straus's views, see *Under Four Administrations* (Boston: Houghton Mifflin, 1922), 218–230; Tichenor, *Dividing Lines,* 128–132; Straus, *Under Four Administrations,* 180. On Root's views, see Philip C. Jessup, *Elihu Root* (New York: Dodd, Mead, 1938), 2:458. On Straus, see Straus to Charles Bonaparte, U.S. Attorney General, January 30, 1907, and Wilber F. Crafts to Straus, August 27, 1907, both Box 7, OSP; "Jordan Explains President Was in Bad Temper," *San Francisco Call,* February 16, 1907, 2; Letter, Theodore Roosevelt to John Hay, September 2, 1904, in *Letters of Theodore Roosevelt,* ed. Elting E. Morison et al. (Cambridge, MA: Harvard University Press, 1951), 4:917, quoted in Warren I. Cohen, "From Contempt to Containment: Cycles in American Attitudes toward China," in *Twentieth Century American Foreign Policy,* ed. John Braeman et al. (Columbus: Ohio State University Press, 1971), 507. I thank Warren Cohen for the reference.

11. See Kramer, "Outside Agitators," 5; Jeremiah W. Jenks, "The Japanese in Manchuria," *The Outlook,* March 11, 1911, 549.

12. David Folkmar and Elnora Folkmar, USIC, 5:98, 147. Ichihashi, *Japanese Immigration*, 46. He likely got the term from his mentor David Starr Jordan; see quotations in Gordon H. Chang, *Morning Glory, Evening Shadow: Yamato Ichihashi and His Internment Writings, 1942–1945* (Palo Alto, CA: Stanford University Press, 1999), 19–20; quotation from Ichihashi, *Japanese Immigration*, 54.

13. Esthus, *Theodore Roosevelt and Japan*, 143, 148–149, and quotations from Root and Roosevelt, 132, 139. For more detail on the press in Japan, see Kramer, "Outside Agitators." And see Masuda Hajimu, "Rumors of War: Immigration Disputes and the Social Construction of American-Japanese Relations, 1905–1913," *Diplomatic History* 33, no. 1 (January 2009): 1–37.

14. Esthus, *Theodore Roosevelt and Japan*, 139, 156, 145–147, 166. As pernicious as segregation was, Roosevelt was exaggerating, since the Oriental School was, of course, public. It should be pointed out, however, that Roosevelt was working to increase naval appropriations at the same time, so it made sense for him to emphasize the military aspect of the conflict.

15. Letter, Theodore Roosevelt to Henry Cabot Lodge, July 10, 1907, in *Selections from the Correspondence of Theodore Roosevelt and Henry Cabot Lodge, 1884–1918*, ed. Henry Cabot Lodge (New York: C. Scribner's Sons, 1925), 2:274–275.

16. What IRL lobbyist James Patten called "some fool distribution schemes." See Chapters 3 and 7. James Patten to Joseph Lee, March 8, 1906, Carton 1, JLP; and see Barbara Miller Solomon, *Ancestors and Immigrants: A Changing New England Tradition* (Chicago: University of Chicago Press, 1956), 118–119, 124.

17. Robert F. Zeidel, *Immigrants, Progressives, and Exclusion Politics: The Dillingham Commission, 1900–1927* (DeKalb: Northern Illinois University Press, 2004), 27; USIC, 1:11; on splits in the Republican party at this time, see Tichenor, *Dividing Lines*, chap. 5, esp. 123–128; on Bartholdt, *Joint Resolution to Create a Commission to Examine the Subject of Immigration*, H.J.Res. 161, 59th Cong., 1st sess., May 22, 1906, Box 347, Records of the United States House of Representatives, HR59A, and see Donna Gabaccia, *Foreign Relations: American Immigration in Global Perspective* (Princeton, NJ: Princeton University Press, 2012).

18. Zeidel, *Immigrants, Progressives*, 31–35. This came from a recollection of IRL lobbyist James Patten three years later, so it is hard to know the reliability of the information. See J. H. Patten to Joseph Lee, May 16, 1910, Carton 1, JLP.

19. On Japanese attitudes, see Kramer, "Outside Agitators"; William S. Rossiter, "The Immigration Law of 1907," *The American Monthly Review of Reviews* 35, no. 4 (April 1907): 470.

20. Months before, he had already discussed the commission idea with Charles Neill. Zeidel, *Immigrants, Progressives*, 24–25, and 34; on the IRL and the literacy test, see John Higham, *Strangers in the Land: Patterns of American Nativism, 1860–1925* (New York: Atheneum, 1968), 101–105. The conference committee's opponents of the literacy test

found that they were, in Congressman William Bennet's words, "up against Henry Cabot Lodge." *Reminiscences of William Stiles Bennet* (1951), 37, Rare Book & Manuscript Library, Columbia University in the City of New York; "Restriction of Immigration," 3089.

21. Technically, the executive branch could not add new material to a bill in conference, as a violation of the separation of powers. However, it happened in this case and does in others as well. On the power of Straus's agency, see Diary, April 17, 1907, and January 10, 1907, both in Box 22, OSP.

22. "Restriction of Immigration," 3218, 3098; Letter, Oscar Straus to Isidor Straus, December 19, 1906, Box 20, OSP; Kornel Chang, "Circulating Race and Empire: Transnational Labor Activism and the Politics of Anti-Asian Agitation in the Anglo-American Pacific World, 1880–1910," *Journal of American History* 96, no. 3 (December 2009): 678–701; "Senate Passes Coolie Measure," *New York Times,* February 17, 1907, 1.

23. Esthus, *Theodore Roosevelt and Japan,* 159; Consider Arizona's 2010 state law, SB1070, and related laws passed in several other states and opposed by the Obama administration. In the early twentieth century, Alien Land Laws in Arizona and California caused similar problems. Jerry Markon, "Obama Administration Widens Challenges to State Immigration Laws," *Washington Post,* September 29, 2011, www.washingtonpost .com/politics/obama-administration-widens-challenges-to-state-immigration-laws/2011 /09/28/gIQA8HgR7K_story.html. Theodore Roosevelt killed a California version in 1909 that was later passed in 1913. See H. A. Millis, *The Japanese Problem in the United States* (New York: Macmillan, 1915), 197, 211; Christopher Mitchell, "Introduction: Immigration and U.S. Foreign Policy toward the Caribbean, Central America, and Mexico," in *Western Hemisphere Immigration and United States Foreign Policy,* ed. Christopher Mitchell (University Park: Pennsylvania State University Press, 1992), 13.

24. "Restriction of Immigration," 3222, 3097. The language of southern legislators mirrored that used by exclusionists in California. Kazin, *Barons of Labor,* 64.

25. "Restriction of Immigration," 3222.

26. Ibid., 3227, 3222.

27. Scott Kurashige, *The Shifting Grounds of Race: Black and Japanese Americans in the Making of Multiethnic Los Angeles* (Princeton, NJ: Princeton University Press, 2008), 18, *L.A. Times* quotation on p. 20. On population, see Ichihashi, *Japanese Immigration,* 19, 20; *The Wasp* [San Francisco], December 8, 1906, quoted in Doremus Scudder, "The Japanese Question" (unpublished paper attached to Letter, Wilber F. Crafts to Oscar Straus, August 27, 1907, Box 7, OSP); USIC quotations and citations, 23:162, 73, 55; see also 97.

28. In early February, Roosevelt enjoined Root to meet with four Republican conference committee members—Lodge, Howell, Dillingham, and Bennet (all later named to the commission). Root, like Roosevelt, favored restriction, but he was also a practical diplomat who knew relations with Japan were more important than a literacy test. Esthus, *Theodore Roosevelt and Japan,* 152–160; see also "Jordan Explains"; Andrea Geiger,

Subverting Exclusion: Transpacific Encounters with Race, Caste, and Borders, 1885–1928 (New Haven, CT: Yale University Press, 2011), 105; Straus Diary, OSP, 215.

29. I am indebted to Zeidel, *Immigrants, Progressives,* for this account, esp. 26–34. The jockeying for appointments to the commission began nearly right away. See the letters of the IRL, for example, Letter, Prescott Hall to James Patten, February 4, 1907, JLP.

30. Root, "Real Questions," 7.

31. Ibid., 8, 11, 14, 22, 23; Rhee says that by summer of 1907, even after the Gentlemen's Agreement, relations with Japan were so bad that President Roosevelt sent a coded cable to General Leonard Wood in the Philippines, warning him to ready his troops for attack by Japan. Roosevelt later told Root that the Europeans thought that Japan could beat the United States in a war, in T. C. Rhee, "A Postscript on the Japanese-American 'Immigration' Dispute, 1868–1924: A Diplomatic Tinderbox," *University of Dayton Review* 9 (Winter 1972), 135.

32. "Substitutes for Asiatics," *Los Angeles Times,* May 8, 1908, 1. On "facts" and commissions, see Sunmin Kim, "Reworking Whiteness: Challenges to the Racial Ideology of the Dillingham Commission (1907–1911)" (unpublished conference paper, Legal Studies Association Conference, July 2017, in author's possession).

33. Jeremiah W. Jenks, "The Character and Influence of Recent Immigrants," in *Questions of Public Policy: Addresses Delivered in the Page Lecture Series, 1913, Before the Senior Class of the Sheffield Scientific School, Yale University* (New Haven, CT: Yale University Press, 1913), 2.

34. Higham, *Strangers in the Land,* 126, On IRL attitudes see, generally, File Nov. 10–30, 1910, Carton 2[?], JLP; Letter, John Burnett to Prescott Hall, June 22, 1912, Folder 203, IRLR; Zeidel, *Immigrants, Progressives,* 26.

35. Letter, Theodore Roosevelt to [?] Jesse Taylor, secretary, National Council Junior Order United American Mechanics, February 1, 1907, Carton 1, JLP.

36. Paul B. Cook, *Academicians in Government from Roosevelt to Roosevelt* (New York: Garland, 1982), 64: after Taft was elected in 1908, Jenks lobbied unsuccessfully for the China ambassadorship. Jerry Israel, *Progressivism and the Open Door: America and China, 1905–1921* (Pittsburgh, PA: University of Pittsburgh Press, 1971), 44–51, 65; Daniel J. Tichenor and Alexandra Filindra, "Raising *Arizona v. United States:* Historical Patterns of American Immigration Federalism," *Lewis & Clark Law Review* 16, no. 4 (2012): 1215. On the states as a model for federal legislation, see Hidetaka Hirota, "The Moment of Transition: State Officials, the Federal Government, and the Formation of American Immigration Policy," *Journal of American History* 99, no. 4 (2013): 1092–1108; "Coast Man Selected: W. R. Wheeler, of Oakland, on Immigration Body," *Washington Post,* March 27, 1907, 4 (though the IRL was suspicious of him for his ties to railway companies, a notorious employer of Asian immigrants). Patten to Lee, November 25, 1910, File Nov. 10–30, 1910, Carton 2, JLP; Letter, Theodore Roosevelt to William R.

Wheeler, March 19, 1907, quoted in Letter, Wheeler to William Howard Taft, April 21, 1909, Reel 351, William H. Taft Papers, Manuscript Division, Library of Congress, Washington, DC.

37. Letter, Wheeler to Taft, April 21, 1909, Reel 351, Taft Papers; "Nation Aroused: The Need of Exhaustive Investigation into Immigration Problem Recognized," *Berea (KY) Citizen,* April 25, 1907, 6; USIC, 1:12.

38. "Coast Man Selected"; USIC, 4:231. On the SS *Canopic,* http://www.titanic -titanic.com/canopic.shtml; USIC, 1:165; "Decide to Tour Europe," *New York Times,* April 23, 1907; Claude G. Bowers, *Beveridge and the Progressive Era* (Boston: Houghton Mifflin, 1932), 263.

39. USIC, 4. The National Liberal Immigration League sent a representative who sent weekly reports on the commission's activities, and sent them, for no discernible reason, to the IRL. See, e.g., Herbert G. Sherwood, series of reports, June 1, 1907–September 13, 1907, enclosed in Nathan Bijur, NLIL, to Prescott Hall, Folder 5 of 9 Immigration Commission, IRLR; Unidentified news clipping, summer 1907, New Brunswick, New Jersey, in Folder A2, Benjamin Howell Papers, Rutgers University Library Special Collections, New Brunswick, NJ; NCF had also considered one until President Roosevelt decided the trip might step on the State Department's diplomatic toes. What had once been a private think tank's purview was becoming more clearly the business of the state. Letter, Ralph Easley to Nicholas Murray Butler, August 9, 1907, Reel 167, NCFP. On Root's support see Telegram, Easley to Butler, August 16, 1907, and on Neill, see Easley to MacVeagh, September 8, 1907; Reynolds to Easley, December 9, 1907, and sarcastic response denigrating Taft in Easley[?] to Reynolds, December 12, 1907, and, generally for discussion of the discussion of the Japanese investigation, see correspondence, Reel 167, NCFP.

40. USIC, 40; U.S. Congress, Senate, *Importing Women for Immoral Purposes: A Partial Report from the Immigration Commission on the Importation and Harboring of Women for Immoral Purposes,* 61st Cong., 2nd sess., 1909, S.Doc. 136. And see Gunther Peck, "Feminizing White Slavery in the United States: Marcus Braun and the Transnational Traffic in White Bodies, 1890–1910," in *Workers across the World: The Transnational Turn in Labor History,* ed. Leon Fink (New York: Oxford University Press, 2011), 221–244; See Gruenberg reports, Files 52066, 52066A, Box 386, Entry 9, Record Group 85, Bureau of Immigration Records, NADC.

41. Patrick Weil, "Races at the Gate: A Century of Racial Distinctions in American Immigration Policy (1865–1965), *Georgetown Immigration Law Journal* 15 (2000–2001): 637. My thanks to Professor Weil for pointing this work out to me.

42. Marilyn Lake and Henry Reynolds, *Drawing the Global Colour Line: White Men's Countries and the International Challenge of Racial Equality* (New York: Cambridge University Press, 2008). See "Investigation of Immigration," *Salt Lake Herald,* April 21, 1907, and Frederic J. Haskin, "Our Immense Immigration," *Washington (DC)*

Herald, February 1, 1908, 7. Aristide Zolberg, *A Nation by Design: Immigration Policy in the Fashioning of America* (Cambridge, MA: Harvard University Press, 2006), 230–231; Diary, November 8, 1908, Box 22, OSP. In the end, the trip to Europe and one by Dillingham to Hawaii proved to be the extent of the commission's investigative work outside the nation's boundaries, besides the reports they purchased from agents of the Immigration Service.

43. Thomas J. Archdeacon, *Becoming American: An Ethnic History* (New York: Free Press, 1983), 118.

44. "Secondary Topics: The Immigration Problem," *Washington (DC) National Tribune,* April 25, 1907, 1. See also "Substitutes for Asiatics"; Notebook, "USIC Records 1907–1910," 87, HP. William Wheeler to Charles Neill (as Commissioner of Labor), August 11, 1910, Entry of Hindu and Sikh immigrants to U.S., and San Francisco, California, and West Coast labor movement and exclusion movement, Accession #: 001738-022-0704, Records of the Immigration and Naturalization Service, Series A: Subject Correspondence Files, Part 1: Asian Immigration and Exclusion, 1906–1913, Date: Jan 01, 1910–Dec 31, 1910, from Bureau of Immigration Papers, RG 85, NADC, reproduced in Proquest History Vault Database; USIC, 23:3–4; "Warns Jenks of Brown Peril," *Los Angeles Times,* August 17, 1907, I3.

45. Takaki, *Strangers,* 186, and USIC, 23:131, 48. The shingle mill story was a disheartening one—the shingle workers faced opposition from white unions, so they worked to buy their own mills, only to find they could not get insurance for their mills when one burned down. USIC, 23:3, 48.

46. Thomas J. Archdeacon, *Becoming American: An Ethnic History* (New York: Free Press, 1983), 118. These tables of contents were compiled in the summer of 1910; the abstracts in the first two volumes of the commission's report, compiled in December, did list Mexicans in a simplified table of contents organized around national origin. On the cuts, see Zeidel, *Immigrants, Progressives,* 82–85. The 1908 statistics gathering was made possible by a provision in the Immigration Act of 1907. On Mexicans, see Katherine Benton-Cohen, "Other Immigrants: Mexicans and the Dillingham Commission," *Journal of American Ethnic History* 30, no. 2 (2011): 33–57.

47. Millis, *Japanese Problem.* It was funded in part by the Federal Council of Churches in America. See Review of *The Japanese Problem in the United States,* by H. A. Millis, *Journal of Political Economy* 23, no. 10 (1915): 1020–1021. Millis's work on the Japanese began a lifelong interest in labor relations, and he served on the first National Labor Relations Board; USIC, 24:59. Ichihashi said he was hired "through the kind effort of Prof. Millis" to work with him on the "investigation of Japanese engaged in agricultural pursuits." Ichihashi to Jordan, n.d., Box 60, Folder 60–578, Jordan Papers; USIC, 23:141, 148–149, 160, 59.

48. I have learned from the work of Paul Kramer and Alicia Ratterree about the world of Asian university students. I found translators' names in payroll reports in LP and HP.

Typewritten article, "Classroom Ambassadors," Yamato Ichihashi Papers (SC0071), Dept. of Special Collections and University Archives, Stanford University Archives, Stanford, CA.

49. Takaki, *Strangers,* 143, 148.

50. USIC, 23:40, 67, 41 and 24:186.

51. USIC, 23:4, 41, 43 and 24:228. This effect was, in fact, the argument for policy makers' support of immigration restriction.

52. USIC, 24:187. A special report on the small South Asian population in California (largely Punjabi) was included in the same volume. They were described in the Japanese reports as "a filthy, ignorant, and despised race . . . considered the least desirable immigrants in the state." USIC, 24:28. Among many discussions of this strike, see Takaki, *Strangers,* 198–199, and Tomas Almaguer, *Racial Fault Lines: The Historical Origins of White Supremacy in California* (Berkeley: University of California Press, 2008).

53. USIC, 23:54–55; Geiger, *Subverting Exclusion,* 17, 66–70, quotation on 67. Some Japanese diplomats blamed prejudice in the American West on the preponderance of lower-caste Japanese there. Geiger, *Subverting Exclusion,* 56–57.

54. USIC, 24:21, 36, 23:55, 57, 24:29.

55. USIC, 24:141. On immigration policy and concerns over free labor, see Peck, *Reinventing Free Labor.*

56. See for example, USIC, 23:80–82. In some places, though, there were no Japanese farmers—in Colorado, for example, where general opinions of the Japanese were higher than in California, "only one Japanese landowner—a half breed with a white wife—was reported." USIC, 24:123.

57. Geiger argues Japanese immigrants found it rude to ask one another personal questions that might reveal an outcaste status obscured by upward mobility. *Subverting Exclusion,* 70. In 1909, the California Assembly came close to passing an alien land law forbidding Japanese from owning land, but President Roosevelt intervened with the governor, who managed its narrow defeat. An Alien Land Act succeeded in 1913, however, and even before that California State's constitution forbade land sale to aliens ineligible for citizenship. Ichihashi, *Japanese Immigration,* 65–66; USIC, 24:236, 189.

58. USIC, 24:56 and 23:82–88. On the number of women, see K. K. Kawakami, "Japanese Immigration: A Study in Official Documents and Statistics," *Japan Review: A Herald of the Pacific Era* 4 (January 1920): 76.

59. Quoted in Takaki, *Strangers,* 201.

60. Proclamation cited in USIC, 23:162. These fears would animate anti-Japanese attacks for years to come. In hearings in 1913 to promote an alien land act, one white California farmer testified, "Near my home is an eighty-acre tract of as fine land as there is in California. On that tract lives a Japanese. With that Japanese lives a white woman. In that woman's arms is a baby. What is that baby? It isn't Japanese. It isn't white. I'll tell you

what that baby is. It is a germ of the mightiest problem that ever faced this state; a problem that will make the black problem of the South look white. All about us the Asiatics are gaining a foothold." Quoted in Takaki, *Strangers,* 204. Ichihashi himself appears to have lied about his age in high school to avoid criticism. Chang, *Morning Glory,* 14.

61. Report of mass meeting in San Francisco, May 8, 1900, cited in USIC, 24:167.

62. USIC, 23: 160, 164.

63. Ibid., 23:3; Ichihashi to Jordon, n.d., Jordan papers.

64. Victor Clark, "Immigration Conditions in Hawaii," in USIC, 1:696–722; Notebook, "USIC Records 1907–1910," December 14, 1909, 105, HP; See Letter, H. C. Stevens, Acting Private Secretary, to "Sir," July 1, 1907, and August 27, 1907, Box 7, OSP.

65. James A. LeRoy, American Consular Service, Durango, Mexico, to Victor S. Clark, January 31, 1905; Edward Treagor to Victor Clark, April 8, 1904; Clark to James LeRoy, January 4, 1906, all Box 1, Victor Clark Papers, Manuscript Division, Library of Congress, Washington, DC; Victor S. Clark, "Mexican Labor in the United States," *Bureau of Labor Bulletin* 78 (1908): 466–522. On Neill and Clark's friendship, see Victor Clark to Mrs. [Charles] Neill, October 5, 1942, Condolences, NP-TRC. On his language training see Janet R. Linde, "Victor S. Clark Papers: A Finding Aid to the Collection in the Library of Congress," rev. Melinda K. Friend (Washington, DC: Manuscript Division, Library of Congress, 2011).

66. Clark, "Immigration Conditions," 700; *Joint Resolution to Provide for Annexing the Hawaiian Islands to the United States,* Pub. L. 55–55, 30 Stat. 751 (1898), known as the Newlands Resolution. Clark was an expert on debt peonage. In 1906 and 1907 he went to the American South to investigate debt peonage of immigrants and African Americans. See Oscar Straus to Bishop Gailor, January 13, 1908, Scrapbook 3, Box 20, OSP.

67. Clark, "Immigration Conditions," 702, 712, 722. His use of the term "Caucasia" in this context was doubly confusing—the commission's *Dictionary of Races or Peoples* classified Siberians as "Caucasians" but also criticized the term for its confusion. See USIC, 5:98, 147. For more on the Siberia scheme, see Aline Simone, "Inside the Bizarre, Racist Scheme to Import Siberian Workers to Hawaii in 1909," *Atlas Obscura.com,* May 2, 2016.

68. Letter, Ichihashi to Jordan, April 17, 1908, Folder 568, Box 59, Jordan Papers; Chang, *Morning Glory,* 20; Typewritten article, "Classroom Ambassadors," and typewritten article, "Autobiographical Clipping," both, Ichihashi Papers; Yamato Ichihashi, *Japanese in the United States* (1932; repr., New York: Arno Press, 1969).

69. On horse stalls, see encyclopedia.densho.org/Santa_Anita_(detention_facility)/; Gordon H. Chang, "We Almost Wept," *Stanford Today,* November / December 1996, https://web.stanford.edu/dept/news/stanfordtoday/ed/9611/9611fea401.shtml; Chang, *Morning Glory.*

70. See, for example Rhee, "A Postscript," 135; Notes for a lecture called "Facts around the Pacific," Ichihashi Papers.

3. Hebrew or Jewish Is Simply a Religion

1. See, e.g., the articles in *The Outlook,* esp. December 15, 1906, December 29, 1906, June 1, 1907, which offered a western—specifically California—perspective; for an eastern point of view, see "Schmitz's Deal with President," *New York Times,* February 19, 1907, 5. In an ironic turn, in 1900, Ross had been fired from Stanford University for supporting Asian exclusion. Julius Weinberg, "The Progressive as Nativist," *Wisconsin Magazine of History* 50, no. 3 (1967): 244. Edward A. Ross, *Old World in the New: The Significance of Past and Present Immigration to the American People* (New York: Century, 1913), 163. On lobbying, see Christopher M. Loomis, "The Politics of Uncertainty: Lobbyists and Propaganda in Early Twentieth-Century America," *Journal of Policy History* 21, no. 2 (2009): 187–213.

2. Ross, *Old World,* 144–145. Ross's work is cited by Kevin MacDonald, a scholar who has become associated with white nationalism, in, "Jewish Involvement in Influencing United States Immigration Policy, 1881–1965: A Historical Review," *Population and Environment* 19, no. 4 (1998): 295–355. On his politics, see Tony Ortega, "In the Hot Seat," *New Times Los Angeles,* May 25, 2000; Gary Dean Best, *To Free a People: American Jewish Leaders and the Jewish Problem in Eastern Europe, 1890–1914* (Westport, CT: Greenwood Press, 1982), 6. The term "negotiation" is from Eric Goldstein, *The Price of Whiteness: Jews, Race, and American Identity* (Princeton, NJ: Princeton University Press, 2006), 5.

3. Jeremiah W. Jenks, "The Japanese in Manchuria," *The Outlook,* March 11, 1911.

4. Minutes of an "informal conference . . . at the residence of Louis Marshall," Box 1, Folder 4, LMP.

5. See Simon Wolf, *Presidents I Have Known from 1860–1918,* 2nd ed. (Washington, DC: Press of Byron S. Adams, 1918). Biographical information on Wolf is from Esther L. Panitz, *Simon Wolf: Private Conscience and Public Image* (Rutherford, NJ: Farleigh Dickinson University Press, 1987), intro. and chap. 1. On Washington Hebrew Congregation, see "About Us," *Washington Hebrew Congregation,* www.whctemple.org/about-us.

6. On this point, see Jonathan Sarna, "Cyrus Adler and the Development of American Jewish Culture: The 'Scholar-Doer' as a Jewish Communal Leader," *American Jewish History* 78, no. 3 (1989): 382–394, esp. 393.

7. One exception was financier Jacob Schiff, who came to the United States from Germany at age eighteen.

8. Sheldon Morris Neuringer, "American Jewry and United States Immigration Policy, 1881–1953" (PhD diss., University of Wisconsin-Madison, 1969), 23. On Wolf's testimony, see Wolf, *Presidents,* 286. On Kohler, see Libby Garland, *After They Closed the Gates: Jewish Illegal Immigration to the United States, 1921–1965* (Chicago: University of Chicago Press, 2014), 164; *United States v. Lee Yen Tai,* 185 U.S. 213 (1902). The relationship between Jewish lobbyists and Chinese exclusion deserves further research. See for example Max Kohler's correspondence with individuals, including prominent

Chinese scholar Mary Coolidge and Oscar Straus, in Box 1, Folders 13, 14, and 37, MJKP. Most interesting, perhaps, is a letter from Coolidge to Kohler urging him to offer some positive reflections on Chinese immigration to Jeremiah Jenks. See Letter, Coolidge to Kohler, June 13, 1907, Box 12, Folder 12, MJKP. Also see link to Japanese in Kohler's work in Letter, Oscar Straus to attorney general Charles Bonaparte, January 30, 1907, Box 20, OSP.

9. See the stirring first lines of Irving Howe's famous *World of Our Fathers: The Journey of the East European Jews to America and the Life They Found and Made* (1976; repr., New York: Schocken Books, 1989), 5; Neuringer, "American Jewry," 10–11, 8.

10. Quoted in Neuringer, "American Jewry," 17–18.

11. See, among others, Moon-Ho Jung, *Coolies and Cane: Race, Labor, and Sugar in the Age of Emancipation* (Baltimore, MD: Johns Hopkins University Press, 2008), and Gunther Peck, *Reinventing Free Labor: Padrones and Immigrant Workers in the North American West, 1880–1930* (New York: Cambridge University Press, 2000).

12. Quoted in Neuringer, "American Jewry," 25.

13. Ibid., 25. The main organizations were the Jewish Colonization Society and the Jewish Agricultural Society.

14. Initially the most vocal opponents were German American gentiles, who had an extensive language program in parochial schools and maintained many German-language newspapers.

15. Neuringer, "American Jewry," 56–63. On Wolf's work in getting exclusions overturned or preventing deportations, see his papers in general, but especially "Not a Time to Despair: Mr. Simon Wolf of Washington is Apprehensive of the Large Immigration But It Cannot Be Stemmed: Influential Jews Must Help Us," which appears to be a typescript of a newspaper article, n.d.; and Wolf to Cowen, July 31, 1906, Box 1, Folder 1, SWP. Jeanne Petit, *The Men and Women We Want: Gender, Race, and the Progressive Era Literacy Test* (Rochester, NY: University of Rochester Press, 2010), esp. 322.

16. Britt Tevis, " 'The Hebrews Are Appearing in Court in Great Numbers: Toward a Reassessment of Early Twentieth-Century American Jewish Immigration History," *American Jewish History* 100, no. 3 (2016): 319–347, fig. on 322. See Ronald H. Bayor, *Encountering Ellis Island: How European Immigrants Entered America* (Baltimore, MD: Johns Hopkins University Press, 2014). Deirdre Moloney, *National Insecurities: Immigrants and U.S. Deportation Policy since 1882* (Chapel Hill: University of North Carolina Press, 2012), esp. 108–109, 125–126, 83–84. For discussion of the poor-physique clauses and challenges to them, see also Box 10, Folder 2, MJKP. On Williams and new policies, see Esther Panitz, "In Defense of the Jewish Immigrant, 1891–1924," *American Jewish Historical Quarterly* 55, no. 1 (1965): 60.

17. Neuringer, "American Jewry," 94. On kosher meals, see Anna Herkner, "Steerage Conditions," in USIC, 37:19. Wolf spent much of his time challenging these rulings. On Wolf's efforts, and his opposition to the Committee of Fifty, see Letter, Wolf to Philip Cowen, July 31, 1906, SWP.

18. Wolf had lobbied Congress on the plight of immigrant Jews since as early as 1870. He had protested to Congress about the plight of Romanian Jews, and by the twentieth century he was a fixture at the Bureau of Immigration. Best, *To Free a People*, 6. Historian Deirdre Moloney calls the rule a "physical manifestation of the LPC provision," especially because its authors thought that physique was purely hereditary. Moloney, *National Insecurities*, 126. On 1909, see Panitz, "In Defense," 60. As my student Chad Frazier has pointed out, there was also an effort to use the Immigration Act of 1907 to reduce the personal sway and power of the secretary of commerce and labor, Oscar Straus, the first Jewish cabinet secretary. Critics—especially centered in the IRL—felt Straus was far too sympathetic to people who challenged their exclusion in the boards of inquiry. When Roosevelt appointed Straus, he told him, "I want to show Russia and such countries what we think of a Jew in this country." Best, *To Free a People*, 123. Chad Frazier, "Power and Expectation: Oscar Straus, the Boards of Special Inquiry, and the Implementation of U.S. Immigration Law, 1906–1909" (unpublished seminar paper, Georgetown University, December 16, 2011, in author's possession); Tevis, "Hebrews Are Appearing."

19. Fiorella LaGuardia's mother was Jewish, although he was a practicing Episcopalian. New York did not have another Jewish mayor until Abraham Beame in the 1970s.

20. Letter, Cyrus Adler to Max Kohler, July 26, 1909, Box 12, Folder 4, MJKP. Also in Ira Robinson, *Cyrus Adler: Selected Letters*, ed. Cyrus Adler (Philadelphia: Jewish Publication Society of America, 1985), 1:166.

21. Jerome Karabel, *The Chosen: The Hidden History of Admission and Exclusion at Harvard, Yale, and Princeton* (Boston: Houghton Mifflin, 2005).

22. Speech, "Summer Hotels and Kindred Insanity," Box 2, Folder 7, SWP.

23. Unidentified newspaper clipping in Box 2, Folder 6, SWP.

24. Best, *To Free a People*, 88; "FOR FAIR IMMIGRATION LAW: Mass Meeting Called to Protest against the Bill before Congress," *New York Times*, June 10, 1906, 16. Also see Neuringer, "American Jewry," 91–92. On the NLIL, see Rivka Shpak Lissak, "The National Liberal Immigration League and Immigration Restriction, 1906–1917," *American Jewish Archives* 46, no. 2 (1994): 197–246. Although the Jewish effort was probably the most high-profile and transformative of their own ethnic politics, the major German and Irish benevolent groups also committed themselves to fighting restriction in 1907. During the 1907 debates, for example, the National German American Alliance wrote to Congress calling for "the entire subject [to] . . . be referred to a Commission . . . whose report and recommendations could be made the basis for stable laws." The German lobbyists called "immigration . . . as much a local as a national question, and the solution lies more in distribution than in restriction." File 59a-H8.3, Box 412, USHR. See also John Higham, *Strangers in the Land: Patterns of American Nativism, 1860–1925* (New York: Atheneum Books, 1968), 123.

25. See for example Sulzberger to Adler, February 8, 1907, Box 1, Folder 9, CAP; Neuringer, "American Jewry," 91–93, quotation on 93. My views on this point have been

heavily influenced by William E. Forbath, "Jews, Law and Identity Politics" (paper presented at the annual meeting of the Law and Society Association, San Francisco, CA, May 30, 2011).

26. Panitz, *Simon Wolf,* 103–104; Marshall to Wertheim, February 2, 1907, and Marshall to Judge [M. Warley Platzek], February 4, 1907, both in Box 1, Folder 1, LMP. Marshall was aware that Roosevelt already "would be entirely satisfied" with a bill that substituted a commission for restrictions. On Marshall and the New York Commission, see USIC, 41:209; Marshall to Lauterbach, February 9, 1907, Box 1, Folder 1, LMP. For pressure on other members of the immigration committee, see [Marshall?], United Cigar Manufacturer's Co., New Brunswick, NJ, to Hon. B. F. Howell (R-NJ), February 4, 1907, Box 1, Folder 1, LMP.

27. Adler to Herbert Friedenwald, February 21, 1907, in Robinson, *Cyrus Adler,* 1:132. In addition, an amendment to exempt political and religious refugees from the LPC charge (an early attempt at refugee policy) introduced by a German Jewish congressman from upstate New York did not survive the conference committee (in spite of E. A. Ross's complaints, Jews did not get everything they wanted). Neuringer, "American Jewry," 95–96. Straus was either completely clueless about what was going on with the legislation just before its passage, or he was purposely trying to throw Jewish leaders off. See Straus to Schiff, January 30, 1907, and Straus to Nathan Bijur, February 4, 1907, both in Box 20, OSP. Yet in a letter a few days later to his brother Isidor, Straus expresses confidence that the legislation will pass and happiness with its details. See Oscar Straus to Isidor Straus, February 16, 1907, Box 20, OSP; Cyrus Adler to Herbert Friedenwald, February 21, 1907, in Robinson, *Cyrus Adler,* 1:133. On the comparison between anti-Asian sentiment and anti-Semitism, especially in Great Britain, see Aristide Zolberg, "The Great Wall against China: Responses to the First Immigrants," in *Migration, Migration History, History,* ed. Jan Lucassen and Leo Lucassen (New York: Peter Lang, 1997), 291–316.

28. One potential candidate, Cyrus Sulzberger (who was related to Adler by marriage), was problematic because he had played a prominent role in the Galveston immigration scheme. Edward Lauterbach to Straus, February 19, 1907, and Adler to Herbert Friedenwald, February 21, 1907, both in Box 20, OSP; Telegram, Adolf Kraus to Oscar Straus, March 12, 1907, Box 6, OSP; Bijur to Straus, February 25, 1907, Box 20, OSP. For other suggestions for appointees, see for example Telegram, R. M. Easley to Oscar Straus, February, 26, 1907, Box 20, OSP; R. M. Easley, National Civic Federation, to Oscar Straus, March 13, 1907, Box 6, OSP.

29. Straus to Kraus, March 13, 1907, Box 20, OSP. He repeated a similar line to another request by a Jew for a Jew that promised the candidate was "able, fair, just and yet not too favorably prejudiced." Lauterbach to Straus, March 14, 1907, Box 20, OSP. Straus replied briefly that Roosevelt had decided and did not want "to select anyone who might, directly or indirectly, be the representative of any special interest so far as the elements composing the immigration are concerned." Straus to Lauterbach, March 15, 1907, Box

20, OSP. Adler lobbied against James Reynolds, a government investigator close to Roosevelt and affiliated with the IRL. Reynolds had investigated debt peonage, and coauthored a report on the Chicago stockyards with Charles Neill that had been ordered by Roosevelt after the publication of *The Jungle* in 1906. Adler to Herbert Friedenwald, March 18, 1907, in Robinson, *Cyrus Adler*, 1:133–134. Neuringer counts supporters differently. See Neuringer, "American Jewry," 98–99.

30. On lobbying in the era, see Loomis, "Politics of Uncertainty." For an argument similar to mine about Jewish institutions and modern state building, see Carol Nackenoff, "The Private Roots of American Political Development: The Immigrants' Protective League's 'Friendly and Sympathetic Touch,' 1908–1924," *Studies in American Political Development* 28, no. 2 (2014): 129–160.

31. For text of the law, see U.S. Department of Commerce and Labor, Bureau of Immigration and Naturalization, *Immigration Laws and Regulations of July 1, 1907*, 11th ed. (Washington, DC: Government Printing Office, 1910), 3–23, quotations on 21; "Restriction of Immigration," *Cong. Rec.* 59th Cong., 2nd sess., 1907, vol. 41, pt. 4, 3229.

32. USIC, 41:18.

33. Higham, *Strangers in the Land*, generally, chaps. 4–5, esp. 175; Neuringer, "American Jewry," 103–105; Robinson, *Cyrus Adler*, 1:46; Aviva S. Zuckerman, Hadassah Rutman, and Adina Aflink, "Guide to the Papers of Philip Cowen (1853–1943), undated, 1873–1935, P-19," *American Jewish Historical Society*, http://findingaids.cjh.org/PhilipCowen02.html.

34. In Robinson, *Cyrus Adler*, 1:133; John M. Lund, "Vermont Nativism: William Paul Dillingham and U.S. Immigration Legislation," *Vermont History* 63 (Winter 1995): 15–29, 22; John Lund, "Boundaries of Restriction: The Dillingham Commission," *University of Vermont History Review* 6 (December 1994), www.uvm.edu/~hag/histreview/vol6/lund.html. The commission's two volumes on immigrants in cities began, "Congestion of immigrants in large cities has long been considered one of the most unfavorable features of the modern problem of immigration." The problems of the city that Jacob Riis, the reports, and many others described were chicken and egg. Were the poverty, illness, and vice among southern and eastern European immigrants responsible for their dismal living conditions, or vice versa? Could better conditions create better new Americans? In fact, the commission's report, released in January 1910, would lean toward the "environmentalist" thesis, acknowledging that many immigrant city-dwellers did their best, and that "the undesirable conditions prevailing in congested quarters often are not brought about by the residents, but largely in spite of them." USIC, 26:3.

35. Not everyone was impressed by the Jews' role in distribution policy. The IRL's president, Prescott Hall, called distribution "a bluff of the Jews and the steamship companies to throw dust in the eyes of the ignorant" who think it might make a difference. Neuringer, "American Jewry," 105; Simon Wolf speech, "Immigration and Its Possibilities," Box 2, Folder 6, SWP. Schiff echoed Wolf; see p. 85.

36. Neuringer, "American Jewry," 63, 34. Schiff chose Galveston rather than the larger port in New Orleans because he wanted to avoid sending Jews into the South, where he feared they would be used "in competition with Negro labor." Gary Dean Best, "Jacob H. Schiff's Galveston Movement: An Experiment in Immigrant Deflection, 1907–1914," *American Jewish Archives Journal* 30, no. 1 (1978): 49. On the IRL's views, see the statement that the Bureau of Information would "stimulate immigration" and was "liable to create the impression that this Government is running an employment bureau." The Junior Order of American Mechanics also opposed distribution, in part because, it argued, immigrants in rural places got bored. In contrast, the Sons of American Revolution wanted it "expanded and enlarged": "Where there are but a few immigrants they quickly become Americanized, and it is only a question of time when they become assimilated." Quotations from statements in USIC, 41:109, 18, 8.

37. For the personal histories, I have relied on Neuringer, "American Jewry," and Deborah Dash Moore, *B'nai B'rith and the Challenge of Ethnic Leadership* (Albany: State University of New York Press, 1981); USIC, 41:238.

38. Cyrus Adler to Racie Adler, November 20, 1911, in Robinson, *Cyrus Adler,* 1:198.

39. Best, *To Free a People,* 144–146, 47, 63, 72, 77–78, and Bernard Marinbach, *Galveston, Ellis Island of the West* (Albany: State University of New York Press, 1984); Kohler to Wolf, September 28, 1910, Kohler to Wolf, Box 10, Folder 2, MJKP. On the internal debates, see the papers of Max Kohler, Jacob Schiff, and Simon Wolf at the American Jewish Historical Society. The correspondence between Wolf and Kohler in late 1910 in Box 10, Folder 2, MJKP, is particularly enlightening. Nagel, although not Jewish, had been married to Louis Brandeis's sister. Panitz, *Simon Wolf,* 103. Another program, called the Industrial Removal Office, distributed 22,500 people outside eastern urban cities, or a little more than 5 percent of the Jewish immigrant population at that time.

40. See USIC, vols. 21–22. Some settlements were socialist, not Orthodox, experiments. See, e.g., Robert Alan Goldberg, *Back to the Soil: The Jewish Farmers of Clarion, Utah, and Their World* (Salt Lake City: University of Utah Press, 2011); "Agriculture," *Yivo Encyclopedia of Jews in Eastern Europe,* www.yivoencyclopedia.org/article.aspx/Agriculture.

41. Letter to the editor, Simon Wolf, *Washington Times,* January 11, 1918, Box 1, Folder 5, SWP. Wolf once dismissed the views of two opponents, scoffing that whatever they "may do or say . . . both of them have Zionistic tendencies." Wolf to Kohler, January 17, 1910, Box 10, Folder 2, MJKP. Wolf's insistence on equal rights rather than on a specific nationalism for Jews persisted after World War I. See Speech, "Jewish Nationalism at Versailles," December 1, 1918, Box 2, Folder 7, SWP. For more on this crowd's view on Zionism, see Oscar Straus to Cyrus Adler, November 12, 1905, Box 1, Folder 7, CAP; Schiff to Wolf, May 23, 1917, Box 1, Folder 9, SWP. Even after the commission submitted its recommendations for further restrictions, one Jewish commentator continued to believe that "the great problem, as we all know, is an intelligent distribution of

immigration, to which end every effort should be directed." D[illeg.] to Kohler, April 26, 1911, Box 12, Folder 16, MJKP.

42. See the classic Richard Hofstadter, *The Age of Reform: From Bryan to F. D. R.* (New York: Vintage Books, 1955), but the field of women's history most carefully traces the rise of the welfare state from private philanthropy to public social democracy. See for example Lori Ginzberg, *Women and the Work of Benevolence: Morality, Politics, and Class in the Nineteenth-Century United States* (New Haven, CT: Yale University Press, 1990), and, inter alia, Linda Gordon, *Pitied But Not Entitled: Single Mothers and the History of Welfare* (New York: Free Press, 1994), Linda Gordon, ed., *Women, the State, and Welfare* (Madison: University of Wisconsin Press, 1990), and Theda Skocpol, *Protecting Soldiers and Mothers: The Political Origins of Social Policy in the U.S.* (Cambridge, MA: Belknap Press, 1995).

43. The book was nearly in press when I discovered a concurrent argument in Sunmin Kim, "Reworking Whiteness: Challenges to the Racial Ideology of the Dillingham Commission (1907–1911)" (unpublished paper in author's possession, Legal Studies Association, July 2017), esp. 4.

44. The classic Howe, *World of Our Fathers,* deals with the question fairly if briefly.

45. Wolf to Doctor [Adler], October 21, 1907, Box 1, Folder 10, CAP. I have not found a reply. Panitz, *Simon Wolf,* 102.

46. Neuringer, "American Jewry," 87; Lance J. Sussman, "The Myth of the Trefa Banquet: American Culinary Culture and the Radicalization of Food Policy in American Reform Judaism," *American Jewish Archives* 51, no. 1/2 (2005): 29–52. On the menu, see "The Trefa Dinner," *Cleveland Jewish History,* http://www.clevelandjewishhistory.net /res/cyber-gems-trefa-dinner.htm.

47. The American Jewish Congress, with which the AJC was often confused, was founded in 1918. Naomi W. Cohen, *Jacob H. Schiff: A Study in American Jewish Leadership* (Hanover, NH: University Press of New England, 1999), xiiil; Neuringer, "American Jewry," 85; Panitz, *Simon Wolf,* 15, 97. The editor of the *Jewish Encyclopedia,* Joseph Jacobs, told Adler in 1906 that "I do grudge [Wolf] his] 'national fame.' . . . I certainly think something ought to be said about the way he rushes into print. However, I am not vindictive, and have accepted almost all your recommendations." Joseph Jacobs to Adler, October 31, 1906, Box 1, Folder 12, CAP. Straus quoted in Best, *To Free a People,* 103.

48. By 1910, the population of the Lower East Side was five million, the majority of them Jews. Lauren Price, "Mapping the Evolution of the Lower East Side through the Jewish Lens, 1880–2014," *6sqft,* September 19, 2014, www.6sqft.com/mapping-the -evolution-of-the-lower-east-side-through-a-jewish-lens-1880-2014. Wolf to Cowen, May 21, 1906, Box 1, Folder 1, SWP.

49. On conflicts, see Best, *To Free a People,* 132. On attitudes, see Adler to Wolf, November 25, 1905[?], Box 1, Folder 10, CAP. The groups managed to get along at the key moments of lobbying in 1906–7, and in 1909–1910 while crafting a statement for the U.S.

Immigration Commission, but fired off a heap of ugly correspondence in 1908. Panitz, *Simon Wolf,* 95–96. Adler to Marshall, January 1, 1906, in Robinson, *Cyrus Adler,* 1:127; Cohen, *Jacob H. Schiff,* xiii.

50. See also Goldstein, *Price of Whiteness,* 103–108, and, for a similar interpretation to mine, Joel Perlmann, *America Classifies the Immigrants: From Ellis Island to the 2020 Census* (Cambridge, MA: Harvard University Press, 2018), esp. chap. 4.

51. All of those statements were submitted in writing after being solicited by the commission. The joint Jewish organizations (about which more below) decided to send the transcript of their hearing, perhaps to highlight their special status in having an in-person meeting with the commission. USIC, 1:16; USIC, 41:265–266. This disdain for hearings may have come from Jenks or Lauck, who opposed them in his work for the Industrial Commission a few years later. Carmen Grayson Brissette, "W. Jett Lauck: Biography of a Reformer" (PhD diss., University of Virginia, 1975), 74–75. On Wolf's request, see Meeting Minutes, December 1, 1909, and December 3, 1909, in Notebook, "U.S. Immigration Commission Records 1907–1910," 100–101, HP.

52. Jews were not quite the only group in the race / religion position: the commission and census also used the term "Hindoo." A year before the hearing, Wolf had raised the issue with the commission's secretary, Walter W. Husband, who told him that the com-mission followed the practice of the Bureau of Immigration and that it had avoided all references to religion in its investigations. Rather, the terms "Jew" and "Hebrew" were supposed to be racial terms and "nothing more." Husband to William W. Wheeler, December 15, 1908, Box 1, HP. This was hardly a comfort to Wolf—or other Jewish leaders, for that matter. Max Kohler shared Wolf's view, because if it revealed religion, then it was a violation of privacy and caused a "serious constitutional question." Panitz, *Simon Wolf,* 123–124.

53. Forbath, "Jews, Laws, and Identity Politics," 16–17, On the history of the "List," see Perlmann, *America Classifies the Immigrants.* The category stayed there until 1952. On its later guise, see Patrick Weil, "Races at the Gate : A Century of Racial Distinctions in American Immigration Policy (1865-1965)," *Georgetown Immigration Law Journal* 15, no. 4 (2001): 645–646.

54. As Perlmann points out, this action was the most important thing—and a nearly unknown one—that Guggenheim did in an otherwise unimpressive one-term Senate career, *America Classifies the Immigrants,* 138.

55. This is, of course, a central insight of Michel Foucault's work. But see also Margot Canaday, *The Straight State: Sexuality and the State in Twentieth-Century America* (Princeton, NJ: Princeton University Press, 2009).

56. Mitchell B. Hart, "Jews and Race: An Introductory Essay," in *Jews & Race: Writ-ings on Identity and Difference, 1880–1940,* ed. Mitchell B. Hart (Waltham, MA: Brandeis University Press, 2011), xxvi. Consider Sarah Pulliam Bailey, "How the Jewish Identity of 'Wonder Woman' 's Star Is Causing a Stir," *Washington Post,* June 7, 2017, which noted,

"The debate 'Are Jews white?' has seen a resurgence since the presidential election last year and was resurrected surrounding the release of 'Wonder Woman.'" See the astute discussion of Jews and race in Goldstein, *Price of Whiteness.*

57. Wolf quoted in Neuringer, "American Jewry," 44; William Lawrence, *Henry Cabot Lodge: A Biographical Sketch* (Boston: Houghton Mifflin, 1925), 128–129.

58. USIC, 41:267.

59. Ibid., 266. On the false consciousness observation, I thank my colleague Adam Rothman.

60. USIC, 41:266.

61. Panitz, *Simon Wolf,* 122–123. For Wolf's version of these events, see Wolf, *Presidents,* 238–241. This definition was somewhat consistent with Chinese exclusion policy, which defined Chinese as Chinese no matter their national origin. In other words, an ethnically Chinese person who was a citizen of Mexico, for example, could not legally immigrate to the United States. For Cyrus Adler's response to this inquiry, see Adler to Wolf, August 6, 1903, reprinted in Wolf, *Presidents,* 245–247. His answer anticipated the arguments of Maurice Fishberg in a book published in 1908. Mayer Sulzberger, with whom Wolf would later have a nasty split, wrote that in terms of the law, "The Jews are not a race, but that latter term is applied to them chiefly as a periphrastic method of denoting their religion"—the important thing, he noted, in the era of Asian exclusion, was that they were definitely Caucasian. B. Felsenthal to Wolf, August 7, 1903, in Wolf, *Presidents,* 249; Leo Levi, the president of B'nai B'rith until 1903, used the term "Jewish race." Moore, *B'nai B'rith,* 86. On Zionists and racial thinking, see Hart, "Jews and Race," xxix.

62. Wolf, *Presidents,* 244–245.

63. USIC, 41:267. He also cited a statement in the encyclopedia by Joseph Jacobs, formerly president of the Jewish Historical Society of England: "'Anthropologically considered, the Jews are a race of markedly uniform type, either to unity of race or to similarity of environment.'" This was a sly move because anti-Semitism and Zionism, and thus racialism of Jews, were far more developed in England than they were in the United States. See Zolberg, "Great Wall." The 1906 *Jewish Encyclopedia* has been digitized (www.jewishencyclopedia.com). These examples had actually been gathered at least two years earlier, by the commission's secretary, William Husband, who quoted these exact sources in a letter to William Wheeler on the same subject. Husband to Wheeler, December 15, 1908.

64. After a recent political debate, the census had suffered from this exact problem: defining most people (though not Jews) by nationality, not "race." Thus the 1910 census would call everyone in the Austro-Hungarian empire "Austrian," whether they were Slavic, Montenegrin, and so on. "I think it was a great mistake," Lodge announced at the hearing in a statement that betrayed his belief that the point of the census was to measure race. "It makes the [census] returns almost valueless." USIC, 41:269.

65. USIC, 41:271. In fact, there is some discussion that Benjamin continued to consider himself a Jew.

66. USIC, 41:271. Wolf had written *The American Jew as Soldier, Patriot and Citizen* in 1895. In a cursory review, I was not able to find anyone in the book who had converted from Judaism, but it bears a more careful look.

67. USIC, 41:271. This practice of classification by race, not nationality, had been first codified with the Chinese Exclusion Act—which excluded the Chinese, no matter their nation of citizenship or residencies, and continued with the quota laws of the 1920s.

68. Husband, cited in Joel Perlmann, "'Race or People': Federal Race Classifications for Europeans in America, 1898–1913" (paper, Jerome Levy Economics Institute Working Paper No. 320, January 2001), http://papers.ssrn.com/sol3/papers.cfm?abstract_id=257921.

69. Wolf brought up the LPC charge, the powers of the boards of special inquiry, and the poor-physique rulings. He was urged to submit statements rather than make his points orally. USIC, 41:275–276.

70. Adler to Friedenwald, December 14, 1909, and December 17, 1909, in Robinson, *Cyrus Adler,* 1:176–177. On the bill, see Maurice Fishberg, "Preface from *Jews, Race, and Environment,*" reprinted in Hart, *Jews & Race,* 23.

71. USIC, 1:19–20.

72. Friedenwald to Mayer Sulzberger, president of the AJC, December 4, 1909, and others quoted in Perlmann, "'Race or People.'" The statement appears in USIC, 41:276–278; Panitz, *Simon Wolf,* 127; Goldstein, *Price of Whiteness,* 89, 93–96; Forbach, "Jews, Law and Identity Politics," 23.

73. Quoted in Perlmann, *America Classifies the Immigrant,* 115.

74. I am counting the NLIL as Jewish. Since the commission solicited the statements and some organizations may have declined to reply, the reasons for the overrepresentation of Jewish groups cannot be certain. Still, the strength of the Jewish response clearly shows their own commitment, as well as recognition of it on the part of the commission. On invitations to submit recommendations, see USIC, 1:16. These exhibits added to, and in some cases reproduced, statements and data the major Jewish organizations had already sent (both solicited and unsolicited) to the commission.

75. Speech, "Immigration and Its Possibilities," Box 2, Folder 6, SWP. To emphasize this was not just a Jewish cause, he also acknowledged "a valuable adjunct in the 'Liberal Immigration League,' which [is] guided, directed, and stimulated by persons not of our faith" (although in fact largely led by Jews). Speech, "Immigration and Its Possibilities," Box 2, Folder 6, SWP; Wolf to Kohler, September 16, 1910, Kohler to Wolf, September 28, 1910, Wolf to Kohler, October 1, 1910, and Louis Marshall to "Doctor" [Friedenwald? Adler?], October 27, 1910, all in Box 10, Folder 2, MJKP.

76. Panitz, *Simon Wolf,* 127–129. See also all three men's correspondence at the time, especially Box 1, Folder 3, and Marshall to "Doctor," October 27, 1910, Box 12, Folder 9, LMP.

77. Jeremiah Jenks, "The Racial Problem in Immigration," *Proceedings of the National Conference of Charities and Corrections* 36 (June 1909): 216; Marshall to "Doctor," October 27, 1910, Box 12, Folder 9, MJKP.

78. USIC, 41:141.

79. USIC, 41:142. The statement also called for publication of a "compilation of [relevant] judicial decisions and opinions," which I think was mandated by the 1907 law but had not yet happened, and said there had not been one since 1899. USIC, 41:143. For a recent investigation into immigrants' access to legal representation and its effect on the U.S. government's handling of their case, see Ingrid V. Eagly and Steven Shafer, "A National Study of Access to Counsel in Immigration Court," *University of Pennsylvania Law Review* 164, no. 1 (2015): 1–91.

80. On the later development of Jews' involvement in refugee and human rights work, see James Loeffler's "'The Conscience of America': Human Rights, Jewish Politics, and American Foreign Policy at the 1945 United Nations San Francisco Conference," *Journal of American History* 100, no. 2 (2013): 401–428. Victims of a 1908 Sicily earthquake were unfairly excluded, in Kohler's view, "and similarly, the able-bodied, industrious Jewish victims of Russia's fiendish fanaticism can not be lawfully excluded under existing law, even if they have been aided in their passage by sympathetic friends or charitable organizations." USIC, 41:147.

81. USIC, 41:147–151.

82. With a nod to colonialism, the statement also recommended that "in the Territories it should itself establish similar classes." USIC, 41:155–156.

83. USIC, 41:152–155. Note that their number was much higher than other estimates of the Industrial Removal Office's work. The finding aid for the IRO's papers says, "From 1901 to 1922, the IRO distributed approximately 79,000 individuals throughout the United States and Canada. From 1901 to 1913, IRO distributions represented close to 6 or 7 per cent of the US total immigration figures." "Guide to the Records of the Industrial Removal Office undated, 1899–1922, I-91," *American Jewish Historical Society*, http://findingaids .cjh.org//IRO5.html. Here was an interesting parallel to one of the issues driving concern over immigration's costs, especially to border states, today. The Immigration and Reform Control Act of 1986 (IRCA) established State Legalization Impact Assistance Grants (SLIAG) to reimburse states and municipalities for education and welfare, as well as for other costs of legalization.

84. Statement by "Immigrants' Protective League," in USIC, 41:63, also 156. The IPL is the subject of Nackenoff, "Private Roots," which argues a similar point to mine. Quoted in Henry B. Leonard, "The Immigrants' Protective League of Chicago, 1908–1921," *Journal of the Illinois State Historical Society* 66, no. 3 (1973): 276.

85. USIC, 1:42–43.

86. With only the most minor of exceptions, immigrant integration is still left to private organizations; public funding for programs pales in comparison to other immigrant-receiving

countries. For recent research on this topic, see "Immigration Integration," *Migration Policy Institute,* www.migrationpolicy.org/topics/immigrant-integration.

87. Wolf to Kohler, November 3, 1910, Box 10, Folder 2, MJKP.

88. USIC, 1:17–20; USIC, 2:719, emphasis in original.

89. Ross, *Old World,* table of contents and 144–145.

4. The Vanishing American Wage Earner

1. Isaac Hourwich, *Immigration and Labor: The Economic Aspects of European Immigration to the United States* (New York: G. P. Putnam's Sons, 1912). Oscar Handlin's *Race and Nationality in American Life* (New York: Atheneum Books, 1950), chap. 5, made a similar critique, and it has appeared in generations of scholarship on the commission. See for example Karen Schoenewaldt Buchholz, "The Politics of Research: Social Scientists and the New Immigrant Labor, 1880–1924" (PhD diss., Temple University, 1992), 79.

2. Carmen Brissette Grayson, "W. Jett Lauck: Biography of a Reformer" (PhD diss., University of Virginia, 1975), 31–32. Grayson used the statistics from W. Jett Lauck, "The Economic Investigations of the United States Immigration Commission," *Journal of Political Economy* 18, no. 7 (1910): 540.

3. My deduction regarding the timing of Lauck's hiring by the Immigration Commission comes from William Walter Husband to Lauck, January 22, 1909, Box 80, LP. The postcards "Charleroi, Pa. Lock #4 Monongehela River" and "High Water, Lock No. 4, March 1907, North Charleroi, Pa," both in Box 401, LP, suggest that he was there doing work for the commission, because he returned there later for greater study. In any case, it is certain he was employed by June 1907.

4. USIC, vols. 6–18, which focused on the role of immigrants in industries east of the Rockies, plus vols. 19–20, which were the summary reports, were officially authored by Lauck. More specialized reports organized under his general economic investigation concerned trade unions, labor and employment agencies, the floating immigrant labor supply, immigrant banks and steamship agents, exploitation [trafficking], and the economic effects of immigration. From Lauck, "Economic Investigations," 531.

5. USIC, 1:45.

6. Two or three Lauck children, including the oldest, died in childhood. *West Virginia, Deaths Index, 1853–1973* [database on-line]. Provo, UT, USA: Ancestry.com Operations, Inc., 2011. Original data: "West Virginia Deaths, 1853–1970." Index. FamilySearch, Salt Lake City, Utah. From originals housed in county courthouses throughout West Virginia. The first major railroad in the United States, the Birmingham & Ohio, had itself been the subject of bitter conflicts over its employment of Irish and black workers and was a harbinger of industrial change. Leon Fink, *Progressive Intellectuals and the Dilemmas of Democratic Commitment* (Cambridge, MA: Harvard University Press, 1998), 216. For

more information about the life and career of Lauck's father, see "William Blackford Lauck," *Find a Grave,* www.findagrave.com.

7. Department of the Interior, U.S. Census, *Statistics of the Population of the United States, at the Tenth Census* (Washington, DC: Government Printing Office, 1882), 84 and 534, table xiv. Background in part from Fink, *Progressive Intellectuals,* chap. 7.

8. *The Calyx,* Washington & Lee College Yearbooks, 1902 and 1903; "College Notes," Box 353, LP. See Roger T. Johnson, *Historical Beginnings: The Federal Reserve* (Boston: Federal Reserve Board of Boston, Public and Community Affairs Department, 2010), 18.

9. Grayson, "W. Jett Lauck," 12–13, 23.

10. A. L. Richmond to Dr. Webster, March 5, 1905, University of Chicago. Office of the President. Harper, Judson and Burton Administrations. Records, Box 23, Folder 6, UCL; James Laurence Laughlin, *Twenty-five Years of the Department of Political Economy, University of Chicago* (Chicago: Privately Printed, 1916), 20.

11. "Propagandist" in Ellen Fitzpatrick, *Endless Crusade: Women Social Scientists and Progressive Reform* (New York: Oxford University Press, 1990), 49. On his mentoring of women, see Fitzpatrick, *Endless Crusade,* 40–41. See also A. W. Coats, "The American Economic Association, 1904–1929," *American Economic Review* 54, no. 4, pt. 1 (1964): 262. On Laughlin's friendly relationship with Jeremiah Jenks, see Alvin Johnson, *Pioneer's Progress: An Autobiography* (New York: Viking Press, 1952), 199; University of Chicago, *Annual Register, July, 1904–July, 1905. With announcements for 1905–1906* (Chicago: University of Chicago, 1905), 190–191, 212. "Government officials often play the leading role in deciding what conditions will be recognized as problems, how their causes and effects will be defined, and what policy alternatives will be considered." See Mary O. Furner and Barry Supple, "Ideas, Institutions, and State in the United States and Britain: An Introduction," in *The State and Economic Knowledge: The American and British Experiences,* ed. Mary O. Furner and Barry Supple (Washington, DC: Woodrow Wilson International Center for Scholars, 1990), 28.

12. Johnson, *Pioneer's Progress,* 198. At the time, the department also included Wesley Clark Mitchell, a currency expert and pioneer in the theory of business cycles, who briefly oversaw the commission's Pacific Coast reports; University of Chicago, *Annual Register,* 1903, 183–192.

13. Abbott and Lauck both worked with Laughlin, but I have found no evidence of any correspondence between them, and she later printed a book criticizing the commission's data on criminality. Abbott, who later served as a graduate dean at the University of Chicago, recalled that "when I was a graduate student here it was the only one of the great centers of graduate study in the United States in which all the graduate professional schools were open to women. . . . In all departments we were tolerated and in most of them were officially welcomed." Typescript of a talk about women in graduate school at the University of Chicago, n.d., Abbott, Edith and Grace Abbott Papers, Box 5, Folder 13, UCL, and on Abbott's criticism of the commission, see typescripts in Box 5, Folder 6.

14. William Jett Lauck official transcript, University of Chicago, in author's possession. On Lauck's essay, see Fink, *Progressive Intellectuals,* chap. 7.

15. Mary O. Furner and Barry Supple, "Ideas," 5. Lauck's own summary of his vita suggests he took the position with the commission before resigning his position at Washington & Lee University. Lexington's proximity to the bituminous coal region might explain why it was the first to be studied. See Typescript, W. Jett Lauck, "General Record of Word Done," 1, Box 25, LP. On the precarious class status of Progressive Era social scientists, see Buchholz, "Politics of Research," xvii. Lauck's correspondence with Jenks, with whom he did business and coauthored books, was laced with similar slobbering. Lauck to Laughlin, August 16, 1910, Box 1, LLP; Lauck, "Economic Investigations," 525–549.

16. In available payroll and minutes, I have found only three other employees hired before Lauck. See the Dillingham Commission employee database (in author's possession), compiled from payroll records and minutes in HP; Frederick Croxton Oral History Transcript, 55, FCC; W. Jett Lauck to W. W. Husband, n.d., 2, 11; Croxton to Husband, [April] 1908, 1, Box 80, LP.

17. Lauck to Husband, n.d., 3, Box 80, LP.

18. Notebook: titled "U.S. Immigration Commission Records 1907–1910," April 25, 1908, 56, HP. Lauck retained Croxton's questionnaires on family units, individuals, employers, payroll surveys, community officials, boarding houses, and neighborhood blocks but added questions to garner more economic data from these. Grayson, "W. Jett Lauck," 63. See modifications suggested by Lauck to Husband, 7–8; Husband to Lauck, January 22, 1909, Box 80, LP; W. Jett Lauck, "The Bituminous Coal Miner and Coke Worker of Western Pennsylvania," *The Survey* 26, no. 1 (1911): 34.

19. The Pacific Coast studies went first to University of California economist Wesley Clark Mitchell and then, after his resignation, to Stanford University's Henry A. Millis. Not long after, the separate committees on the south and the Pacific Coast were disbanded and put under the charge of the general office, with Lauck and Falkner overseeing all investigations. Notebook: titled "U.S. Immigration Commission Records, 1907–1910," September 12, 1908, 75–76, HP.

20. Notebook, July 10, 1908, 66, HP.

21. Lauck, "Economic Investigations," 533, 535; Grayson, "W. Jett Lauck," 29; Alice O'Connor, *Poverty Knowledge: Social Science, Social Policy, and the Poor in Twentieth-Century U.S. History* (Princeton, NJ: Princeton University Press, 2009), chap. 1. Lauck called it "a common method." Lauck to Husband, n.d., 2, Box 80, LP.

22. Quoted in Fink, *Progressive Intellectuals,* 238. Letter of recommendation for United States Industrial Commission, Croxton to John Commons, August 12, 1913, Box 239, LP. For a similar description, see clipping from unnamed newspaper in New York, "Collecting Data about Workmen," n.d., Box 29, LP. Quoted in Grayson, "W. Jett Lauck," 52.

23. Notebook, July 10, 1908, 66, HP. Lauck, "Economic Investigations," 539. Lauck to Allan Dunlap, December 5, 1908, Box 401, LP.

24. Lauck to [Eleanor Dunlap Lauck], December 5, 1907 [1908?], Box 401, LP. Quotation from Polish immigrant Anthony Cyburt in "This Was the America I Saw," interpretation panel at the Johnstown Immigration Museum in Johnstown, Pennsylvania.

25. See explanation in USIC, 8:231, 189. Lauck's personal notes and correspondence confirm these reports were done first, and therefore they have more extensive work than others.

26. "As regards the immigration problem, the fact of great significance . . . in connection with the extraordinary development of the iron and steel industry has been the constant increase in the number of iron and steel workers." USIC, 8:4, 18, 32. Lauck, "Bituminous Coal Miner," 35.

27. Note on the back side of photograph of the Susquehanna River at Steelton, PA, n.d., Box 401, LP.

28. On ethnic variety, see Lauck, "Bituminous Coal Miner," 36. See also W. Jett Lauck, "Industrial Communities," *The Survey* 25, no. 15 (1911): 585.

29. Eileen Janes Yow, "Social Surveys in the Eighteenth and Nineteenth Centuries," in *The Cambridge History of Science*, ed. Theodore M. Porter and Dorothy Ross (New York: Cambridge University Press, 2003), 7:83–99, esp. 98–99; *The Pittsburgh Survey*, 6 vols. (New York: Russell Sage Foundation, 1909–1914).

30. Buchholz, "Politics of Research," 35. For a brief description of the major findings of the Pittsburgh Survey, see Edward T. Devine, "Results of the Pittsburgh Survey," *American Journal of Sociology* 14, no. 5 (1909): 661. Buchholz sees a "startling contrast" between the Dillingham Commission and the Pittsburgh Survey, which she clearly favors: "The Survey team made no secret of its reformist political agenda, and approached the same issues with far more compassion. The Dillingham Commission had its own agenda, yet insisted on its objectivity and emotionally detached investigation." Buchholz, "Politics of Research," 83. Secondary sources on the Pittsburgh Survey include Roy Lubove, *Twentieth Century Pittsburgh: Government, Business, and Environmental Change* (New York: John Wiley and Sons, 1969), 6–19; John F. McClymer, *War and Welfare: Social Engineering in America, 1890–1925* (Westport, CT: Greenwood Press, 1980), 30–49; Allen F. Davis, *Spearheads for Reform: The Social Settlements and the Progressive Movement, 1890–1914* (New York: Oxford University Press, 1967), 172–173; Charles Hill and Stephen Cohen, "John Fitch and the Pittsburgh Survey," *Western Pennsylvania Historical Magazine, 1918–2015* 67, no. 1 (1984): 17–32; Maurine Greenwald and Margo Anderson, eds., *Pittsburgh Surveyed: Social Science and Social Reform in the Early Twentieth Century* (Pittsburgh, PA: University of Pittsburgh Press, 1996).

31. Lauck to Husband, n.d., 6, 9–10, Box 80, LP; Grayson, "W. Jett Lauck," 31–32.

32. Statistics from an interpretation panel at Johnstown Immigration Museum, Johnstown, Pennsylvania.

33. Cyburt and Charles Schwab, quoted in "This Was the America I Saw" exhibit.

34. Lauck, "Bituminous Coal Miner," 34–35; W. Jett Lauck, "The Lesson from Lawrence," *North American Review* 195, no. 678 (1912): 665.

35. Lauck, "Bituminous Coal Miner," 38.

36. Ibid., 38–39.

37. Ibid., 47.

38. Ibid., 50.

39. Raymond A. Mohl, *The New City: Urban America in the Industrial Age, 1860–1920* (Arlington Heights, IL: Harlan Davidson, 1985), 166–179. A famous early example of what was known as "environmentalism" is Jacob Riis, *How the Other Half Lives: Studies among the Tenements of New York* (New York: Charles Scribner's Sons, 1890).

40. Irving Fisher, "Impending Problems of Eugenics," *The Scientific Monthly* 13, no. 3 (1921): 214–231, quotation on 226, cited in Thomas D. Boston, ed., *A Different Vision: Race and Public Policy* (New York: Routledge Books, 1996), 2:20.

41. Political scientists and economists are less attentive than historians to the precise chronology of the rise of eugenics in the United States and have been especially prone to these conclusions. Daniel Tichenor, *Dividing Lines: The Politics of Immigration Control in America* (Princeton, NJ: Princeton University Press, 2002), 42. The same passage says that during "this period" the House Immigration Committee put an "expert eugenics agent" on staff (Harry Laughlin), but in fact that did not occur until 1920. On Tichenor's unsubstantiated claims about Jenks's relationship to eugenics, see Chapter 3. For another example, see Buchholz, "Politics of Research," esp. 230. Desmond King, *Making Americans: Immigration, Race, and the Origins of the Diverse Democracy* (Harvard, MA: Cambridge University Press, 2000), 52. See also Thomas C. Leonard, *Illiberal Reformers: Race, Eugenics, and American Economics in the Progressive Era* (Princeton, NJ: Princeton University Press, 2016); Keith Fitzgerald, *The Face of the Nation: Immigration, the State, and National Identity* (Palo Alto, CA: Stanford University Press, 1996), 75 (where he only mentions the restrictionist groups who contributed to vol. 41), 127–128, 137–140; and Joel Perlmann, *America Classifies the Immigrants: From Ellis Island to the 2020 Census* (Cambridge, MA: Harvard University Press, 2018); King, *Making Americans,* 58.

42. King, *Making Americans,* 61; Barbara M. Solomon, *Ancestors and Immigrants, and Changing New England Tradition* (Cambridge, MA: Harvard University Press, 1956), 199.

43. It was funded by the Carnegie Institution and later by millionaire philanthropist Mrs. E. L. Harriman; Charles Davenport, *Heredity in Relation to Eugenics* (New York: Henry Holt, 1911), 273–287.

44. Lee to Jenks, August 9, 1906, Carton 1, JLP. See also Lee to Ralph M. Easley, May 1, 1906, Carton 1, JLP.

45. Lee to Joseph Glenn, April 20, 1907, Carton 1, JLP.

46. Robert DeCourcy Ward, "National Eugenics in Relation to Immigration," *North American Review,* 192 (July 1910): 56–57, 62, 65–66.

47. IRL president Prescott Hall asked Davenport to join the organization in lobbying Congress for immigration restriction. One of the better chronologies of this aspect of the eugenics movement appears in the Eugenics Archives, which includes Harry Laughlin's appointment. Paul Lombardo, "Eugenics Laws Restricting Immigration," *Image Archive on the American Eugenics Movement,* www.eugenicsarchive.org/html/eugenics/essay9text.html.

48. USIC, 41:103, 106–107; USIC, 5:4; USIC, 38:155. Because his objection to immigrants was racial, Hall opposed the "distribution schemes" of those who hoped to funnel more immigration to the South and to the West, thus relieving eastern industrial cities of the crush of new immigrants. USIC, 41:109.

49. Richards M. Bradley to Lee, March 16, 1911, Carton 1, JLP.

50. Isaac A. Hourwich, *Immigration and Labor: The Economic Aspects of European Immigration to the United States,* rev. ed. (New York: B. W. Huebsch, 1922), iii.

51. Lee to Ellis, December 11, 1911, Carton 1, JLP. See Alan M. Kraut, *Silent Travelers: Germs, Genes, and the "Immigrant Menace"* (New York: Basic Books, 1994).

52. I only found even the term "racial stock" once in the commission's reports, in a letter from a liberal rabbi who maintained that Jews were not a distinct race because over the years "the Modern Jew . . . had lost their purity of *racial stock.*" USIC, 41:289; American Breeders Association, Eugenics Section, Immigration Committee, 1st Report, December 30, 1911, Reel 12, BP-APS. On fecundity studies, see for example Katrina Irving, *Immigrant Mothers: Narratives of Race and Maternity, 1890–1925* (Urbana: University of Illinois Press, 2000); King, *Making Americans.* On Joseph Hill and the national-origins quota system, see Mae M. Ngai, "The Architecture of Race in American Immigration Law: A Reexamination of the Immigration Act of 1924," *Journal of American History* 86, no.1 (1999): 67–92; "The Eugenics Committee," *Journal of Heredity* 5, no. 8 (1914): 340. On the Folkmars, see Daniel Folkmar to Davenport, August 6, 1913, and September 8, 1913, Reel 14, BP-APS. Tichenor says that the *Dictionary* included "eugenicist methods and findings," which has some truth, and declared the "definitive physical qualities of races," which is less clear. Tichenor, *Dividing Lines,* 131. In addition, Dillingham and the commission's chief administrator, secretary William W. Husband, both hailed from Vermont—which developed an extensive eugenics program for sterilization and institutionalization. But this program, begun in the 1920s, focused more on poverty-stricken rural Vermonters in general than on immigrants. See Nancy L. Gallagher, *Breeding Better Vermonters: The Eugenics Project in the Green Mountain State* (Hanover, NH: University Press of New England, 1999).

53. I have found no connection in Jenks's personal papers or published works to the eugenics movement per se, although he did cooperate with the IRL later. See Jeanne D. Petit, *The Men and Women We Want: Gender, Race, and the Progressive Era Literacy Test Debate* (Rochester, NY: University of Rochester Press, 2010), 64, 160, n. 24, citing Box 5, JLP; Jeremiah W. Jenks and W. Jett Lauck, *The Immigration Problem: A Study of American Immigration Conditions and Needs,* 4th ed. (New York: Funk & Wagnalls, 1913), 79. Leonard's

argument about what might be called Jenks and Lauck's "soft" racism does not distinguish between ideas about inherent racial inequalities and social differences. Leonard, *Illiberal Reformers,* 149–151. On Tichenor's views, see his *Dividing Lines,* 131. Tichenor also erroneously argues that Jenks's "key staff assistant" was Daniel Folkmar, a conclusion not supported by the commission's minutes in the Husband Papers.

54. Lauck, "Bituminous Coal Miner," 50; USIC, 9:331–332.

55. USIC, 9:387.

56. Ibid., 387, 486–487 (noting, those who do evince an interest have "ludicrously erroneous" ideas about politics), 477; USIC, 8:387–388. Lauck was more sympathetic about citizenship lessons than the more conservative Jenks, although he taught civics classes to working-class students. Jeremiah W. Jenks, "The Character and Influence of Recent Immigrants," in *Questions of Public Policy: Addresses Delivered in the Page Lecture Series, 1913, before the Senior Class of the Sheffield Scientific School, Yale University* (New Haven, CT: Yale University Press, 1913), 7, cited in Buchholz, "Politics of Research," 132.

57. Lauck, "Economic Investigations," 537.

58. Ibid., 539, 537. Notebook, "U.S. Immigration Commission Records, 1907–1910," March 16, 1909, 85, HP. On data, see Grayson, "W. Jett Lauck," 50, 32.

59. Lauck, "Industrial Communities," 580; USIC, vols. 8–9, 12, and 18–19.

60. Copy, U.S. Department of Commerce and Labor, Bureau of Labor, B.L. 110—Individual Nationality Slip: Chicago and Northwestern Railroad Company, 1906, Box 80, LP. Grayson, "W. Jett Lauck," 31–32, using Lauck, "Economic Investigations," 540.

61. Lauck, "Economic Investigations," 534–540.

62. Ibid., 535, 529.

63. Questions from Industrial Family Schedule—H, described in Lauck to Husband, n.d., 7, Box 80, LP.

64. W. Jett Lauck, "Lesson from Lawrence," 672; Hall quotation from Grayson, "W. Jett Lauck," 40.

65. Lauck, "Lesson from Lawrence," 672; [W. J. Lauck], "Solving Great Labor Problems," *Richmond Times-Dispatch,* December 31, 1911, Box 80, LP. Indeed, Leslie Hayford, the author of the volume on immigrants and crime, found their overall rates no worse than the native-born, and took a job as field secretary for the North American Civic League for Immigrants, which was an assimilationist, not exclusionist, organization.

66. [Lauck], "Solving Great Labor Problems." In other stories, he extolled the virtues of distribution to the South as a possible solution to the "immigration problem." See, among others, W. J. Lauck, "North Carolina Italian Farmers," *Richmond-Times Dispatch,* May 5, 1912, Industrial Section, 1; and W. Jett Lauck, "The Right Kind of Immigration," *Richmond Times-Dispatch,* May 2, 1912, Main Section, 6. The impact of immigrants on wages is an ongoing debate, and Isaac Hourwich challenged Lauck's argument in his 1912 analysis of the commission's reports. But here I am interested in the argument, not its validity.

67. See Buchholz, "Politics of Research," 12. For more on eugenics, see Chapter 6. Mayo-Smith quoted in Aristide Zolberg, *A Nation by Design: Immigration Policy in the Fashioning of America* (Cambridge, MA: Harvard University Press, 2009), 212. See also Thomas C. Leonard, "'More Merciful and Not Less Effective': Eugenics and American Economics in the Progressive Era," *History of Political Economy* 34, no. 4 (2003): 693.

68. This outline was an elaboration of the initial one he prepared for William Walter Husband. "Explanation of Outline," 2, Box 80, LP. See also his distinction in his initial plan, Lauck to Husband, n.d., 12, Box 80, LP.

69. "Explanation of Outline," 5, Box 80, LP; Lauck, "Lesson from Lawrence," 666–667.

70. See Grayson, "W. Jett Lauck," 30; "Explanation of Outline," 2, Box 80, LP; Paul U. Kellogg, "The Minimum Wage and Immigrant Labor," *Proceedings of the National Conference of Charities and Correction at the Third-eighth Annual Session, Held in Boston, Mass., June 7–14, 1911,* ed. Alexander Johnson (Fort Wayne, IN: Fort Wayne Printing, 1911), 171.

71. It also matched Jenks's approval of collective bargaining and interest in wages during his work at the National Civic Federation. Clarence Wunderlin, *Visions of a New Industrial Order* (New York: Columbia University Press, 1992), 19–22. Again, see Fink, *Progressive Intellectuals,* 217. On the other hand, Lauck's article on the IWW strike in Lawrence in 1912 argued for immigration restriction. See Lauck, "Lesson from Lawrence," 665–672. Buchholz discusses Lauck's work on Lawrence but does not mention his criticism of employers. Buchholz, "Politics of Research," 63–64.

72. In 1875, economist Carroll Wright, who would later head the U.S. Census, had mentioned the similar concept of the "minimum wage" as head of the Massachusetts Bureau of Labor Statistics.

73. See for example Christine Stansell, *City of Women: Sex and Class in New York, 1789–1860* (New York: Alfred A. Knopf, 1986); Fink, *Progressive Intellectuals,* 217–219. Fink also identifies the standard of living as the central guiding principle of Lauck's career, but he dates it to Lauck's time at the U.S. Industrial Commission, probably because he did not read Grayson's dissertation and so had less information on Lauck's previous work at the Dillingham Commission.

74. Irving, *Immigrant Mothers,* chap. 4; George J. Sánchez, *Becoming Mexican American: Ethnicity, Culture and Identity in Chicano Los Angeles, 1900–1945* (New York: Oxford University Press, 1993), chap. 4.

75. Lauck's mentor, H. Parker Willis, noted that the high percentage of immigrant women who worked for wages showed "the extent to which the immigrant has been reduced not merely personally, but in family life, to a basis of commercial exploitation." H. Parker Willis, "The Findings of the Immigration Commission," *The Survey* 25, no. 15 (1911): 576.

76. Lauck, "Bituminous Coal Miner," 47; USIC, 9:388. In general, on women's work in Johnstown, see USIC, 8:57–79.

77. "Explanation of Outline," 5, Box 80, LP.

78. Ibid. It also reflected Jenks's work with the Anthracite Coal Commission and his preoccupation with language challenges in industrial workplaces. See Wunderlin, *Visions.*

79. W. Jett Lauck, "The Alien Contract Labor Delusion," *New York Times Annalist,* August 11, 1913, clipping in Box 80, Folder 1910–1928 Immigration Press 3 of 4, LP.

80. See Hourwich, *Immigration and Labor,* and Handlin, *Race and Nationality,* but also the astute critique by Lauck's biographer, Grayson, "W. Jett Lauck," esp. 42–46; Leonard, *Illiberal Reformer,* 150; Hourwich, *Immigration and Labor,* 48–50. For the source of the quotation by Lauck's mentor, see H. Parker Willis, "Immigration Commission," 571. On how quantification truncates meaning, see Theodore M. Porter, *Trust in Numbers: The Pursuit of Objectivity in Science and Public Life* (Princeton, NJ: Princeton University Press, 1995), 85.

81. Memorandum, U.S. Immigration Commission, "Instructions to Paymasters, Foremen, and Others in Charge of Filling Out Individual Cards," n.d., Box 80, LP.

82. Ibid.

83. "Individual Schedule or Slip G," USIC, 2:712.

84. USIC, 6:viii–ix.

85. Grayson, "W. Jett Lauck," 40, 51, 22–23. As Theodore Porter notes, "Critics of quantification in the natural sciences as well as in social and humanistic fields have often felt that reliance on numbers simply evades the deep and important issues." Porter, *Trust in Numbers,* 5; Susan Herbst, "Polling in Politics and History," *The Cambridge History of Science,* ed. Theodore M. Porter and Dorothy Ross (New York: Cambridge University Press, 2003), 7:581. In fact, as she notes, the foundational work on sampling did not appear until 1934. The high percentage of workers noted was possible because all of the southern iron and steel workers were in either Maryland or Birmingham, Alabama, which was represented by commission member John Burnett. USIC:9, 8–9, 18–19.

86. Grayson, "W. Jett Lauck," 42–45.

87. Clipping, *New York Evening Post,* October 31, 1912, LP; Lauck, "Explanation of Outline," 5, Box 80, LP.

88. This is a debate that still rages today about new immigration's impact. See for example Room for Debate, "Do Immigrants Take Jobs from American-Born Workers?," *New York Times,* January 6, 2015, www.nytimes.com/roomfordebate/2015/01/06/do -immigrants-take-jobs-from-american-born-workers; Hourwich, *Immigration and Labor,* iii.

89. Porter, *Trust in Numbers,* 77; Jenks and Lauck, *Immigration Problem,* 6, 9.

90. Lauck, "Lesson from Lawrence," 669.

91. Ibid., 665.

92. Grayson, "W. Jett Lauck," 56.

93. Ibid., 57–60.

94. On labor's pursuit of "industrial democracy" in the early twentieth century, see Joseph A. McCartin, *Labor's Great War: The Struggle for Industrial Democracy and the Origins of Modern American Labor Relations, 1912–1921* (Chapel Hill: University of North Carolina Press, 1997); W. Jett Lauck, "A Real Myth," *Atlantic Monthly* 110, no. 3 (1912): 388; Lauck, "Lesson from Lawrence," 665; Lauck, "A Real Myth," 388–393.

95. Scrapbook 1913–1914, Box 439, LP; Grayson, "W. Jett Lauck," 60, 72–75.

96. Lauck quoted in Grayson, "W. Jett Lauck," 111, 121. On the relationship of "non-economic" ideas to the family wage debate—including and especially eugenics, see Leonard, *Illiberal Reformers;* Box 441, LP. On the union, see Mary Ann Clawson, *Constructing Brotherhood: Class, Gender, and Fraternalism* (Princeton, NJ: Princeton University Press, 1989), esp. 129–130; Jenks in Jenks to O. P. Van Sweringen, March 18, 1926, copy, Box 38, LP.

97. W. Jett Lauck, "The Industrial Significance of Immigration," *The Annals of the American Academy of Political and Social Science* 93, Present-Day Immigration with Special Reference to the Japanese (January 1921), 189.

98. W. Jett Lauck, *Political and Industrial Democracy, 1776–1926* (New York: Funk & Wagnalls, 1926), 7–8.

99. "The Industrial Organization of Immigrants," *Immigrants in American History: Arrival, Adaptation, and Integration,* Vol. 1, ed. Elliott Robert Barkan (New York: ABC-CLIO, 2013), 1727; Announcement of the American Association for Economic Freedom, n.d. [1937?], Box 376, LP; Fink, *Progressive Intellectuals,* 226, quotation from 216.

100. Scrapbook, Religious Clippings and Personal Notes, Box 28, LP.

101. Lauck to Jenks, July 1, 1929, Box 38, LP. David Coppola, "River Island Has a Name—and a History," *Freelance Star,* Fredericksburg.com, April 6, 2012; see correspondence in Lauck Papers, Box 38, especially in 1926; Fink, *Progressive Intellectuals,* 232.

5. Women's Power and Knowledge

1. Meeting Minutes, May 22, 1908, in Notebook: titled "U.S. Immigration Commission Records 1907–1910," 67, Box 1, HP. I have also drawn on the outstanding biography created by my undergraduate students, led by Tiana Baheri, in History 292, Fall 2015 (referred to from here as Baheri et al., "Herkner Biography"); USIC, 37:2. Information on agents from the Dillingham Commission database created by author, based on payroll records in HP and other references to agents elsewhere.

2. Historians of women's work have overlooked this fact, probably because the commission's records were destroyed, so the extant evidence is obscure. In addition, the commission's purview was not exclusively or obviously women (unlike the Women's Bureau or, as we shall see, even the Bureau of Labor Statistics), and the most explicit evidence is from the obscure Croxton oral history, FCC, 53–57. The BLS studies on women, too, were absorbed in 1912 into the Children's Bureau and in 1920 the Women's Bureau, both in

the Department of Labor, which became bulwarks of women's federal employment and influence. See Molly Ladd-Taylor, *Mother-Work: Women, Child Welfare, and the State, 1890–1930* (Urbana: University of Illinois Press, 1995). Cindy Sondik Aron, *Ladies and Gentlemen of the Civil Service: Middle-Class Workers in Victorian America* (New York: Oxford University Press, 1987), 90; A. Ross Eckler, *The Bureau of the Census* (New York: Praeger, 1972), 15. Female employees lobbied Congress for the Census to become a permanent bureau so that they could keep their jobs. Walter F. Willcox's story about the women's threats to Congress[?] appears in Eckler, *Bureau of the Census,* 10. On Neill and the BLS studies, see U.S. Bureau of Labor Statistics, "Commissioners: Charles P. Neill, February 1905-March 1913," *BLS History,* www.bls.gov/bls/history/commissioners/neill .htm.

3. FCC, 53. On the back and forth between the commission and the Census Bureau, see also Joel Perlmann, "Views of European Races among the Research Staff of the US Immigration Commission and the Census Bureau, ca. 1910" (paper, Levy Economics Institute of Bard College, Working Paper No. 648, January 2011), www.levyinstitute.org/pubs /wp_648.pdf.

4. Personnel data also collected in database created by author from payroll records in HP, and augmented by Google and archival searches for biographical details. My thanks to Andres Blanco for his assistance creating the database. I counted everyone who used initials instead of a first name as a man, unless I knew otherwise, but probably a few of these were actually women. In other words, my estimate of women employed by the commission was conservative. In addition, there is no reason to believe the extant payrolls include every employee of the commission for its entire duration (1907–1911). Also, the numbers actually exaggerate the number of male rank-and-file employees, since I included senior administrators and the nine commission members in the database. And this figure is only if everyone who used initials was a man. Cindy Sondik Aron reports that, that year, federal agencies employed 6,882 women and 18,793 men in Washington, DC. See Aron, *Ladies and Gentlemen,* 5, table 1.1. Most of the women were tabulators, which did not require special skills in statistics but probably involved training on special machines originally created for the U.S. Census. Margo J. Anderson, *The American Census: A Social History* (New Haven, CT: Yale University Press, 1988), 120. Women with high positions included Elnora Folkmar on the *Dictionary of Races or Peoples,* Mary Louise Mark and Nellie F. Sheets on *Immigrants in Cities,* Mary Simonds on *Children of Immigrants in Schools,* and Mary Mills West on the sections on Brazil and Argentina in *Immigrants in Other Countries.*

5. Thomas D. Snyder, ed., *120 Years of American Education: A Statistical Portrait* (Washington, DC: U.S. Department of Education, Office of Educational Research and Improvement, National Center for Education Statistics, 1993), 76, 82.

6. See author's database on the employees of the U.S. Immigration Commission, and Meeting Minutes, April 13, 1910, in Notebook: titled "U.S. Immigration Commission

Executive Committee Records, 1908–1910," 44–47, Box 1, HP. So, too, somewhat surprisingly, did the Japanese interpreters working on the Pacific Coast. On Herkner, see Baheri et al., "Herkner Biography"; Aron, *Ladies and Gentlemen,* 83. On teacher earnings, see U.S. Bureau of the Census, *Historical Statistics of the United States, Colonial Times to 1970* (Washington, DC: U.S. Department of Commerce, Bureau of the Census, 1975), 167, Series D 763. On comparable salaries, see United States Committee on Grades and Salaries, *Estimates for Salaries in the Executive Departments and Establishments* (Washington, DC: Government Printing Office, 1908), esp. 4–6.

7. Meeting Minutes, May 29, 1908, Notebook, "U.S. Immigration Commission Records, 1907–1910," 65, Box 1, HP.

8. Meeting Minutes, January 9, 1908, 34, Box 1, HP.

9. Immigration Commission Executive Committee Minutes, April 1, 1908; Notebook: titled "U.S. Immigration Commission Executive Committee Records, 1908–1910," 18, Box 1, HP.

10. Jenks to Richard Ely, March 23, 1910, Box 41, Folder 2, Richard Ely Papers, Wisconsin Historical Society, Madison, Wisconsin. Alice Durand's brother E. Dana Durand was the director of the U.S. Census at the time, and Jenks called her "a worthy sister" to him.

11. My assumption about married couples is based on common surnames in the database; Rima D. Apple, *Perfect Motherhood: Science and Childrearing in America* (New Brunswick, NJ: Rutgers University Press, 2006), 50. White married women with children were the least likely group to be in the paid-wage labor group, although this statistic excludes the very sizable percentage of married women—in some working-class communities sometimes approaching half—who took in boarders or roomers or did some other remunerative labor within their home or "off the books." See U.S. Bureau of the Census, *Historical Statistics,* 129–134; Neill to Dana Durand, July 26, 1911, and, on Mrs. Neill, see unlabeled clipping, both in Folder (A) 1905–1907, NP-TRC. That said, the statistics in the schools reports were a mess.

12. In fact, their employment later became a political issue (although not because they were married). See Geo. A. Traylor to Hon. Lee S. Overman, U.S. Senate, March 3, 1913, Box 3, NP-CUA. Cindy Aron argues most female clerks joined federal employment because of unforeseen family financial problems. Aron, *Ladies and Gentlemen,* 60. Daisy Lee Worcester to Neill, October 13, 1908, Box 1, NP-CUA; Neill to Worcester, October 15, 1908, Box 1, NP-CUA; Mary E. Cookingham, "Bluestockings, Spinsters, and Pedagogues: Women College Graduates," *Population Studies* 38, no. 3 (1984): 350–351.

13. J. E. Hagerty to Miss Mark, June 26, 1907, MP. My characterization of Mark as a minister's daughter is based on the results of the 1900 census, which indicated that her father, Lewis Peter Mark, was a minister in Marion, Ohio. See Ancestry.com. *1900 United States Federal Census* [database on-line] (Provo, UT: Ancestry.com Operations Inc., 2004).

14. USIC, 26:3. Goldenweiser was a Jewish immigrant from Kiev whose brother, Alexander, an anthropologist, also worked for the commission; "SHEETS, M. A.

'08-LORENZ, Ph. D. '06," *Wisconsin Alumni Magazine* 13, no. 3 (1911): 139. Those of the first generation of college-educated women who did marry, often married other academics / social scientists: Sheets's husband, Max Lorenz, was a government economist with a PhD from the University of Wisconsin.

15. J. E. Hagerty to Whom It May Concern, June 11, 1903, MP.

16. Dorothy Ross, *The Origins of American Social Science* (New York: Cambridge University Press, 1991), 158; Jasper A. Smith to Miss Mark, March 5, 1905, MP. He, along with Kellogg, also ran the influential social work and reform magazine, *Survey.*

17. Edward T. Devine to My Dear Miss Mark, June 19, 1907, MP; J. E. Hagerty to Miss Mark, June 26, 1907, MP.

18. Reprinted as chapter six of Jane Addams, *Twenty Years at Hull-House, with Biographical Notes* (New York: Macmillan, 1911); Devine to Jane Addams, February 28, 1908, MP.

19. Mary Louise Mark, "The Upper East Side: A Study in Living Conditions and Migration," *Publications of the American Statistical Association* 10, no. 79 (1907): 345–368; J. W. Jenks to E. Dana Durand, October 18, 1909, MP.

20. Mark, "Upper East Side," 347.

21. Charles P. Neill to E. Dana Durand, October 15, 1909, MP; [Frederick Croxton] to Durand, October 23, 1909, MP; Jenks to Durand, October 18, 1909, MP.

22. Jenks to Durand, October 18, 1909, MP; "Mary Louise Mark (1878–1975)," *Find a Grave,* www.findagrave.com.

23. She might have had an earlier condition—her undergraduate adviser had also mentioned her health. J. W. Jenks to E. Dana Durand, October 18, 1909, MP. On her leave of absence, see Meeting Minutes, July 10, 1908, 67, Notebook: titled "U.S. Immigration Commission Records, 1907–1910," Box 1, HP. Volume 37 contained another study, on immigrant homes, that featured a woman author, Martha Dodson, and undercover work. For reasons of brevity, I have not included it in my analysis, although prominent reformer and special agent to the commission Kate Waller Barrett clearly saw it as of a piece with the other investigations. See Clipping, "Protecting Immigrant Girls," *Washington Times,* n.d. [c.1912], KWB.

24. In 1910, Elizabeth Goodnow wrote about prostitution in *The Market for Souls.* This suggests she may also have worked on the white slavery investigation, and reminds us of the concern over sexual coercion in the steerage study. She may also have been married to prominent academic Frank Goodnow.

25. USIC, 37:6.

26. Ibid., esp. 18–23. See Jennifer Fronc, *New York Undercover: Private Surveillance in the Progressive Era* (Chicago: University of Chicago Press, 2009). The practice was closely related to "slumming." See Tobie Higbie, "Crossing Class Boundaries: Tramp Ethnographers and Narratives of Class in Progressive Era America," *Social Science History* 21, no. 4 (1997): 559–592. Elizabeth Zanoni also makes this point in "'In the Guise of

Immigrants': Anna Herkner, Immigration Policy, and the Gendering of the Transatlantic Voyage during the Progressive Era" (unpublished paper presented at the Berkshire Conference on the History of Women, June 2008, in author's possession).

27. USIC, 37:22.

28. "Topics of the Times: Strangers in the Steerage," *New York Times,* December 15, 1909, cited in Zanoni, " 'In the Guise of Immigrants.' "

29. USIC, 37:1. See also Glen Edwards, "Steerage Legislation," in USIC, 39:339–485. (These laws resembled early laws regulating the slave trade. I thank Adam Rothman for this observation.) Bennet, who opposed almost all numerical immigration restrictions, admitted, "The labor people were for that, because that cut down immigration," Reminiscences of William Stiles Bennet (1951), Biographical Interview, 39, Columbia Center for Oral History, Rare Book and Manuscript Library, Columbia University in the City of New York. Steamships had to pay for the return passage of anyone rejected by immigration officials, so it was in their interest to comply with regulations. The U.S. Public Health Service grew out of the Marine health officers who served at Ellis Island. See Alan Kraut, *Silent Travelers: Germs, Genes, and the "Immigrant Menace"* (New York: Basic Books, 1994).

30. Aristide R. Zolberg calls this "remote control" in *A Nation by Design: Immigration Policy in the Fashioning of America* (Cambridge, MA: Harvard University Press, 2006), 4–5 (first mention). Zanoni makes the same point about Herkner's endorsement of "remote control" in " 'In the Guise of Immigrants.' " The earliest example of "remote control" was "An Act regulating passenger ships and vessels, Pub. L. No. 15–46, 3 Stat. 488 (1819)." Herkner addresses the law in her report's introduction; USIC, 37:41; USIC, 1:46.

31. See Mara Keire, "Vice Trust: Reinterpretation of White Slavery, 1907–1917," *Journal of Social History* 35, no. 1 (2001): 7, and esp. Gunther Peck, "Feminizing White Slavery in the United States: Marcus Braun and the Transnational Traffic in White Bodies, 1890–1910," in *Workers across the Americas: The Transnational Turn in Labor History,* ed. Leon Fink (New York: Oxford University Press, 2011), 221–244. Whitlock quoted in Pamela Haag, *Consent: Sexual Rights and the Transformation of American Liberalism* (Ithaca, NY: Cornell University Press, 1999), 70.

32. The Bureau of Investigation was created by Theodore Roosevelt by executive order in 1908. John Allen Noakes estimates that by 1913—just three years after the Mann Act was passed—20 to 32 percent of its budget was spent on white slavery investigations. See John Allen Noakes, "Enforcing Domestic Tranquility: State Building and the Origin of the (Federal) Bureau of Investigation, 1908–1920" (PhD diss., University of Pennsylvania, 1993), 17. Quotation from Don Whitehead, *The FBI Story: A Report to the People* (New York: Random House, 1956), 23; Athan G. Theoharis, *The FBI and American Democracy: A Brief Critical History* (Lawrence: University Press of Kansas, 2004), 16. For a similar argument about other undercover vice investigations, see Fronc, *New York Undercover.* On the role of the Mann Act in putting policing sexuality at the center of the FBI's

work, see Jessica Pliley, *Policing Sexuality: The Mann Act and the Making of the FBI* (Cambridge, MA: Harvard University Press, 2014), esp. 7–8, 56. Pliley also argues that the Mann Act expanded government power not just at the federal level but also at state and local, where FBI agents encouraged local investigators to pursue prostitution cases. By targeting women prostitutes, not pimps or johns, this power, Pliley argues, disproportionately affected women.

33. Thomas M. Pitkin, *Keepers of the Gate: A History of Ellis Island* (New York: New York University Press, 1975), 101–103. On William's skepticism, see Zanoni, "'In the Guise of Immigrants.'" On the WCTU's impact on journalistic and legislative coverage of white slavery, see Gretchen Soderlund, *Sex Trafficking, Scandal, and the Transformation of Journalism, 1885–1917* (Chicago: University of Chicago Press, 2014), chap. 3.

34. *Keller v. United States,* 213 U.S. 138 (1909); Pitkin, *Keepers of the Gate,* 101–103.

35. See Jane Addams, *A New Conscience and an Ancient Evil* (New York: Macmillan, 1912).

36. Meeting Minutes, January 18, 1908, and December 11, 1909, both in Notebook: titled "U.S. Immigration Commission Executive Committee Records, 1908–1910," 6, 104, Box 1, HP; Fronc, *New York Undercover,* 30; Soderlund, *Sex Trafficking,* 159–160.

37. Fronc, *New York Undercover,* chap. 3, on Bennet, 66. See also Soderlund, *Sex Trafficking.*

38. Its president, coincidentally, was David Starr Jordan, president of Stanford University and Yamato Ichihashi's mentor. Clifford G. Roe, "American Vigilance Association," *Journal of the American Institute of Criminal Law and Criminology* 3, no. 5 (1913): 806; Edward J. Bristow, *Prostitution and Prejudice: The Jewish Fight against White Slavery, 1870–1939* (New York: Schocken Books, 1983), 161. Similar figures in Chicago were prosecutors Clifford Roe and Edwin Sims.

39. Keire, "Vice Trust," 16; Bristow, *Prostitution and Prejudice,* 160; New York Police Department, *Annual Report of the Police Commissioner, City of New York, for the Year Ending December 31, 1908* (New York: Martin R. Brown, 1909), 20.

40. Their investigation had originally concluded in April 1909, but the commission decided to delay the publication of this report, the steerage conditions, and immigrant homes until other reports were completed. In the meantime, it is clear from the report that they continued collecting materials and writing, since some appendices were dated December 1909, the date the report was actually released.

41. As far as I know, no scholarship on the Dillingham Commission, white slavery, or the Mann Act has identified Philbrook as the author of the report. Biographical and archival material on her mentions her work on white slavery for the commission but without necessarily attributing the whole report to her. I discovered her authorship by reading the commission's minutes and payroll in HP; USIC, 37:57.

42. USIC, 37:76–80, 60–61.

43. Ibid., 65, 81.

44. Ibid., 37, 65, 67, 73.

45. Ibid., 86. On Braun's reports, see Pliley, *Policing Sexuality*, 50. On the role of the Bureau of Immigration in the construction of sexual identity, and the way it policed—and recognized—homosexuality and queerness, see Margot Canaday, *The Straight State: Sexuality and the State in Twentieth-Century America* (Princeton, NJ: Princeton University Press, 2009). Historian Gunther Peck has determined that few of those reported on were actually "boys." See Gunther Peck, *Reinventing Free Labor: Padrones and Immigrant Workers in the North American West, 1880–1930* (New York: Cambridge University Press, 2000), 96–97.

46. "Protecting Immigrant Girls," KWB.

47. Kate Waller Barrett, "Tribute to Children's Bureau," n.d. [c. 1914], KWB. The comment was prescient. In 2008, when New York governor Elliott Spitzer was arrested under the Mann Act for fraternizing with a prostitute, he resigned six days later.

48. USIC, 37:92. At the same time, Philbrook and others assailed the double standard in which prostitutes got arrested, but johns did not. In the 1920s, the NWP, in which Philbrook was very active, would launch a campaign for "Anti-johns laws," an attempt to hold those who hired prostitutes as responsible as those who practiced or organized prostitution. Thomas Mackey, *Pursuing Johns: Criminal Law Reform, Defending Character and New York City's Committee of Fourteen, 1920–1930* (Columbus: Ohio State University Press, 2005).

49. The law was called the Howell-Bennet Act after commission members Benjamin Howell and William Bennet. Bennet sponsored it as part of his general effort to restrict "undesirables" to avoid quantitative restriction. But note that his action strengthened federal power, even though he was a "liberal" on immigration. And see "Tribute to Children's Bureau," KWB.

50. An Act To further regulate interstate and foreign commerce by prohibiting the transportation therein for immoral purposes of women and girls, and for other purposes, Pub. L. No. 61–277, 36 Stat. 825 (1910). The antitrust point is Maura Kiele's central argument, though Soderlund says that the Rockefeller Commission's report denied that there was a vice trust. See Soderburgh, *Sex Trafficking*, xv. On Jenks and Lauck specifically, see Gabriel J. Chin, "Regulating Race: Asian Exclusion and the Administrative State," *Harvard Civil Rights-Civil Liberties Law Review* 37, no. 1 (2002): 2. On the anti-monopoly aspects of the law, see Mark Thomas Connelly, *The Response to Prostitution in the Progressive Era* (Chapel Hill: University of North Carolina Press, 1980), 59, and Veire, "Vice Trust," 5–41, esp. 5–6, 16, 18. Ironically, as I have noted, Philbrook argued that there was not, in fact, a white slavery monopoly or "trust."

51. On the legal points, the best source is Connelly, *Response to Prostitution,* esp. 56–60, Section 6, quoted on 57; *United States v. Holte,* 236 U.S. 140 (1915), discussed in Connelly, *Response to Prostitution,* 129; "Seeks Case against Johnson: Department of Justice Inquires If Pugilist Violated White Slave Act," *New York Times,* October 27, 1912, 11. Singer

Chuck Berry and actor Charlie Chaplin were also both arrested for violations of the Mann Act, for largely political reasons. Berry (whose case involved a fourteen-year-old) served twenty months in prison, but Chaplin was not convicted. See Bernard A. Weisberger, "Morals, Mobility, and the Law," *Reviews in American History* 24, no. 3 (1996): 474; Pliley, *Policing Sexuality,* 7–8, 56.

52. Christopher J. Cyphers, *The National Civic Federation and the Making of a New Liberalism, 1900–1915* (Westport, CT: Praeger, 2002), chap. 3.

53. I use Linda Gordon's definition of maternalism in "Gender, State, and Society: A Debate with Theda Skocpol," *Contention* 2, no. 3 (1993): 146–147. On maternalism versus paternalism, see *Pitied But Not Entitled: Single Mothers and the History of Welfare* (Cambridge, MA: Harvard University Press, 1994), esp. 55–56. On strategic suffrage, see *inter alia* Mary Ting Yi Lui, "Saving Young Girls from Chinatown: White Slavery and Woman Suffrage, 1910–1910," *Journal of the History of Sexuality* 18, no. 3 (2009): 393–417. On protective labor, see Alice Kessler-Harris, *In Pursuit of Equity: Women, Men, and the Quest for Economic Citizenship in 20th-Century America* (New York: Oxford University Press, 2003).

54. In effect, the Brandeis brief argued that women were all current or future mothers of citizens, so laws preserving women's health were necessary for the protection of the citizenry. The so-called Brandeis brief, the first to use nonlegal evidence to defend the constitutionality of a law, created a precedent for presenting sociological evidence in legal cases—the most famous example being psychologist Kenneth Clark's famous experiments with black-and-white dolls presented in *Brown v. Board of Education* (1953). On the lasting negative effects on women's economic citizenship of protective labor laws, see Kessler-Harris, *In Pursuit of Equity.*

55. On early feminists, see Jill Lepore, *The Secret History of Wonder Woman* (New York: Alfred A. Knopf, 2014); Jayme Rae Hill, "From the Brothel to the Block: Politics and Prostitution in Baltimore during the Progressive Era" (MA thesis, University of Maryland, Baltimore County, 2008), 47–48; Baheri et al., "Herkner Biography," and David W. McFadden and Claire Gorfinkel, *Constructive Spirit: Quakers in Revolutionary Russia* (Pasadena, CA: Intentional Productions, 2004), 184.

56. Only a very few women in industrial work competed directly with men. Among these were a few women in the printing trades, who opposed protective labor legislation because it hampered their ability to compete with men for well-paid skilled jobs. Mary Walton, *A Woman's Crusade: Alice Paul and the Battle for the Ballot* (New York: Palgrave Macmillan, 2010), 247; Alva Belmont, cited in Christine A. Lunardini, *From Equal Suffrage to Equal Rights: Alice Paul and the National Woman's Party* (New York: New York University Press, 1986), 152; Kessler-Harris, *In Pursuit of Equity,* 41–42.

57. I have relied heavily here on Barbara Petrick, *Mary Philbrook: The Radical Feminist in New Jersey* (Trenton: New Jersey Historical Commission, 1981). Philbrook's papers have a correspondence index that lists no one related to the Dillingham Commission, so

that portion of her work must not survive. A researcher I hired found nothing in her papers, either.

58. Mary Philbrook, "Woman's Legal Status—Should It Be Altered?," *New Jersey Law Journal* 20, no. 11 (1897): 326, quoted in Petrick, *Mary Philbrook*, 3.

59. On women, including Philbrook, and legal aid, see Felice Batlan, *Women and Justice for the Poor: A History of Legal Aid, 1863–1945* (New York: Cambridge University Press, 2015).

60. "The Portrait," *New Jersey Law Journal* 27, no. 6 (1904): 188–189, quoted in Petrick, *Mary Philbrook*, 21.

61. Walton, *A Woman's Crusade*, 247. On the NWP's efforts, including the alliance with the Committee of Fourteen, see Mackey, *Pursuing Johns*, esp. 131. On the NWP's archives, now housed at the Library of Congress Manuscript Division, see Petrick, *Mary Philbrook*; Abigail M. Markwyn, *Empress San Francisco: The Pacific Rim, the Great West, and California at the Panama-Pacific International Exposition* (Lincoln: University of Nebraska Press, 2014), 230–231.

62. Quoted in "Juliet Stuart Poyntz, Class of 1907: Suffragist, Feminist, Spy," *Barnard Archives and Special Collections*, https://barnardarchives.wordpress.com/2012/02/20/juliet-stuart-poyntz-class-of-1907/.

63. I have surmised that she worked on the seasonal unemployment report in Volume 18 because it included Utica, where Points said she worked, and because a couple years later she wrote memos on the seasonal unemployment in Massachusetts. See Alexander Keyssar, *Out of Work: The First Century of Unemployment in Massachusetts* (New York: Cambridge University Press, 1986), 383.

64. Quoted in "Suffragist, Feminist, Spy."

65. 1912 Barnard Yearbook, Barnard College Archives. My thanks to researcher Shannon O'Neill at Barnard. On feminists, see Christine Stansell, *American Moderns: Bohemian New York and the Creation of a New Century* (New York: Metropolitan Books, 2000).

66. Juliet Stuart Poyntz, "Suffragism and Feminism at Barnard," *Barnard Bear* 9, no. 7 (1914): 3–4. On the rising popularity of these clubs, see Lepore, *Wonder Woman*.

67. On her work at the ILGWU, see Annelise Orleck, *Common Sense and a Little Fire: Women and Working-Class Politics in the United States, 1900–1965* (Chapel Hill: University of North Carolina Press, 1995), 175, 177–179, 181–183.

68. Quoted in Annelise Orleck, Review of *All Together Different: Yiddish Socialists Garment Workers and the Roots of Multiculturalism*, by Daniel Katz, *ILR Review* 66, no. 3 (2013): 531.

69. On the founding of the Communist Party in the United States, see Paul Buhle and Dan Georgakas, "Communist Party, USA," *Encyclopedia of the American Left*, www.marxists.org/history/usa/parties/cpusa/encyclopedia-american-left.htm. See "Juliet Stuart Poyntz, Class of 1907," *Barnard Archives and Special Collections*, http://

barnardarchives.wordpress.com/2012/02/20/juliet-stuart-poyntz-class-of-1907, and "Juliet Stuart Poyntz," *Wikipedia,* http://en.wikipedia.org/wiki/Juliet_Stuart_Poyntz.

6. The American Type

1. Boas to Jenks, March 19, 1908, Reel 9, BP-LoC.

2. The older "science" of phrenology focused more on personality and character; craniometry, while sometimes linking physical characteristics with mental, on measurement.

3. Franz Boas, *Materials for the Study of Inheritance in Man.* Vol. 6, *Columbia University Contributions to Anthropology* (New York: Columbia University Press, 1928). On budget cuts that curtailed the full scope of his proposed study, see Boas to Jenks, March 11, 1909, Reel 10, BP-LoC. For a good overview of recent analyses, see Tracy Teslow, *Constructing Race: The Science of Bodies and Cultures in American Anthropology* (New York: Cambridge University Press, 2014), 34. See also Charles Fergus, "Boas, Bones, and Race," *Penn State News,* May 1, 2003, http://news.psu.edu/story/140739/2003/05/01/research/boas-bones-and-race.

4. Vernon J. Williams, Jr., "What Is Race? Franz Boas Reconsidered," in *Race, Nation, and Empire in American History,* ed. James T. Campbell, Matthew Pratt Guterl, and Robert G. Lee (Chapel Hill: University of North Carolina Press), 41.

5. Clarence C. Gravlee, H. Russell Bernard, and William R Leonard, "Heredity, Environment, and Cranial Form: A Reanalysis of Boas' Immigrant Data," *American Anthropologist* 105, no. 1 (2003): 126; Franz Boas, "Human Faculty as Determined by Race," 1894, reprinted in George Stocking, ed., *A Franz Boas Reader: The Shaping of American Anthropology, 1883–1911* (Chicago: University of Chicago Press, 1974), 222.

6. Franz Boas, *The Mind of Primitive Man* (New York: Macmillan, 1911); George W. Stocking, *Delimiting Anthropology: Occasional Essays and Reflections* (Madison: University of Wisconsin Press, 2001), 41.

7. Maurice Fishberg, *The Jews: A Study of Race and Environment* (New York: Walter Scott Publishing, 1911), 21.

8. Desmond King comes to a similar conclusion about Boas, although he argues for a greater role for eugenics in the commission than I do. Desmond S. King, *Making Americans: Immigration, Race, and the Origins of Diverse Democracy* (Cambridge, MA: Harvard University Press, 2000), 67, 69, 75.

9. *Time Magazine,* May 11, 1936.

10. Regina Darnell, "Toward Consensus on the Scope of Anthropology: Daniel Garrison Brinton and the View from Philadelphia," in *Philadelphia and the Development of Americanist Archaeology,* ed. Don D. Fowler and David R. Wilcox (Tuscaloosa: University of Alabama Press, 2003), 22–23; Julia E. Liss, "German Culture and the German Science in the *Bildung* of Franz Boas," in *Volksgeist as Method and Ethic: Essays on Boasian*

Ethnography and the German Anthropological Tradition, ed. George W. Stocking (Madison: University of Wisconsin, 2006), 155–184; George W. Stocking, Jr., *The Shaping of American Anthropology, 1883–1911* (New York: Basic Books, 1974), vi; Mead, quoted in Marvin Harris, *The Rise of Anthropological Theory: A History of Theories of Culture* (New York: Thomas W. Crowell, 1968), 252.

11. Harris, *Rise of Anthropological Theory,* 263, 268; Benoit Massin, "From Virchow to Fischer: Physical Anthropology and 'Modern Race Theories' in Wilhelmine Germany," in Stocking, *Volksgeist,* 80–100.

12. Harris, *Rise of Anthropological Theory,* 263–264; Stocking, *Delimiting Anthropology,* 51.

13. Harris, *Rise of Anthropological Theory,* 253; Franz Boas, "Rudolf Virchow's Anthropological Work," *Science* 16 (1902), reprinted in Stocking, ed., *A Franz Boas Reader,* 257–258, and Boas "The Methods of Ethnology," *American Anthropologist* 22, no. 4 (1920): 314.

14. Harris, *Rise of Anthropological Theory,* chap. 9. Fishberg's influence begins on the first page of the report. See USIC, 38:1, 99. On Fishberg, see Mitchell Hart, "Maurice Fishberg and the Ambiguities of Jewish Identity," *AJS Perspectives: The Magazine of the Association for Jewish Studies,* Fall 2007, 20–22. On changing views in German anthropology, see Massin, "From Virchow to Fischer," 104–121; Sunmin Kim, "Different Kind of Naturalization: Quantification and Race in Franz Boas's Work in the Dillingham Commission" (unpublished conference paper in author's possession, presented at Social Science History Association Annual Meeting, Baltimore, Maryland, November 2015).

15. Harris, *Rise of Anthropological Theory,* 286, 278, White quotation, 261; Boas to Husband, January 27, 1909, Reel 9, BP-LoC.

16. The two were not brothers, but both came from small towns in Michigan and clearly knew each other and were of a similar generation. I thank my research assistant Chad Frazier for doing this genealogical research. Letters between Boas and Albert Jenks date back at least to 1902. See A. Jenks to Boas, May 13, 1902, BP-APS.

17. USIC, 38:1.

18. Darnell, "Toward Consensus," 21; Benedict quoted in Harris, *Rise of Anthropological Theory,* 253.

19. John W. Weeks, *The Library of Daniel Garrison Brinton* (Philadelphia: University of Pennsylvania Museum of Archaeology and Anthropology, 2002), 3. On Brinton's work as the basis for the *Dictionary of Races or Peoples,* see USIC, 5:8; Douglas Cole, *Franz Boas: The Early Years, 1858–1906* (Seattle: University of Washington Press, 1999), 121.

20. William McGee, "Some Principles of Nomenclature," *American Anthropologist* 8 (1895), quoted in Harris, *Rise of Anthropological Theory,* 255, 256.

21. On the dictionary, see Husband to Boas, September 29, 1909; Boas to Husband, October 9, 1909, October 11, 1909; Husband to Boas, October 12, 1909; Boas to Husband, October 14, 1909; Husband to Boas, October 15, 1909, Reel 10, BP-LoC. On "descent," see Husband to Boas, January 9, 1909; Boas to Husband, January 12, 1909,

Folder Husband, W. W. #1, BP-APS. On consulting on other volumes, see W. W. Husband to Boas, January 29, 1909, Husband to Boas, February 23, 1909; Boas to Husband, and insert, February 24, 1909, Folder, Husband, W. W. #1; Husband to Boas, October 12, 1909, Folder, Husband, W. W. #4, BP-APS.

22. Stocking, *Delimiting Anthropology,* 23, 15, 20; Teslow, *Constructing Race,* 35; Boas, *Mind of Primitive Man,* rev. ed. (Westport, CT: Greenwood Press, 1938; 1983), 138.

23. Yu Xie, "Franz Boas and Statistics," *Annals of Scholarship* 5 (1988): 276–277, Boas quoted on 272.

24. M. Eileen Magnello, "Karl Pearson and the Origins of Modern Statistics: An Elastician Becomes a Statistician," *Rutherford Journal: The New Zealand Journal for the History and Philosophy of Science* 1 (2005–2006), www.rutherfordjournal.org/.

25. L. L. Bernard and Jessie Bernard, *Origins of American Sociology* (New York: Russell & Russell, 1965), 824; Charles Camic and Yu Xie, "The Statistical Turn in American Social Science: Columbia University, 1890 to 1915," *American Sociological Review* 59, no. 5 (1994): 789; see for example Franz Boas, "Determination of the Coefficient of Correlation," *Science,* May 21, 1909, 823–824; Cole, *Franz Boas,* 134, 146; Xie, "Franz Boas and Statistics," 287–288.

26. Boas quotations in Xie, "Franz Boas and Statistics," 280–281, 287; Theodore M. Porter, *Karl Pearson: The Scientific Life in a Statistical Age* (Princeton, NJ: Princeton University Press, 2004), 263; USIC, 38:93. On the challenges of using new correlation methods, see A. Goldenweiser to Boas, August 29, 1909, Folder: Goldenweiser, Alexander #1, BP-APS.

27. Boas was the only one of the four leading statisticians at Columbia University who was not an ardent restrictionist. It was at Columbia that statistical methods became an established part of the social sciences. Camic and Xie, "Statistical Turn," 778.

28. Teslow, *Constructing Race,* 62. Among these was his own son Ernst, because in Boas's view, he was one of the few candidates with the skills necessary for the job. Boas to Morton E. Crane, May 25, 1910, Reel 10, BP-LoC.

29. See for example Boas to Prof. R. S. Woodward, President Carnegie Institution, Washington, DC, May 4, 1908, Reel 9, and Boas to Davenport, October 10, 1913, Reel 10, BP-LoC; Garland E. Allen, "Eugenics and Modern Biology: Critiques of Eugenics, 1910–1945" (article, Biology Faculty Publications and Presentations, Washington University Open Scholarship, May 2011), 2, http://openscholarship.wustl.edu/bio_facpubs/5; Boas to H. W. Hodge, Bureau of American Ethnology, March 14, 1910; Hodge to Boas, March 18, 1910, Reel 10, BP-LoC.

30. Quoted in Lee D. Baker, "Franz Boas Out of the Ivory Tower," *Anthropological Theory* 4, no. 1 (2004): 33. See also Cole, *Franz Boas,* 60–61.

31. William Z. Ripley, "Races in the United States," *Atlantic Monthly,* December 1908, www.theatlantic.com/past/docs/unbound/flashbks/immigr/rip.htm. *Atlantic Monthly* turned down Boas's reply, but see Franz Boas, "Race Problems in America," *Science,*

May 28, 1909, 839–849, quotations on 839, 846; A. T. Sinclair, Allston, Mass., to Boas, June 5, 1909, Folder: *Atlantic Monthly,* BP-APS.

32. Mark H. Haller, *Eugenics: Hereditarian Attitudes in American Thought* (New Brunswick, NJ: Rutgers University Press, 1963; 1984), chap. 5; Boas to Dr. Maurice Fishberg, March 1, 1909; and see Boas to Davenport, June 13, 1910; Helene M. Boas (Franz's daughter) to Davenport, June 30, 1910, all Reel 10, BP-LoC.

33. Cance oversaw the Dillingham Commission's reports on recent immigrants in agriculture; see Chapter 7. Secretary, Immigration Committee to Boas, July 19, 1912, Sec. Imm. Assn. ABA to Boas, August 28, 1912, Folder: American Breeders Association Eugenics Section, Immigration Committee, BP-APS; Boas to Davenport, October 10, 1913, BP-APS.

34. Economic historian Joel Perlmann concurs that "there was a dramatic range of contradictory views" among staff. But he also uses commission staff's queries to Boas about racial definitions as evidence of their flexibility on race. This argument mistakenly assumes that the Boas of 1909 was the Boas of the 1930s. But in 1909, he was in fact not yet rigidly identified with cultural relativism or critiques of race. See Joel Perlmann, "Views of European Races among the Research Staff of the US Immigration Commission and the Census Bureau, ca. 1910" (Working Paper No. 648, Levy Economics Institute of Bard College, January 2011); dictionary quoted in Joel Perlmann, " 'Race or People': Federal Race Classifications for Europeans in America, 1898–1913" (Working Paper No. 320, January 2001, unpag.).

35. Boas to Jenks, March 19, 1908, Reel 9 (the original is partly illegible: says Russian Jews or someone else, but unclear), BP-APS.

36. Boas to Jenks, August 6, 1909; H. Lischmer, Pt. Loma, CA to Boas, August 20, 1909, Reel 10, BP-LoC. Boas to Husband, January 12, 1909; Boas to Crane, May 19, 1909, Reel 10, BP-LoC, Boas to Jenks, March 23, 1908, Jenks to Boas, April 8, 1908, Reel 9, BP-LoC.

37. Boas to Jenks, March 23, 1908, April 15, 1908, Reel 9, BP-LoC. The field of physical anthropology had been especially interested in children's development. Xie, "Franz Boas and Statistics," 277–278.

38. I assume that Jenks shared Boas' correspondence with the rest of the Commission before the vote. Jenks to Boas, April 29, 1908, BP-APS; Executive Committee Notebook, May 8, 1908, 21, HP, and Jenks to Boas, March 6, 1909, BP-LoC.

39. On Lodge's support for Boas, see Jenks to Boas, March 29, 1909; on Bennet's, see Husband to Boas, May 26, 1909, Folder Husband, W. W. #3, BP-APS; Jenks to Boas, March 22, 1910; Walcott, Smithsonian Institution to Boas, May 4, 1910, BP-LoC. I thank my research assistant Chad Frazier for his research on ancestry.com to demonstrate Albert and Jeremiah were not brothers, as I had previously assumed. It's almost certain they were cousins, though, given that they were both from small towns in Michigan. Letters between Albert Jenks and Boas date back at least that far, and it appeared that

they worked together at the Smithsonian Institution's Bureau of American Ethnology. A. Jenks to Boas, May 13, 1902, BP-APS. On Albert Jenks's work, see Tim Brady, "Primitive Thinking," *Minnesota,* March–April 2008, www.minnesotaalumni.org/s/1118/content .aspx?sid=1118&gid=1&pgid=1096. On Boas's mixed opinion of Albert Jenks, see Boas to Mr. E. W. Brock, Director Geological Survey, Ottawa, Canada, May 14, 1910, BP-LoC.

40. Boas to Jenks, March 23, 1908, Reel 9, BP-LoC.

41. Boas to Jenks, March 23, 1908, May 2, 1908, BP-LoC. On intermarriage and eugenics, see for example Robert DeC. Ward, "National Eugenics in Relation to Immigration," *North American Review* 192, no. 656 (1910): 56–67. Ironically, race scientists in Italy who were pioneers in criminal anthropology provided much of the initial theoretical material that American scientists used to argue that southern Italians were racially inferior.

42. See for example USIC, 38:65, 100. See also Boas to Jenks, November 15, 1909, Reel 10; Boas to Jenks, March 23, 1908, Reel 9, BP-LoC. On "abnormality" and the LPC charge, see Margot Canaday, *The Straight State: Sexuality and the State in Twentieth-Century America* (Princeton, NJ: Princeton University Press, 2009).

43. The term appears to have been invented by a hospital lawyer in 1957. "P. G. Gebhard, Developer of the Term 'Informed Consent,'" *New York Times,* August 26, 1997; Ruth R. Faden, Thomas L. Beauchamp, and Nancy M. King, *History and Theory of Informed Consent* (New York: Oxford University Press, 1986), 84–85, 65.

44. Faden et al., *History and Theory,* 3, 59; Susan E. Lederer, *Subjected to Science: Human Experimentation in America before the Second World War* (Baltimore, MD: Johns Hopkins University Press, 1995). The topic of scientific research, as opposed to medical research, deserves much more historical study; Joel Sparks, comp., "Timeline on Laws Related to the Protection of Human Subjects," 2002, http://history.nih.gov/about/timelines _laws_human.html; "History of Research Ethics," http://ors.umkc.edu/research -compliance-%28iacuc-ibc-irb-rsc%29/institutional-review-board-%28irb%29/history -of-research-ethics.

45. The tension between democracy and social control is a central theme in Progressive Era historiography. This historiography is too vast to list here, but a rather striking and recent variant of the coercion argument—in the form of what amounts to a libertarian brief—appears in Thomas Leonard's *Illiberal Reformers: Race, Eugenics and American Economics in the Progressive Era* (Princeton, NJ: Princeton University Press, 2015).

46. USIC, 38:82; Boas to Husband, March 23, 1908, Reel 9, BP-LoC.

47. Teslow, *Constructing Race,* 52; *Worcester Daily Telegram,* quoted in Baker, "Franz Boas," 33–34. See also Cole, *Franz Boas,* 142–143.

48. Baker, "Franz Boas," 35–36.

49. USIC, 38:82.

50. Gaylord White, Union Settlement, to Boas, May 27, 1908; Boas to Husband, February 6, 1909; Husband to Boas, February 15, 1909, Folder Husband, W. W. #2, BP-APS.

Interestingly, one private school they identified as keeping useful records was Lawrenceville Academy, which Secretary of Commerce and Labor Oscar Straus's son attended. George L. Meylan, Director, Columbia University Gymnasium, to Boas, May 13, 1908, Reel 9, BP-LoC. A principal at the Newark Academy gave Boas several years of student health records, presumably without permission from them. USIC, 38:3; Samuel[?] Dutton, Teachers College to Boas, February 10, 1909, Reel 10, BP-LoC. The superintendent of the Ethical Culture schools had to "consider the matter very carefully together with some of his colleagues" but eventually consented to some measurements. Franklin Lewis, Ethical Culture School, to Boas, February 1, 1909, Reel 10, BP-LoC.

51. Martin Beck, General Manager, Orpheum Circuit to [?], May 4, 1909, BP-APS.

52. Harvey to Boas, February 5, 1909, Reel 10, BP-LoC.

53. He hoped to conduct his own research with the findings. Dr. Ward Crampton, Department of Education the City of New York Office of the City Superintendent of Schools to Boas, June 3, 1908, August 29, 1908, Reel 9, BP-LoC; D. P. Macmillan, Director, Department of Child Study and Pedagogical Investigation, Board of Education, City of Chicago Tribune Building to Boas, June 5, 1908, Boas to Jenks, October 23, 1908, both Reel 9, BP-LoC; USIC, 38:2–3; Boas to Mr. B. Veit, Principal Public School No. 1, Henry & Oliver Sts., March 9, 1909, March 13, 1909, Reel 10, BP-LoC. On the use of children in medical research (there is very little literature on the history of academic research outside of biomedical fields), see Susan E. Lederer, "Children as Guinea Pigs: Historical Perspectives," *Accountability in Research* 10 (2003): 1–16.

54. Jenks to "TO WHOM IT MAY CONCERN," enclosed with Jenks to Boas, June 5, 1908, Reel 9, BP-LoC. Another example of a letter appears in "Agent in Charge" [not Boas] to Mr. A. B. Poland, Supt. Of Schools, Newark, NJ, n.d. [probably late 1909, early 1910], Reel 10, BP-LoC.

55. Boas to Husband, Folder W. W. Husband #3, May 24, 1909, BP-APS; Boas to General Theodore A. Bingham, Commissioner of Police, New York City, May 12, 1909, Reel 10, BP-APS, emphasis added.

56. Husband to Boas, April 16, 1909, Husband to Boas, June 12, 1909, Boas to Husband, April 3, 1909, all in Folder: W. W. Husband #3, BP-APS.

57. Boas to Mr. W. M. Brittain, Caledonia Club, May 13, 1909; Boas to Goldenweiser, June 21, 1909, Goldenweiser to Boas, July 2, 1909, all in Folder: Goldenweiser, Alexander #1, BP-APS. On his focus on children, see Boas to Jenks, April 15, 1908, Reel 9, and Boas to Prof. C. L. Sperazas, Columbia University, February 13, 1909, Reel 10, BP-LoC.

58. Boas to Mr. Felix M. Warburg, Care of Messrs. Kuhn, Loeb, & Co., May 29, 1908, Reel 9; Warburg[?] to Dr. Henry Fleischman, Supt., Education Alliance, 197 East Broadway, New York, June 1, 1908, Reel 9, BP-LoC. Jewish lawyer and immigration lobbyist Louis Marshall served on the board of the Educational Alliance. USIC 41:206.

59. Boas to Warburg, June 2, 1908; See also Fleischman to Boas, June 4, 1908, both in Reel 9, BP-LoC.

60. See for example Boas to Nicholas Murray Butler, June 14, 1909, and Boas and mother's correspondence throughout 1907–1910, in BP-APS. Mentions of Immigration Commission in letters appear in Folder: Boas-Corresp—1909, Jan-Feb., and Boas-Corresp.—1909, July-Aug, Corresp.—1911, Jan.-Feb., Boas-Corresp.—1911, April-June; "A Study of the Jewish Race," *New York Times* February 12, 2011; Boas to Jenks, December 21, 1909; Osiah Schwarz, *General Types of Superior Men: A Philosophico-Psychological Study of Genius, Talent and Philistinism in Their Bearings upon Human Society and Its Struggle for a Better Social Order* (Boston: Badger Books, 1916).

61. Boas to Jenks, May 12, 1908, Reel 9, BP-LoC. See also Boas to Jenks, June 6, 1910, Reel 10, BP-LoC. On another female physician, Dr. Annie Daniels, who did home health work, recommended to Boas, see Gaylord White, Union Settlement, to Boas, May 27, 1908, Reel 9, BP-LoC. For list of women see Boas to Crane, June 9, 1910, Reel 10, BP-LoC.

62. See Boas to Dr. Ridolfo Livi, Rome, Italy, January 10, 1910, Reel 10, BP-LoC; Boas to Felix Antonsachio, November 20, 1908, Reel 9, BP-LoC; Peter D'Agostino, "Craniums, Criminals, and the 'Cursed Race': Italian Anthropology in American Racial Thought, 1861–1924," *Comparative Studies in Society and History* 44, no. 2 (2002): 323; Boas to Camillo Cianfarra, editor, *L'araldo Italiano,* April 18, 1909, Reel 10, BP-LoC; David Rappaport to Boas, July 19, 1909, Reel 10, BP-LoC.

63. See for example Jenks to Boas, April 8, 1908, Reel 9; Dr. J. Morgan Howe, May 29, 1908, Reel 9; Boas to Dr. Charles B. Minot, Harvard Medical School, April 30, 1910, Reel 10; Minot to Boas, May 20, 1910, Reel 10, BP-LoC; Executive Committee Notebooks, April 24, 1908, 42, HP; Jenks to Boas, June 8, 1909 Boas to Jenks, March 11, 1909, Reel 10, BP-LoC. See also Boas to Jenks, February 28, 1910; Boas to Jenks, May 28, 1909; Boas to Jenks, October 18, 1909, all in Reel 10, BP-LoC.

64. Boas to Jenks, December 23, 1909. See also Jenks to Boas, February 14, 1910; Crane to Boas, February 23, 1910; Boas to Jenks, February 28, 1910; Jenks[?], on board T. S. S. Lapland to Boas, March 30, 1910; Boas to Jenks, November 14, 1910; Boas to Davenport, January 25, 1913; Boas to Jacob Schiff, April 12, 1909, June 11, 1910; Boas to Adler, January 20, 1910; Jenks to Boas about Lodge, inter alia, April 20, 1910; Boas to Jenks, January 25, 1910. For other examples, see Boas to Prof. W. I. Thomas, University of Chicago, October 1, 1910. See also Boas to Vladimir Simkhovitch, January 26, 1910, all in Reel 10, BP-LoC. I thank my colleague John McNeill for pointing out the contrast with W. T. Thomas's studies on immigrants generously funded by industrialists.

65. Boas to Dr. Berthold Laefer, October 21, 1908, Reel 9, BP-LoC. On where he found his subjects, see Boas to Jenks, October 18, 1909, Reel 10, BP-LoC; USIC, 38:82; 55, 57, 1. On research on Scots and Bohemians, see Schwarz to Boas, July 12, 1909, Reel 9, BP-LoC.

66. "Cranial assimilation" in Boas to Nicholas Murray Butler, President of Columbia University, November 13, 1908, Reel 9, BP-LoC; USIC, 1:44.

67. USIC, 38:2, 5–7.

68. Boas to Jenks, December 31, 1909, Reel 10, BP-LoC. Quotation in "America Molding the Races," newspaper clipping, n.d., BP-APS; USIC, 38:12.

69. Ludy T. Benjamin, Jr., "The Birth of American Intelligence Testing," *Monitor on Psychology* 40, no. 1 (2009): 20, www.apa.org/monitor/2009/01/assessment.aspx; Boas to Jacob Schiff, April 12, 1909, Reel 10, BP-LoC; USIC, 38:5, 76, emphasis added.

70. Boas to Jenks, December 23, 1909; Boas to Crane, April 30, 1910. See also Husband to Boas, April 30, 1910; Crane to Boas, May 2, 1910; Boas to Husband, May 2, 1910, all in Reel 10, BP-LoC; Franz Boas, *Changes in Bodily Form of Descendants of Immigrants* (New York: Columbia University Press, 1912); "Aliens Change in America," *Baltimore Sun,* December 17, 1909, 11; Boas to Jenks, December 21, 1909, Reel 10, BP-LoC.

71. Boas to Husband, December 20, 1909, Reel 10, BP-LoC; "America Molding the Races."

72. News clipping, *Leslie's Weekly,* March 10, 1916, 231, Reel 10, BP-LoC.

73. Ward, "National Eugenics," 58. See Gary Gerstle, *American Crucible: Race and Nation in the Twentieth Century* (Princeton, NJ: Princeton University Press, 2001), and Gail Bederman, *Manliness and Civilization: A Cultural History of Gender and Race in the United States, 1880–1917* (Chicago: University of Chicago Press, 1995). On desire to study intermarriage, see Boas to Jenks, January 29, 1909, February 24, 1909, December 31, 1909, all in Reel 10, BP-LoC. On leaving it out of the study, see USIC, 38:2.

74. Allen, "Eugenics and Modern Biology"; Franz Boas, "Eugenics," *Scientific Monthly,* July–December 2016, 471–478.

75. G. M. Morant and Otto Samson, "An Examination of Investigations by Dr. Maurice Fishberg and Professor Franz Boas Dealing with Measurements of Jews in New York," *Biometrika* 28, no. 1/2 (1936): 1–31; Karl Pearson, "On Jewish-Gentile Relationships," *Biometrika* 28, no. 1/2 (1936): 32–33. On their own assumptions, see Elazar Barkan, *The Retreat of Scientific Racism: Changing Concepts of Race in Britain and the United States between the World Wars* (New York: Cambridge University Press, 1993), 161–162. See Teslow, *Constructing Race,* 35, chap. 5. Shapiro served as president of the American Eugenic Society from 1955–1962. Shapiro biographical memoir, http://nasonline.org/publications/biographical-memoirs/.

76. James M. Tanner, cited in Gravlee, Bernard and Leonard, "Heredity," 125–126; Gravlee, Bernard, and Leonard, "Heredity," 331; Michael A. Little and Paul A. Leslie, quoted in Gravlee, Bernard, and Leonard, "Heredity," 136.

77. USIC, 1:44; Boas to Jenks, April 18, 1917, Folder: Jenks, Jeremiah, W. #3, BP-APS.

7. Not a Question of Too Many Immigrants

1. USIC, 22:235; USIC, 1:567; "An Important Task," *New-York Daily Tribune,* May 5, 1907. On William Wheeler's interest in distribution, see for example "Immigration

Investigated," *Los Angeles Times,* November 10, 1907, and "Substitutes for Asiatics," *Los Angeles Times,* May 8, 1908.

2. On Neill's southern allegiances and work there for the Bureau of Labor, see B. R. Tillman, to D. D. Wallace, March 13, 1913, Box 3, NP-CUA; Neill to C. W. Stiles, August 7, 1907, Folder 1907, NP-TRC, and Neill to Mr. Ethelbert Stewart, 2, October 21, 1906, Box 1, NP-CUA; Neill to Tillman, March 15, 1913, Box 3, NP-CUA.

3. USIC, vols. 7, 9, 11, 15, and 16. On the other hand, the South had no entries in the studies on immigrants in cities or on the fecundity of immigrant women. In his work outline, W. Jett Lauck had noted that investigations of the South would include topics such as "inducements and obstacles, sentiment of the people, distribution of immigrants, and the stability and progress of immigrants," as well as "economic effects and assimilation." "This general investigation," he noted, "will cover practically all of the problems" of the South, "except peonage," which was planned for a separate study. Lauck, "Explanation of Outline," 3, Box 80, LP; USIC, vol. 39. On the head, W. A. Rauch, see minutes, July 10, 1908; USIC, vols. 29–35.

4. Cance sought "to determine accurately the position of the immigrant farmer in the southern rural economy, his economic and social status, his progress in Americanization, his effect upon the community, and the effect of the environment on him." USIC, 21:236. One section covered "extinct or partially extinct Italian Agricultural colonies," including at least one in Alabama. Volume 22 had reports on Italians in the Delta, Bohemians in Texas, Slovaks in Arkansas and Missouri, and Japanese in Texas and Florida. USIC, 21:235–388, Sunnyside on 319–334, extinct colonies on 431–433; USIC, 22:383–389, 435–441, 463–488; USIC, 1:567. In the 1906 immigration bill debates, Congressman Bennet had quoted a telegram from Percy enthusing about the possibilities of distribution. Robert F. Zeidel, *Immigrants, Progressives, and Exclusion Politics: The Dillingham Commission, 1900–1927* (DeKalb: Northern Illinois University Press, 2004), 47 n. 31.

5. Percy lived in Greenville, Mississippi, across the Mississippi River from the plantation.

6. Percy to Will Percy, December 1, 1910, Reel 5, PP. On the rush to approve reports and the impossibility of reading them, see also Patten to Lee, November 25, 1910, Carton 1, JLP.

7. Meeting Minutes, November 25, 1910, Notebook: titled "U.S. Immigration Commission Records, 1907–1910," 117, Box 1, HP.

8. Percy to Will Percy, April 19, 1907, Reel 3, PP.

9. Rowland T. Berthoff, "Southern Attitudes toward Immigration, 1865–1914," *Journal of Southern History* 17, no. 3 (1951): 359–360.

10. Julie M. Wiese, *Corazón de Dixie: Mexicanos in the U.S. South since 1910* (Chapel Hill: University of North Carolina Press, 2015); David Herbert Donald, "A Generation of Defeat," in *From the Old South to the New: Essays on the Transitional South,* ed. Walter J.

Fraser and Winfred B. Moore, Jr. (Westport, CT: Greenwood Press, 1981), 3–4; Berthoff, "Southern Attitudes," 331; "Says Laws Are Ample," *Washington Post,* June 8, 1906.

11. Carolyn G. Phelps, "John L. Burnett: A Southern Congressman and the Immigration Problem, 1905–1919" (MA thesis, Auburn University, 1970), 25. As my colleague Chandra Manning has pointed out, the South could support federal power when it served its interests; take, for example, the Fugitive Slave Act of 1850, which had empowered the federal government to punish northern law-enforcement officials who failed to return escaped slaves. But the rhetoric and reputation of southern legislators was of states' rights and limited government, especially the elites.

12. "The Immigration Problem," *Washington Post,* August 16, 1907. See also *New-York Daily Tribune,* December 16, 1907. On Latimer, see Memorandum in re: Senate Bill No. 2246, File 51538/5, Box 80, Entry 9, Record Group 85, BIP; Advertising Matter, Commissioner of Immigration to Mr. F. Missler, Bremen, Germany, File: 52066/3, Box 387, Entry 9, Record Group 85, BIP; Daniel J. Tichenor, *Dividing Lines: The Politics of Immigration Control in America* (Princeton, NJ: Princeton University Press, 2002), 83, 119–120; Berthoff, "Southern Attitudes," 339–341.

13. Berthoff, "Southern Attitudes," 342. To compare the distribution of immigrants across the South with the rest of the country, see Matthew Bloch and Robert Gebeloff, "Immigration Explorer," *New York Times,* March 10, 2009, www.nytimes.com/interactive /2009/03/10/us/20090310-immigration-explorer.html; Orleans Parish, home of New Orleans, accounted for 10 percent of the South's foreign-born population. U.S. Department of Commerce and Labor, Bureau of the Census, *Thirteenth Census of the United States Taken in the Year 1910: Statistics for Louisiana, Containing Statistics of Population, Agriculture, Manufactures, and Mining for the State, Parishes, Cities, and Other Divisions* (Washington, DC: Government Printing Office, 1913), 583; USIC, 21:235, 308, 95.

14. USIC, 21:329–330.

15. Ibid., 329–334.

16. Bertram Wyatt-Brown, *The House of Percy: Honor, Melancholy, and Imagination in a Southern Family* (New York: Oxford University Press, 1994), 175, 10, 12, 3. See for instance Percy to Hon. W. H. Powell, Canton, Miss., April 29, 1905, Reel 2, PP.

17. Wyatt-Brown, *House of Percy,* 4.

18. Patten to Lee, January 3, 1910, and Patten to Lee, January 18, 1910, both in Carton 1, JLP. Legendary southern historian C. Vann Woodward called men such as Percy the "conservatives" of the South. Bertram Wyatt-Brown, "LeRoy Percy and Sunnyside: Planter Mentality and Italian Peonage in the Mississippi Delta," *Arkansas Historical Quarterly* 50, no. 1 (1991): 78. On the bear hunt and teddy bears, see Wyatt-Brown, "LeRoy Percy and Sunnyside," 77, and J. William Hunt, *Deep Souths: Delta, Piedmont, and Sea Island Society in the Age of Segregation* (Baltimore, MD: Johns Hopkins University Press, 2001), 120.

19. Wyatt-Brown, "LeRoy Percy and Sunnyside," 73; Wyatt-Brown, *House of Percy,* 174.

20. Alfred Stone was also a sworn enemy of Vardaman. Both Percy and Stone saw themselves as paternal overseers of southern African Americans. Burnett's opinions of Jews were much more favorable than his views on Italians: he favored the refugee exemptions to immigration restrictions, and the chair of his 1912 reelection campaign was Jewish. In general, Jews in the South had a favorable experience, at least before the 1920s. Phelps, "Burnett," 36, 18–19, 24, 49–50.

21. USIC, 41:205–206.

22. Most of this summary relies on Willard B. Gatewood, Jr., "Sunnyside: Evolution of an Arkansas Plantation, 1840–1945," *Arkansas Historical Quarterly* 50, no. 1 (1991): esp. 6–22.

23. There is a long-standing, but also recently burgeoning, literature on capitalism and the southern economy. See, most recently, Martin Ruef, *Between Slavery and Capitalism: The Legacy of Emancipation in the American South* (Princeton, NJ: Princeton University Press, 2014); Sven Beckert, *Empire of Cotton: A Global History* (New York: Penguin, 2014); and Edward Baptist, *The Half Has Never Been Told: Slavery and the Making of American Capitalism* (New York: Basic Books, 2014). For older works see James Cobb, *The Most Southern Place on Earth: The Mississippi Delta and the Roots of Regional Identity* (New York: Oxford University Press, 1994), and Susan Mann, *Agrarian Capitalism in Theory and Practice* (Chapel Hill: University of North Carolina Press, 1989). On the particular methods of capitalist plantation formation and horizontal and vertical integration in the Arkansas Delta, see Jeannie M. Whayne, *Delta Empire: Lee Wilson and the Transformation of Agriculture in the New South* (Baton Rouge: Louisiana State University Press, 2011). On the Delta, see Nan Elizabeth Woodruff, *American Congo: The African-American Freedom Struggle in the Delta* (Cambridge, MA: Harvard University Press, 2003), chap. 1; Cobb, *Most Southern Place on Earth*.

24. "Mr. Corbin's Career: The Very Embodiment of Energy throughout His Life," *New York Times*, June 5, 1896.

25. USIC, 21:319; Ernesto R. Milani, "Peonage at Sunnyside and the Reaction of the Italian Government," *Arkansas Historical Quarterly* 50, no. 1 (1991): 31; USIC, 21:319. Emilia is now part of Emilia-Romagna.

26. USIC, 21:320.

27. Percy to H. P. Trezevant, March 27, 1907, Reel 3, PP.

28. "Pietro Bandini," *Encyclopedia of Arkansas*, www.encyclopediaofarkansas.net /encyclopedia/entry-detail.aspx?entryID=1583, and "Moses in the Ozarks: The Parable of Italians in the South," *The Economist*, May 27, 2017; "Austin Corbin Dead," *New York Times*, June 5, 1896; Percy to H. P. Trezevant, March 27, 1907, Reel 3, PP. Quackenbos's report on debt peonage in the southern States, January 10, 1908, 95, with Charles J. Bonaparte to Root, January 22, 1908, RG 59, M862, Reel 539, USDS. Corbin's son-in-law George Edgell had tried unsuccessfully to sell the property to Percy. On the proposed sale, see Percy to Mr. Austin Corbin, November 2, 1906, Reel 2, PP. On Corbin's anti-Semitism,

see Robert C. Kennedy, "On this Day," http://www.nytimes.com/learning/general /onthisday/harp/0728.html. LeRoy Percy's hometown of Greenville had a large Jewish community who intermingled—and intermarried—with Christians. The town's first mayor was a Jew. The Sunnyside Company's Morris Rosenstock had a daughter who married into a Protestant planter family; her son grew up to be the Civil War novelist Shelby Foote. David L. Cohn, "I've Kept My Name," *Atlantic Monthly* 181, no. 4 (1948): 42–44; Wyatt-Brown, *House of Percy*, 290.

29. Percy to H. Soegaard, July 19, 1905, Reel 2, PP; Percy to Capt. W. F. Randolph, March 8, 1905, Reel 2, PP; Percy to August Corbin, November 19, 1906, Reel 2, PP; Percy to H. P. Trezevant, March 27, 1907, Reel 3, PP.

30. Percy to John T. Savage, March 6, 1907, Reel 3, PP; Percy to Chevalier A. Rossi, July 18, 1906, Reel 2, PP. He showed his hand the year before, however, when he told the Danish consul that Italians "offered little in the way of good citizenship." Percy to Mr. H. Soegaard, Royal Danish Consulate, New Orleans, Louisiana, July 19, 1905, Reel 2, PP.

31. Gatewood, "Sunnyside," 25; Percy to Rossi, Rome, Italy, July 18, 1906, Reel 2, PP; USIC, 24:238; Henry Cabot Lodge, "Lynch Law and Unrestricted Immigration," *North American Review* 152 (1891): 602–612; Norton H. Moses, comp., *Lynching and Vigilantism in the United States: An Annotated Bibliography* (Westport, CT: Greenwood Press, 1997), 125.

32. Percy to Will Percy, April 19, 1907, Reel 3, PP.

33. Wyatt-Brown, "LeRoy Percy and Sunnyside," 71; Edward Ayers, *The Promise of the New South: Life after Reconstruction* (New York: Oxford University Press, 1992), 195; U.S. Department of Commerce, Bureau of the Census, *Thirteenth Census of the United States Taken in the Year 1910, Vol. II, Population 1910: Reports by States, with Statistics for Counties, Cities, and other Civil Divisions, Alabama-Montana* (Washington, DC: Government Printing Office, 1913), 118.

34. Of course, all lynching statistics are estimates. I used the Tuskegee Institute data, reproduced at "Lynching: By Year and Race," *Famous American Trials: The Trial of Sheriff Joseph Shipp et al., 1907*, http://law2.umkc.edu/faculty/projects/ftrials/shipp /lynchingyear.html. On the Great Migration, see, among others, James R. Grossman, *Land of Hope: Chicago, Black Southerners, and the Great Migration* (Chicago: University of Chicago Press, 1991), and Isabel Wilkerson, *The Warmth of Other Suns: The Epic Story of America's Great Migration* (New York: Random House, 2010).

35. Recent interviews and reminiscences testify to these relationships among the Italian migrants to Mississippi and Arkansas, too. See "Moses in the Ozarks"; Percy to H. P. Trezevant, March 27, 1907, Reel 3, PP.

36. On the "black boss" of Chicot County, who served in the State Senate, see Willard B. Gatewood., Jr., and Jeannie M. Whayne, *The Arkansas Delta: Land of Paradox* (Fayetteville: University of Arkansas Press, 1993), 104; Percy to H. P. Trezevant, March 27, 1907, Reel 3, PP.

37. H. P. Trezevant to Percy, March 24, 1907, emphasis in original, Reel 3, PP. Stone's article was later reprinted in his *Studies in the American Race Problem* (New York: Doubleday, Page, 1908); Percy to H. P. Trezevant, March 27, 1907, Reel 3, PP; James G. Hollandsworth, Jr., *Portrait of a Scientific Racist: Alfred Holt Stone of Mississippi* (Baton Rouge: Louisiana State University Press, 2008), 137, 151.

38. William Humphreys, in a 1908 speech about peonage investigation, quoted in Hollandsworth, *Stone,* 23; Wyatt-Brown, "LeRoy Percy and Sunnyside," 69; Alfred H. Stone, "The Italian Cotton Grower: The Negro's Problem," *South Atlantic Quarterly* 4 (1905): 42–47, and Alfred H. Stone, "The Negro in the Yazoo-Mississippi Delta," *Publications of the American Economic Association*, 3rd ser., 3, no. 1 (1901): 235–278; quotation from Hollandsworth, *Scientific Racist*, 22.

39. For a local paper he told fellow Mississippians, "If the thief and the thug be kept out[,] the Italian immigrant is as good as any we receive." He is a better worker than the "Negro," because he has equal stamina, "with none of his propensity for shirking." Stone, "Italian Immigration," *Greenville Times,* May 11, 1901, quoted in Hollandsworth, *Scientific Racist,* 138; "A Modern Italian Colony in Arkansas," *American Monthly Review of Reviews* 34, no. 3 (1906): 361–362.

40. USIC, 21:326, 328.

41. Carnegie Institution of Washington, *Yearbook No. 7, 1908* (Washington, DC: Published for the Institution by Judd & Detweiler, 1909), 76. The two served on the same panel. See "Proceedings of the Seventy-third Annual Meeting of the American Statistical Association, Washington, D.C., December 28–29, 1911," *Publications of the American Statistical Association* 13, no. 97 (1912): 28.

42. Alfred Holt Stone, "Italian Cotton-Growers in Arkansas," *American Monthly Review of Reviews* 35, no. 2 (1907): 209–210, 213.

43. On Dubois and Stone, see Hollandsworth, *Scientific Racist,* 139–151. For Stone and Du Bois's correspondence around the turn of the twentieth century, see Reel 3, from around 210, DBP.

44. USIC, 21:332–333. On similar reasoning about Mexicans, see Katherine Benton-Cohen, "Other Immigrants: Mexicans and the Dillingham Commission," *Journal of American Ethnic History* 30, no. 2 (2011): 33–57.

45. USIC, 21:334; Percy to George Edgell, February 14, 1907; Percy to Baron des Planches, February 14, 1907; and Percy to Trezevant, March 27, 1907, all Reel 3, PP. For correspondence between Percy and Stone, see Percy to Mr. Alfred K. Stone, February 5, 1906, Reel 2, PP.

46. A well-reasoned argument for expanding the definition of slavery appears in Andrés Reséndez, *The Other Slavery* (New York: Houghton Mifflin, 2016); U.S. Department of Justice, *The Peonage Files of U.S. Department of Justice, 1901–1945,* comp. Pete Daniel (Frederick, MD: University Publications of America, 1989), v; Aviam Soifer, "Federal

Protection, Paternalism, and the Virtually Forgotten Prohibition of Voluntary Peonage," *Columbia Law Review* 112, no. 7 (2012): 1607–1640.

47. Victor H. Metcalf to Percy, November 10, 1906, Reel 2, PP.

48. Roosevelt backed the Department of Justice's peonage investigations, and Taft acceded to them when he became president. Pete Daniel, *The Shadow of Slavery: Peonage in the South, 1901–1969* (Urbana: University of Illinois Press, 1972), 44, 93.

49. *Clyatt v. United States,* 197 U.S. 207 (1905), quoted in USIC, 2:444. Arkansas banned convict lease labor in 1913. An act to prohibit the importation and migration of foreigners and aliens under contract or agreement to perform labor in the United States, its Territories, and the District of Columbia, Pub. L. No. 48–164, 23 Stat. 332 (1885). The law was nearly impossible to enforce and was amended several times, adding, for example, a ban on the use of "advertisements printed or published in any foreign city" to induce immigration on the basis of promised employment. Samuel P. Orth, "The Alien Contract Labor Law," *Political Science Quarterly* 22, no. 1 (1907): 49–60.

50. Robert J. Steinfeld, *Coercion, Contract, and Free Labor in the Nineteenth Century* (New York: Cambridge University Press, 2001), 5.

51. *Ex Parte Drayton,* 153 F. 986, at 996 (D.S.C. 1907), quoted in Benno Schmidt, Jr., "Principle and Prejudice: The Supreme Court and Race in the Progressive Era. Part 2: The *Peonage Cases,*" *Columbia Law Review* 82, no. 4 (1982): 657.

52. Department of Justice, *Peonage Files,* v–vi.

53. Daniel, *Shadow of Slavery.* See especially Richard Barry, "Slavery in the South To-Day," *Cosmopolitan Magazine,* March 1907, 481–491.

54. On the murky racial and political meanings of peonage, see Shelley Streeby, "Imagining Mexico in Love and War: Nineteenth-Century U.S. Literature and Visual Culture," in *Mexico and Mexicans in the Making of the United States,* ed. John Tutino (Austin: University of Texas Press, 2012), 110–140.

55. Percy to Will Percy, March 19, 1906 [probably 1907], Reel 2, PP; Robert Rose, Chicago, Ill., to LeRoy Percy, March 12, 1905, Reel 2, PP; Percy to John T. Savage, March 6, 1907, Reel 3, PP.

56. Percy to John T. Savage, March 8, 1907, Reel 3, PP.

57. Ibid.

58. Percy to Will Percy, April 19, 1907, Reel 3, PP. Percy later hosted the ambassador on a carefully choreographed visit to the Sunnyside Plantation, hoping in vain to win him over. See Milani, "Peonage at Sunnyside," 35–36; Percy to Will Percy, April 19, 1907, Reel 3, PP; Percy to John T. Savage, March 6, 1907, Reel 3, PP. See also Percy to Merry, July 22, 1905, Reel 2, PP; Percy to Trezevant, July 27, 1907, Reel 3, PP.

59. This section relies heavily on the Justice Department's correspondence, as cited below, but I also relied on the useful overview of Randolph H. Boehm, "Mary Grace Quackenbos and the Federal Campaign against Peonage: The Case of Sunnyside Plantation,"

Arkansas Historical Quarterly 50, no. 1 (1991): 40–59; Des Planches to Root, June 4, 1907, USDS; Bonaparte to Root, January 22, 1908, USDS. See also Bonaparte to Root, January 15, 1908, and Bonaparte to Des Planches, January 20, 1908, both in USDS.

60. Stimson, quoted in Daniel, *Shadow of Slavery*, 104. For Stimson's comparison of Quackenbos to a recalcitrant team of horses, see File 50–162, Box 10800, Record Group 60, DoJ-GR. Bonaparte to President Theodore Roosevelt, September 10, 1907, File Special Correspondence, Aug.-Sep. 1907; President Theodore Roosevelt, Oyster Bay, NY, to Hon. Charles Bonaparte, Care Dr. R. H. Harte, Articou, Mt. Desert, Maine, September 7, 1907; Bonaparte to Roosevelt, September 10, 1907, 2, all CBP.

61. "Woman Will Help in War against Trusts," *New York Times*, September 15, 1907. Quotations from Daniel, *Shadow of Slavery*, 83, 101.

62. At one time, Quackenbos's grandfather had published a newspaper with abolitionist William Lloyd Garrison; Bonaparte to Roosevelt, 3, CBP; Percy to Bonaparte, August 19, 1907, quoted in Wyatt-Brown, "LeRoy Percy and Sunnyside," 70.

63. Quoted in Wyatt-Brown, "LeRoy Percy and Sunnyside," 71, 76, 80; Boehm, "Mary Grace Quackenbos," 53.

64. Quackenbos report, 8, USDS.

65. Quackenbos report, esp. 5–8, 15, USDS.

66. Quackenbos report, 96, 32–33, USDS; "Moses in the Ozarks," and Camille Elise Mullins, "Italians in the Delta: The Evolution of an Unusual Migration" (MA thesis, University of Mississippi, 2015).

67. Barry, "Slavery in the South To-day," 481, 484.

68. Quackenbos report, 89, 4, USDS. About Italians recruited to cotton-mill work, she reported, "Little white children must serve grown people six days in the week for abusively long hours." Quackenbos report, 21, USDS.

69. Bonaparte to Roosevelt; Wyatt-Brown, "LeRoy Percy and Sunnyside," 69–70, 76–77; Percy to Will Percy, January 16, 1908, Reel 3, PP.

70. I have reversed the "nursing" quotation's grammar because it was very confusing. Percy to Mrs. F. L. McLaurin, January 14, 1908, Reel 3, PP; Percy to Will Percy, January 16, 1908, Reel 3, PP. In his various defenses of his business partner E. O. Crittenden, Percy also noted that Crittenden was accused of breaking a law that did not yet exist at the time of the violation.

71. See Daniel, *Shadow of Slavery*, 103; quoted in "Ire Is Aroused by Peonage Cases," *San Francisco Call*, March 3, 1908.

72. March 2, 1908: "Mr. Humphreys, of Mississippi, submitted the following: "Resolution: *Resolved*, . . ." See Meeting Minutes, 41, HP. There had been complaints about overspending and debates over funding, but no mandates about content.

73. Morton Crane to Henry Cabot Lodge, May 23, 1907, Reel 24, HCLP; Meeting Minutes, January 9, 1908, Notebook: titled "U.S. Immigration Commission Executive Committee Records, 1908–1910," 28–29, Box 1, HP; Lucian Lamar Knight, *A*

Standard History of Georgia and Georgians (Chicago: Lewis Publishing, 1917), 5:2543–2544.

74. In fact, McLaurin had been the original nominee to the commission and had initially declined; Latimer was appointed in his place, but with his death McLaurin returned to the position. On Heard's resignation, see Meeting Minutes, May 22, 1908, Notebook: titled "U.S. Immigration Commission Executive Committee Records, 1908–1910," 25, Box 1, HP; Meeting Minutes, July 10, 1908, Notebook: titled "U.S. Immigration Commission Records, 1907–1910," 78, Box 1, HP.

75. Meeting Minutes, May 15, 1908, Notebook: titled "U.S. Immigration Commission Records, 1907–1910," 62, Box 1, HP.

76. The commission already had a five-person subcommittee on southern investigation made up of McLaurin, Neill, Howell, Bennet, and Burnett, which hired "Messrs. Bell, Kellett, and Bacon," Notebook: titled "U.S. Immigration Commission Records," 59, 58, 30, 62, Box 1, HP. Jeremiah Jenks had already been in correspondence with Quackenbos, who claimed she worked with the Dillingham Commission. Jenks to Quackenbos, attached to Quackenbos to Guass, Container 130, CBP.

77. USIC, 2:443. On the raise that Elder received for his work on peonage, see Meeting Minutes, June 1, 1910, Notebook: titled "U.S. Immigration Commission Executive Committee Records, 1908–1910," 48, Box 1, HP. The decision to table Elder's report is recorded in an unpaginated scrapbook in Box 1, HP. Elder's report ultimately landed in the DoJ-GR.

78. See also Daniel, *Shadow of Slavery*, 107–108. Meeting Minutes, May 15, 1908, and June 10, 1909, Notebook: titled "U.S. Immigration Commission Records, 1907–1910," 62, 89, Box 1, HP; USIC, 2:444, 447–449, quotation on 449.

79. Percy to Will Percy, December 1, 1910, Reel 5, PP.

80. Mary Grace Quackenbos, "Why They Come," *Pearson's Magazine*, December 1910, 737–747; Patten to Lee, November 25, 1910, Carton 1, JLP; Patten to Lee, December 11, 1910, Carton 1, JLP.

81. One legal scholar calls them "the most lasting of the [Justice Edward Douglas] White Court's contributions to justice for black people, and among its greatest achievements." Schmidt, "Principle and Prejudice," 646.

82. I have relied here on Schmidt, "Principle and Prejudice," 646–718.

83. USIC, 1:46–47; Des Planches to Root, June 4, 1907, USDS. See also Daniel, *Shadow of Slavery*, 95; Thomas A. Guglielmo, *White on Arrival: Italians, Race, Color, and Power in Chicago, 1890–1945* (New York: Oxford University Press, 2004); and, for a similar point about Jamaican guest workers versus African Americans, see *No Man's Land: Jamaican Guestworkers and the Global History of Deportable Labor* (Princeton, NJ: Princeton University Press, 2011), 65.

84. More than one-third, a plurality, of Louisiana's foreign-born population was Italian. Bureau of the Census, *Statistics for Louisiana*, 583. The new Ku Klux Klan was also strong outside the South, notably in Indiana and Colorado.

85. Patten to Lee, November 8, 1910, Patten to Lee, November 25, 1910, Carton 1, JLP. Percy had previously expressed the same idea in less vulgar terms, writing three years before: "It would be out of the question to permit them to sell their cotton until their accounts with us were paid, as it would require a regiment of Pinkerton Detectives to keep them from stealing it. They are industrious, but no more honest than the negro, and much more enterprising." Percy to John T. Savage, March 9, 1907, Reel 3, PP.

86. Across the Delta the number of Italian families had fallen by half, to just 350, according to Italian government reports. Milani, "Peonage at Sunnyside," 38. USIC, 22: 359–368, and Quackenbos report, 111. An Italian community still lives in Tontitown, Arkansas, and there are a few elsewhere in the Delta; Gatewood, "Sunnyside," 28.

87. Translated and quoted in Milani, "Peonage," 36. On the "pushing system" of southern capitalism and its roots in slavery, see Baptist, *The Half Has Never Been Told.*

88. He opposed it for these reasons, as well as because it jettisoned the literacy test. Phelps, "Burnett," 22–24.

89. I thank my colleague John Tutino for making this point to me.

90. "President Wilson's Veto of the Immigration Bill—1915: Extracts from Speech of Hon. William P. Dillingham of Vermont, in the Senate of the United States, February 11 and 12, 1915," 8, Box 10, William P. Dillingham Papers, Special Collections, University of Vermont Library, Burlington, Vermont.

Epilogue

1. Joseph Lee to Charles Nagel, December 31, 1910, File J. Lee Immigration Restriction League Correspondence, December 1910, Carton 1, JLP, and, generally, November and December 1910 correspondence.

2. USIC:1, 45. I am indebted to Robert F. Zeidel's meticulous reconstruction of the commission's internal debates over the final recommendations in *Immigrants, Progressive, and Exclusion Politics: The Dillingham Commission, 1900–1927* (DeKalb: Northern Illinois University Press, 2004), chap. 6, esp. 112–115. We share the belief that the Dillingham Commission did not act out of eugenically minded racism, although my emphasis is on state power. On the recommendations' harshness, I concur with other historians, notably with Oscar Handlin and Robert Zeidel. Oscar Handlin, "Old Immigrants and New," chap. 5, in *Race and Nationality in American Life* (Boston: Little, Brown, 1957).

3. Jeremiah Jenks praised the Gentlemen's Agreement for relying on diplomacy rather than on "exclusion by drastic legislation" and proposed a different quota system in his private writings. Theodore Roosevelt also preferred international cooperation to a quota system or legislation for full Asian exclusion. USIC, 1:45–48, 40. Jeremiah W. Jenks, "The Japanese in Manchuria," *The Outlook*, March 11, 1911, 549. See also Paul Kramer, "Empire against Exclusion in Early 20th-Century Trans-Pacific History," *Nanzan Review of American Studies* 33 (2011): 13–32; Patrick Weil, "Races at the Gate: A Century of

Racial Distinctions in American Immigration Policy," *Georgetown Immigration Law Journal* 15 (2000–2001): 637–638.

4. Charles Nagel to Wolf, February 21, 1913, SWP.

5. Zeidel, *Immigrants, Progressives,* 125–128.

6. USIC, 1:48.

7. Max Kohler and others preferred the term "immigration question" to "immigration problem," and with good reason. It left open many different answers. "The immigration question, with particular reference to the Jews of America. Addresses by Max J. Kohler, honorable Charles Nagel, and Jacob Schiff, delivered at the twenty-second council of the Union of American Hebrew Congregations on January 18, 1911, at New York," New York, 1911, https://babel.hathitrust.org/cgi/pt?id=umn.31951002461139x;view=1up;seq=23.

8. "EUGENIC TEST FOR ALIENS; Prof. Ward of Harvard Urges Its Application at American Ports," *New York Times,* December 25, 1913; Jeremiah W. Jenks, "The Character and Influence of Recent Immigrants," in *Questions of Public Policy: Addresses Delivered in the Page Lecture Series, 1913, Before the Senior Class of the Sheffield Scientific School, Yale University* (New Haven, CT: Yale University Press, 1913), 1–40; Paul Lombardo, "Eugenics Laws Restricting Immigration," *Image Archive on the American Eugenics Movement,* www.eugenicsarchive.org/html/eugenics/essay9text.html.

9. These quotas, based on the demographics of the 1910 census, proved to be less restrictive than many had hoped.

10. Husband's plan was similar to one created by reformer Sidney Gulick. See Sidney L. Gulick, "A Comprehensive Immigration Policy and Program," *Scientific Monthly* 6, no. 3 (1918), 214–223, and Son-Thierry Ly and Patrick Weil, "The Antiracist Origin of the Quota System," *Social Research* 77, no. 1 (2010): 45–78. In 1941, a year before he died, Husband wrote a speech in which he claimed to have come up with an idea for a quota system in the spring of 1913 while talking to his brother-in-law, because of his frustration over the continued failure and recent veto by Taft of the literacy test. He told Dillingham and Lodge, and was disappointed that neither seemed "over-enthusiastic about the idea," because, he claimed, they had invested so much time and energy into the literacy test. He then went to a lunch meeting in New York with Jenks "and a few leaders in the restrictionist group in that city, and discussed it with Prescott Hall, Joseph Lee, and Robert deC Ward of the IRL." They said they would continue to pursue the literacy test but when that was complete, they would move on to the quota plan. William W. Husband, "How the Quota Limit System of Regulating Immigration Happened," Washington, September 4, 1941, Box 1, HP.

11. Erez Manela, "Imagining Woodrow Wilson in Asia: Dreams of East-West Harmony and the Revolt against Empire in 1919," *American Historical Review* 111, no. 5 (2006): 1327–1351; Naoko Shimaza, *Japan, Race, and Equality: The Racial Equality Proposal of 1919* (London: Routledge, 1998); Phelan, "Letter to a Japanese Gentleman," in *Japanese Exclusion,* comp. Julia E. Johnsen (New York: H. W. Wilson, 1925), 126; Andrea Geiger,

Subverting Exclusion: Transpacific Encounters with Race, Caste, and Borders, 1885–1928 (New Haven, CT: Yale University Press, 2011), 188; Donna R. Gabaccia, *Foreign Relations: American Immigration in Global Perspective* (Princeton, NJ: Princeton University Press, 2012), 142.

12. USIC, vol. 28, whose author was Joseph Hill. On Hill's work on the quota laws, see Mae M. Ngai, "The Architecture of Race in American Immigration Law: A Reexamination of the Immigration Act of 1924," *Journal of American History* 86, no. 1 (1999): 67–92. The annual quotas appear on p. 74, and they show that Asian countries received a quota of 100. But it was reserved for people who were not of the Asian "races." On Husband and Dillingham's commitment to avoiding legislative Asian exclusion and preserving harmonious diplomatic relations, see esp. Ly and Weil, "Antiracist Origin." On Dillingham's death, see p. 69.

13. At the end of the passage, Kohler conceded that some immigration limits might have been necessary during World War I (when the literacy test was passed), but the quota laws came afterward. Kohler to Husband, March 23, 1927, MJKP, quoted in Joel Perlmann, " 'Race or People': Federal Race Classifications for Europeans in America, 1898–1913" (paper, Jerome Levy Economics Institute Working Paper No. 320, January 2001), http://papers.ssrn.com/sol3/papers.cfm?abstract_id=257921; Simon Wolf, *Presidents I Have Known from 1860–1918,* 2nd ed. (Washington, DC: Press of Byron S. Adams, 1918), 240–241.

14. Mark Reisler, *By the Sweat of Their Brow* (Westport, CT: Greenwood Press, 1977).

15. See Katherine Benton-Cohen, "Other Immigrants: Mexicans and the Dillingham Commission," *Journal of American Ethnic History* 30, no. 2 (2011): 33–57; Gilberto Cárdenas, "United States Immigration Policy towards Mexico: A Historical Perspective," *Chicano Law Review* 2 (Summer 1975): 68–70; Mae M. Ngai, *Impossible Subjects: Illegal Aliens and the Making of Modern America* (Princeton, NJ: Princeton University Press, 2004); Lynne M. Getz, "Biological Determinism in the Making of Immigration Policy in the 1920s," *International Social Science Review* 70, no. 1 (1995): 26–33, esp. 29.

16. "Address of Hon. W. W. Husband, Second Assistant Secretary of Labor, on the present immigration problem," Station WJSV, April 20, 1931, p. 12, Box 2, Folder 1927–1931, HP. Also interesting is a 1931 set of articles on deportation drive, half of them of Mexicans, with comments by Husband, in Box 2, Folder 1927–1931, HP.

17. I must credit Mae Ngai with this insight.

Acknowledgments

I have incurred many debts (financial, intellectual, academic, and personal) in completing this book. Georgetown University provided generous time and money (in the form of summer grants, research grants, a senior sabbatical, and a senior research fellowship). I have also benefited from the National Endowment for the Humanities' summer stipend, a fellowship at the Woodrow Wilson International Center for Scholars—where I did my first year of research—and the Franklin Fellowship at the American Philosophical Society. This book is based on research in more than two dozen archives—from the National Archives to the Waterbury Historical Society above the Vermont town's library. Everywhere, the assistance of staff and volunteers—both online and in-person—has been generous and prompt. Thank you.

My first published foray into this topic was in "The Rude Birth of Immigration Reform," *Wilson Quarterly* 34, no. 3 (2010): 16–22, which informs Chapter 5 of this book. Chapter 2 builds on ideas first discussed in "Japanese Immigrants and the Dillingham Commission: Federal Immigration Policy and the American West," *Immigrants in the Far West: Historical Identities and Experiences,* ed. Bryan Cannon and Jessie Embry (University of Utah Press, 2014), 122–150. Concepts I treat in "Other Immigrants: Mexicans and the Dillingham Commission," *Journal of American Ethnic History* 30, no. 2 (2011): 33–57, are developed further in the Introduction, Chapter 2, and the Epilogue of this book. I am grateful to the publishers for giving me the opportunity to first present some of these views.

Along the way, I have also presented my research in many places. Each audience and commenter improved this work in critical ways (and I mean that in both senses). At the Immigration History Revisited Summer Institute (funded by the National Endowment for the Humanities, the National History Center, and the Library of Congress), I learned the field and did some of my earliest writing and research for the project. My thanks to my classmates there, as well as to the coleaders, Alan Kraut and Maureen Nutting. At Georgetown University, my audiences included Georgetown College's Americas Initiative, the Department of History's faculty workshop, the Pacific Empires working group, and the faculty manuscript reading group. I took the show on the road to talks sponsored by the Historical Society; American Studies Workshop, Princeton University; the Zolberg Institute on Migration and Mobility, New School for Social Research; Rutgers University Graduate Student Interpreting American History Speaker Series; the American Historical Association; the Organization of American Historians; the Social Science Historical Association; the Labor and Empire Conference, University of California, Santa Barbara; Stokes History Seminar, Dalhousie University; the University of California, Los Angeles, Immigration Workshop; the American Society for Legal History; the Western History Association; the Redd Center for the American West, Brigham Young University; the New America Foundation; the Wilson Center; Friends House, Sandy Spring, Maryland; the U.S. Citizenship and Immigration Services (USCIS); the University of Texas-El Paso Department of History Seminar Series; the American Studies Association; the Historical Society; the Congregation Tifereth Israel; and the Foreign Service Institute.

For reading portions or all of the manuscript and making useful suggestions, I thank, in no particular order, Alan Kraut, Tyler Anbinder, Carol Benedict, Deirdre Moloney, Chad Frazier, Maddalena Marinari, Marcia Chatelain, Kate DeLuna, Jordan Sand, Paul Weil, Judith Resnik, Sunmin Kim, Leon Fink, Sheldon Garon, Hendrik Hartog, Joseph McCartin, Brian Hochmann, Chandra Manning, Tommaso Astarita, Adam Rothman, John Tutino, James Shedel, John McNeill, Paul Kramer, Rebecca Kobrin, Roger Waldinger, Joel Perlmann, Michael Kazin, Thomas Andrews, Flannery Burke, Michael Werz, Brian Foster, Mark Choate, Warren Cohen, Jenice Benton, Hal Cohen, Edna Friedberg, and two anonymous readers at Harvard University Press, who gave the book their close attention and considerable expertise. Those of you who read the whole thing deserve my extra thanks, as does Robert Zeidel, whose book on the Dillingham Commission has been an indispensable guide for me. Bob has been unfailingly generous with his insight and resources, a model of scholarly grace and collegiality.

Susan Martin and Linda Gordon wrote letters of recommendation that helped me get my start on this project at the Woodrow Wilson Center, where the fellows and Sonya Michel were so encouraging. Early on, Carmen Grayson met with me, and I learned a lot from her. Mae Ngai gave me some fascinating sources about Jeremiah Jenks. Joel Perlmann shared his page proofs on his important, related book in my final days of editing. My editor, Kathleen Mc-Dermott, championed this book from the first, discussed it over many delicious dinners, and was patient, thoughtful, and encouraging. My agent, Michelle Tessler, jumped in at a crucial moment. Louise Robbins, Daniel Sentance, and Melody Negron lent their expert production skills and copyediting eyes. If I've forgotten anyone, please forgive me. The mistakes that remain are mine alone.

It turns out two-year-olds do not help get books written (written *on*—with crayons—is a different story). But they are a lot more fun. Asher always wants to do "homework" on mommy's "compooter." So, I could not have completed this book without the outstanding child care provided by Connie Romani, Blanca Johnson, Dale and Sandra Knock, BCDC, John and Jenice Benton, Natasha Vargas, and the fellow parents of the Chevy Chase and Friendship Co-Ops. Julius took on the burdens and joys of big brother status in enormously helpful and gratifying ways, mostly for free.

While those intrepid souls were chasing Asher, a series of research assistants were chasing footnotes for me. Andres Blanco, Meredith Hall, and Jose Madrid all helped me do this work. My greatest debt is to my graduate student Chad Frazier, whom I entrusted with a great deal of responsibility—all of which he handled with great aplomb.

I agree with federal immigration official Charles Nagel, who said in 1913, explaining why he had not read anything but the commission reports' abstracts: "As to the forty volumes I feel constrained to consider my limited time and my obligations to my family." In my case, this one book has taken me twice as long as it took the Dillingham Commission to finish 41 volumes. With a staff of more than three hundred and absolute certainty in my authority, I might have finished more quickly, too. I am not sorry, though, because life intervened. I wrote much of this book in Lunenburg, Nova

Scotia, during the summers and one snowy winter and spring. That work was balanced—precariously—between family adventures and meals with my parents, friends, siblings and spouses, and fun-loving nephews. For your love, companionship, and general zaniness, thank you to Pop-Pop, Gigi, JT, Betsy, Jennie, Zach, Miller, and Colt. Though I see them more frequently in midwestern locales than maritime ones, I treasure my time with Beth, "Muncle Mike," Eebie, and Nay-pin. My in-laws, Steve Cohen and Debbie Mendeloff, have cheered me on in my every endeavor. A special thanks to my parents, John and Jenice, who made space for me in the final days of writing by looking after a very energetic young human, and sending me off to my own little writing retreat in their Airstream trailer (stocked with coffee and booze). As I write these words, I am overlooking the Atlantic Ocean, which so many of the people in this book crossed a century ago.

Editing by my husband, Hal Cohen, has improved every part of this book I let him mark up. The book could have been better had I let him do more with it. He has improved everything else in my life instead.

This book is dedicated to our sons, Julius Zbinden Cohen and Asher Merritt Cohen. Three of my husband's grandparents were immigrants, as were four of my great-grandparents, all in the years just before the quota laws went into effect. Our children's ancestors and namesakes range from Puritan New Englanders to Illinois Swiss-Germans to Eastern European Jews from Brooklyn to Akron to Beaumont to Nogales. Their stories informed every page of this book.

Illustration Credits

153 Image from Scannell's *New Jersey's First Citizens, 1917–1918: Biographies and Portraits of the Notable Living Men and Women of New Jersey with Informing Glimpses into the State's History and Affairs* (Paterson, NJ: J. J. Scannell, 1917), 1:399.

164 Courtesy Barnard College Archives.

172 Franz Boas Papers (Mss. B. B61), American Philosophical Society.

193 USIC, 38:9.

208 Library of Congress Prints and Photographs Division, Washington, DC (LC-USZ62-57646).

212 J. C. Coovert Collection. Courtesy of the Archives and Records Services Division, Mississippi Department of Archives and History.

Index